Critical Infrastructure

Homeland Security and Emergency Preparedness

Critical Infrastructure

Homeland Security and Emergency Preparedness

Robert Radvanovsky

Taylor & Francis
Taylor & Francis Group
Boca Raton   London   New York

CRC is an imprint of the Taylor & Francis Group
an informa business

Published in 2006 by
CRC Press
Taylor & Francis Group
6000 Broken Sound Parkway NW, Suite 300
Boca Raton, FL 33487-2742

International Standard Book Number-10: 0-8493-7398-0 (Hardcover)
International Standard Book Number-13: 978-0-8493-7398-5 (Hardcover)
Library of Congress Card Number 2005036212

Library of Congress Cataloging-in-Publication Data

Radvanovsky, Robert.
    Critical infrastructure : Homeland Security and Emergency Preparedness / Robert Radvanovsky.
        p. cm.
    Includes index.
    ISBN 0-8493-7398-0 (9780849373985)
    1. Civil defense--United States. 2. War damage, industrial--United States. I. Title.

UA927.R34 2006
363.34'70973--dc22   2005036212

Taylor & Francis Group
is the Academic Division of Informa plc.

Visit the Taylor & Francis Web site at
http://www.taylorandfrancis.com

and the CRC Press Web site at
http://www.crcpress.com

Dedication

This book is dedicated to my loving and endearing wife, Tammy, who has been through some very hard and trying times with me since that fateful day on September 11, 2001. Both of our lives have been touched in ways that we can never forget. My wife has been with me through many hardships, as well as endured long and arduous hours spent researching and writing this book.

To my wife — all of my love — always.

To secure ourselves against defeat lies in our own hands, but the opportunity of defeating the enemy is provided by the enemy himself.

— Sun Tzu, The Ancient Art of War

Preface

This book represents a culmination of research activity that has stemmed over the past several years. The intent of the materials contained within and referenced throughout this book is to represent significant strides made in understanding the fundamentals behind securing, protecting, and safekeeping our nation's infrastructures — all relevant industries, national landmarks, and national assets — that are considered critically vital to the continued economic success and operation of the United States.

Since September 11, 2001, many people (including the author) were utterly and forever changed by the magnitude of that catastrophic event on that fateful day. Our lives have been altered and scarred by reminders that we are no longer safe, that we cannot feel safe anymore, and must take action to safeguard our families, friends, and colleagues. The federal government has taken initiatives, starting as early as mid-1996, to implement a foundational framework that would be useful in the years following 9/11. Little did anyone know how soon that was going to be, only to struggle with something as vast and enormous as the contemplation of the how's, what's, where's, and when's in securing our infrastructures. This is (by no means) a science ... yet. However, this is a development process that is subdivided into individual methodological components and subcomponents.

Many interesting developments have been conceived by several very intelligent individuals, whom we must thank dearly for thinking in ways that we could not have thought of before. From those developments, new and useful department/agency-level protocols, procedures, and guidelines have been formulated and are now either currently in use or will shortly be implemented. These procedures and guidelines provide a base, a foundation, on which our nation's infrastructures (as listed within President Clinton's President Decision Directive focusing on the formulation and definition of the term "critical infrastructure," PDD-63) now (or soon will) depend upon. As such, those who implement their operation, maintain their integrity and functional status, or safeguard and prevent acts of terrorism from occurring depend upon those procedures and guidelines and must demonstrate their fundamental understanding and comprehension. Key factors, terms, and guidelines must be conveyed to those individuals in a manner that is generally understood and (more importantly) accepted. Without acceptance and the fundamental understanding of that knowledge being conveyed, our nation may not prosper.

It is felt that you, the reader, will grasp what is being conveyed within this book, understanding the fundamental, general knowledge that some individuals and organizations consider important.

Acknowledgments

Some materials used within this publication were taken in part or in their entirety from several very reliable and useful sources. Any information that may appear to be repetitive in its content from those sources was taken to provide a more introspective perception of what defines "critical infrastructure preparedness."

The author, editor, and publisher wish to thank the following organizations for their contributions of references and materials:

The United States Department of Homeland Security: www.dhs.gov

The Office of Domestic Preparedness (ODP), which is part of the United States Department of Homeland Security's Office of State and Local Government Coordination and Preparedness (SLGCP): www.ojp.usdoj.gov/odp

The Federal Emergency Management Agency (FEMA), which is part of the United States Department of Homeland Security's Emergency Preparedness and Response Directorate: www.fema.gov

The United States Fire Administration, which is part of FEMA, which is part of the United States Department of Homeland Security's Emergency Preparedness and Response Directorate: www.usfa.fema.gov

The National Fire Prevention Association: www.nfpa.org

Author's Note

This publication offers an aid in maintaining professional competence, with the understanding that the author, editor, and publisher are not rendering any legal, financial, or any other professional advice.

Due to the rapidly changing nature of the homeland security industry, the information contained within this publication may become outdated and therefore the reader using this publication should consider researching for alternative or other professional or more current sources of authoritative information. The significant portion of this publication was based on research conducted over the past three years from several government resources, publications, and Internet-accessible Web sites, some of which may no longer be publicly available, or may have been restricted due to the Critical Infrastructure Information Act of 2002.

The views expressed in this book are those of a variety of sources (and their authors) and may not necessarily reflect the position of the author.

Synopsis of the Chapters

This book is broken into 11 categories that represent months (if not years) of research, as well as strategic and tactical development, which emphasize those factors that comprise functions within and throughout critical infrastructures.

These factors are categorically subdivided into unique and prioritized levels, beginning with Chapter 1 being the foremost and vitally important chapter of the book, Chapter 2 slightly less important than Chapter 1, and so on and so forth. Each subsequent chapter emphasizes a different meaning that is being conveyed such that it can be structured and remembered in an easy, cognitive fashion. The listing of each chapter (with a brief summary of its description and function) is provided below.

CHAPTER 1: INTRODUCTION TO CRITICAL INFRASTRUCTURE PREPAREDNESS

This chapter provides the base for the entire book and what is described in some of the historical backgrounds of "critical infrastructure," and why it is important to the United States. There will be some terms and definitions covering a brief synopsis of the intent of the book, and what is to be expected from Critical Infrastructure Protection and Preparedness Specialists (CIPS) professionals.

CHAPTER 2: REGULATIONS AND LEGISLATION

This chapter outlines laws that are currently in effect (since 9/11) that apply to critical infrastructure protection. It is nothing more than a small journal listing each law, with a brief synopsis of the law and its summary.

CHAPTER 3: NATIONAL RESPONSE PLAN (NRP)

In December 2004, the Department of Homeland Security (DHS) introduced a comprehensive 500+ page report outlining "what if" scenarios in case of disasters, national emergencies, and potential acts of terrorism. Since the NRP is rather comprehensive and very detailed, this chapter merely summarizes and highlights some of the content from the NRP.

CHAPTER 4: NATIONAL INCIDENT MANAGEMENT SYSTEMS (NIMS)

This chapter applies strictly to NIMS and how to apply a "chain of command" for any given incident; there is some crossover between this chapter and Chapter 5, which specifically involves Incident Command Systems (ICS) (ICS is a subset of NIMS), and Chapter 6, which outlines scenarios and instructions on Emergency Preparedness and Readiness (EMR).

CHAPTER 5: INCIDENT COMMAND SYSTEMS (ICS)

This chapter elaborates further about the chain of command structure during a crisis and summarizes the appropriate course of action, definition of Incident Action Plans (IAP), and more.

CHAPTER 6: EMERGENCY PREPAREDNESS AND READINESS (EMR)

This chapter deals with the overall concept behind emergency preparedness and summarizes "what if" scenarios with explanations from the Office of Domestic Preparedness (ODP) and the U.S. Fire Administration.

CHAPTER 7: SECURITY VULNERABILITY ASSESSMENTS (SVA)

This chapter is the meat of the book, and provides the backbone for reasons of what, where, why, and how risk assessments are to be performed, why they are needed, and what causes them to be needed. This chapter is representative of a set of guidelines that both military and government agencies currently are using or improving.

CHAPTER 8: STANDARDS AND GUIDELINES

This chapter outlines relevant standards, guidelines, and protocols from various agencies, associations, and councils such as the National Fire Prevention Association (NFPA) and how they might apply to critical infrastructure. It also outlines two new standards from NFPA that are established for onsite premise security sometime in 2005, mostly applying to electrical wiring for security systems Closed-Circuit Television (CCTV) cameras, perimeter control systems, and so forth.

CHAPTER 9: INFORMATION SHARING AND ANALYSIS CENTERS (ISAC)

This chapter outlines and summarizes all relevant Information Sharing and Analysis Centers (ISAC), which are information dissemination and distribution points for critical information that may pertain to that particular sector. Not all sectors listed within the President's Report on Critical Infrastructure (PDD-63 and HSPD-7/HSPD-8) outline all ISAC organizations; however, an effort was made to provide as much information as possible and how it is relevant and pertains to critical infrastructure environments.

CHAPTER 10: SUPERVISORY CONTROL AND DATA ACQUISITION (SCADA)

This chapter discusses control systems used within and throughout (just about) each sector. Control systems consist of two subset topics: Distributed Control Systems (DCS), which are the distribution mechanisms of a large geographical area; and Supervisory Control and Data Acquisition (SCADA) systems, which are devices that interface with noncomputing functions that are critical to that sector (value control, switch control, flow metering, and so forth).

CHAPTER 11: CRITICAL INFRASTRUCTURE INFORMATION (CII)

This chapter outlines and attempts to summarize all classifications of information that would apply to critical infrastructures. Additionally, any legal ramifications, enforcement capabilities, along with the definition of the term "critical infrastructure information" are outlined as well.

Table of Contents

Chapter 5

1 Introduction to Critical Infrastructure Preparedness

1.1 INTRODUCTION

Officials from both public and private sectors of the United States have been actively promoting and applying critical infrastructure protection and preparedness methods well before the attacks on September 11, 2001. Yet it was not too long ago that most citizens never heard of such words, at least until 9/11. So why is there now so much attention being given to critical infrastructure?

The urgent call for the protection of critical infrastructures began on September 11, 2001, when leaders of government and industry, and its citizens, were awakened on issues of national safety and security. Since that unforgettable day, the American people have been confronted with the possibility of living and working without one or more of the many basic necessities we have come to expect and depend on. For example, can you imagine surviving without water, electricity, home heating oil, natural gas, transportation (train, airplane, or automotive), communications (telephones, cellular telephones, the Internet), emergency services, and more? Neither can the government.

The operations of protecting a critical infrastructure does not depend upon any unique intelligence collection method, nor does it require any unique integrated intelligence function. What is more important are the specific analytical methodologies which may be used to assess vulnerabilities, perform risk analysis relative to the infrastructure being protected, and its remediation, or the mitigation of any (hopefully, all) risk. These tasks involve businesses at thinking in terms of self-protection at a business-level capability; the same goes for whatever government or agency is implementing the policy.[1]

For example, one analytical method for prevention is performing penetration tests (formerly referred to as *tiger teams*,[2] now referred to as *red teams*[3]). *Tiger teams* (now called *red teams*[4]) is a former U.S. military term[5] (in which private sector, commercial security groups, but in a more specific sense) defining government or industry-sponsored teams of experts and professionals who attempt to break down [or through] any defenses or perimeters in an effort to uncover, and eventually patch, any security holes.[6] This concept is useful for short-lived projects or tasks that involve designating individuals within a given organization to think like, act like, and behave in manners that support the way criminals (referred to as *bad guys*) or terrorists would think, would attack, and study their approach to target sets and priorities.

In former years of U.S. military history, these people were paid professionals who performed hacker-type tricks, for example, leaving cardboard signs displaying the words "bomb" within critical defense installations, or leaving handwritten notes stating "Your codebooks have been stolen" (even though they usually were not) that were placed inside safes or locked, secured areas. In some instances, after a successful penetration mission, when there was an official security review, the next morning for that review, officials found signs, notes, and so forth, emplaced by the security team(s) from the previous day or week, which sometimes resulted in early retirements of the base commanders or their security officers. It is generally assumed that with any critical infrastructure protection initiative, that the *bad guys* are determined adversaries — flexible, creative, resourceful — and able to learn how to target vulnerable areas while avoiding those that are more protected and predictable. In many situations, modern, sophisticated, or technologically advanced societies are perfect targets for terrorists; and businesses that are not flexible enough also make perfect targets.[7]

1.2 HOMELAND SECURITY PRESIDENTIAL DIRECTIVES (HSPD)

Homeland Security Presidential Directives (HSPD) are presidential directives specifically relating to Homeland Security. Each directive has specific meaning and purpose and is carried out (almost immediately) by the U.S. Department of Homeland Security.[8] For each directive (and its meaning), see the subsequent sections which summarize each directive.

1.2.1 HSPD-1: ORGANIZATION AND OPERATION OF THE HOMELAND SECURITY COUNCIL

Established on October 29, 2001, this is the first in a series of Homeland Security Presidential Directives that shall record and communicate presidential decisions about the homeland security policies of the United States. This directive formed the organizational structure that now makes up the U.S. Department of Homeland Security, as well as defined the Operation of the Homeland Security Council. The Homeland Security Council (HSC) was defined to ensure coordination of all homeland security-related activities among executive departments and agencies and to promote the effective development and implementation of all homeland security policies. The HSC is broken into several coordinated committees, each with their own specific direction and function.[9]

1.2.2 HSPD-2: COMBATING TERRORISM THROUGH IMMIGRATION POLICIES

Established on October 29, 2001, this directive defined border and immigration security policies.[10]

1.2.3 HSPD-3: HOMELAND SECURITY ADVISORY SYSTEM

Established on March 11, 2002, this directive established the color-coded national security advisory system. The Homeland Security Advisory System provides a comprehensive and effective means to disseminate information regarding the risk of terrorist acts to federal, state, and local authorities and to its citizens. This system provides warnings in the form of a set of graduated "Threat Conditions" that increase as the risk of the threat increases. At each Threat Condition, federal departments and agencies would implement a corresponding set of "Protective Measures" to further reduce vulnerability or increase response capability during a period of heightened alert.[11]

1.2.4 HSPD-4: NATIONAL STRATEGY TO COMBAT WEAPONS OF MASS DESTRUCTION

Signed into effect on September 17, 2002, and established sometime in December 2002, this directive provides specific directions in proliferation and counter-proliferation strategies and tactics relating to Weapons of Mass Destruction (WMD).[12]

1.2.5 HSPD-5: MANAGEMENT OF DOMESTIC INCIDENTS

Established February 28, 2003, this directive is defined to enhance the ability of the United States to manage domestic incidents by establishing a single, comprehensive National Incident Management System (NIMS).[13]

1.2.6 HSPD-6: INTEGRATION AND USE OF SCREENING INFORMATION

Established September 16, 2003, this directive defined methods and policies to protect against terrorism It is the policy of the United States to (1) develop, integrate, and maintain thorough, accurate, and current information about individuals known or appropriately suspected to be or have been engaged in conduct constituting, in preparation for, in aid of, or related to terrorism (Terrorist Information); and (2) use that information as appropriate and to the full extent permitted by law to support (a) federal, state, local, territorial, tribal, foreign-government, and private-sector screening processes, and (b) diplomatic, military, intelligence, law enforcement, immigration, visa, and protective processes.[14]

1.2.7 HSPD-7: CRITICAL INFRASTRUCTURE IDENTIFICATION, PRIORITIZATION, AND PROTECTION

HSPD-7[15] was issued on December 17, 2003, and established the policy of the United States to enhance and protect its national critical infrastructures against acts of terrorism or criminal activities that would significantly diminish the responsibility of federal, state, and local governments, and to perform essential security services that would ensure stability, safety, and security to its citizens. The USA PATRIOT Act of 2001 defines critical infrastructures as "those physical and cyber-based systems so vital to the operations of the United States that their incapacity or destruction would have a debilitating impact on national defense, economic security, or public safety."[16] More specifically, critical infrastructures are those people, things, or systems that must be intact and operational in order to make daily living and working possible. This directive supersedes Presidential Decision Directive (PDD)/National Security Council (NSC)-63 of May 22, 1998 (entitled "Critical Infrastructure Protection"), and any Presidential directives issued prior to this directive to the extent of any inconsistency.

1.2.8 HSPD-8: National Preparedness

Established on the same date as HSPD-7, December 17, 2003, this directive established policies to strengthen the preparedness of the United States to prevent and respond to threatened or actual domestic terrorist attacks, major disasters, and other emergencies by requiring a national domestic all-hazards preparedness goal, establishing mechanisms for improved delivery of federal preparedness assistance to state and local governments, and outlining actions to strengthen preparedness capabilities of federal, state, and local entities.[17]

1.2.9 HSPD-9: Defense of United States Agriculture and Food

Established on January 30, 2004, this directive establishes a national policy to defend the agriculture and food system against terrorist attacks, major disasters, and other emergencies.[18]

1.2.10 HSPD-10: Biodefense for the 21st Century

Also referred as National Security Presidential Directive (NSPD)-33[19], HSPD-10 was established on April 28, 2004, and it expands on defending against biological weapons attacks requiring further modifications of government policies, coordination, and planning that integrate the biodefense capabilities at federal, state, local, and private sector levels.[20]

1.2.11 HSPD-11: Comprehensive Terrorist-Related Screening Procedures

Established on August 27, 2004, this directive defines more effectively methods in detecting and interdicting individuals known or reasonably suspected to be or have been engaged in conduct constituting, in preparation for, in aid of, or related to terrorism.[21]

1.2.12 HSPD-12: Policy for a Common Identification Standard for Federal Employees and Contractors

Established on the same date as HSPD-11, August 27, 2004, this directive initiated methods of enhancing security, increasing government efficiency, reducing identity fraud, and protecting personal privacy by establishing a mandatory, government-wide standard for secure and reliable forms of identification issued by the federal government to its employees and contractors.[22]

1.2.13 HSPD-13: NATIONAL STRATEGY FOR MARITIME SECURITY

The National Strategy for Maritime Security[23], which defined the National Maritime Domain Awareness (MDA) Plan, was also referred to as NSPD-41.[24] This directive defines an "effective understanding of anything associated with the Maritime Domain that could impact the security, safety, economy, or environment of the United States" with the Maritime Domain defined as " ... all areas and things of, on, under, relating to, adjacent to, or bordering on a sea, ocean, or other navigable waterway, including all maritime-related activities, infrastructure, people, cargo, vessels, and other conveyances." [25]

1.3 WHAT IS CRITICAL INFRASTRUCTURE?

The term *critical infrastructure* refers to assets of physical and computer-based systems that are essential to the minimum operations of the economy and government. They include, but are not limited to, telecommunications, energy, banking and finance, transportation, water systems and emergency services, both governmental and private. Many of the nation's critical infrastructures have historically been physically and logically separated systems that had little interdependence, at least, until 9/11. As a result, advances in information technology and with efforts performed to improve efficiencies in these systems, infrastructures have become increasingly automated and more interlinked. These improvements have created new vulnerabilities relating to equipment failure, human error, weather and other natural causes, as well as physical and computer-related attacks. Addressing these vulnerabilities necessitates flexibility, a massive evolutionary approach that spans both public and private sectors, protecting both domestic and international interests.

Every department and agency of federal, state, and local governments is responsible for protecting their own infrastructure; each department and agency should have measures to assure that information is valid and accurate, protecting that information as if it were considered an asset. Part of the assurance process is through consistent testing and evaluation of their infrastructures, performing vulnerability assessments periodically against physical and computer-based systems, and obtaining expedient and valid authorities to validate those systems. This applies to both public and private sectors.[26]

1.4 WHAT IS THE PRIVATE SECTOR?

The private sector of a nation's economy consists of those entities which are not controlled by the state, that is, a variety of entities such as private firms and companies, corporations, private banks, nongovernmental organizations, etc.[27] The U.S. Department of Homeland Security (DHS) has an Office of Private Sector Affairs which provides the American business community with a direct line of communication to the U.S. Department of Homeland Security. The Office works with businesses, trade associations, and other nongovernmental organizations to foster dialogue between the private sector and the department on the full range of issues and challenges faced by America's business sector. In addition to ensuring open communication between the department and the private sector, the Office provides strategic guidance to the Secretary on prospective policies and regulations and their impact, and promotes public–private partnerships and best practices to improve the nation's homeland and economic security.[28]

1.5 WHAT IS THE PUBLIC SECTOR?

The public sector consists of federal, state, local, and tribal governments, government-owned or controlled corporations and government monetary institutions.[29] This includes offices, departments, and agencies of these organizations or entities that receive monies and/or appropriations from public interest groups, public funding committees, or tax revenue centers (such as the Internal Revenue Service [IRS]).

1.6 WHAT IS CRITICAL INFRASTRUCTURE PROTECTION?

The term *critical infrastructure protection* (CIP) pertains to the activities for protecting critical infrastructures. This includes people, physical assets, and communication (cyber) systems that are indispensably necessary for national, state, and urban security, economic stability, and public safety. CIP methods and resources deter or mitigate attacks against critical infrastructures caused by people (terrorists, other criminals, hackers, and so forth), by nature (hurricanes, tornadoes, earthquakes, floods, and so on), and by hazardous materials (HAZMAT) accidents involving nuclear, radiological, biological, or chemical substances. Quite simply put, CIP is about protecting assets considered invaluable to society that promotes social well-being.[30] CIP is (oftentimes) considered a reactionary response to threats, risks, vulnerabilities, or hazardous conditions. It does entail some preventative measures and countermeasures, but usually are reactive by nature.

1.7 WHAT IS CRITICAL INFRASTRUCTURE PREPAREDNESS?

In contrast to critical infrastructure protection, the term *critical infrastructure preparedness* (sometimes referred to as *critical infrastructure protection and readiness*, or *CIPR*) represents proactive measures taken in preventing (in some cases, reducing) serious or dangerous levels of threats, risks, vulnerabilities, or hazardous conditions which exist in nature or are man-made. This includes training of preventative measures and countermeasures for both public and private sectors, and public awareness programs, which encourage the general public to think more securely[31], be and feel more safe about their surroundings and environments, and define reporting mechanisms of any unusual or suspicious activities. Also, this includes reading and interpreting visually represented materials for risk mitigation (and its remediation), vulnerability assessments (as part of periodic assurance tests), and competency or accreditation courses for those who validate, protect, and safeguard our infrastructures. The term *preparedness* refers to the existence of plans, procedures, policies, training, and equipment necessary at the federal, state, and local level to maximize the ability to prevent, respond to, and recover from major events. The term *readiness* is used interchangeably with preparedness, such that the term *prevention* refers to activities undertaken by the first responder community during the early stages of an incident to reduce the likelihood or consequences of threatened or actual terrorist attacks. More general and broader efforts to deter, disrupt, or thwart terrorism are not addressed in this directive. All of these factors combined create critical infrastructure protection and preparedness, and its efforts.[32]

1.8 CRITICAL INFRASTRUCTURE FUNCTIONS

Defining, using, and maintaining critical infrastructures are a process of themselves, such that it is an analytical model or template that guides the systematic protection of itself. More importantly, it is a reliable decision-making, sequential set of methodologies that assists decision makers in determining possible needs of what methods should be used for whatever is being safeguarded. The process ensures the protection of only those infrastructures upon which survivability, continuity of operations, and their mission successes depend upon. Thus, these methodologies safeguard only those infrastructures which are deemed important and vital for the continued operation of large scales of economies.

1.9 ORIGINS OF CRITICAL INFRASTRUCTURE

What U.S. policymakers consider to be critical infrastructure has been evolving and is often ambiguous. Twenty years ago, the word *infrastructure* was defined primarily with respect to the adequacy of the nation's public works. In the mid-1990s, however, the growing threat of international terrorism led policy makers to reconsider the definition of *infrastructure* in the context of national security. Successive federal government reports, laws, and executive orders have refined and generally expanded the number of infrastructure sectors and the types of assets considered to be deemed "critical" for purposes of homeland security.[33]

This definition was adopted, by reference, in the Homeland Security Act of 2002 (P.L. 107-296, Sec. 2.4) and it established the "U.S. Department of Homeland Security" (DHS). The National Strategy also adopts the definition of "critical infrastructure" in P.L. 107-56, and provides the following list of specific infrastructure sectors (and its assets) falling under that definition:

- Information technology
- Telecommunications
- Chemicals
- Transportation systems
- Emergency services
- Postal and shipping services
- Agriculture and food
- Public health and health care
- Drinking water/water treatment

- Energy
- Banking and finance
- National monuments and icons
- Defense industrial base
- Key industry/technology sites
- Large gathering sites

The critical infrastructure sectors within the National Strategy contain many physical assets, but only a fraction of these could be viewed as critical according to the DHS definition. For example, out of 33,000 individual assets cataloged in the DHS national asset database, the agency considers only 1700, or 5%, to be nationally critical.[34] Of the 33,000 assets listed within the DHS database, only a small subset of all assets listed are defined as critical infrastructure sectors.[35] Because federal, state, and local governments, as well as the private sector, often have different views of what constitutes criticality, compiling a consensus list of nationally critical assets has been an ongoing challenge for DHS.

1.10 QUESTIONS

1. The definition of "red teaming" means the same thing as conducting a security assessment against a targeted facility or location. True or False?

   Answer: *True*. The term *red team* replaced the term *tiger team*, which was the same.

2. HSPD-1 was defined and established on_____.

   Answer: HSPD-1 (*Homeland Security Presidential Directive-1*) established the Department of Homeland Security on October 29, 2001.

3. National threat conditions were defined and established under _____.

   Answer: *HSPD-7, established on March 11, 2002.*

4. Presidential Decision Directive (PDD)/National Security Council (NSC)-63 was issued on which date?
   a. March 23, 1997
   b. May 22, 1998
   c. March 22, 1998
   d. May 22, 1996

   Answer: Despite the fact that initial efforts started in 1996, the actual Presidential directive was refined and issued on *May 22, 1998* by President Bill Clinton, only to be superseded by President George W. Bush's HSPD-7 on December 17, 2003.

5. PDD/NSC-63 was superseded by which Presidential directive? _____.

   Answer: *HSPD-7: Critical Infrastructure Identification, Prioritization and Protection*, which was established on December 17, 2003.

6. The definition of the term "critical infrastructure" refers to assets of physical and computer-based systems that are essential to the minimum operations of the economy, government, and military. True or False?

   Answer: *True*. This definition is what is provided within the Critical Infrastructure Protection Act of 2001.

7. Each department, each agency, from the federal level down to the local level, are individually responsible for protecting and ensuring the continued operation of each of their own infrastructures. True or False?

   Answer: *True*. Each department or agency is individually responsible for their course of actions that are to be taken in protecting a given infrastructure. This applies to all levels of government, from federal to local level.

8. The *private sector* consists of entities that are _____ by the _____.

   Answer: (1) *Not controlled*; (2) *state* (or *government*).

9. The "public sector" is strictly limited to law enforcement and fire protection. True or False?

   Answer: *False*. The *public sector* consists of all departments and agencies at federal, state, local, and tribal levels that are government-owned or controlled corporations as well as government monetary institutions (such as the Internal Revenue Service and the Federal Reserve Banks).

10. Can "critical infrastructure protection" pertain to circumstances of nature such as hurricane? Yes or No.

    Answer: *Yes*. It can pertain to man-made events or natural events (such as acts of God), hazardous materials spills involving nuclear, radiological, biological, or dangerous chemical substances, or can be computer-based (such as the Internet).

11. The definition of the term critical infrastructure preparedness refers to _____ taken in _____ risks, threats, or vulnerabilities from occurring.

    Answer: (1) *Proactive measures*; (2) *preventing*.

12. The term "critical infrastructure" was introduced when?
    a. Mid-1980s
    b. Mid-1990s
    c. Late 1990s
    d. Early 2001

    Answer: *Mid-1990s*. Actually, the term *infrastructure* was first introduced during the years of President Ronald Reagan. This definition has undergone several modifications with each successor, but was further refined into the term *critical infrastructure* that is used today as being attributed to President Bill Clinton.

NOTES

1. http://www.usfa.fema.gov/subjects/emr-isac/what_is.shtm
2. http://www.tsl.state.tx.us/ld/pubs/compsecurity/glossary.html
3. http://www.sandia.gov/idart/index.html
4. http://www.sandia.gov/idart/index.html
5. http://www.comedia.com/hot/jargon-4.2.3/html/entry/tiger-team.html
6. http://catb.org/~esr/jargon/html/T/tiger-team.html
7. http://faculty.ncwc.edu/toconnor/431/431lect06.htm
8. http://www.whitehouse.gov/query.html?col=colpics&qt=hspd
9. http://www.fas.org/irp/offdocs/nspd/hspd-1.htm
10. http://www.fas.org/irp/offdocs/nspd/hspd-2.htm
11. http://www.fas.org/irp/offdocs/nspd/hspd-2.htm
12. http://www.fas.org/irp/offdocs/nspd/nspd-17.html
13. http://www.whitehouse.gov/news/releases/2003/02/20030228-9.html
14. http://www.whitehouse.gov/news/releases/2003/09/20030916-5.html
15. http://www.whitehouse.gov/news/releases/2003/12/20031217-5.html
16. http://thomas.loc.gov/cgi-bin/bdquery/z?d107:HR03162:@@@L&summ2=m&
17. http://www.whitehouse.gov/news/releases/2003/12/20031217-6.html
18. http://www.whitehouse.gov/news/releases/2004/02/20040203-2.html
19. http://www.fas.org/irp/offdocs/nspd/biodef.html
20. http://www.fas.org/irp/offdocs/nspd/hspd-10.html
21. http://www.whitehouse.gov/news/releases/2004/08/20040827-7.html
22. http://www.whitehouse.gov/news/releases/2004/08/20040827-8.html
23. http://66.102.7.104/search?q=cache:v8T1EXa---8J:www.sddc.army.mil/CONTENT/13554/PORTPLANNINGORDERPROCESSES.pdf+hspd-13&hl=en
24. http://www.sddc.army.mil/CONTENT/13554/PORTPLANNINGORDERPROCESSES.pdf
25. http://www.maritimesecurityexpo.com/advcomm/advcomm-member-karol.html
26. http://www.usfa.fema.gov/subjects/emr-isac/what_is.shtm
27. http://en.wikipedia.org/wiki/Private_sector
28. http://www.dhs.gov/dhspublic/display?theme=37&content=3363
29. http://nscbru10.norminet.org.ph/glossary/glossmab.htm
30. http://www.usfa.fema.gov/subjects/emr-isac/what_is.shtm
31. http://www.ready.gov
32. http://www.whitehouse.gov/news/releases/2003/12/20031217-6.html

33. The Library of Congress, CRS Report for Congress, Guarding America: Security Guards and U.S. Critical Infrastructure Protection, CRS-RL32670 (November, 2004).

34. Liscouski, Robert, Asst. Sec., Infrastructure Protection, Department of Homeland Security, Testimony before the House Select Committee on Homeland Security; Infrastructure and Border Security Subcommittee. April 21, 2004. Note that DHS's list of 1700 critical assets may not include the 430 U.S. commercial airports with passenger screeners, whose security is primarily administered by the Transportation Security Administration.

35. For example, in the chemicals sector, DHS has identified 4000 facilities as potentially critical out of 66,000 total U.S. chemical sites. See Liscouski, Robert, Asst. Sec. Infrastructure Security, Department of Homeland Security (DHS). Testimony before the House Committee on Government Reform, Subcommittee on National Security, Emerging Threats and International Relations. Combating Terrorism: Chemical Plant Security. Serial No. 108-156. Feb. 23, 2004. p13.

2 Regulations and Legislation

2.1 INTRODUCTION

This chapter outlines any and all laws, bills, and regulations that have been created since September 11, 2001. This chapter outlines those laws which may apply and summarizes them based upon their level of severity. All laws, bills, and regulations listed are displayed alphabetically (as best as possible). As a representative of a critical infrastructure, individuals should know which laws pertain to their sector and are advised to be (at least) somewhat familiar with them, their overall function, and what (if any) ramifications may come from their use.

> Author's Note: At the time of writing this book, there were additional bills and regulations currently under resolution with either the U.S. Congress or the U.S. House of Representatives that were found or established. Not all laws, bills, or regulations may be listed within this book, and as such, may be revised for future releases.

2.2 WHAT ARE THE CATEGORIES OF THE LAWS LISTED?

Any laws, bills, and regulations that pertain to or could be remotely associated with *critical infrastructure* are broken down into several subcomponents, not necessarily similar to those outlined or defined within the National Strategy identified as a "critical infrastructure sector." These subcomponents are represented within several grouped sectors, which are listed sequentially in alphabetic order, and are listed as follows:

- Border Security and Immigration
- Communications and Network Security
- Cyberterrorism
- Domestic Safety and Security
- Economic and Financial Security
- Emergency Preparedness and Readiness
- Hazardous Materials (includes Weapons of Mass Destruction [WMD])
- Infrastructure (not to be confused with the term *critical infrastructure*)
- Medical and Healthcare Security
- Transportation Security (includes Maritime Security)

2.3 BORDER SECURITY AND IMMIGRATION

This section pertains to laws, bills, and regulations for protecting and safeguarding American borders, as well as immigration enforcement.

2.3.1 AN ACT TO MODIFY CERTAIN DEADLINES PERTAINING TO MACHINE-READABLE, TAMPER-RESISTANT ENTRY AND EXIT DOCUMENTS (H.R. 4417)[1]

Presented to the President on July 28, 2004, for signature, this act amends the Enhanced Border Security and Visa Entry Reform Act of 2002 (8 U.S.C. 1732) to extend the deadline by 1 year to 2005 for (a) U.S. ports of entry to install equipment and software capable of processing machine-readable, tamper-resistant entry and exit documents and passports that contain biometric identifiers; (b) Visa Waiver Program (VWP) countries to certify that they are issuing machine-readable, tamper-resistant passports that contain biometric and document authentication identifiers comporting with specified standards; and (c) VWP participants who are issued passports on or after the new deadline to present passports that comply with those requirements.

2.3.2 A BILL TO AMEND THE IMMIGRATION AND NATIONALITY ACT TO PROVIDE PERMANENT AUTHORITY FOR THE ADMISSION OF "S" VISA NONIMMIGRANTS (S. 1424, PUBLIC LAW NO. 107-45)[2]

Signed into law on October 1, 2001, this act grants permanent authority for the provision of nonimmigrant "S" visas to aliens who possess, and will supply (or have supplied) to law enforcement agencies, critical information concerning criminal or terrorist organizations.

2.3.3 ENHANCED BORDER SECURITY AND VISA ENTRY REFORM ACT OF 2002 (H.R. 3525, PUBLIC LAW NO. 107-173)[3]

Signed into law on May 14, 2002, this act provides for increased numbers of U.S. Immigration and Naturalization Service (INS) investigators and inspectors; authorizes appropriations for INS, Border Patrol, and consular personnel, training, facilities, and security-related technology; and calls for information sharing among border security, law enforcement, and intelligence agencies (including technology standard and interoperability requirements), among other provisions.

2.3.4 IMMIGRATION AND NATIONALITY ACT OF 1952 (U.S. CODE TITLE 8)[4]

The INS has asked state and local police to voluntarily arrest aliens who have violated criminal provisions of the U.S. Immigration and Nationality Act or civil provisions that render an alien deportable, and who are wanted as recorded by the National Crime Information Center. The National Security Entry-Exit Registration System Fact Sheet details the purpose and procedures called for by the INS National Security Entry-Exit Registration System. On December 6, 2002, INS issued a statement emphasizing the registration requirements for visiting foreign nationals from the 18 countries affected.

2.3.5 REAL ID Act of 2005 (H.R. 418[5] and H.R. 1268,[6] Public Law No. 109-13)

An extremely controversial piece of legislation was passed unanimously on May 11, 2005, as *Division B of the Emergency Supplemental Appropriations Act for Defense, the Global War on Terror, and Tsunami Relief, 2005*, and became effective on the date of enactment.[7] It is intended to deter terrorist activities through: (1) establishing national standards for state-issued driver's licenses and nondriver's identification cards; (2) waiving laws that interfere with construction of physical barriers at the borders; (3) updating and tightening the laws on application for asylum and deportation of aliens for terrorist activity; (4) introducing rules covering "delivery bonds" (rather like bail bonds, but for aliens that have been released pending hearings); (5) funding for some reports and pilot projects related specifically to border security; and (6) changing visa limits for temporary workers, nurses, and Australians.[8] The act amends the *INA* provisions concerning asylum to: (1) authorize the Secretary of Homeland Security, in addition to the Attorney General, to grant asylum (retroactive to March 1, 2003); (2) require asylum applicants to prove that race, religion, nationality, membership in a particular social group, or political opinion was or will be (if removed) the central reason for their persecution; and (3) provide that an applicant's testimony may be sufficient to sustain this burden of proof only if the trier of fact determines that it is credible, persuasive, and fact-specific. The legislation requires corroborating evidence where requested by the trier of fact unless the applicant does not have the evidence and cannot reasonably obtain it without departing the United States. It also states that the inability to obtain corroborating evidence does not excuse the applicant from meeting his or her burden of proof.[9]

2.4 COMMUNICATIONS AND NETWORK SECURITY

This section pertains to laws, bills, and regulations for protecting and safeguarding any devices connected to our telephone systems, radio, and two-way communications networks, and computer-based networks, such as the Internet.

2.4.1 Communications Assistance for Law Enforcement Act (CALEA) (H.R. 4922, Public Law No. 103-414, 108 Stat. 4279)[10]

Signed into law on October 25, 1994, this act amends the federal criminal code to make clear a telecommunications carrier's duty to cooperate in the interception of communications for law enforcement purposes. The CALEA Web site[11] is an information clearinghouse for those interested in CALEA; it provides information on capability, capacity, cost recovery, flexible deployment, liaison, and reimbursement requirements and standards.

2.4.2 E-911 Implementation Act of 2003 (H.R. 2898)[12]

The bill would authorize the U.S. Department of Commerce's National Telecommunications and Information Administration to make matching grants to state and local governments and tribal organizations to enhance emergency communications services through planning, infrastructure improvements, equipment purchases, and personnel training and acquisition.

2.4.3 GOVERNMENT INFORMATION SECURITY REFORM ACT OF 2002 (GISRA) (S. 3067)[13]

This act was passed on November 14, 2002, and amends Title 44, United States Code, to extend certain government information security reform for one year.[14]

2.4.4 GOVERNMENT INFORMATION SECURITY ACT OF 2000 (GISA) (S. 1993)[15]

Signed into law on October 12, 2000, by the Senate as part of the conference report on the National Defense Authorization Act for Fiscal 2001 (H.R. 4205), this act provides a comprehensive framework for establishing and ensuring the effectiveness of controls over information and information resources that support federal operations and assets. This legislation maintains the existing distinction between: (1) policy and oversight for national security systems and information; and (2) policy and oversight for unclassified systems and information, in a manner generally consistent with existing law, policy, and practice.[16] The act will ensure that: (1) basic management practices for agencies are followed and establish accountability at agency levels; (2) requires an annual independent evaluation of agencies' security, a practice suggested by many of the leading security experts in both government and industry; and (3) authorizes the Federal Cyber Services Scholarship for Service program, an initiative aimed at increasing federal security expertise by paying the tuition of students studying security in college in return for a term of employment in the federal government.[17]

2.5 CYBERTERRORISM

The Gilmore Commission[18] noted that the "cyber attacks incident" to conflicts in the Middle East "emphasized the potentially disastrous effects that such concentrated attacks can have on information and other critical government and private sector electronic systems."[19] The Commission concluded that while not "mass destructive," attacks on our critical infrastructure would certainly be "mass disruptive." It also concluded that the most likely perpetrators of cyber attacks on critical infrastructures are terrorists and criminal groups rather than nation-states. As a result, the Commission predicted that detection of these attacks would fall primarily to the private sector and to local law enforcement authorities.[20]

2.5.1 CYBER SECURITY RESEARCH AND DEVELOPMENT ACT (H.R. 3394, PUBLIC LAW NO. 107-305)[21]

Signed into law on November 27, 2002, this legislation will establish computer security research centers and fellowship programs through the National Science Foundation and the National Institute of Standards and Technology.[22]

Under the bill, the National Science Foundation (NSF) will create new cyber-security research centers, undergraduate program grants, community college grants, and fellowships. The National Institute of Standards and Technology (NIST) will create new program grants for partnerships between academia and industry, new postdocs, and a new program to encourage senior researchers in other fields to work on computer security. The Cyber Security Act authorized $880 million over 5 years for these new programs, ensuring that the U.S. is better prepared to prevent and combat terrorist attacks on private and government computers.[23]

Other cyber-related legislation that may be considered equally as important as others in an effort of securing critical infrastructure is detailed in the following.

2.5.2 Computer Security Act of 1987 (40 U.S.C. Chapter 25 Section 1441, Public Law No. 100-235)[24]

This Act provides for a computer standards program within the National Bureau of Standards, to provide for government-wide computer security, and to provide for the training in security matters of persons who are involved in the management, operation, and use of federal computer systems.[25]

2.5.3 Computer Security Enhancement Act of 1997 (H.R. 1903[26])[27]

This bill amends the *Computer Security Act of 1987* which was enacted on September 16, 1997, to give the National Institute of Standards and Technology the primary role in establishing guidelines for the protection of computer systems in the federal government.[28] The amendment states that the *National Institute of Standards and Technology Act* will require the National Institute of Standards and Technology, in fulfilling its responsibilities under the computer standards program, to: (1) upon request from the private sector, assist in establishing voluntary interoperable standards, guidelines, and associated methods and techniques to facilitate and expedite the establishment of nonfederal public key management infrastructures that can be used to communicate with and conduct transactions with the federal government; and (2) provide assistance to federal agencies in the protection of computer networks, and coordinate federal response efforts related to unauthorized access to federal computer systems.[29] The law also requires NIST to perform evaluation and tests of: (1) information technologies to assess security vulnerabilities; and (2) commercially available security products for their suitability for use by federal agencies for protecting sensitive information in computer systems.[30]

2.5.4 Federal Information Security Management Act of 2002 (FISMA) (H.R. 2458,[31] S. 803, Public Law No. 107-347)[32]

This act was enacted on December 17, 2002, authorizing and strengthening the information security program, evaluation, and reporting requirements for federal agencies.[33] The *Federal Information Security Management Act of 2002 (FISMA)* is contained within the *E-Government Act of 2002 (P.L. 107-347)* as *Title III*, replacing the *Government Information Security Reform Act (GISRA)*. FISMA, effective throughout the federal government, places requirements on government agencies and components with the goal of improving the security of federal information and information systems.[34] FISMA's purpose is to: (1) provide a framework for enhancing the effectiveness of information security in the federal government, which means protecting information and information systems from unauthorized access, use, disclosure, disruption, modification, or destruction to ensure integrity, confidentiality, and availability; (2) provide effective government-wide management of risks to information security; (3) provide for the development and maintenance of minimum controls required for protecting federal information and information systems; and (4) provide a mechanism for effective oversight of federal agency information security programs.[35] The act requires every government agency to secure the information and information systems that support its operations and assets, including those provided or managed by another agency, contractor, or other source. FISMA defines three (3) security objectives for information and information systems: *confidentiality*, *integrity*, and *availability*. All agencies covered by the Paperwork Reduction Act must implement the requirements of FISMA and report annually to the Office of Management and Budget and Congress on the effectiveness of the agency's security programs. It codifies existing OMB security policies, including those specified in *Circular A-130, Management of Federal Information Resources*, under *Appendix III*, and reiterates security responsibilities outlined within the *Computer Security Act of 1987*, the *Paperwork Reduction Act of 1995*, and the *Clinger-Cohen Act of 1996*.[36] The reports must also include independent evaluations by the agency Inspector General.[37] *NOTE: FISMA is applicable only to the government sector or private sector industries that operate within the government sector.*

2.5.5 E-GOVERNMENT ACT OF 2002 (H.R. 2458, S. 803, PUBLIC LAW NO. 107-347)[38]

This piece of legislation, along with the *Federal Information Security Management Act of 2002 (FISMA)*, was combined within H.R. 2458/S. 803, and enacted on December 17, 2002. This act enhances the management and promotion of electronic government services and processes by establishing an Office of Electronic Government within the Office of Management and Budget, and established a broad framework of measures that require using Internet-based information technology to enhance citizen access of government information and services.[39]

2.5.6 INFORMATION TECHNOLOGY MANAGEMENT REFORM ACT OF 1996 (PUBLIC LAW NO. 104-106) (NOW REFERRED TO AS THE CLINGER-COHEN ACT)[40]

The Information Technology (IT) Management Reform Act of 1996 (that is, ITMRA or the *Clinger-Cohen Act*), which took effect August 8, 1996, abolished the Brooks Act (it repealed Section 111 of the Federal Property and Administrative Services Act of 1949 [40 U.S.C. 759]). The Brooks Act made the General Services Administration (GSA) the central authority for procurement of automatic data processing

(ADP) resources. The Federal Information Resources Management Regulation (FIRMR) was issued to implement the Brooks Act and established a process that required federal agencies to obtain a Delegation of Procurement Authority (DPA) from GSA to acquire ADP, initially, and telecommunications (TC) resources. Passage of the ITMRA caused a major paradigm shift in the process for acquiring and managing IT as the task of understanding the objectives of ITMRA and establishing a program or process to manage IT in a federal agency is a major undertaking.[41] Although the Paperwork Reduction Act specifically addresses IT, other related legislation attempted had made the federal government operations more efficient and effective without concentrating specifically upon IT functions. Congress was concerned about the expenditure of funds on IT since the executive branch started spending large sums of money for mainframe computers and systems. The track record on the acquisition and implementation of large IT systems has included a number of spectacular successes and spectacular failures.[42]

2.6 INFRASTRUCTURE

This section pertains (mostly) to buildings, bridges, and spans — essentially, the fabrication of an infrastructure, rather than one of the listed sectors defined as a *critical infrastructure.*

2.6.1 ENERGY POLICY ACT OF 2005 (H.R. 6; ALSO REFERRED TO AS THE ELECTRIC RELIABILITY ACT OF 2005)

The Energy Policy Act of 2005 (H.R. 6; also referred to as the "Electric Reliability Act of 2005") was passed by the U.S. House of Representatives on April 21, 2005.[43] The Senate passed its version of the energy bill on June 28, 2005. The law was instrumental in several key aspects, but primarily one: it provides for enforceable mandatory reliability standards, incentives for transmission grid improvements and reform of transmission rules. The improvements implemented will attract new investment into the industry and ensure the reliability of the nation's electricity grid to prevent future blackouts.[44] This law should not be confused with the *Energy Policy Act of 1992 (EPACT) (Public Law No. 102-486)*; EPACT created a competitive wholesale framework such that transmission access was opened to wholesale power generation organizations (wholesale buyers of electricity, such as electric utilities, who buy electricity at wholesale prices to sell it on a retail basis).[45]

2.6.2 NATIONAL CONSTRUCTION SAFETY TEAM ACT (H.R. 4687, PUBLIC LAW NO. 107-231)[46]

In response to the September 11, 2001, terrorist attack on the World Trade Center (WTC), this act was signed into law on October 1, 2002, granting broad investigative authority to the National Institute of Standards and Technology (NIST) concerning major U.S. building failures. NIST's WTC Web site[47] offers additional information.

2.6.3 PIPELINE SAFETY IMPROVEMENT ACT OF 2002 (H.R. 3609, PUBLIC LAW NO. 107-355)[48]

Signed by President Bush on December 17, 2002, this law was enacted to further enhance the security and safety of pipelines. It amends Title 49, Subtitle VIII[49] of the U.S. Code.

2.7 DOMESTIC SAFETY AND SECURITY

This section represents legislation introduced to the U.S. to protect its citizens and infrastructure. The Homeland Security Act of 2002 was the beginning of such efforts by the federal government to safeguard and protect human life, property, assets, and its infrastructure.

2.7.1 EFFECTIVE COUNTERTERRORISM ACT OF 1996 (H.R. 3071)[50]

Signed into law on April 24, 1996 (as S.735,[51] Public Law No. 104-132[52]), this bill sets penalties for providing terrorist organizations with material support, expands federal jurisdiction over bomb threats, adds terrorism offenses to the money laundering statute, and establishes or increases other penalties related to acts of terrorism. It also authorizes funding for specialized training or equipment to enhance the capability of metropolitan fire and emergency service departments to respond to terrorist attacks.

2.7.2 HOMELAND SECURITY ACT OF 2002 (H.R. 5005, PUBLIC LAW NO. 107-296)[53]

Signed into law on November 25, 2002, this act restructures and strengthens the executive branch of the federal government to better meet the threat posed by terrorism. In establishing a new U.S. Department of Homeland Security, the act for the first time creates a federal department whose primary mission will be to help prevent, protect against, and respond to acts of terrorism.

2.7.3 FY 2005 HOMELAND SECURITY APPROPRIATIONS ACT[54]

Signed into law on October 18, 2004, the Appropriations Act provides $28.9 billion in net discretionary spending for the U.S. Department of Homeland Security.

2.7.4 INTELLIGENCE REFORM AND TERRORISM PREVENTION ACT OF 2004 (CONFERENCE REPORT)[55]

This conference report accompanies S.2845[56] (National Intelligence Reform Act of 2004). Referred to the President on December 8, 2004, the Intelligence Reform Bill creates a national counterterrorism center and an independent civil liberties board. Once signed into law, this bill will create the position of Intelligence Chief. This person will oversee the nation's intelligence community and related agencies. In addition, the act will increase security measures for airports, create national standards for drivers' licenses and other identification cards, increase incidents of mandatory sentencing for terrorist-related crimes, provide more border security agents and inspectors, and increase the number of detention spaces available for terrorists.

2.7.5 A JOINT RESOLUTION EXPRESSING THE SENSE OF THE SENATE AND HOUSE OF REPRESENTATIVES REGARDING THE TERRORIST ATTACKS LAUNCHED AGAINST THE UNITED STATES ON SEPTEMBER 11, 2001 (S.J. RES. 22, PUBLIC LAW NO. 107-39)[57]

Signed into law on September 18, 2001, this act condemns the terrorists who planned and carried out the September 11, 2001, attacks against the United States; extends condolences to the victims and their loved ones; commends the heroic actions of the rescue workers, volunteers, and public officials who responded to these tragic events; declares that the nation will stand united as recovery and rebuilding are carried out; and declares that the United States is entitled to respond under international law.

2.7.6 NATIONAL INTELLIGENCE REFORM ACT OF 2004[58]

Passed by both houses of Congress and cleared for The White House on December 8, 2004, the National Intelligence Act of 2004[58] overhauls U.S. intelligence. (See also the description of the conference report, as shown above, entitled as the "Intelligence Reform and Terrorism Prevention Act of 2004.") The act creates a Director of National Intelligence with broad authority to unify intelligence gathering and operations. Additional provisions (a) require standards for state-issued identification; (b) authorize the Federal Bureau of Investigation to conduct surveillance of foreign nationals suspected of terrorism; (c) create a uniform security-clearance process; (d) allow federal prosecutors to share information from grand jury proceedings with law enforcement to prevent terrorist attacks; and (e) shift the burden of proof for (release/continued detention of) those detained for terrorist offenses from the government to the defense.

2.7.7 PREPAREDNESS AGAINST TERRORISM ACT OF 2000 (H.R. 4210)[59]

Referred to the Senate committee on July 26, 2000, this bill requires the President to ensure that federal emergency preparedness plans and programs are adequate and carried out in the event of an act of terrorism or other catastrophic event. *This bill predates September 11, 2001.*

2.7.8 ROBERT T. STAFFORD DISASTER RELIEF AND EMERGENCY ASSISTANCE ACT (PUBLIC LAW NO. 93-288, AS AMENDED, 42 U.S.C. 5121, ET SEQ.)[60]

The Disaster Relief and Emergency Assistance Act provide the federal government with the authority to respond to disasters and emergencies in order to provide assistance, save lives, and protect public health, safety, and property. Such responses include establishing disaster preparedness programs; providing funding for preparedness and prevention plans, and ensuring that all appropriate federal agencies are prepared to issue disaster warnings to state and local officials.

2.7.9 TERRORIST PENALTIES ENHANCEMENT ACT OF 2004 (H.R. 2394)[61]

This act increases criminal penalties for fatal acts of terrorism and denies federal benefits for convicted terrorists.

2.7.10 UNITED STATES FIRE ADMINISTRATION REAUTHORIZATION ACT OF 2003 (S. 1152, PUBLIC LAW NO. 108-169)[62]

Signed by the President on December 6, 2003, this bill reauthorizes appropriations for the U.S. Fire Administration and authorizes increased federal assistance in evaluating and standardizing fire prevention and control technologies in preparation for state and local fire service responses to national emergencies.

2.7.11 UNITING AND STRENGTHENING AMERICA BY PROVIDING APPROPRIATE TOOLS REQUIRED TO INTERCEPT AND OBSTRUCT TERRORISM ACT (ALSO KNOWN AS THE USA PATRIOT ACT) OF 2001 (H.R. 3162, PUBLIC LAW NO. 107-56)[63]

Signed into law on October 26, 2001, this act provides for enhanced domestic security against terrorism, enhanced surveillance and intelligence procedures, mechanisms to detect and report money laundering and currency crimes, enhanced immigrations provisions, and procedures for cooperation and information sharing in investigating terrorism. The Web site,[64] dedicated to the USA PATRIOT Act, is organized by specialized topics: major speeches, dispelling the myths about the act, congressional votes, congressional explanations of the act, support of the people, stories and articles, the full text of the act, and the antiterror record of accomplishments. The U.S. Department of Justice's first priority is to prevent future terrorist attacks. Since its passage following the September 11, 2001, attacks, the USA PATRIOT Act has played a key part (often the leading role) in a number of successful operations of protecting innocent Americans from the deadly plans of terrorists dedicated to destroying America and our way of life. While the results have been important, in passing the USA PATRIOT Act, Congress provided for only modest, incremental changes in the law. Congress simply took existing legal principles and retrofitted them to preserve the lives and liberty of the American people from the challenges posed by a global terrorist network.[65]

2.7.12 CRITICAL INFRASTRUCTURE PROTECTION ACT OF 2001 (USA PATRIOT ACT S. 1016, 42 U.S.C. 5195c)[66]

Declares and defines national policy such that: (1) any physical or virtual disruption of the operation of the critical infrastructures of the United States be rare, brief, geographically limited in effect, manageable, and minimally detrimental to the economy, human and government services, and national security; (2) actions necessary to achieve this policy be carried out in a public–private partnership involving corporate and nongovernmental organizations; and (3) a comprehensive and effective program to ensure the continuity of essential federal government functions under all circumstances be in place. This act establishes the National Infrastructure Simulation and Analysis Center (NISAC) to serve as a source of national competence to address critical infrastructure protection and continuity through support for activities related to counterterrorism, threat assessment, and risk mitigation.[67] Finally, it defines the term *critical infrastructure* as meaning "systems and assets, whether physical or virtual, so vital to the United States that the incapacity or destruction of such systems and assets would have a debilitating impact on security, national economic security, national public health or safety, or any combination of those matters."[68]

2.7.13 WIRELESS COMMUNICATIONS AND PUBLIC SAFETY ACT OF 1999 (H.R. 438, S. 800)[69]

This act establishes "911" as a nationwide emergency number, limits commercial disclosure, as well as the reuse of location information from mobile telephones.[70]

2.8 ECONOMIC AND FINANCIAL SECURITY

The banking and finance sector is building an already resilient foundation. Financial institutions have been targets of criminal activity since the first bank was charted in the United States in 1781. Since 1985, over 60% of terrorist attacks worldwide have targeted financial institutions. This sector dedicates significant resources in the protection of its assets and its customers, ensuring the safety of its employees and customers. Over the past few years, there have been examples of this kind of resilience; for example, the U.S. economy endured the pressure of an economic recession, the terrorist attacks of September 11, corporate governance scandals, and the power outage of August 2004. This sector responded effectively when the threat level was elevated, and institutions that were targeted experienced no disruptions.[71]

2.8.1 1984 ACT TO COMBAT INTERNATIONAL TERRORISM (H.R. 6311, PUBLIC LAW NO. 98-533)[72]

This act established the Rewards for Justice Program,[73] under which the U.S. Secretary of State may offer rewards for information that prevents or favorably resolves acts of international terrorism against U.S. persons or property worldwide. Rewards also may be paid for information leading to the arrest or conviction of terrorists attempting, committing, and conspiring to commit, or aiding and abetting the commission of such acts. *This law predates September 11, 2001.*

2.8.2 2001 EMERGENCY SUPPLEMENTAL APPROPRIATIONS ACT FOR RECOVERY FROM AND RESPONSE TO TERRORIST ATTACKS ON THE UNITED STATES (H.R. 2888, PUBLIC LAW NO. 107-38)[74]

Signed into law on September 18, 2001, this act makes emergency supplemental appropriations for fiscal year 2001 for emergency expenses to respond to the September 11 terrorist attacks, provide assistance for the victims, and deal with other consequences of the attacks.

2.8.3 CLEAN DIAMOND TRADE ACT (H.R. 1584)[75]

On April 25, 2003, President Bush signed into law this act to ban illegal diamonds that finance the illicit proliferation of arms and armed conflict and the resulting destabilization of legitimate governments and violations of human rights. Upon implementation, this law will bring the United States into compliance with the Kimberley Process Certification Scheme for Rough Diamonds,[76] an international agreement that bans the import or export of "conflict" or "blood" diamonds.

2.8.4 HOMELAND SECURITY GRANT ENHANCEMENT ACT OF 2003 (S. 1245)[77]

The text of a Senate bill provides for homeland security grant coordination and simplification. This bill was referred to the Committee on Governmental Affairs on June 12, 2003.

2.8.5 INTELLIGENCE AUTHORIZATION ACT FOR FISCAL YEAR 2004 (H.R. 2417, S. 1025)[78]

This bill, presented to the White House on December 2, 2003, authorizes appropriations for fiscal year 2004 for intelligence and intelligence-related activities of the U.S. government, the Community Management Account, and the Central Intelligence Agency Retirement and Disability System. This bill was signed by President George Bush on December 13, 2003, and enacted as Public Law No. l08-177, 117 Stat. 2599.

2.8.6 INTERNATIONAL EMERGENCY ECONOMIC POWERS ACT (IEEPA) (U.S. CODE TITLE 50, CHAPTER 35)[79]

This act authorizes the President to regulate foreign economic transactions when a national emergency is declared to deal with any unusual and extraordinary threat to the United States that has its source in whole or substantial part outside the United States. As amended after the September 11, 2001, terrorist attacks, it also provides the President with the authority to freeze assets in which any foreign country or national has an interest. (For further information, please see the U.S. Department of the Treasury's Web page for the Office of Foreign Assets Control,[80] Specially Designated Nationals and Blocked Persons and 31 Code of Federal Regulation, Part 595,[81] Part 596,[82] and Part 597.[83])

2.8.7 PUBLIC SAFETY OFFICER BENEFITS BILL (H.R. 2882, PUBLIC LAW NO. 107-37)[84]

Signed into law on September 18, 2001, this act provides for expedited payment of death or permanent disability benefits to qualified beneficiaries of public safety officers who were killed or suffered a catastrophic injury in the line of duty in connection with the terrorist attacks of September 11, 2001.

2.8.8 REWARDS FOR INFORMATION CONCERNING TERRORIST ACTS AND ESPIONAGE (U.S. CODE TITLE 18, PART II, CHAPTER 204)[85]

An amendment to Section 3071[86] of this law authorizes the U.S. Attorney General to pay for information that uncovers espionage activity, leads to the arrest and conviction of any persons charged with an act of espionage against the United States (for example, conspiring or attempting to commit an act of espionage against the United States), or leads to the prevention or frustration of an act of espionage against the United States.

2.8.9 TERRORISM RISK INSURANCE PROGRAM[87]

On November 26, 2002, President Bush signed into law the Terrorism Risk Insurance Act of 2002.[88] This new law established a temporary federal program that provides for a transparent system of shared public and private compensation for insured losses resulting from acts of terrorism.

2.9 EMERGENCY PREPAREDNESS AND READINESS

Although owners, operators, and regulators of critical infrastructures are responsible for the protection and emergency preparedness of their facilities, services, assets, and information systems, codependencies and interrelationships between systems makes it very difficult to fully protect these on their own. Partnerships and information sharing are crucial. Some of the legislation recently passed helps enable better communications and information sharing strategies between agencies and promotes better interagency relationships.

2.9.1 COMMUNITY PROTECTION AND RESPONSE ACT OF 2003 (H.R. 2878)[89]

Introduced by Representative Carolyn B. Maloney (New York), the Community Protection and Response Act of 2003 amends the Robert T. Stafford Disaster Relief and Emergency Assistance Act to improve federal response efforts after a terrorist strike or other major disaster affecting homeland security.

2.9.2 EMERGENCY PREPAREDNESS AND RESPONSE ACT OF 2003 (S. 930)[90]

Introduced by Senator James M. Jeffors (Vermont), the Emergency Preparedness and Response Act of 2003 amends the Robert T. Stafford Disaster Relief and Emergency Assistance Act to establish a program that provides assistance to enhance the ability of first responders to prepare for and respond to all hazards.

2.9.3 FIRST RESPONDERS PARTNERSHIP GRANT ACT OF 2003 (S. 466)[91]

The text of a Senate bill that authorizes the Secretary of Homeland Security to make grants to states, local governments, and Indian tribes to support public safety officers in protecting homeland security and responding to acts of terrorism.

2.9.4 Mychal Judge Police and Fire Chaplains Public Safety Officers' Benefit Act of 2002 (S. 2431, Public Law No. 107-196)[92]

This law was enacted on June 24, 2002, and applies to incidents that occurred on and after September 11, 2001. It amends the Omnibus Crime Control and Safe Streets Act of 1968[93] to ensure that chaplains killed in the line of duty receive public safety officer death benefits.

2.9.5 First Responders Assistance Act of 2001 (H.R. 3162, Public Law No. 107-56)[94]

This law is subset to the USA PATRIOT Act of 2001 and directs the Attorney General to make grants to state and local governments and Indian tribes to improve the ability of state and local law enforcement, fire department, and first responder departments and agencies to respond to and prevent acts of terrorism as well as certain costs relating to the mobilization of reserves who are first responder personnel of such governments or tribes.

2.10 MEDICAL AND HEALTH CARE SECURITY

Until recently, contamination of water with biological, chemical, or radiological agents generally resulted from natural, industrial, or unintentional man-made accidents. Unfortunately, current terrorist activity has forced the medical community, public health agencies, emergency medical services, and water utilities to consider the possibility of deliberate contamination of American water supplies as part of an organized effort to disrupt and damage important elements of our national infrastructure. Now there is growing concern that chemical, biological, and radiological weapons may be used against the U.S. population with water as one possible vehicle of transmission or mode of dispersal. Some of the recently passed legislation (outlined below) is a result of these concerns.[95]

2.10.1 Patient Safety and Quality Improvement Act (PSQIA) of 2005 (S. 544/H.R. 3205, Public Law No. 109-41)[96]

Signed into law by President Bush on July 29, 2005, this act would establish certification procedures for "patient safety organizations" (PSOs) and require the Secretary of Health and Human Services to maintain a list of certified PSOs.[97] PSOs would collect patient safety data voluntarily submitted by health care providers for inclusion in a network of databases, and it would require the Secretary to develop a uniform database, establish national standards for the collection and maintenance of patient safety data, and provide technical assistance to PSOs; it would also establish privacy protections and impose civil monetary penalties for violations of those protections. The law would require two (2) reports, including a report by the Government Accountability Office (GAO) on the overall effectiveness of the program and a report by the Secretary on effective strategies for increasing patient safety. The act would preempt any state laws that govern the disclosure of information provided to patient safety organizations. While that preemption would be an inter-governmental mandate as defined in the Unfunded Mandates Reform Act (UMRA), it would impose no requirements on states that would result in additional spending; thus, the threshold established by UMRA would not be exceeded ($62 million in 2005, adjusted annually for inflation).[98,99] The law would impose a private-sector mandate on health care providers, as defined in UMRA, by not allowing them to use the fact that an employee reported patient safety data in an adverse employment action against an employee. That mandate would not have any direct cost, however, because patient safety data as defined in the bill does not exist under current law.[100]

2.10.2 PROJECT BIOSHIELD ACT OF 2004 (S. 15)[101]

Signed into law by President Bush on July 21, 2004, Project Bioshield authorizes appropriations to develop, procure, and make available countermeasures against chemical, biological, radiological, or nuclear weapons that could cause public health emergencies affecting national security.[102]

2.10.3 PUBLIC HEALTH SECURITY AND BIOTERRORISM PREPAREDNESS AND RESPONSE ACT OF 2002 (H.R. 3448, PUBLIC LAW NO. 107-188)[103]

Signed into law on June 12, 2002, this act was crafted by Congress to improve the ability of the United States to prevent, prepare for, and respond to bioterrorism and other public health emergencies. The Food and Drug Administration is charged with implementing this legislation and has prepared a Web site[104] to provide updates and allow continuing public discussion on this process via the National Institutes of Health electronic mailing list server, FDA-BIOTERRORISMACT.[105]

2.10.4 SAFE FOOD ACT OF 2005 (H.R. 1507)[106]

At the time of writing, this act was under review by the Subcommittee on Health. This bill establishes the Food Safety Administration to administer and enforce food safety laws. It directs the Administrator of the Food Safety Administration to: (1) promulgate regulations to ensure the security of the food supply from all forms of contamination; (2) implement federal food safety inspection, enforcement, and research efforts to protect the public health; (3) develop consistent and science-based standards for safe food; (4) coordinate and prioritize food safety research and education programs with other federal agencies; (5) prioritize federal food safety efforts and deployment of resources to achieve the greatest possible benefit in reducing food-borne illness; (6) coordinate the federal response to food-borne illness outbreaks with other federal and state agencies; and (7) integrate federal food safety activities with state and local agencies.[107]

2.10.5 SMALLPOX EMERGENCY PERSONNEL PROTECTION ACT OF 2003 (H.R. 1770, PUBLIC LAW NO. 108-20)[108]

Signed into law on April 30, 2003, this act authorizes benefits and other compensation for certain individuals with injuries resulting from administration of smallpox countermeasures.

2.11 TRANSPORTATION SECURITY (INCLUDES MARITIME SECURITY)

Recent events within and through the United States, as well as with other sections worldwide, have focused considerable attention on the potential occurrence of major incidents of public terrorism. In our own country, such incidents have included the bombings of the World Trade Center in New York City, the Federal Building in Oklahoma City, and the Olympic Park in Atlanta. Throughout the rest of the world there have been bombings and chemical weapon attacks in Japan, Europe, the Middle East, South America, and Africa.

The high level of concern about terrorism is reflected in the President's creation of a Presidential Commission on Critical Infrastructure Protection and a White House Commission on Aviation Safety and Security.

Historically, transportation has been among the most visible and frequently targeted of terrorist attacks, and recent terrorist incidents have reinforced that observation (case in point, the attacks conducted on September 11, 2001). Yet another security concern in transportation is cargo theft and tampering. Estimates place the losses from either resulting from such thefts or tampering at well over $13 billion a year.[109]

On May 5, 2003, (68 FR 23831-23842), the Research and Special Programs Administration (RSPA),[110] U.S. Department of Transportation (DOT), issued an interim final rule (49 CFR parts 107, 171, 176, and 177) that incorporates into the Hazardous Materials Regulations (HMR) a requirement that shippers and transporters of certain hazardous materials comply with federal security regulations that apply to motor carrier and vessel transportation. In addition, this interim final rule revises the procedures for applying for an exemption from the HMR to require applicants to certify compliance with applicable federal transportation security laws and regulations.

2.11.1 AIR TRANSPORTATION SAFETY AND SYSTEM STABILIZATION ACT (H.R. 2926, PUBLIC LAW NO. 107-42)[111]

Signed into law on September 22, 2001, this act directs the President to take certain actions to preserve the continued viability and security of the U.S. air transportation system. Title IV: Victim Compensation establishes a victim compensation program for any individual who was injured or killed as a result of the terrorist-related aircraft crashes of September 11, 2001. See the U.S. Department of Justice's September 11th Victim Compensation Fund of 2001.[112]

2.11.2 AIRPORT SECURITY IMPROVEMENT ACT OF 2000 (S. 2440, PUBLIC LAW NO. 106-528)[113]

This law was enacted on November 22, 2000, and amended Title 49, United States Code, to improve airport security. Primarily, it directs the Administrator of the Federal Aviation Administration (FAA) to develop an electronic fingerprint transmission pilot project for individual criminal history record checks into an aviation industry-wide program, and exempts any airport, air carrier, or screening company from participating in such program if they determine it would not be cost effective and notify the administrator of such determination.[114] This law essentially helps protect those who travel by air by improving controls on access to secure areas in airports, increasing training for security screeners at U.S. airports, requiring criminal history record checks for baggage screeners and security personnel, and requiring the FAA to improve security at its own air traffic control facilities.[115]

2.11.3 ANTITERRORISM AND PORT SECURITY ACT OF 2003 (S. 746)[116]

The text of a Senate bill details how to prevent and respond to terrorism and crime at or through ports.[117] This law amends the federal criminal code making it unlawful to[118]: (1) destroy or interfere with vessels or maritime facilities; (2) put devices in U.S. waters that can destroy a ship or cargo or interfere with safe navigation or maritime commerce; (3) use a dangerous weapon or explosive to try to kill someone on board a passenger vessel; (4) fail to heave to (that is, to slow or stop) a vessel at the direction of a Coast Guard or other authorized federal law enforcement official seeking to board that vessel, or to interfere with boarding by such an officer; (5) destroy an aid to maritime navigation (such as a buoy or shoal/breakwater light) maintained by the Saint Lawrence Seaway Development Corporation or the Coast Guard if this would endanger the safe navigation of a vessel; or (6) knowingly discharge or release oil, a hazardous substance, a noxious liquid substance or any other substance (malicious dumping) into U.S. navigable waters or the adjoining shoreline with intent to endanger human life, health, or welfare.[119]

2.11.4 AVIATION AND TRANSPORTATION SECURITY ACT (S. 1447, PUBLIC LAW NO. 107-71)[120]

Signed into law on November 19, 2001, this law amends federal transportation law to establish in the U.S. Department of Transportation (DOT) the Transportation Security Administration, to be headed by an Under Secretary of Transportation for Security responsible for security in all modes of transportation, including:[121] (1) civil aviation security, and related research and development activities; (2) security responsibilities over other modes of transportation that are exercised by DOT; (3) day-to-day federal security screening operations for passenger air transportation and intrastate air transportation; (4) policies, strategies, and plans for dealing with threats to transportation; (5) domestic transportation during a national emergency (subject to the Secretary of Transportation's control and direction), including aviation, rail, and other surface transportation, and maritime transportation, and port security; and (6) management of security information, including notifying airport or airline security officers of the identity of individuals known to pose a risk of air piracy or terrorism or a threat to airline or passenger safety.[122] Essentially, the act improves security in all modes of transportation, creates and implements protocols for dealing with threats to transportation, manages domestic transportation during a national emergency, and manages security information; it issued qualification standards for federal airport security screeners. In order to be hired screeners must be U.S. citizens, pass a background and security investigation, including a criminal records check and pass a standardized examination among other requirements.[123]

2.11.5 AVIATION INVESTMENT AND REFORM ACT FOR THE 21ST CENTURY (AIR-21) (H.R. 1000, PUBLIC LAW NO. 106-181)[124]

This law amended federal aviation law that reauthorized funding through FY 2003: (1) the Airport Improvement Program (AIP); and (2) the FAA Facilities and Equipment Program. This law also earmarked specified amounts for: (1) the voluntary purchase and installation of universal access systems; (2) the Alaska National Air Space Interfacility Communications System; and (3) the implementation and use of upgrades to the current automated surface observation system-automated weather observing system (if the upgrade is successfully demonstrated). It specifically directed the Administrator of the FAA to establish life-cycle cost estimates for any air traffic control modernization project whose costs equal or exceed $50 million.[125] This law also provided the FAA $40 billion through FY 2003 for operations, facilities, and equipment, and for the Airport Improvement Fund, thus promoting a competitive aviation industry and improving airline customer service and passenger safety during this time of ever-increasing demand for airport and airway usage.[126]

2.11.6 MARITIME TRANSPORTATION SECURITY ACT OF 2002 (PUBLIC LAW NO. 107-295)[127]

Signed into law on November 25, 2002, this bill amends the Merchant Marine Act of 1936 to establish a program to ensure greater security for U.S. seaports. The act directs the Secretary of Transportation to assess port vulnerability and to prepare a National Maritime Transportation Antiterrorism Plan for deterring catastrophic emergencies.

2.11.7 NOTIFICATION OF ARRIVAL IN U.S. PORTS; CERTAIN DANGEROUS CARGOES; ELECTRONIC SUBMISSION, 69 FED. REG. 51,176 (2004) (33 C.F.R. PARTS 104, 105, 160)[128]

The U.S. Coast Guard is changing its definition of *certain dangerous cargo* to include ammonium nitrate and certain ammonium nitrate fertilizers shipped in bulk, as well as propylene oxide, alone or mixed, with ethylene oxide in bulk. The Coast Guard is also adding two options for vessels to submit notices of arrival electronically. This temporary final rule was published August 18, 2004, and became effective on September 17, 2004.

The Office of Hazardous Materials Safety (OHM)[129] formulates issues and revises Hazardous Materials Regulations (HMR) under the Federal Hazardous Materials Transportation Law.[130] The HMR cover hazardous materials definitions and classifications, hazard communications, shipper and carrier operations, training and security requirements, and packaging and container specifications.[131]

2.12 HAZARDOUS MATERIALS

Some of the legislation available does not fit under any one particular category or group, and so therefore, is placed here. Typically, most hazardous materials (HAZMAT) handling is covered by the U.S. Department of Transportation or some emergency management group or agency; however, some of these regulations may not apply in those areas, as these imply an intent for use to harm life or damage property. For HAZMAT transportation regulations, refer to the Office of Hazardous Materials Safety's (subset to the U.S. Department of Transportation) Web site[132]; for WMD investigations, there is the Commission on the Intelligence Capabilities of the United States Regarding Weapons of Mass Destruction.[133]

2.12.1 CHEMICAL SAFETY INFORMATION, SITE SECURITY, AND FUELS REGULATORY RELIEF ACT (S. 880, PUBLIC LAW NO. 106-40)[134]

This law, signed by President Clinton on August 5, 1999, requires the promulgation of regulations that address public access to information about the worst possible impact that a release of toxic or flammable chemicals from a facility could have on the nearby populace and environment. The U.S. Department of Justice, which was tasked with describing the risks associated with the release of off-site consequence analysis data, has documented its findings in the Department of Justice Assessment of the Increased Risk of Terrorist or Other Criminal Activity Associated with Posting Off-Site Consequence Analysis Information on the Internet. *This law predates September 11, 2001.*

2.12.2 CHEMICAL WEAPONS (U.S. CODE TITLE 18, PART I, CHAPTER 11B)[135]

This portion of the United States Code defines and prohibits illegal development, acquisition, delivery, possession, and use of a chemical agent as a weapon and delineates investigative and prosecutorial procedures for interdiction, which include military assistance to enforce prohibition in certain emergencies.

2.12.3 CRIMES AND CRIMINAL PROCEDURE, CRIMES, BIOLOGICAL WEAPONS (U.S. CODE TITLE 18, PART I, CHAPTER 10)[136]

This portion of the United States Code defines and prohibits illegal development, acquisition, delivery, possession, and use of a biological agent as a weapon and delineates investigative and prosecutorial procedures for interdiction, which include military assistance to enforce prohibition in certain emergencies.

2.12.4 DEFENSE AGAINST WEAPONS OF MASS DESTRUCTION (PUBLIC LAW NO. 104-201, U.S. CODE TITLE 50, CHAPTER 40)[137]

This chapter of the U.S. Code directs the President and Secretary of Defense to take immediate actions both to enhance the capability of the federal government to respond to terrorist incidents and to support improvements in the capabilities of state and local emergency response agencies.

2.12.5 SAFE EXPLOSIVES ACT (HOMELAND SECURITY ACT OF 2002, PUBLIC LAW NO. 107-296, SECTION 1121)[138]

Included as part of the Homeland Security Act of 2002 and signed by President Bush on November 25, 2002, the Safe Explosives Act empowers the Bureau of Alcohol,

Tobacco and Firearms (ATF) to apply stricter controls on the purchase of explosives. Effective May 24, 2002, any person who wants to transport, ship, cause for transportation, or receive explosive materials must first obtain a federal permit. ATF has prepared a special online reference page[139] to keep the public informed of resulting regulations.

2.12.6 TERRORIST BOMBINGS CONVENTION IMPLEMENTATION ACT OF 2002 (TITLE I) AND SUPPRESSION OF THE FINANCING OF TERRORISM CONVENTION IMPLEMENTATION ACT OF 2002 (TITLE II) (H.R. 3275, PUBLIC LAW NO. 107-197)[140]

This law was enacted as Public Law No. 107-197 on June 25, 2002. Title I implements the International Convention for the Suppression of Terrorist Bombings,[141] which was signed by the United States on January 12, 1998. This convention imposes legal obligations on state parties either to submit for prosecution or to extradite any person within their jurisdiction who unlawfully and intentionally delivers, places, discharges, or detonates an explosive or other lethal device in, into, or against a place of public use, a state or government facility, a public transportation system, or an infrastructure facility. Title II implements the International Convention for the Suppression of the Financing of Terrorism,[142] which was signed by the United States on January 10, 2000. This convention imposes legal obligations on state parties either to submit for prosecution or to extradite any person within their jurisdiction who unlawfully and willfully provides or collects funds with the intention that they should be used to carry out various terrorist activities. State parties are subject to the obligations of these conventions without regard to the place where the alleged acts included in these conventions take place.

2.12.7 THE TOXIC SUBSTANCES CONTROL ACT (TSCA) (PUBLIC LAW NO. 94-469)[143]

This legislation was passed in 1976 (effective January 1, 1997) to reduce the threat from new chemicals that present or will present an unreasonable risk of injury to health or the environment. As a result, chemical producers are required to research the effects of new chemicals and notify the Environmental Protection Agency (EPA) before they are manufactured. The EPA has the authority to ban or restrict chemical uses if there is sufficient evidence that the substance poses an "unreasonable risk" to public health or the environment.[144] Under earlier laws the EPA had authority to control toxic substances only after damage had occurred. The earlier laws did not require the screening of toxic substances before they entered the marketplace. TSCA closed the gap in the earlier laws by requiring that the health and environmental effects of all new chemicals be reviewed before they are manufactured for commercial purposes.[145]

2.12.8 THE OCCUPATIONAL SAFETY AND HEALTH ACT

The Occupational Safety and Health Act of 1970 (29 U.S.C. 5651 et seq. 29 CFR Parts 1900 to 2400) created the Occupational Safety and Health Administration (OSHA),[146] which sets standards for work exposure to hazardous substances and requires that such substances display warning labels. It also mandates that employees be given training and other information on dangers posed by chemicals and are given instructions as to how to use these chemicals safely. OSHA has the authority to inspect a workplace to determine whether it is in compliance with these regulations.[147]

2.12.9 SUPERFUND AMENDMENTS AND REAUTHORIZATION ACT (SARA) OF 1986

In 1986, Congress enacted the Superfund Amendments and Reauthorization Act (SARA), and under Title III of the Act, the Emergency Planning and Community Right-to-Know Act of 1986, subjects over 300 "extremely hazardous substances" to routine and detailed reporting to designated local, state, and federal government agencies. It also requires local planning committees to use this (and other data about local hazards that may be present) information to provide effective plans for hazardous materials emergencies.[148] This piece of legislation amended the Comprehensive Environmental Response, Compensation, and Liability Act (CERCLA)[149] on October 17, 1986.

2.12.10 CHEMICAL SECURITY ACT OF 2005 (H.R. 2237)[150]

At the time of writing, this act was under review by the Subcommittee on Environment and Hazardous Materials. If enacted, this piece of legislation would direct the Administrator of the U.S. EPA to promulgate regulations to: (1) designate certain combinations of chemical sources and substances of concern as high priority categories based on the severity of the threat posed by an unauthorized release from the chemical sources; and (2) require each owner and operator of a high priority category chemical source to conduct an assessment of the vulnerability of the source to a terrorist attack or other unauthorized release, identify hazards that may result from an unauthorized release, and prepare a prevention, preparedness, and response plan.[151] It also (1): establishes a publicly available clearinghouse to compile and disseminate information on the use and availability of inherently safer technologies; (2) permits the Secretary of Energy to establish and administer a Technology Transition Fund to provide grants to assist chemical facilities that demonstrate financial hardship in implementing inherently safer technologies; and (3) establishes grants to provide for training of first responders and of employees at chemical sources in identifying opportunities to reduce the chemical source's vulnerability to a release of a substance of concern through the use of safer technologies or in emergency response procedures.[152]

2.12.11 CHEMICAL FACILITY SECURITY ACT OF 2005 (H.R. 1562)[153]

At the time of writing, this act was under review by the Subcommittee on Environment and Hazardous Materials. The Chemical Facility Security Act of 2005 requires the Secretary of Homeland Security to designate certain combinations of chemical sources and substances of concern as high-priority categories based on the severity of the threat of a terrorist release, taking into account specified factors. It requires the Secretary of Homeland Security to promulgate regulations requiring owners or operators of chemical sources to conduct vulnerability assessments and develop and implement site security plans that address the results, and directs chemical sources not in high-priority categories to certify completion of such assessments and implementation of such plans. This bill also requires the Secretary of Homeland Security, in promulgating regulations and establishing procedures, protocols, and standards for such assessments and plans, to consider specified factors, including the likelihood that a chemical source will be the target of terrorism and the potential scope of injury, authorizing the Secretary to: (1) designate or exempt certain categories of stationary sources as chemical sources; and (2) designate, exempt, and adjust threshold quantities of substances of concern. The bill establishes five assessments and plans a review requirement for chemical sources not in high-priority categories, requiring high-priority chemical sources to provide the Secretary with any changes to assessments and plans within 90 days.[154]

2.13 QUESTIONS

1. The USA PATRIOT Act of 2001 contains additional acts of legislation within it. True or False?

   Answer: *True*. The USA PATRIOT Act of 2001 contains several smaller, lesser known acts of legislation, all of which have significant roles in our National Security laws. The one law that should be noted is the Critical Infrastructure Protection Act of 2001.

2. The E-Government Act of 2002 was enacted in late 2002 to enhance the federal government's capabilities and reduce (mostly) paperwork filed with, within, and throughout government locations utilizing which medium?
   a. Internet
   b. Telephone
   c. Facsimile
   d. E-mail

   Answer: *Internet*. The E-Government Act, implemented along with the Federal Information Security Management Act of 2002 (FISMA), was intended to reduce paperwork by allowing individuals the ability to electronically submit information through a web interface via the Internet.

3. The Cyber Security Research and Development Act of 2002 was formally introduced into Congress by the _____.

   Answer: *The Gilmore Commission*. This was an advisory panel that assessed governmental capabilities for responding to terrorist incidents within and throughout the United States that involved weapons of mass destruction and acts of terrorism. Response capabilities were at several levels — federal, state, and local levels — which were examined with particular emphasis on state and local (county, city, village, township) levels.

The Secretary of Defense, along with consulting with the Attorney General, the Secretary of Energy, the Secretary of Health and Human Services, as well as the Director of the Federal Emergency Management Agency (FEMA), entered into an agreement with the RAND National Defense Research Institute (NDRI), establishing the advisory panel, which released its report sometime in December 2003.

4. The "National ID" is about a controversial piece of legislation described within the _____ Act.

   Answer: *The REAL ID Act of 2005*, signed into law on May 11, 2005.

5. The Energy Policy Act of 2005 was introduced to improve the _____ .

   Answer: *Power grid*.

6. The Department of Homeland Security was formed under which part of legislation?
   a. USA PATRIOT Act
   b. Homeland Security Act
   c. Effective Counterterrorism Act
   d. Intelligence Reform and Terrorism Prevention Act

   Answer: *The Homeland Security Act of 2002*, which was signed into law on November 25, 2002, helped restructure key, critical departments and agencies throughout the federal government into a streamlined organization, while strengthening the Executive Branch (President of the United States) of the federal government.

7. The USA PATRIOT Act is an acronym. True or False?

   Answer: *True*. The USA PATRIOT Act means "Uniting and Strengthening America by Providing Appropriate Tools Required to Intercept and Obstruct Terrorism Act?

8. Does the Critical Infrastructure Protection Act of 2001 reintroduce the term "critical infrastructure?" Yes or No?

   Answer: *Yes*. The act, which is a part of the USA PATRIOT Act, refines and reintroduces the definition of *critical infrastructure*, which was later used within HSPD-7.

9. Which piece of legislation introduced the term "first responder?"
   a. Emergency Preparedness and Response Act
   b. First Responders Assistance Act
   c. First Responders Partnership Grant Act
   d. Community Protection and Response Act

   Answer: *First Responders Assistance Act* of 2001, which provides funding for training of first responders for prevention of acts of terrorism, biological, or radiological decontamination, and more.

10. Which piece of legislation (primarily) safeguards our nation's ports?
    a. Aviation and Transportation Security Act
    b. Maritime Transportation Security Act
    c. Antiterrorism and Port Security Act
    d. Airport Security Improvement Act

    Answer: *Antiterrorism and Port Security Act*, which enhanced the already implemented Maritime Transportation Security Act, but focused on acts of vandalism, terrorism, and environmental safety.

NOTES

1. http://frwebgate.access.gpo.gov/cgi-bin/getdoc.cgi?dbname=108_cong_bills& docid =f:h4417enr.txt.pdf
2. http://thomas.loc.gov/cgi-bin/bdquery/z?d107:s.01424:
3. http://thomas.loc.gov/cgi-bin/bdquery/z?d107:h.r.03525:
4. http://www.fourmilab.ch/uscode/8usc/www/contents.html
5. http://thomas.loc.gov/cgi-bin/bdquery/z?d109:h.r.00418:
6. http://thomas.loc.gov/cgi-bin/bdquerytr/z?d109:HR01268:
7. http://thomas.loc.gov/cgi-bin/bdquery/z?d109:HR01268:@@@D&summ2=m&.
8. http://en.wikipedia.org/wiki/Real_id
9. http://thomas.loc.gov/cgi-bin/bdquery/z?d109:HR00418:@@@D&summ2=m&
10. http://thomas.loc.gov/cgi-bin/bdquery/z?d103:HR04922:|TOM:/bss/d103query.html
11. http://www.askcalea.net
12. http://frwebgate.access.gpo.gov/cgi-bin/getdoc.cgi?dbname=108_cong_bills&docid =f:h2898ih.txt.pdf
13. http://thomas.loc.gov/cgi-bin / bdquery /z? d 107 : SN03067: @@@ L&summ2 = m& #summary
14. http://thomas.loc.gov/cgi-bin/bdquery/z? d107:SN03067:@@@ L&summ 2=m&# summary
15. http://clinton4.nara.gov/OMB/legislative/sap/106-2/S1993-s.html
16. http://clinton4.nara.gov/OMB/legislative/sap/106-2/S1993-s.html
17. http://www.fcw.com/fcw/articles/2000/1016/web-gisa-10-16-00.asp
18. The Gilmore Commission is an advisory panel that assesses the capabilities for responding to terrorist incidents in the U.S. involving weapons of mass destruction. Response capabilities at the federal, state, and local levels are examined, with a particular emphasis on the latter; the Secretary of Defense, in consultation with the

Attorney General, the Secretary of Energy, the Secretary of Health and Human Services, and the Director of the Federal Emergency Management Agency entered into a contract with the RAND National Defense Research Institute (NDRI), a federally funded research and development center (FFRDC), to establish the advisory panel, which released its fifth and final report in December 2003.

19. 80–337PS/2003 HOMELAND SECURITY: THE FEDERAL AND NEW YORK RESPONSE, FIELD HEARING BEFORE THE COMMITTEE ON SCIENCE HOUSE OF REPRESENTATIVES, ONE HUNDRED SEVENTH CONGRESS, SECOND SESSION, JUNE 24, 2002, Serial No. 107–71, http://commdocs.house.gov/committees/science/hsy80337.000/hsy80337_0.htm

20. COMMITTEE ON SCIENCE, U.S. HOUSE OF REPRESENTATIVES, HEARING CHARTER, Cyber Terrorism — A View From the Gilmore Commission, Wednesday, October 17, 2001, http://www.house.gov/science/full/oct17/full_charter_101701.htm

21. http://www.house.gov/science/cyber/hr3394.pdf

22. http://www.house.gov/science/cyber.htm

23. http://www.house.gov/science/press/107pr/107-139.htm.

24. http://www.army.mil.ciog6/references/legislation_docs/CSA.doc

25. http://www.house.gov/science_democrats/archive/compsec1.htm

26. http://thomas.loc.gov/cgi-bin/bdquery/z?d105:HR01903:@@@R

27. http://www.house.gov/science_democrats/archive/compsec.htm

28. http://www.house.gov/science_democrats/archive/compsec.htm

29. http://thomas.loc.gov/cgi-bin/bdquery/z?d105:HR01903:@@@D&summ2=m&

30. http://thomas.loc.gov/cgi-bin/bdquery/z?d105:HR01903:@@@D&summ2=m&

31. http://thomas.loc.gov/cgi-bin/bdquery/z?d107:HR02458:@@@D&summ2=1&

32. http://frwcbgate.access.gpo.gov/cgi-bin/getdoc.cgi?dbname=107_cong_public_laws&docid=f:publ347.107

33. http://www.nasact.org/IISAF/laws_FIS.html

34. http://www.chips.navy.mil/archives/04_winter/Web_Pages/FISMA.htm

35. http://www.chips.navy.mil/archives/04_winter/Web_Pages/FISMA.htm

36. Federal Information Security Management Act FY 2004 Executive Summary Report U.S. Securities and Exchange Commission Office of Inspector General September 10, 2004; http://www.sec.gov/about/oig/audit/391fin.pdf

37. http://www.va.gov/budget/report/HTML/management-discussion-analysis/controls systems-compliance/information-security.html

38. http://frwebgate.access.gpo.gov/cgi-bin/getdoc.cgi?dbname=107_cong_public_laws&docid=f:publ347.107

39. http://thomas.loc.gov/cgi-bin/bdquery/z?d107:SN00803:@@@L&summ2=m&# summary

40. http://irm.cit.nih.gov/policy/itmra.html

41. http://irm.cit.nih.gov/itmra/background.html

42. http://irm.cit.nih.gov/itmra/background.html

43. http://energycommerce.house.gov/108/energy_pdfs_2.htm

44. http://energycommerce.house.gov/108/0205_Energy/05policy_act/EPACT% 202005%20Committee%20Print%20Highlights.pdf

45. http://www.kannerandassoc.com/energy%20laws.html

46. http://frwebgate.access.gpo.gov/cgi-bin/getdoc.cgi?dbname=107_cong_bills&docid=f:h4687enr.txt.pdf

47. http://wtc.nist.gov

48. http://www.oalj.dol.gov/public/WBLOWER/REFRNC/107_355.htm

49. http://www4.law.cornell.edu/uscode/49/stVIII.html

50. http://thomas.loc.gov/cgi-bin/bdquery/z?d104:h.r.03071:
51. http://thomas.loc.gov/cgi-bin/bdquery/z?d104:S.735:
52. http://thomas.loc.gov/cgi-bin/bdquery/z?d104:SN00735:|TOM:/bssd104query.html
53. http://frwebgate.access.gpo.gov/cgi-bin/getdoc.cgi?dbname=107_cong_bills&docid
    =f:h5005enr.txt.pdf
54. http://www.dhs.gov/dhspublic/interapp/press_release/press_release_0541.xml
55. http://govt-aff.senate.gov/_files/IntelligenceReformconferencereportlegislativelangu
    age12704.pdf
56. http://frwebgate.access.gpo.gov/cgi-bin/getdoc.cgi?dbname=108_cong_bills&docid
    =f:s2845pp.txt.pdf
57. http://thomas.loc.gov/cgi-bin/bdquery/z?d107:s.j.res.00022:
58. http://frwebgate.access.gpo.gov/cgi-bin/getdoc.cgi?dbname=108_cong_bills&docid
    =f:s2845pp.txt.pdf
59. http://thomas.loc.gov/cgi-bin/bdquery/z?d106:h.r.04210:
60. http://www.fema.gov/library/stafact.shtm
61. http://frwebgate.access.gpo.gov/cgi-bin/getdoc.cgi?dbname=108_cong_reports&
    docid=f:hr588.108.pdf
62. http://frwebgate.access.gpo.gov/cgi-bin/getdoc.cgi?dbname=108_cong_public_laws
    &docid=f:publ169.108.pdf
63. http://thomas.loc.gov/cgi-bin/bdquery/z?d107:h.r.03162:
64. http://www.lifeandliberty.gov
65. http://www.lifeandliberty.gov/highlights.htm
66. http://frwebgate.access.gpo.gov/cgi-bin/getdoc.cgi?dbname=107_cong_public_laws
    &docid=f:publ056.107
67. http://thomas.loc.gov/cgi-bin/bdquery/z?d107:HR03162:@@@L&summ2=m&
68. http://frwebgate.access.gpo.gov/cgi-bin/getdoc.cgi?dbname=107_cong_public_laws
    &docid=f:publ056.107
69. http://thomas.loc.gov/cgi-bin/query/z?c106:H.R.438:
70. http://thomas.loc.gov/cgi-bin/query/z?c106:H.R.438:
71. http://www.treas.gov/press/releases/js1881.htm
72. http://thomas.loc.gov/cgi-bin/bdquery/z?d098:HR06311:@@@D|TOM:/bss/d098
    query.html
73. http://www.rewardsforjustice.net
74. http://thomas.loc.gov/cgi-bin/bdquery/z?d107:h.r.02888:
75. http://frwebgate.access.gpo.gov/cgi-bin/getdoc.cgi?dbname=108_cong_bills&docid
    =f:h1584enr.txt.pdf
76. http://www.kimberleyprocess.com
77. http://frwebgate.access.gpo.gov/cgi-bin/getdoc.cgi?dbname=108_cong_bills&docid
    =f:s1245is.txt.pdf
78. http://frwebgate.access.gpo.gov/cgi-bin/getdoc.cgi?dbname=108_cong_bills&docid
    =f:h2417enr.txt.pdf
79. http://www4.law.cornell.edu/cgi-bin/htm_hl?DB=uscode50&STEMMER=en&
    WORDS=international+emergency+economic+powers+&COLOUR=Red&STYLE
    =s&URL=/uscode/50/ch35.html
80. http://www.treas.gov/offices/eotffc/ofac/sdn/index.html
81. http://www.treas.gov/offices/eotffc/ofac/legal/regs/31cfr595.pdf
82. http://www.treas.gov/offices/eotffc/ofac/legal/regs/31cfr596.pdf
83. http://www.treas.gov/offices/eotffc/ofac/legal/regs/31cfr597.pdf
84. http://thomas.loc.gov/cgi-bin/bdquery/z?d107:h.r.02882:
85. http://www4.law.cornell.edu/uscode/18/pIIch204.html

86. http://www4.law.cornell.edu/uscode/18/3071.html
87. http://www.ustreas.gov/offices/domestic-finance/financial-institution/terrorism-insurance/index.html
88. http://frwebgate.access.gpo.gov/cgi-bin/getdoc.cgi?dbname=107_cong_bills&docid=f:h3210enr.txt.pdf
89. http://frwebgate.access.gpo.gov/cgi-bin/getdoc.cgi?dbname=108_cong_bills&docid=f:h2878ih.txt.pdf
90. http://frwebgate.access.gpo.gov/cgi-bin/getdoc.cgi?dbname=108_cong_bills&docid=f:s930is.txt.pdf
91. http://frwebgate.access.gpo.gov/cgi-bin/getdoc.cgi?dbname=108_cong_bills&docid=f:s466is.txt.pdf
92. http://frwebgate.access.gpo.gov/cgi-bin/getdoc.cgi?dbname=107_cong_public_laws&docid=f:publ196.107.pdf
93. http://www.usdoj.gov/crt/split/42usc3789d.htm
94. http://thomas.loc.gov/cgi-bin/bdquery/z?d107:h.r.03162:
95. http://www.usfa.fema.gov/subjects/emr-isac/infograms/ig2005/igfeb1705.shtm
96. http://www.cbo.gov/showdoc.cfm?index=6582&sequence=0
97. http://thomas.loc.gov/cgi-bin/bdquery/z?d109:s.00544:
98. http://thomas.loc.gov/cgi-bin/bdquery/z?d109:s.00544:
99. http://thomas.loc.gov/cgi-bin/bdquery/z?d109:SN00544:@@@D&summ2=m&
100. http://www.cbo.gov/showdoc.cfm?index=6582&sequence=0
101. http://www.whitehouse.gov/news/releases/2004/07/20040721-2.html
102. http://democrats.senate.gov/dpc/dpc-pf.cfm?doc_name=lb-108-2-139
103. http://www.fda.gov/oc/bioterrorism/PL107-188.html
104. http://www.fda.gov/oc/bioterrorism/bioact.html
105. http://list.nih.gov/cgi-bin/wa?SUBED1=fda-bioterrorismact&A=1
106. http://thomas.loc.gov/cgi-bin/bdquery/z?d109:HR01507:@@@D&summ2=m&
107. http://thomas.loc.gov/cgi-bin/query/z?c109:H.R.1507:
108. http://frwebgate.access.gpo.gov/cgi-bin/getdoc.cgi?dbname=108_cong_bills&docid=f:h1770enr.txt.pdf
109. http://www.volpe.dot.gov/infosrc/strtplns/nstc/nttplan/chap8.html
110. http://www.rspa.dot.gov
111. http://thomas.loc.gov/cgi-bin/bdquery/z?d107:h.r.02926:
112. http://www.usdoj.gov/victimcompensation/index.html
113. http://thomas.loc.gov/cgi-bin/bdquery/z?d105:s.02440:
114. http://thomas.loc.gov/cgi-bin/bdquery/z?d106:SN02440:@@@L&summ2=m&# summary
115. http://www.senate.gov/~rpc/releases/1999/rc110200.htm
116. http://frwebgate.access.gpo.gov/cgi-bin/getdoc.cgi?dbname=108_cong_bills&docid=f:s746is.txt.pdf
117. http://frwebgate.access.gpo.gov/cgi-bin/getdoc.cgi?dbname=108_cong_bills&docid=f:s746is.txt.pdf
118. http://thomas.loc.gov/cgi-bin/query/z?c108:S.746:
119. http://thomas.loc.gov/cgi-bin/bdquery/z?d108:SN00746:@@@D&summ2=m&
120. http://thomas.loc.gov/cgi-bin/bdquery/z?d107:s.01447:
121. http://thomas.loc.gov/cgi-bin/query/z?c107:S.1447:
122. http://thomas.loc.gov/cgi-bin/bdquery/z?d107:SN01447:@@@D&summ2=m&
123. These standards are based on the Aviation and Transportation Security Act (Section 111) and are posted on the DOT Web site at: http://www.dot.gov/affairs/standards.htm
124. http://thomas.loc.gov/cgi-bin/bdquery/z?d106:HR01000:@@@D&summ2=m&

125. http://thomas.loc.gov/cgi-bin/bdquery/z?d106:HR01000:@@@D&summ2=m&

126. http://www.senate.gov/~rpc/releases/1999/rc110200.htm

127. http://thomas.loc.gov/cgi-bin/bdquery/z?d107:SN01214:|TOM:/bss/d107query.html

128 http://a257.g.akamaitech.net/7/257/2422/14mar20010800/edocket.access.gpo.gov/
2004/pdf/04-18899.pdf

129. http://hazmat.dot.gov

130. As amended by the Hazardous Materials Transportation Authorization Act of 1994
(Pub. L. 103-311, August 26, 1994); and as Amended by s 6 & 7 of Pub. L. 103-429,
October 31, 1994 as outlined: http://thomas.loc.gov/cgi-bin/bdquery/z?d103:
HR02178:@@@L&summ2=m&

131. http://hazmat.dot.gov

132. http://hazmat.dot.gov

133. http://www.wmd.gov

134. http://frwebgate.access.gpo.gov/cgi-bin/getdoc.cgi?dbname=106_cong_public_laws
&docid=f:publ040.106.pdf

135. http://www4.law.cornell.edu/uscode/18/pIch11B.html

136. http://www4.law.cornell.edu/uscode/18/pIch10.html

137. http://www4.law.cornell.edu/uscode/50/ch40.html

138. http://news.findlaw.com/hdocs/docs/terrorism/hsa2002.html

139. http://www.atf.gov/press/fy03press/safexpact.htm

140. http://frwebgate.access.gpo.gov/cgi-bin/getdoc.cgi?dbname=107_cong_public_laws
&docid=f:publ197.107.pdf

141. http://www.undcp.org/odccp/resolution_1998-01-09_1.html

142. http://www.undcp.org/odccp/resolution_1998-01-09_1.html

143. http://homer.ornl.gov/oepa/laws/tsca.html

144. Federal Emergency Management Agency, An orientation to Hazardous Materials for
Medical Personnel, IS-346 (September, 1997).

145. http://homer.ornl.gov/oepa/laws/tsca.html

146. http://www.dal.gov/compliance/guide/osha.htm

147. http://homer.ornl.gov/oepa/laws/tsca.html

148. http://homer.ornl.gov/oepa/laws/tsca.html

149. http://www.//epa.gov/superfund/action/law/sara.htm

150. http://thomas.loc.gov/cgi-bin/bdquery/z?d109:h.r.02237:

151. http://thomas.loc.gov/cgi-bin/bdquery/z?d109:h.r.02237:

152. http://thomas.loc.gov/cgi-bin/bdquery/z?d109:h.r.02237:

153. http://thomas.loc.gov/cgi-bin/bdquery/z?d109:HR01562:@@@D&summ2=m&

154. http://thomas.loc.gov/cgi-bin/query/z?c109:H.R.1562:

3 National Response Plan (NRP)

3.1 INTRODUCTION

This chapter outlines the National Response Plan (NRP) issued in December 2004 by the Department of Homeland Security (DHS). It outlines at strategic levels the what, where, and how in case of a crisis or large-scale disaster, usually at a national level. The last sections of this chapter will identify key roles and functions of the NRP and its implementations.

3.2 WHAT IS THE NATIONAL[1] RESPONSE PLAN (NRP)?

The National Response Plan[2] establishes a comprehensive all-hazards approach to enhance the ability of the United States to manage domestic incidents. It incorporates best practices and procedures from incident management disciplines that include homeland security, emergency management, law enforcement, firefighting, public works, public health, first responder and recovery worker health and safety, emergency medical services, and the private sector, integrating them into a unified structure.

It forms the basis of how the federal government coordinates with state, local, and tribal governments and the private sector during incidents. The goals of the NRP are to:

Protect the health and safety of the public, responder, and recovery workers.
Ensure security of the United States throughout and at its perimeters and borders.
Prevent an imminent incident, including acts of terrorism, from occurring.
Protect and restore critical infrastructures and key resources.
Conduct law enforcement investigations to resolve the incident, apprehend the perpetrators, and collect/preserve evidence for prosecution and/or attribution.
Protect property and mitigate damages and impacts to individuals, communities, and the environment.
Facilitate recovery of individuals, families, businesses, governments, and the environment.

The NRP specifies how the resources of the federal government will work in concert with state, local, and tribal governments and the private sector to respond to "Incidents of National Significance." [3,4] The NRP is predicated on the National Incident Management System (NIMS),[5] in which (together) the NRP and the NIMS provide a nationwide template for working together to prevent or respond to threats and incidents regardless of cause, size, or complexity. The NRP supersedes[6] the Federal Response Plan (FRP),[7] Domestic Terrorism Concept of Operations Plan (CONPLAN),[8] Federal Radiological Emergency Response Plan (FRERP),[9,10] and the Interim National Response Plan (INRP). Many of the concepts and mechanisms associated with these plans were carried over to the NRP, such as the Emergency Support Function (ESF) process from the FRP and introduced critical elements from the INRP such as the Homeland Security Operations Center (HSOC), Interagency Incident Management Group (IIMG), Principal Federal Official (PFO), and the Joint Field Office (JFO).[11]

3.3 NRP TRAINING

The Federal Emergency Management Agency (FEMA) Emergency Management Institute offers an online course designed to introduce the National Response Plan to first responders.[12] The course was designed for DHS and other federal department/ agency staff responsible for implementing the NRP, as well as state, local, and private sector emergency management professionals.

The purpose of the course is to introduce the NRP so that students can[13]:

Describe the purpose of the NRP.
Locate information within the NRP.
Describe the roles and responsibilities of entities as specified within the NRP.
Identify the organizational structure used for NRP coordination.
Describe the field-level organizations and teams activated under the NRP.
Identify the incident management activities addressed by the NRP.

3.4 HOW DOES THE NRP TIE IN WITH EMERGENCY MANAGEMENT

Since the events of September 11, 2001, our nation has now resolved to better prepare itself in preventing potential terrorist attacks within the United States; reduce America's vulnerability to terrorism, major disasters, and other emergencies; and minimize the damage and recover from attacks, major disasters, and other emergencies that occur. These complex and emerging 21st century threats and hazards demand a unified and coordinated national approach to domestic incident management.

3.5 NRP SUBCATEGORIES

The NRP is broken down into subcategories, which include:

Base Plan: Concept of Operations, Coordinating Structures, Roles and Responsibilities, Definitions, etc. This section describes the domestic incident management structures and processes.[14]
Appendixes: Glossary, Acronyms, Authorities, and Compendium of National Interagency Plans.

Emergency Support Function Annexes: Groups capabilities and resources into functions that are most likely needed during an incident (for example, Transportation, Firefighting, Mass Care, etc.). This section describes the structures and responsibilities for coordinating incident resource support.[15]

Support Annexes: Describes common processes and specific administrative requirements (for example, Public Affairs, Financial Management, Worker Safety and Health, etc.). This section provides guidance for the functional processes and administrative requirements.[16]

Incident Annexes: Outlines core procedures, roles, and responsibilities for specific contingencies (for example, Biological, Radiological, Cyber, HAZMAT Spills). This section addresses contingency or hazard situations requiring specialized application of the NRP.[17]

The NRP includes specific directives to be executed in case of a disaster, natural or otherwise, that can be implemented within a relatively short time frame.

3.6 EMPHASIS ON LOCAL RESPONSE[18]

The NRP emphasizes control at the local level and works its way upwards:

Identification of police, fire, public health and medical, emergency management, and other personnel as responsible for incident management at the local level.

Handling of incident response at the lowest organizational and jurisdictional level.

Seamless integration of federal involvement when local or state capabilities are exceeded.

Timely federal response to any catastrophic incidents, which includes both natural and man-made disaster occurrences.

Identification of catastrophic incidents as high-impact, low-probability incidents, including natural disasters and terrorist attacks that result in extraordinary levels of mass casualties, damage, or disruption severely affecting the population, infrastructure, environment, economy, national morale, and/or government functions.

Provides means to swiftly deliver federal support in response to catastrophic incidents.

3.7 WHAT IS THE PURPOSE OF THE NRP?[19]

The purpose of the NRP is to establish a comprehensive, national, all-hazards approach to domestic incident management across a spectrum of activities, including prevention, preparedness, response, and recovery. The NRP incorporates best practices and procedures from various incident management disciplines, including homeland security, emergency management, law enforcement, firefighting, hazardous materials response, public works, public health, emergency medical services, and responder and recovery worker health and safety, and integrates them into a unified coordinating structure.

The NRP provides the framework for federal interaction with state, local, and tribal governments; the private sector; and nongovernmental organizations (NGOs) in the context of domestic incident prevention, preparedness, response, and recovery activities. It describes capabilities and resources and establishes responsibilities, operational processes, and protocols to help protect the nation from terrorist attacks and other natural and man-made hazards; save lives; protect public health, safety, property, and the environment; and reduces adverse psychological consequences and disruptions. Additionally, the NRP serves as the foundation for the development of detailed supplemental plans and procedures to effectively and efficiently implement federal incident management activities and assistance in the context of specific types of incidents.

3.8 TIE BETWEEN NRP AND NIMS[20]

The NRP, using the NIMS, establishes mechanisms to:

Integrate incident prevention, preparedness, response, and recovery activities.

Improve coordination and integration of federal, state, local, tribal, regional, private-sector, and nongovernmental organization partners.

Maximize efficient utilization of resources needed for effective incident management and Critical Infrastructure/Key Resources (CI/KR) protection and restoration.

Improve incident management communications and increase situational awareness across jurisdictions and between the public and private sector.

Facilitate emergency mutual aid and federal emergency support to governments.

Facilitate federal-to-federal interaction and emergency support.

Provide proactive and integrated federal responses for catastrophic events.

Address linkages to other federal incident management and emergency response plans developed for specific types of incidents or hazards.

Author's Note: The NRP (essentially) activates the National Incident Management System (NIMS, see Chapter 4 for further information) when there is a crisis or national emergency (or of significant importance).

3.9 MULTIAGENCY COMMAND STRUCTURE COORDINATION[21]

The NRP outlines a coordinated command structure for multiple agencies during a crisis or national emergency:

Identifies police, fire, public health and medical, emergency management, and other personnel as responsible for incident management at the local level.

Incident responses handled at the lowest organizational and jurisdictional levels.

Seamless integration of federal involvement when local or state capabilities are exceeded.

3.10 COORDINATION RESPONSIBILITIES[22]

The NRP introduces additional responsibility groups, specific to their areas of influence, as part of the structured command coordination control mechanism, which is part of the NRP.

Homeland Security Operations Center (HSOC). The HSOC serves as the primary national level multiagency hub for domestic situational awareness and operational coordination. The HSOC also includes DHS components such as the National Infrastructure Coordinating Center (NICC), which has primary responsibility for coordinating communications with the nation's critical infrastructure during an incident.

National Response Coordination Center (NRCC). The NRCC, a functional component of the HSOC, is a multiagency center that provides overall federal response coordination.

Regional Response Coordination Center (RRCC). At the regional level, the RRCC coordinates regional response efforts and implements both local and federal program support until a Joint Field Office is established.

Interagency Incident Management Group (IIMG). A group of senior federal interagency professionals who provide strategic advice to the Secretary of Homeland Security during an actual or potential Incident of National Significance.

Joint Field Office (JFO). A temporary federal facility established locally to provide a central point to coordinate resources in support of state, local, and tribal authorities.

Principal Federal Official (PFO). The Secretary of Homeland Security may designate a PFO during a potential or actual Incident of National Significance. While individual federal officials retain their authorities pertaining to specific aspects of incident management, the PFO works in conjunction with these officials to coordinate overall federal incident management efforts.

3.11 UPDATES TO THE NRP

The U.S. Department of Homeland Security/Emergency Preparedness and Response (EP&R)/FEMA, in close coordination with the DHS Office of the Secretary, will maintain the National Response Plan. The NRP will be updated to incorporate new Presidential directives, legislative changes, and procedural changes based on lessons learned from exercises and actual events.

3.12 INCIDENT COMMAND STRUCTURE OF THE NRP

The Secretary of Homeland Security declares "Incidents of National Significance"[23] (in consultation with other departments and agencies as appropriate) and provides coordination for federal operations and/or resources, establishes reporting requirements, and conducts ongoing communications with federal, state, local, tribal, private sector, and nongovernmental organizations to maintain situational awareness, analyze threats, assess national implications of threat and operational response activities, and coordinate threat or incident response activities. This plan addresses the full spectrum of activities related to domestic incident management, including prevention, preparedness, response, and recovery actions. The NRP focuses on those activities that are directly related to an evolving incident or potential incident rather than steady-state preparedness or readiness activities conducted in the absence of a specific threat or hazard. Since Incidents of National Significance sometimes result in impacts far beyond the immediate or initial incident area, the NRP provides a framework to enable the management of cascading impacts and multiple incidents as well as the prevention of and preparation for subsequent events. Examples of incident management actions from a national perspective might include:

Increasing nationwide public awareness.

Assessing trends that point to potential terrorist activities.

Elevating the national Homeland Security Advisory System (HSAS) alert condition and coordinating protective measures across multiple jurisdictions.

Increasing countermeasures such as inspections, surveillance, security, counterintelligence, and infrastructure protection.

Conducting public health surveillance and assessment processes and, where appropriate, conducting a wide range of prevention measures to include, but not limited to, immunizations.

Providing immediate and long-term public health and medical response assets.

Coordinating federal support to state, local, and tribal authorities in the aftermath of an incident.

Providing strategies for coordination of federal resources required to handle subsequent events.

Enabling immediate recovery activities while addressing any long-term consequences within the impacted area or zone.

3.13 LEVELS OF AUTHORITY

Various federal statutory authorities and policies provide the basis for federal actions and activities in the context of domestic incident management. The NRP uses the foundation provided by the Homeland Security Act, HSPD-5, and the Robert T. Stafford Disaster Relief and Emergency Assistance Act (Stafford Act) to provide a comprehensive, all-hazards approach to domestic incident management. Nothing within the NRP alters the existing authorities of individual federal departments and agencies. The NRP does not convey new authorities upon the Secretary of Homeland Security or any other federal official.

Rather, this plan establishes the coordinating structures, processes, and protocols required to integrate the specific statutory and policy authorities of various federal departments and agencies in a collective framework for action to include prevention, preparedness, response, and recovery activities. The NRP may be used in conjunction with other federal incident management and emergency operations plans developed under these and other authorities as well as Memorandums of Understanding (MOUs) among various federal agencies.

3.14 KEY CONCEPTS IN THE IMPLEMENTATION OF THE NRP

Summarized key concepts that are reflected throughout the NRP include the following concepts:

Systematic and coordinated incident management, including protocols for: (a) incident reporting; (b) coordinated action; (c) alert and notification; (d) mobilization of federal resources to augment existing federal, state, local, and tribal capabilities; (e) operating under differing threats or threat levels; and, (f) integration of crisis and consequence management functions.

Proactive notification and deployment of federal resources in anticipation of or in response to catastrophic events in coordination and collaboration with state, local, and tribal governments and private organizations (when/where possible).

Organizing interagency efforts to minimize damage, restore impacted areas to preincident conditions (if feasible), and/or implement programs to mitigate vulnerability of future occurrences.

Coordinating incident communication, worker safety and health, private-sector involvement, and other activities that are common to the majority of incidents.

Organize to facilitate the delivery of critical federal resources, assets, and assistance. Federal departments and agencies are assigned to lead or support based on authorities, resources, and capabilities.

Providing mechanisms for vertical and horizontal coordination, communications, and information sharing in response to threats or incidents. These mechanisms facilitate coordination among state, local, and tribal entities and the federal government, as well as between the public and private sectors.

Facilitating federal support to federal departments and agencies acting under the requesting department or agency's own authorities.

Developing detailed supplemental operations, tactical, and hazard-specific contingency plans and procedures.

Providing the basis for coordination of interagency and intergovernmental planning, training, exercising, assessment, coordination, and information exchange.

3.15   ROLES AND RESPONSIBILITIES

Police, fire, public health and medical, emergency management, public works, environmental response, and other personnel are often the first to arrive and the last to leave an incident site. In some instances, a federal agency in the local area may act as a first responder, and the local assets of federal agencies may be used to advise or assist state or local officials in accordance with agency authorities and procedures. Mutual aid agreements provide mechanisms to mobilize and employ resources from neighboring jurisdictions to support the incident command.

When state resources and capabilities are overwhelmed, governors may request federal assistance under a presidential disaster or emergency declaration. Summarized below are the responsibilities of the Governor, Local Chief Executive Officer (CEO), and Tribal Chief Executive Officer.

3.15.1   ROLE OF THE GOVERNOR

As a state's chief executive, the Governor is responsible for the public safety and welfare of the people of that state or territory, such that the Governor:

Is responsible for coordinating state resources to address the full spectrum of actions to prevent, prepare for, respond to, and recover from incidents in an all-hazards context to include terrorism, natural disasters, accidents, and other contingencies.

Under certain emergency conditions, typically has police powers to make, amend, and rescind orders and regulations.

Provides leadership and plays a key role in communicating to the public and in helping people, businesses, and organizations cope with the consequences of any type of declared emergency within state jurisdiction.

Encourages participation in mutual aid and implements authorities for the state to enter into mutual aid agreements with other states, tribes, and territories to facilitate resource-sharing.

Is the Commander-in-Chief of state military forces (National Guard when in State Active Duty or Title 32 Status and the authorized State militias).

Requests federal assistance when it becomes clear that state or tribal capabilities will be insufficient or have been exceeded or exhausted.

3.15.2   ROLE OF THE LOCAL CHIEF EXECUTIVE OFFICER

A mayor or city or county manager, as a jurisdiction's chief executive, is responsible for the public safety and welfare of the people of that jurisdiction, such that the Local Chief Executive Officer:

Similar to the Governor, the Local CEO ("Mayor") is responsible for coordinating local resources to address the full spectrum of actions to prevent, prepare for, respond to, and recover from incidents in an all-hazards context to include terrorism, natural disasters, accidents, and other contingencies.

Dependent upon state and local law, has extraordinary powers to suspend local laws and ordinances, such as to establish a curfew, direct evacuations, and, in coordination with the local health authority, to order a quarantine.

Provides leadership and plays a key role in communicating to the public, and in helping people, businesses, and organizations cope with the consequences of any type of domestic incident within the jurisdiction.

Negotiates and enters into mutual aid agreements with other jurisdictions to facilitate resource-sharing.

Requests state and, if necessary, federal assistance through the Governor of the state when the jurisdiction's capabilities have been exceeded or exhausted.

3.15.3 ROLE OF THE TRIBAL CHIEF EXECUTIVE OFFICER

The Tribal Chief Executive Officer is responsible for the public safety and welfare of the people of that tribe, such that the Tribal Chief Executive Officer, as authorized by tribal government:

Has all of the similar roles to that of the Local CEO, except that the Tribal CEO is not dependent upon state and local law insofar as to be able to suspend tribal laws and ordinances, and others.

Can elect to deal directly with the federal government (although a state Governor must request a presidential disaster declaration on behalf of a tribe under the Stafford Act, federal agencies can work directly with the tribe within existing authorities and resources).

3.16 ROLES OF THE FEDERAL GOVERNMENT

The Homeland Security Act of 2002 established DHS to prevent terrorist attacks within the United States; reduce the vulnerability of the United States to terrorism, natural disasters, and other emergencies; and minimize the damage and assist in the recovery from terrorist attacks, natural disasters, and other emergencies. The act also designates DHS as "a focal point regarding natural and manmade crises and emergency planning."[24]

Pursuant to HSPD-5,[25] the Secretary of Homeland Security is responsible for coordinating federal operations within the United States to prepare for, respond to, and recover from terrorist attacks, major disasters, and other emergencies. HSPD-5[26] further designates the Secretary of Homeland Security as the "principal federal official"[27] for domestic incident management. In this role, the Secretary is also responsible for coordinating federal resources utilized in response to or recovery from terrorist attacks, major disasters, or other emergencies if and when any of the following four conditions apply:

1. Federal department or agency acting under its own authority has requested DHS assistance.
2. Resources of state and local authorities are overwhelmed and federal assistance has been requested.

3. More than one federal department or agency has become substantially involved in responding to the incident.
4. The Secretary has been directed to assume incident management responsibilities by the President of the United States.

In accordance with HSPD-5[28] and other relevant statutes and directives, the Attorney General has lead responsibility for criminal investigations of terrorist acts or threats by individuals or groups inside the United States, or directed at U.S. citizens or institutions abroad, where such acts are within the federal criminal jurisdiction of the United States, as well as for related intelligence-collection activities within the United States, subject to applicable laws, executive orders, directives, and procedures. Generally acting through the U.S. Department of Justice Federal Bureau of Investigation (FBI), the Attorney General, in cooperation with other federal departments and agencies engaged in activities to protect national security, coordinates the activities of the other members of the law enforcement community to detect, prevent, preempt, and disrupt terrorist attacks against the United States. This includes actions to prevent, preempt, and disrupt specific terrorist threats or actual incidents that are based upon specific intelligence or law enforcement information. Nothing in this plan derogates the Attorney General's status or responsibilities.

Following a terrorist threat or an actual incident that falls within the criminal jurisdiction of the United States, the full capabilities of the United States will be dedicated to assisting the Attorney General to identify the perpetrators and bring them to justice, consistent with U.S. law and with authorities of other federal departments and agencies to protect national security.

The Department of Defense (DoD) has significant resources that may be available to support the federal response to an Incident of National Significance. The Secretary of Defense authorizes Defense Support of Civil Authorities (DSCA) for domestic incidents as directed by the President or when consistent with military readiness operations and appropriate under the circumstances and the law. The Secretary of Defense retains command of military forces under DSCA, as with all other situations and operations.[29] Concepts of "command" and "unity of command" have distinct legal and cultural meanings for military forces and operations. For military forces, command runs from the President to the Secretary of Defense to the Commander of the combatant command to the commander of the forces. The "Unified Command" concept utilized by civil authorities is distinct from the military chain of command.

The Department of State has international coordination responsibilities. The Secretary of State is responsible for coordinating international prevention, preparedness, response, and recovery activities relating to domestic incidents, and for the protection of U.S. citizens and interests overseas.

During an Incident of National Significance, other federal departments or agencies may play primary, coordinating, and/or support roles based on their authorities and resources and the nature of the incident. In situations where a federal agency has jurisdictional authority and responsibility for directing or managing a major aspect of the response, that agency is part of the national leadership for the incident and participates as a Senior Federal Official (SFO) or Senior Federal Law Enforcement Official (SFLEO) in the Joint Field Office (JFO) Coordination Group at the field level, and as part of the Interagency Incident Management Group (IIMG) and/or Homeland Security Council (HSC)/National Security Council (NSC) Policy Coordination Committees (PCC). Some federal agencies with jurisdictional authority and responsibility may also participate in the Unified Command at the Incident Command Post (ICP). Federal departments and agencies participate in a structure as coordinators, primary agencies, and/or support agencies and/or as required to support incident management activities.

HSPD-5[30] directs the heads of all federal departments and agencies, in the context of domestic incident management, to provide their full and prompt cooperation, resources, and support, as appropriate and consistent with their own responsibilities for protecting our national security, to the Secretary of Homeland Security, the Attorney General, the Secretary of Defense, and the Secretary of State. Several federal agencies have independent authorities to declare disasters or emergencies. These authorities may be exercised concurrently with or become part of a major disaster or emergency declared under the Stafford Act.

Some examples of agencies exercising independent authorities include the following scenarios:

The Secretary of Agriculture may declare a disaster in certain situations in which a county sustained production loss of 30% or greater in a single major enterprise, authorizing emergency loans for physical damages and crop loss.

The Administrator of the Small Business Administration may make a disaster declaration based on physical damage to buildings, machinery, equipment, inventory, homes, and other property as well as economic injury.

The Secretary of Commerce may make a declaration of a commercial fisheries failure or fishery resources disaster.

The Secretary of Health and Human Services may declare a public health emergency.

The U.S. Army Corps of Engineers (USACE) Chief of Engineers may issue a disaster declaration in response to flooding and coastal storms. USACE is authorized to undertake emergency operations and activities.

A federal On-Scene Coordinator (OSC), designated by the U.S. Environmental Protection Agency (EPA), DHS/U.S. Coast Guard (DHS/USCG), DoD, or the U.S. Department of Energy (DOE) under the NCP, has the authority to direct response efforts at the scene of a discharge or release of oil, hazardous substance, pollutants, or contaminants, depending on the substance and the location and source of release.

The NRP applies a functional approach that groups the capabilities of federal departments and agencies and the American Red Cross into ESFs to provide the planning, support, resources, program implementation, and emergency services that are most likely to be needed during Incidents of National Significance. The federal response to actual or potential Incidents of National Significance is typically provided through the full or partial activation of the ESF structure as necessary. The ESFs serve as the coordination mechanism to provide assistance to state, local, and tribal governments or to federal departments and agencies conducting missions of primary federal responsibility. ESFs may be selectively activated for both Stafford Act and non-Stafford Act incidents where federal departments or agencies request DHS assistance or under other circumstances as defined in HSPD-5.[31] The ESFs provide staffing for the National Response Coordination Center (NRCC), Regional Response Coordination Center (RRCC), JFO, and ICP as required by the situation at hand.

3.17 NRP EMERGENCY SUPPORT FUNCTIONS (ESFS)

As merged from the Federal Response Plan (FRP) the NRP introduced several corresponding ESFs into the NRP. Previously, the FRP ESFs were as follows:

- Transportation
- Communications
- Public Works and Engineering
- Firefighting
- Information and Planning
- Mass Care
- Resource Support
- Health and Medical Services
- Urban Search and Rescue
- Hazardous Materials
- Food
- Energy

Now, with merged functions from the FRP, the NRP ESFs are as follows:

- Transportation
- Communications
- Public Works and Engineering
- Firefighting
- Emergency Management
- Mass Care, Housing, and Human Services
- Resource Support
- Public Health and Medical Services
- Urban Search and Rescue
- Oil and Hazardous Materials Response
- Agriculture and Natural Resources
- Energy
- Public Safety and Security
- Long-Term Community Recovery and Mitigation
- External Affairs

3.18 SCOPE OF ESFs

Each ESF is composed of primary and support agencies. The NRP identifies primary agencies on the basis of authorities, resources, and capabilities. Support agencies are assigned based on resources and capabilities in a given functional area. The resources provided by the ESFs reflect the resource-typing categories identified in the NIMS. ESFs are expected to support one another in carrying out their respective roles and responsibilities. The federal response to actual or potential Incidents of National Significance is typically provided through the full or partial activation of the ESF structure as necessary.[32] Not all Incidents of National Significance result in the activation of ESFs.[33] It is possible that an Incident of National Significance can be adequately addressed by DHS and other federal agencies through activation of certain NRP elements (for example, Principal Federal Official [PFO], IIMG) without the activation of ESFs.[34] Similarly, operational security considerations may dictate that activation of NRP elements be kept to a minimum, particularly in the context of certain terrorism prevention activities. ESF services (and their scope) are broken into subcategories based upon functionality.[35]

3.18.1 ESF 1: TRANSPORTATION

- Federal and civil transportation support
- Transportation safety
- Restoration and recovery of the transportation infrastructure
- Movement restrictions
- Damage and impact assessments

3.18.2 ESF 2: COMMUNICATIONS

- Coordination with the telecommunications industry
- Restoration and recovery of the telecommunications infrastructure
- Protection, restoration, and sustainment of national computer and information technology resources

3.18.3 ESF 3: PUBLIC WORKS

- Public infrastructure protection and emergency repair services
- Infrastructure restoration
- Engineering services and construction management
- Critical infrastructure liaison

3.18.4 ESF 4: FIRE SERVICES

- Firefighting activities on federal lands
- Resource support to rural and urban firefighting operations

3.18.5　ESF 5: Emergency Management

- Coordination of incident management efforts
- Issuance of mission assignments
- Resource and human capital assessment management
- Incident Action Plan (IAP)
- Financial management

3.18.6　ESF 6: Human Services

- Mass casualty care
- Disaster housing
- Human services

3.18.7　ESF 7: Resource Management

- Resource support for finding facility space, office equipment and supplies, contracting services, etc.

3.18.8　ESF 8: Public Health and Medical Services

- Public health services
- Medical services
- Mental health services
- Mortuary services

3.18.9　ESF 9: Urban Search and Rescue Services

- Lifesaving assistance
- Urban search and rescue

3.18.10　ESF 10: Hazardous Materials (HAZMAT) Response

- Oil and hazardous materials (chemical, biological, radiological, etc.) response
- Environmental safety and short- and long-term cleanup

3.18.11　ESF 11: Agriculture and Natural Resources

- Nutrition assistance
- Animal and plant disease/pest response
- Food safety and security
- Natural and cultural resources and historic properties protection and restoration

3.18.12 ESF 12: ENERGY

- Energy infrastructure assessment, repair, and restoration
- Energy industry utilities coordination
- Energy forecast

3.18.13 ESF 13: PUBLIC SAFETY AND SECURITY

- Facility and resource security
- Security planning and technical and resource assistance
- Public safety/security support
- Support to access, traffic, and crowd control

3.18.14 ESF 14: LONG-TERM COMMUNITY RECOVERY AND MITIGATION

- Social and economic community impact assessment
- Long-term community recovery assistance to states, local governments, and the private sector
- Mitigation analysis and program implementation

3.18.15 ESF 15: EXTERNAL AFFAIRS

- Emergency public information and protective action guidance
- Media and community relations
- Congressional and international affairs
- Tribal and insular affairs

3.19 QUESTIONS

1. The acronym NRP means:
   a. National Response Plan
   b. National Registry Program
   c. New Reparation Plan
   d. National Responder Plan

   Answer: *National Response Plan*, introduced sometime in December 2004 by the Department of Homeland Security.

2. The _____ is an acronym and is a subcomponent of the NRP.

   Answer: *National Incident Management System* or *NIMS*.

3. The NRP supersedes the FRP. True or False?

   Answer: *True*. The NRP supersedes the Federal Response Plan, the Domestic Terrorism Concept of Operations Plan, the Federal

Radiological Emergency Response Plan, and the Interim National Response Plan.

4. ESF is an acronym for the _____.

Answer: *Emergency Support Function.*

5. NRP training is provided by which organization?
   a. Federal Emergency Management Agency
   b. Department of Homeland Security
   c. United States Fire Administration
   d. Office of Emergency Management

   Answer: It is the *Federal Emergency Management Agency* (also known as *FEMA*) Emergency Management Institute that provides the training on the NRP, NIMS, and other subcomponents and topics of the NRP.

6. The NRP consists of primarily how many topics?
   a. 4
   b. 5
   c. 6
   d. 7

   Answer: *5.* The topics, or sections, that make up the NRP consist of the following: (1) Base Plan; (2) Appendixes; (3) Emergency Support Function Annexes; (4) Support Annexes; and (5) Incident Annexes.

7. The NRP emphasizes control at the local level, and works it way upwards. True or False?

   Answer: *True.* The intention of the NRP is to place emphasis of support and control beginning at the lowest level of the government: the local governments, as they often have more incidents locally than at a national level, but can be escalated upwards to a national, or federal, level should it require such a response.

8. Fill in the missing piece: The NRP provides the framework for federal interaction with state, local, and tribal governments; the private sector; and nongovernmental organizations (NGOs) in the context of domestic incident prevention, preparedness, response, and recovery activities. It describes capabilities and resources and establishes responsibilities, operational processes, and protocols to help _____ and other natural and manmade hazards; save lives; protect public health, safety, property, and the

environment; and reduces adverse psychological consequences and disruptions.

Answer: *Protect the nation from terrorist attacks.*

9. The following definition refers to scenarios in which (1) a federal department or agency, responding under its own authorities, requests DHS assistance and/or if resources of state and local authorities are overwhelmed; (2) enactment of the Stafford Act pertaining to major disasters or emergencies; (3) other catastrophic incidents not necessarily covered or pertaining other categorically defined events or circumstances; (4) situations involving more than one (1) federal department or agency is involved; (5) credible threats or indications of imminent terrorist attack; (6) threats/incidents related to high-profile, large-scale events; (7) and/or lastly, in which The President of the United States directs DHS to assume responsibility for incident management. What is the definition called?
   a. Homeland Security Advisory System (HSAS)
   b. Levels of Authority
   c. Interagency Incident Management Coordination Group
   d. Incidents of National Significance

   Answer: *Incidents of National Significance.* Since Incidents of National Significance sometimes result in impacts far beyond the immediate or initial incident area, the NRP provides a framework to enable the management of cascading impacts and multiple incidents as well as the prevention of and preparation for subsequent events.

10. NRP ESFs total in number by how much?
    a. 15
    b. 14
    c. 13
    d. 10

    Answer: *15.*

11. "Chemical Materials Response" is an ESF function. True or False?

    Answer: *False.* It is actually "Oil and Hazardous Material Response", and includes chemical, biological, radiological, and nuclear.

NOTES

1. http://www.dhs.gov/dhspublic/interapp/editorial/editorial_0566.xml
2. U.S. Department of Homeland Security, National Response Plan (December, 2004).

3. By definition, the term *"Incidents of National Significance"* refers to scenarios in which (1) a federal department or agency, responding under its own authorities, requests DHS assistance and/or if resources of state and local authorities are over-whelmed; (2) enactment of the Stafford Act pertaining to major disasters or emergencies; (3) other catastrophic incidents not necessarily covered or pertaining other categorically defined events or circumstances; (4) situations involving more than one (1) federal department or agency is involved; (5) credible threats or indications of imminent terrorist attack; (6) threats/incidents related to high-profile, large-scale events; (7) and/or lastly, in which The President of the United States directs DHS to assume responsibility for incident management.

4. Department of Homeland Security National Response Plan, One Plan, One Goal: a safer, more secure America Federal Partners Briefing, November 2004. http://www.bhs.idaho.gov/bhslibrary/nrp-full-brief_files/frame.htm#slide0054.htm

5. http://www.fema.gov/nims

6. http://www.bhs.idaho.gov/bhslibrary/nrp-full-brief_files/frame.htm#slide0047.htm

7. In response to a presidential-declared disaster, FEMA may work with up to 28 federal agencies and the American Red Cross to provide assistance. These agencies provide state and local governments with personnel, technical expertise, equipment and other resources, and assume an active role in managing the response. To coordinate the federal efforts, FEMA recommends and the President appoints a Federal Coordinating Officer (FCO) for each state that is affected by a disaster. The FCO and the state response team set up a Disaster Field Office (DFO) near the disaster scene. It is from there that the federal and state personnel work together to carry out response and recovery functions. These functions are grouped into 12 Emergency Support Functions (ESFs), each headed by an agency supported by other agencies. http://www.fema.gov/about/frp.shtm

8. United States Government Interagency Domestic Terrorism Concept of Operations Plan, January 2001. http://www.fbi.gov/publications/conplan/conplan.pdf

9. On December 7, 1979, following the March 1979 Three Mile Island nuclear power plant accident in Pennsylvania, President Carter transferred the federal lead role in offsite radiological emergency planning and preparedness activities from the U.S. Nuclear Regulatory Commission (NRC) to FEMA. FEMA established the Radiological Emergency Preparedness (REP) Program to: (1) ensure that the public health and safety of citizens living around commercial nuclear power plants would be adequately protected in the event of a nuclear power station accident and (2) inform and educate the public about radiological emergency preparedness. FEMA's REP Program responsibilities encompass only "offsite" activities; that is, state and local government emergency preparedness activities that take place beyond the nuclear power plant boundaries. http://www.fema.gov/rrr/rep

10. FEMA REP PLANNING GUIDANCE, http://www.fema.gov/doc/rrr/rep/repplan 101702.doc

11. EIIP Virtual Forum Presentation — September 15, 2004, The National Response Plan, An Update by Barbara S. Yagerman and Amy Sebring. http://www.emforum.org/vforum/lc040915.htm

12. Federal Emergency Management Agency, An Introduction to the National Response Plan (NRP) (IS-800), Self-Study Guide (December, 2004).

13. FEMA Independent Study Program: IS-800 National Response Plan (NRP), An Introduction. http://training.fema.gov/EMIWeb/IS/is800.asp

14. Department of Homeland Security National Response Plan, One Plan, One Goal: a safer, more secure America Federal Partners Briefing, November 2004. http://www.bhs.idaho.gov/bhslibrary/nrp-full-brief_files/frame.htm#slide0047.htm

15. Department of Homeland Security National Response Plan, One Plan, One Goal: a safer, more secure America Federal Partners Briefing, November 2004. http://www.bhs.idaho.gov/bhslibrary/nrp-full-brief_files/frame.htm#slide0047.htm

16. Department of Homeland Security National Response Plan, One Plan, One Goal: A safer, more secure America Federal Partners Briefing, November 2004. http://www.bhs.idaho.gov/bhslibrary/nrp-full-brief_files/frame.htm#slide0047.htm

17. Department of Homeland Security National Response Plan, One Plan, One Goal: A safer, more secure America Federal Partners Briefing, November 2004. http://www.bhs.idaho.gov/bhslibrary/nrp-full-brief_files/frame.htm#slide0047.htm

18. http://www.dhs.gov/dhspublic/interapp/press_release/press_release_0581.xml

19. U.S. Department of Homeland Security, National Response Plan (December, 2004).

20. U.S. Department of Homeland Security, National Response Plan (December, 2004).

21. U.S. Department of Homeland Security, National Response Plan (December, 2004).

22. U.S. Department of Homeland Security, National Response Plan (December, 2004).

23. By definition, the term *"Incidents of National Significance"* refers to scenarios in which (1) a federal department or agency, responding under its own authorities, requests DHS assistance and/or if resources of state and local authorities are overwhelmed; (2) enactment of the Stafford Act pertaining to major disasters or emergencies; (3) other catastrophic incidents not necessarily covered or pertaining other categorically defined events or circumstances; (4) situations involving more than one (1) federal department or agency is involved; (5) credible threats or indications of imminent terrorist attack; (6) threats/incidents related to high-profile, large-scale events; (7) and/or lastly, in which The President of the United States directs DHS to assume responsibility for incident management; Department of Homeland Security National Response Plan, One Plan, One Goal: a safer, more secure America Federal Partners Briefing, November 2004. http://www.bhs.idaho.gov/bhslibrary/nrp-full-brief_files/frame.htm#slide0047.htm

24. http://www.uscg.mil/legal/Homeland_legislation/text/032101%20HR1158.htm

25. http://www.whitehouse.gov/news/releases/2003/02/20030228-9.html

26. http://www.whitehouse.gov/news/releases/2003/02/20030228-9.html

27. http://www.uscg.mil/legal/Homeland_legislation/text/032101%20HR1158.htm

28. http://www.whitehouse.gov/news/releases/2003/02/20030228-9.html

29. Department of Homeland Security National Response Plan, One Plan, One Goal: A safer, more secure America Federal Partners Briefing, November 2004. http://www.bhs.idaho.gov/bhslibrary/nrp-full-brief_files/frame.htm#slide0047.htm

30. http://www.whitehouse.gov/news/releases/2003/02/20030228-9.html

31. http://www.whitehouse.gov/news/releases/2003/02/20030228-9.html

32. Department of Homeland Security National Response Plan, One Plan, One Goal: A safer, more secure America Federal Partners Briefing, November 2004. http://www.bhs.idaho.gov/bhslibrary/nrp-full-brief_files/frame.htm#slide0047.htm

33. Department of Homeland Security National Response Plan, One Plan, One Goal: A safer, more secure America Federal Partners Briefing, November 2004. http://www.bhs.idaho.gov/bhslibrary/nrp-full-brief_files/frame.htm#slide0047.htm

34. Department of Homeland Security National Response Plan, One Plan, One Goal: A safer, more secure America Federal Partners Briefing, November 2004. http://www.bhs.idaho.gov/bhslibrary/nrp-full-brief_files/frame.htm#slide0047.htm

35. U.S. Department of Homeland Security, National Response Plan (December, 2004).

4 National Incident Management Systems (NIMS)

4.1 INTRODUCTION

This chapter summarizes the need and use for the National Incident Management System (NIMS), which was implemented in March 2004 by the Department of Homeland Security (DHS). The NIMS is vital in terms of best practices, principles, and methods used for an incident command framework structure. This is useful especially for disasters involving critical infrastructures and the requirement of coordinated efforts between critical infrastructure owners and emergency responders.

4.2 WHAT IS NIMS?

On February 28, 2003, the President of the United States issued Homeland Security Presidential Directive (HSPD)-5, Management of Domestic Incidents, which directs the Secretary of Homeland Security to develop and administer a NIMS. This system provides a consistent nationwide template to enable federal, state, local, and tribal governments and private-sector and nongovernmental organizations to work together effectively and efficiently to prepare for, prevent, respond to, and recover from domestic incidents, regardless of cause, size, or complexity, including acts of catastrophic terrorism. The NIMS provides mechanisms for the further development and refinement of supporting national standards, guidelines, protocols, systems, and technologies.[1] The NIMS integrates effective practices in emergency preparedness and response into a comprehensive national framework for incident management, The NIMS enables responders at all levels to work together more effectively to manage domestic incidents no matter what the cause, size, or complexity.[2]

While most incidents are generally handled on a daily basis by a single jurisdiction at the local level, there are important instances in which successful domestic incident management operations depend on the involvement of multiple jurisdictions, functional agencies, and emergency responder disciplines. These instances require effective and efficient coordination across this broad spectrum of organizations and their activities. The NIMS uses a systems methodological approach to integrate the best of existing processes and methods into a unified national framework for incident management. This framework forms the basis for interoperability and compatibility that will, in turn, enable a diverse set of public and private organizations to conduct well-integrated and effective incident management operations. It does this through a core set of concepts, principles, procedures, and organizational processes, terminology, and standards requirements applicable to a broad community of NIMS users.

Building on the foundation provided by existing incident management and emergency response system methodologies used by jurisdictions and functional disciplines at varied levels, the NIMS integrates best practices that have proven effective over the years into a comprehensive framework that are used by incident management organizations in an all-hazards context (terrorist attacks, natural disasters, and other emergencies) nationwide. It sets in motion mechanisms necessary to leverage new(er) technologies and adopt better approaches, enabling continuous refinement of the NIMS over time. The NIMS document was developed through a collaborative, intergovernmental partnership with significant input from incident management functional disciplines, various private sector industries (and their organizations), and other nongovernmental organizations.[3]

The NIMS represents a core set of doctrine, concepts, principles, terminology, and organizational processes that enable an effective, efficient, and collaborative incident management at all levels. It should be noted that it is *not* an operational incident management or resource allocation plan. HSPD-5 requires the Secretary of Homeland Security to develop a National Response Plan (NRP)[4] that integrates federal government domestic prevention, preparedness, response, and recovery plans into a single, unitary-disciplined all-hazards plan. The NRP, using the comprehensive framework provided by the NIMS, provides the structure and mechanisms for national-level policy and operational direction for federal support to state, local, and tribal incident managers and for exercising direct federal authorities and responsibilities as appropriate under the law.[5]

HSPD-5 requires all federal departments and agencies to adopt the NIMS and to use it in their individual domestic incident management and emergency prevention, preparedness, response, recovery, and mitigation programs and activities, as well as in support of all actions taken to assist state, local, or tribal entities. The directive requires federal departments and agencies to make adoption of the NIMS by state and local organizations a condition for federal preparedness assistance (through grants, contracts, and other activities) beginning in FY 2005.[6] Jurisdictional compliance with certain aspects of the NIMS will be possible for short-term time frames, such as adopting the basic tenets of the Incident Command System (ICS) identified within the document.

Other aspects of the NIMS, however, will require additional development and refinement to enable compliance at a future date (for example, data and communications systems interoperability). To provide this framework for interoperability and compatibility, the NIMS is based on an appropriate balance of flexibility and standardization. In summary, NIMS intent is to:

Be applicable across a full spectrum of potential incidents and hazard scenarios, regardless of its size or complexity.
Improve coordination and cooperation between public and private entities for a variety of domestic incident management activities (and their issues).[7]

4.3 COMPLIANCE

HSPD-5[8] requires federal departments and agencies to make the adoption of NIMS by state and local organizations a condition for federal preparedness assistance (grants, contracts, and other activities) sometime in FY 2005.[9] Jurisdictions can comply in the short term by adopting the ICS, which is subset to NIMS. Other aspects of NIMS require additional development and refinement to enable compliance at a future date.[10,11]

4.4 FLEXIBILITY

The NIMS provides a consistent, flexible, and adjustable national framework within which government and private entities at all levels can work together to manage domestic incidents, regardless of their cause, size, location, or complexity. This flexibility applies across all phases of incident management: prevention, preparedness, response, recovery, and mitigation.[12]

4.5 STANDARDIZATION

The NIMS provides a set of standardized organizational structures such as the ICS,[13] multiagency coordination systems, and public information systems, as well as requirements for processes, procedures, and systems designed to improve interoperability among jurisdictions and disciplines in various areas, including: training; resource management; personnel qualification and certification; equipment certification; communications and information management; technology support; and continuous system improvement. It is important to understand that with the establishment of the NIMS, *there is only one ICS*. As agencies adopt the principles and concepts of ICS as established in the NIMS, the ICS can expand to meet the needs of the response, regardless of the size or number of responders. The key to both NIMS and ICS is a balance between standardization and flexibility.[14]

4.6 NIMS REPRESENTS BEST PRACTICES

The NIMS integrates existing best practices into a consistent, nationwide approach to domestic incident management that is applicable at all jurisdictional levels and across functional disciplines in an all-hazards context. There are six major components that make up this systems approach. Of these components, the concepts and practices for Command and Management (Chapter II) and Preparedness (Chapter III) are the most fully developed, reflecting their regular use by many jurisdictional levels and agencies responsible for incident management across the United States. Chapters IV–VII, which cover Resource Management, Communications and Information Management, Supporting Technologies, and Ongoing Management and Maintenance, introduce many concepts and requirements that are also integral to the NIMS but that will require further collaborative development and refinement over time.[15]

4.7 COMPONENTS OF NIMS

The following provides a brief synopsis of each major component of the NIMS, as well as how these components work together as a system to provide the national framework for preparing for, preventing, responding to, and recovering from domestic incidents, regardless of cause, size, or complexity. A more detailed discussion of each component is included in subsequent chapters of the NIMS document.[16]

NIMS is comprised of several components that work collectively as a complete system providing an overall framework structure for preparing for, preventing, responding to, and recovering from domestic incidents. These components include the following[17]:

- Command and management
- Preparedness
- Resource management
- Communications and information management
- Supporting technologies
- Ongoing management and maintenance

4.8 COMMAND AND MANAGEMENT

NIMS standard incident command structures are based on three key organizational systems:

Incident Command System (ICS): The ICS defines the operating characteristics, interactive management components, and structure of incident management and emergency response organizations engaged throughout the life cycle of an incident.

Multiagency Coordination Systems (MACS): These define the operating characteristics, interactive management components, and organizational structure of supporting incident management entities engaged at the federal, state, local, tribal, and regional levels through mutual-aid agreements and other assistance arrangements.[18]

Public Information Systems: These refer to processes, procedures, and systems for communicating timely and accurate information to the public during crisis or emergency situations. Public information systems are the processes and systems used to communicate with the public during a response.[19]

4.9 PREPAREDNESS

Effective incident management begins with a host of preparedness activities conducted on a ready-state basis, well in advance of any potential incident. Preparedness involves an integrated combination of planning, training, exercises, personnel qualification and certification standards, equipment acquisition and certification standards, and publication management processes and activities.

Planning: Plans describe how personnel, equipment, and other resources are used to support incident management and emergency response activities. Plans provide mechanisms and systems for setting priorities, integrating multiple entities and functions, and ensuring that communications and other systems are available and integrated in support of a full spectrum of incident management requirements.

Training: Training includes standard courses on multiagency incident command and management, organizational structure, and operational procedures; discipline-specific and agency-specific incident management courses; and courses on the integration and use of supporting technologies.

Exercises: Incident management organizations and personnel must participate in realistic exercises, including multidisciplinary, multijurisdictional, and multisector interaction, to improve integration and interoperability and optimize resource utilization during incident operations.

Personnel Qualification and Certification: Qualification and certification activities are undertaken to identify and publish national-level standards and measure performance against these standards to ensure that incident management and emergency responder personnel are appropriately qualified and officially certified to perform NIMS-related functions.

Equipment Acquisition and Certification: Incident management organizations and emergency responders at all levels rely on various types of equipment to perform mission-essential tasks. A critical component of operational preparedness is the acquisition of equipment that will perform to certain standards, including the capability to be interoperable with similar equipment used by other jurisdictions.

Mutual-Aid: Mutual-aid (and Emergency Management Assistance Compacts [EMACS])[20] agreements are the means for one jurisdiction to provide resources, facilities, services, and other required support to another jurisdiction during an incident. Each jurisdiction should be party to a mutual-aid agreement with appropriate jurisdictions from which they expect to receive or to which they expect to provide assistance during an incident.[21]

Publications Management: Publications management refers to forms and forms standardization, developing publication materials, administering publications, including establishing naming and numbering conventions, managing the publication and promulgation of documents, and exercising control over sensitive documents, and revising publications when necessary.

4.10 BENEFITS FROM USING NIMS

Some of the benefits from utilizing NIMS may include one or more of the following[22]:

- Flexible framework that facilitates both public and private entities at all levels to work together in managing domestic incidents.
- Standardized organizational framework structures, processes, procedures, and systems designed to improve interoperability functions.

- Standards for planning, training, and exercising incident command management.
- Personnel qualification standards.
- Equipment acquisition and certification standards.
- Publication management, its processes and activities.
- Interoperability between communications processes, procedures, and systems.
- Information management systems that utilize commonly accepted architectures.
- Supporting technologies such as voice and data communications systems, information systems, data display systems, and specialized technologies.

4.11 RESOURCE RECOVERY

The NIMS defines standardized mechanisms and establishes requirements for processes to describe, inventory, mobilize, dispatch, track, and recover resources over the life cycle of an incident.[23]

4.12 COMMUNICATIONS AND INFORMATION MANAGEMENT

The NIMS identifies the requirement for a standardized framework for communications, information management (collection, analysis, and dissemination), and information sharing at all levels of incident management. These elements are briefly described as follows[24]:

Incident Management Communications: Incident management organizations must ensure that effective, interoperable communications processes, procedures, and systems exist to support a wide variety of incident management activities across agencies and jurisdictions.

Information Management: Information management processes, procedures, and systems help ensure that information, including communications and data, flows efficiently through a commonly accepted architecture supporting numerous agencies and jurisdictions responsible for managing or directing domestic incidents, those impacted by the incident, and those contributing resources to the incident management effort. Effective information management enhances incident management and response and helps insure that crisis decision-making is better informed.

4.13 SUPPORTING TECHNOLOGIES

Technology and technological systems provide supporting capabilities essential to implementing and continuously refining the NIMS. These include voice and data communications systems, information management systems (that is, record keeping and resource tracking), and data display systems. Also included are specialized technologies that facilitate ongoing operations and incident management activities in situations that call for unique technology-based capabilities.[25]

4.14 ONGOING MANAGEMENT AND MAINTENANCE

This component establishes an activity to provide strategic direction for and oversight of the NIMS, supporting both routine review and the continuous refinement of the system and its components over the long term. DHS established the NIMS Integration Center to provide these functions.[26]

4.15 COMMAND STRUCTURING UNDER NIMS

NIMS utilize two levels of incident management structure, depending on the nature of the incident, which are as follows[27]:

Incident Command Systems (ICS): This is a standardized on-scene, all-hazard incident management system. ICS allows users to adopt an integrated organizational structure to match the needs of a single or multiple organizational incidents.

Multiagency Coordination Systems (MACS): These are combined resources of facilities, equipment, personnel, procedures, and communications that are integrated into a common framework structure for coordinating and supporting incident management.

The NIMS requires that all responses for domestic incidents utilize a common management structure. The ICS is a standard, on-scene, all-hazard incident management concept that is critical to the overall framework structure that makes NIMS such a successful and integrated management system.[28]

4.16 INCIDENT COMMAND SYSTEM (ICS)

The ICS is a management system designed to enable effective and efficient domestic incident management by integrating a combination of facilities, equipment, personnel, procedures, and communications operating within a common organizational structure, designed to enable effective and efficient domestic incident management. A basic premise of ICS is that it is widely applicable. It is used to organize both near-term and long-term field-level operations for a broad spectrum of emergencies, from small to complex incidents, both natural and manmade. ICS is used by all levels of government — federal, state, local, and tribal — as well as many private-sector and nongovernmental organizations. ICS is also applicable across disciplines. It is normally structured to facilitate activities in six major functional areas:

- Command
- Operations
- Planning

- Logistics
- Finance
- Administration

ICS is an interdisciplinary and organizationally flexible system that is capable of meeting the needs of any incident of any kind, size, or level of complexity. By utilizing ICS, personnel from several degrees of responsiveness, capabilities, and management can meld their capabilities rapidly into a common management framework structure.[29]

ICS has been tested for more than 30 years and has been used for several incident functionalities including planned events (such as parades, political rallies, demonstrations, and so forth), fires (mostly wildland fires in the Western region of the United States), hazardous materials spills and multiple casualty incidents; also multiple jurisdictional and multiple agency disasters, usually natural disasters involving such events as earthquakes, hurricanes, severe storms (such as tornadoes or heavy rains with flooding); search and rescue missions; biological outbreaks and disease containment, and (of course) acts of terrorism.[30]

Acts of biological, chemical, radiological, and nuclear terrorism represent particular challenges for the traditional ICS structure. Events that are not site specific, are geographically dispersed, or evolve over longer periods of time will require extraordinary coordination between federal, state, local, tribal, private-sector, and nongovernmental organizations. An area command may be established to oversee the management of such incidents.

ICS helps all responders communicate more efficiently, thus getting what they need when they need it. ICS provides a safe, efficient, and (most importantly) cost-effective response and recovery strategy for just about every level of government or organization.[31] This is primarily the main reason of why utilizing ICS is so vitally important.

4.17 ICS FEATURES

ICS has several features that make it very well suited for managing incidents which include the following[32]:

- Common terminology
- Organizational resources
- Manageable span of control
- Organizational facilities
- Use of position titles
- Reliance on an Incident Action Plan (IAP) (defined further in Chapter 5)
- Integrated communications
- Accountability

4.18 COMMON TERMINOLOGY

The ability to communicate within ICS is absolutely crucial as it defines a standard set of common terminology ensuring efficient, clear, concise communications.

ICS requires the use of common terminology, including standard titles for facilities and positions within any given organization. Common terminology includes the use of "clear text"[33]; that is, communications without the use of any organizational-specific codes, jargon, or ciphers. Simply put, "clear text" is a method of utilizing plain, old, simple English for daily activities.[34]

4.19 ORGANIZATIONAL RESOURCES

Resources, including all personnel, facilities, and major equipment and supply items used in supporting incident management activities are assigned common designations. Resources are categorized based on "types"; that is, resources are classified based upon their level of complexity and capabilities, thus helping avoid any confusion as well as enhancing its interoperability functionalities.[35]

4.20 MANAGEABLE SPAN OF CONTROL

Maintaining adequate span of control throughout the organization is critical. Effective span of control may vary from three to seven elements, and a ratio of one supervisor to five reporting elements is (oftentimes) recommended. If the number of reporting elements falls outside of this range, expansion or consolidation of the organization may be necessary. There may be exceptions, usually in lower-risk assignments or where resources work in close proximity to each other.[36]

Higher ratios may be more plausible[37]:

- When team members are highly experienced or operating at lower/lowered capability level(s).
- Where field safety issues may not be applicable (or even an issue).
- Where operating units are running effectively without any disruption to its operations.
- Where there is a defined hierarchy team structure.
- When the supervisor is experienced and highly effective.
- When majority of the team within the unit perform (essentially) similar functionalities and roles.

The definition of "span of control"[38] simply refers to the number of individuals any one given supervisor can manage effectively. Usually there is a specific ratio that is applied, staying between three and seven team members before splitting, or departmentalizing the structure even further.[39]

4.21 ACCOUNTABILITY

The word "accountability"[40] is a concern identified by employees and supervisors alike, particularly by those in organizations with broad spans of control or units in which employees perform work with traditionally high levels of quality control. There may be confusion with some work groups about who is responsible for monitoring results, particularly when it relates to quality control. Employees are openly skeptical that supervisors can be effective at quality control in technical areas for which they have no expertise.[41]

Effective accountability at all jurisdictional levels and within individual functional areas during an incident is both critical as well as essential. To that degree, the ICS framework structure requires the following elements to allow for accountability within any given incident operation[42]:

An orderly chain-of-command such that the line of authority is defined within the ranks of an incident response organization.

Provide check-in capabilities for all responders, regardless of the organization structure or its affiliation.

Provide each individual involved within the incident operations to be assigned to one and only one supervisor (also referred to as the "unity of command"), unless the span of control ratio is higher than anticipated; otherwise, that individual may be reassigned to another supervisor, but still remains under the control of *only one supervisor.*

4.22   INTEGRATE COMMUNICATIONS CAPABILITIES

Communications needs for large incidents may exceed available radio frequencies. Some incidents may be conducted entirely without radio support. In such situations, other communications resources (such as cellular telephones or secured telephone lines) may be the only communications methods used to coordinate communications and to transfer large amounts of data effectively.[43]

Thus, integrated communication systems require or include the following:

Functional communications systems that transfer information efficiently.

Provide for planning capabilities for the use of all available communications systems and resources for any given incident operation (as needed).

Defined and executed procedures and processes for transferring information both internally as well as externally of the incident operations' organizational structure.

4.23   INCIDENT ACTION PLAN

The Incident Action Plan (IAP) provides a coherent means to communicate the overall incident objectives in the context of both operational and support activities. The IAP is developed for operational periods that exceed 12-hour time frames depending on management objectives to accomplish proper response tactics. These objectives are communicated throughout the organization and are used to[44]:

Develop and issue assignments, plans, procedures, and protocols.

Direct efforts to attain the objectives outlined by management necessary for supporting the defined strategic objectives.

Results from the implementation of the IAP are usually documented and provided back into planning processes for the next (or future) incident operational period(s).

4.24 MANAGEMENT COMMAND, COORDINATION, AND CONTROL STRUCTURES

While ICS has proven itself to be effective for all types of incidents, other levels of coordination may be required to facilitate management of:

- Multiple concurrent incidents
- Incidents that are nonsite specific, such as terrorist incidents
- Incidents that are geographically dispersed
- Incidents that evolve over a period of time

NIMS recommended variations in incident management provide two common variations involving the use of Unified Command and/or Area Command.

4.25 UNIFIED COMMAND

Unified Command (UC) is subset of ICS used when[45]:

- There is more than one responding organization for any given incident jurisdiction (and its operations)
- Incidents cross political jurisdictions

Under a Unified Command control structure, organizations work together through the designated members of the Unified Command to:

- Analyze any relevant intelligence information
- Establish, define, and implement a common set of objectives, strategies, and goals for a single Incident Action Plan

The Unified Command control structure does not change any of the other features or aspects of ICS. It merely allows all organizations involved with responsibility for the incident to participate in the decision-making process.[46]

4.26 AREA COMMAND

Area Command (AC) is subset of ICS used when[47]:

- Management oversees multiple incidents that are each being managed by an ICS incident response organization
- Management oversees larger-sized incidents that cross multiple jurisdictional boundaries

The Area Command control structures are particularly relevant to public health emergencies because these incidents are typically[48]:

- Nonsite specific
- Not immediately identifiable
- Geographically dispersed, evolving over a period of time

These types of incidents call for a coordinated response, with larger-scaled coordination typically found at a higher jurisdictional level. The Area Command control structure has the responsibility for [49]:

- Establishing, defining, and implementing the overall strategies and priorities
- Allocating critical resources specific to the priorities defined
- Ensuring incident operations are properly managed
- Ensuring that management objectives are (or have been) met
- Ensuring that management strategies are adhered to

An Area Command control structure may become a Unified Area Command control structure when incidents become multiple jurisdictional or involve multiple organizations. An Area Command control structure is organized similarly to that of an ICS structure; however, because incident operations are conducted on-scene, there is no Operations Section within an Area Command. Other sections and functions are represented within an Area Command control structure.[50]

4.27 MULTIAGENCY COORDINATION SYSTEMS

On larger-scaled emergencies that require higher-level resource management or information management, a Multiagency Coordination System may be required. Multiagency Coordination Systems (MACS)[51] provide for a combination of resources that are integrated into a common framework structure for coordinating and supporting domestic incident management activities. These resources include the following:

- Facilities
- Equipment
- Personnel
- Procedures
- Communications

The primary functions of MACS are to:

- Support incident operations management policies and priorities
- Facilitate logistical support and resource tracking capabilities
- Provide decision capabilities for allocating resources based on incident management priorities and objectives
- Coordinate any incident-related information, both internally and externally
- Coordinate interorganizational and intergovernmental issues regarding incident management policies, priorities, and strategies

Direct tactical and operational responsibility for the conduct of incident management activities rests with the Incident Command.

Multiagency Coordination Systems include Emergency Operations Centers (EOC) and, in certain multiple jurisdictional or complex incidents, Multiagency Coordination Entities.[52] The use of Multiagency Coordination Systems may be utilized at[53]:

- The scene of an incident
- An Area Command (AC)
- A jurisdiction's Emergency Operations Center (EOC)
- An interjurisdictional or regional level
- State and federal levels
- An international level

Type of MACS can include[54] something as simple as a teleconference; or, it can be something as complex as an assembled group with associated support systems. These systems (usually) include one or more of the following:

- Jurisdictional and agency representatives
- Facilities
- Equipment
- Procedures
- Information systems
- Communications systems

4.28 EMERGENCY OPERATIONS CENTERS

The Emergency Operations Centers (EOC) may be staffed by personnel representing multiple jurisdictions and functional disciplines; their size, staffing, and equipment at an EOC will depend on the size of the jurisdiction, the resources available, and the anticipated incident needs. The EOC organization and staffing is flexible, but should include the following[55]:

- Coordination
- Communications
- Resource dispatching and tracking
- Information collection, analysis, and dissemination

EOC activities may also support multiple organizational coordination and joint information activities.[56] Senior elected and appointed officials are located at the EOC, as well as personnel supporting critical functions such as operations, planning, logistics, and finance and administration. The key function of EOC personnel is to ensure that those who are located at the scene have the resources (that is, personnel, tools, and equipment) they need for the response. In large emergencies and disasters, the EOC also acts as a liaison between local responders and the state government. Please note that some states operate EOCs as well and can activate them as necessary to support local operations. Thus, state-level EOC personnel report to the Governor of that state, acting as a liaison between local and federal personnel.[57]

4.29   INCIDENT RESPONSIBILITIES

Regardless of their form or structure, Multiagency Coordination Entities[58] are responsible for the following[59]:

Ensuring each organization involved is providing situation and resource status information.

Establish, define, and implement priorities between incidents and/or Area Command control structures in coordination with the Incident Command or United Command control structures.

Acquire and allocate resources required by incident management.

Coordinate and identify resource requirements for present and future incidents.

Coordinate and resolve any policy issues.

Coordinate strategic operations and decision-making capabilities.

4.30   POSTINCIDENT RESPONSIBILITIES

Following incidents, Multiagency Coordination Entities are typically responsible for ensuring that revisions are acted upon correctly, such that any (or all) revisions may be made to[60]:

- Plans
- Procedures
- Communications
- Staffing and personnel
- Capabilities necessary for improving incident management and operations

Oftentimes, these revisions are based upon lessons learned from the incident, and are usually coordinated with the emergency planning team within the jurisdiction as well as with any mutual aid partners.

4.31   PUBLIC INFORMATION SYSTEMS

Because public information is critical to domestic incident management, it is imperative to establish Public Information Systems and protocols for communicating timely and accurate information to the public during emergency situations, as well as principles needed to support effective emergency Public Information Systems.[61]

Under ICS, the Public Information Officer (PIO) is a member of the command staff. The PIO advises the Incident Command on all public information matters, including media and public inquiries, emergency public information and warnings, rumor monitoring and control, media monitoring, and other functions required to coordinate, clear with proper authorities, and disseminate accurate and timely information related to the incident. The PIO establishes and operates within the parameters established for the Joint Information System (JIS).[62]

4.32 JOINT INFORMATION SYSTEMS (JIS)

The Joint Information Systems (JIS) provides an organized, integrated, and coordinated mechanism for providing information to the public during an emergency. The JIS includes plans, protocols, and structures used to provide information to the public. It encompasses all public information related to the incident.[63]

Key elements of a JIS include interagency coordination and integration, developing and delivering coordinated messages, and support for decision-makers. The PIO, using the JIS, ensures that decision-makers, as well as the general public, are fully informed throughout a domestic incident response.[64]

4.33 JOINT INFORMATION CENTERS (JIC)

During emergencies, the public may receive information from a variety of sources. Part of the PIO's job is ensuring that the information that the public receives is accurate, coordinated, timely, and easy to understand.[65] One way to ensure the coordination of public information is by establishing a Joint Information Center (JIC).[66] Using the JIC[67] as a central location, information can be coordinated and integrated across jurisdictions and agencies, and between all government partners, the private sector, and nongovernmental agencies. The JIC is the physical location where public information staff involved in incident management activities can collocate to perform critical emergency information, crisis communications, and public affairs functions. The JIC provide the organizational structure for coordinating and disseminating critical information.[68]

Incident Commanders and Multiagency Coordination Entities are responsible for establishing and overseeing JICs, including processes for coordinating and clearing public communications. With the case of a Unified Command control structure, those contributing to joint public information management do not lose their individual identities or responsibilities. Essentially, each participating group or organization contributes to the overall unified message.[69]

4.34 JIC LEVELS

JICs may be established at various levels of government.[70] All JICs must communicate and coordinate with each other on an ongoing basis using established JIS protocols. When multiple JICs are established, information must be coordinated among them to ensure that a consistent message is disseminated to the public.[71]

JICs have several characteristics in common:

The JIC includes representatives of just about every member type for managing the incident's response. This may include different jurisdictions, other organizations, private organizations, and other nongovernmental organizations.

Each JIC must have procedures and protocols for communicating and coordinating effectively with other JICs, and with the appropriate components that are representative of the ICS organizational structure.

In most circumstances, a single JIC location is preferable, but the JIS should be flexible enough to accommodate multiple JICs when the circumstances of the incident require larger-scaled responses.[72,73]

4.35 JIC ORGANIZATIONAL STRUCTURE

The typical JIC structure is outlined as follows[74]:

Level I
   Joint Information Center (JIC)

Level II
   Press Secretary (jurisdiction)
   JIC Liaison (as needed)

Level III
   Research Team
   Media Team
   Logistics Team

4.36 PREPAREDNESS AND READINESS

Preparedness is a key phase of the emergency management cycle. Through preparedness, jurisdictions take actions to prevent, mitigate, respond to, and recover from emergencies. Preparedness is critical to emergency management, and involves all of the actions required to establish and sustain the level of capability necessary to execute a wide range of incident management operations. Preparedness is implemented through a continual cycle of planning, training and equipping, exercising and evaluating, and taking action to correct and mitigate.[75]

The significant objective of preparedness is to ensure mission integration and interoperability in response to emergent crises across functional and jurisdictional lines; this also includes efforts to coordinate between public and private organizations. Preparedness is the responsibility of individual jurisdictions, which coordinate their activities among all preparedness stakeholders. Each level of government is responsible for its preparedness activities.[76,77] NIMS provide tools to help ensure and enhance preparedness. These tools include the following[78]:

- Preparedness organization and training programs that define, provide, or establish processes for planning, training, and implementation
- Personnel qualification and certification programs
- Equipment and hardware certification programs
- Mutual-aid assistance programs
- Publication and information management

National-level preparedness standards related to NIMS will be maintained and managed through a multiple-jurisdictional, multiple-disciplined center, using a collaborative process at the NIMS Integration Center. Using NIMS as a basis, all preparedness stakeholders may attain and sustain the level of readiness necessary to respond to the range of domestic incidents throughout the United States.[79]

4.37 PREPAREDNESS ORGANIZATIONS

Preparedness organizations represent a wide variety of committees, planning groups, and other organizations. These organizations meet regularly to coordinate and focus preparedness activities. The needs of the jurisdiction will dictate how frequently the organizations must meet and how they are structured. Preparedness organizations at all levels should follow NIMS standards and undertake the following tasks[80]:

- Establish and coordinate emergency plans and coordination protocols.
- Integrate and coordinate activities and jurisdictions within their purview.
- Establish guidelines and coordination protocols defining greater interoperability between jurisdictions and other organizations.
- Implement and adopt guidelines and protocols for resource management.
- Establish priorities for resources as well as other response requirements.
- Establish and maintain mechanisms implemented for multiple organizational coordination efforts.

4.38 PREPAREDNESS PLANNING AND COORDINATION

Preparedness plans describe how personnel, equipment, and other governmental and nongovernmental resources will be used to support incident management requirements. These plans represent the operational core of preparedness and provide mechanisms for[81]:

- Setting priorities
- Integration of multiple entities, organizations, and their functions
- Establishment of collaborative relationships between all entities
- Ensuring support of established communications systems for incident management activities

4.39 TYPES OF PREPAREDNESS PLANS

Jurisdictions must develop several types of plans, including the following[82]:

Emergency Operations Plans (EOP)[83,84]: These describe how the jurisdiction will respond to emergencies.[85]

Procedures: These include overviews, standard operating procedures, field operations guides, job aids, and other critical information or reference materials needed for response scenarios.

Preparedness Plans: These describe how training needs are identified and met, as well as how resources are obtained via mutual-aid agreements, and the equipment requirements for hazardous situations faced by the jurisdiction.

Corrective Action and Mitigation Plans: These include any activities that are required for implementing procedures based upon lessons leaned from previous incidents, training programs, or exercises (or drills).

Recovery Plans: These describe any actions that will be taken for facilitating any defined long-term recovery mechanisms and their procedures.

4.40 EMERGENCY OPERATIONS PLAN

Generally, the Emergency Operations Plan (EOP) describes how the community will do business in an emergency. The EOP will perform the following[86]:

Assigns responsibilities to organizations and individuals for carrying out specific actions that exceed the capabilities or responsibilities of any single entity or organization.

Establishes lines of authority and organizational relationships, and demonstrates how all actions are coordinated.

Describes how individuals and property will be protected in emergencies and disasters (natural or manmade).

Identifies personnel, equipment, facilities, supplies and other resources that may be made available, within the jurisdiction or through agreement with other jurisdictions, for use during response and recovery operations.

Identifies measures for addressing mitigation concerns during response and recovery operations.

State-level EOPs establish framework structures within which local EOPs are created and through which the federal government is involved with response and recovery operations. Thus, state governments act as the coordinating entity to ensure that all levels of government are able to respond to safeguard the well-being of its citizens.[87]

Federal-level EOP is called the Federal Response Plan (FRP). When activated following a presidential-declared emergency or disaster, the FRP enables FEMA to coordinate the efforts of 27 federal agencies (including The American Red Cross) to assist state and local response and recovery efforts. The FRP is similar to local and state EOPs in terms of its overall goals; however, the federal government may bring highly specialized resources to bear (for example, Nuclear Emergency Support Teams[88] (NEST),[89,90] Metropolitan Medical Response Teams [also called a "Disaster Medical Assistance Team" (DMAT)],[91] and Urban Search and Rescue Task Force[92]) on emergencies and disasters that are outside the response capabilities of local and state governments.[93]

4.41 TRAINING AND EXERCISE DRILLS

Organizations and personnel at all governmental levels and in the private sector must be trained to improve all-hazard incident management capability. These organizations and personnel must also participate in realistic exercises to improve integration and interoperability. To assist jurisdictions in meeting these training and exercise needs, the NIMS Integration Center will[94]:

Facilitate the development of, and dissemination of, national standards, guidelines, and protocols for incident management training.

Facilitate use of modeling and simulations for training and exercise programs.

Define general training requirements and approved training courses for all NIMS users, which include instructor qualifications and course completion documentation.

Review and approve discipline-specific training requirements and courses through the assistance of key stakeholders.

4.42 PERSONNEL QUALIFICATION AND CERTIFICATION

Under NIMS, preparedness is based on national standards for qualification and certification of emergency response personnel. Managed by the NIMS Integration Center,[95] standards help ensure that the participating agencies' and organizations' field personnel possess the minimum knowledge, skills, and experience necessary to perform activities safely and effectively. Standards will include training, experience, credentialing, currency, and physical and medical fitness. Personnel who are certified to support interstate incidents will be required to meet national qualification and certification standards.[96]

4.43 EQUIPMENT AND HARDWARE CERTIFICATION

Incident managers and emergency responders rely on various types of equipment to perform mission-essential tasks. A critical component of operational preparedness is that equipment performs to certain standards, including the capability to be interoperable with equipment used by other jurisdictions. To facilitate national equipment certification, the NIMS Integration Center will perform the following[97]:

Facilitate the development of and/or publication of national equipment standards, guidelines, and protocols.

Review and approve listed emergency responder equipment that meets national requirements and standards.

4.44 MUTUAL-AID AGREEMENTS

Mutual-aid agreements and Emergency Management Assistance Compacts (EMACs)[98] provide the means for one jurisdiction to provide resources or other support to another jurisdiction during an incident. Mutual-aid agreements are formal, written agreements between jurisdictions that provide the conditions under which resource sharing can take place during an emergency. Mutual-aid agreements are most common among fire departments and law enforcement agencies but may be developed to cover other resources and equipment (for example, construction equipment) as well.[99] To facilitate the timely delivery of assistance during incidents, jurisdictions (including states) are encouraged to enter into agreements with the following[100]:

- Other jurisdictions
- Private sector and other nongovernmental organizations
- Private organizations (e.g., The American Red Cross, The Salvation Army)

4.45 STANDBY CONTRACTS

Standby contracts typically are made for equipment, such as dump trucks or other construction equipment, but are also used for supplies, such as plastic sheeting. Under a typical standby contract, the supplier agrees to provide an established quantity of an item at the unit cost in effect on the day before the emergency occurs. Standby contracts are a good way for local governments to meet their resource supply requirements without incurring the costs of stockpiling and without paying the rapidly increasing prices that often follow an emergency.[101]

4.46 PUBLICATION MANAGEMENT

The NIMS Integration Center will manage publications dealing with domestic incident management and response. Publication management will include the following[102]:

- Development of naming and numbering conventions and localizations
- Review and certification of publications made available
- Methods for publication control (documentation management)
- Identification of sources and suppliers for publications and similar services
- Management of publication distribution and dissemination

The NIMS Integration Center will manage a wide range of publications, from qualification information and training courses to computer programs and best practices.[103]

4.47 RESOURCE MANAGEMENT

Resource management[104] involves the coordination and oversight of tools, processes, and systems that provide incident managers with timely and appropriate resources during an incident. Historically, resource management has been an issue at incidents, both large and small; thus, resource management is considered an area of special attention under the NIMS guidelines. Resource management involves four primary tasks[105]:

1. Establish systems for describing, taking inventory, requesting, and tracking resources.
2. Activating systems prior to, during and after an incident.
3. Dispatching resources prior to, during, and after an incident.
4. Deactivating or recalling resources during or after an incident.

The basic concepts and principles that guide resource management and allow these tasks to be conducted effectively are addressed by NIMS. Resource management under NIMS is based on the following[106]:

Providing a uniformed methodology for identifying, acquiring, allocating, and tracking resources.

Classification methods of kinds and types of resources that may be required to support incident management.

Utilization of credentialing systems tied to uniform training and certification standards.

Incorporation of resources that are contributed from private sector and other nongovernmental organizations.

There are (primarily) five key principles towards effective resource management[107]:

1. Advanced planning. Preparedness organizations should work cohesively prior to an incident, to develop plans for managing and utilization of resources.
2. Resource identification and ordering. Using standard processes and methodologies that will identify, order, mobilize, dispatch, and track resources.
3. Resource categorization. Categorizing resources by size, capacity, capabilities, skills required, and other characteristics required making resource ordering and dispatching more efficient.
4. Use of agreements. Develop agreement for preincident management for providing for, or requesting of resources.
5. Effective management. Utilization of validated, established practices for performing key or vital resource management tasks (and their assignments).

4.48 EFFECTIVELY MANAGING RESOURCES

Resource management involves the coordination and oversight of tools, processes, and systems that provide Incident Commanders with the resources that they need during an incident. To assist local managers, NIMS includes standard procedures, methods, and functions in its resource management processes. By following the standards established through NIMS, resource managers are able to identify, order, mobilize, dispatch, and track resources more efficiently.[108]

Resource "typing"[109] involves categorizing resources by capability based on measurable standards of capability and performance. Resource typing[110] defines more precisely the resource capabilities needed to meet specific requirements and is designed to be as simple as possible to facilitate frequent use and accuracy in obtaining resources. Certification and credentialing help ensure that all personnel possess a minimum level of training, experience, physical and medical fitness, or capability for the position they are tasked to fill.[111]

Resource managers use various resource inventory systems to assess the availability of assets provided by public, private, and volunteer organizations; thus, resource managers are able then to identify, refine, and validate resource requirements throughout the incident using a process to identify through the following questions[112]:

- What and how much resources are needed?
- Where and when will it be needed?
- Who will be receiving the resource?

Because resource requirements and availability will change as the incident evolves, all entities must coordinate closely beginning at the earliest possible point in the incident. Request for items that the Incident Commander cannot obtain locally must be submitted through the EOC or Multiagency Coordination Entity using standardized resource-ordering procedures.[113]

Resource managers use established procedures to track resources continuously from mobilization through demobilization. Resource tracking and mobilization are directly linked. When resources arrive on-scene, they must check in to start on-scene in processing and validate the order requirements. Managers should plan for demobilization at the same time they begin the mobilization process. Early planning for demobilization facilitates accountability and makes transportation of resources as efficient as possible.[114]

Recovery involves the final disposition of all resources. During recovery, resources are rehabilitated, replenished, disposed of, or retrograded.[115] Reimbursement provides a mechanism for funding critical needs that arise from incident-specific activities. Processes and procedures must be in place to ensure that resource providers are reimbursed in a timely manner.[116]

4.49 COMMUNICATIONS AND INFORMATION MANAGEMENT PRINCIPLES

Effective communications, information management, and supporting technology are critical aspects of domestic incident management. The concepts and principles on which communications and information management are based include the following[117]:

A common operating process that is accessible across jurisdictions and organizations; the common operating process ensures consistency at all levels, of which all who respond to, or manage incident response scenarios.

A common communications framework and data standards; effective communications, both within and outside of the incident response structure, are enhanced by adherence and compliance to those standards outlined and identified.

NIMS leverages science and technology to improve capabilities at a lowered cost. To accomplish this, NIMS bases its supporting technology standards upon five key principles[118]:

1. Interoperability and compatibility. Systems must be able to work cohesively.
2. Technical support. All organizations using NIMS must be able to enhance any and all aspects of incident management and emergency response management and their scenarios.

3. Technology standards. Adhere and comply with national standards that will facilitate interoperability and compatibility of most communications systems.
4. Broad-based requirements. NIMS provides mechanisms for aggregated and prioritization of newer technologies, procedures, protocols, and standards.
5. Strategic planning. The NIMS Integration Center will coordinate with DHS to create a national research and development agenda (TBD).

NIMS communications and information systems enable the essential functions needed to provide a common operating picture and interoperability for the following[119]:

- Incident management communications
- Information management
- Interoperability standards[120,121]

4.50 QUESTIONS

1. The National Incident Management Systems (NIMS) is a subcomponent of the National Response Plan (NRP). True of False?

   Answer: *True*. The NIMS was implemented in March 2004, and is part of the overall NRP.

2. The NIMS was introduced using which Presidential Directive?
   a. HSPD-3
   b. HSPD-7
   c. HSPD-5
   d. HSPD-6

   Answer: *HSPD-5*. This is the Homeland Security Presidential Directive entitled "Management of Domestic Incidents," which directed the Secretary of Homeland Security to develop and administer a NIMS.

3. The NIMS is an operational incident management or resource allocation plan. True or False?

   Answer: *False*. It is NOT an operational incident management or resource allocation plan. HSPD-5 requires the Secretary of Homeland Security to develop a NRP[122] that integrates federal government domestic prevention, preparedness, response, and recovery plans into a single, unitary-disciplined all-hazards plan. The NRP, using the comprehensive framework provided by the NIMS, provides the structure and mechanisms for national-level policy and operational direction for federal support to state, local, and tribal incident managers and for exercising direct federal authorities and responsibilities as appropriate under the law.

4. The term ICS means what?
   a. Integrated Communication System
   b. Incident Command System
   c. Integrated Command Structure
   d. Incident Command Structure

Answer: *Incident Command System*, and is a subcomponent of NIMS.

5. Of the various factors that makes NIMS valuable and important, which factor is (by far) the most positive feature of NIMS?
   a. Standardization
   b. Interoperability capabilities
   c. Best practices
   d. Flexibility

Answer: *Flexibility.* By far, the most positive and crucial aspect (or factor) of NIMS is the fact that it is extremely flexible and has an adjustable framework within which both government and private organizations — at all levels — can work together to manage just about any incident, regardless of the size, location, or complexity of the situation.

6. MCS, or the Multiagency Coordinating System, describes in one word what functionality or capability?
   a. Mutual-aid agreements
   b. Memorandums of Understanding (MOU)
   c. Multiagency preparedness capabilities
   d. Training and awareness coordination

Answer: *Mutual-aid agreements.* It defines, in specific terms, how one agency will assist another in times of severe or critical situations which would require more than one agency to assist, or require outlining departments and their organizations to assist in an area-wide emergency (such as a natural disaster: tornadoes, floods, hurricanes, and so on, or brush/wild fires, earthquakes, and so on).

7. Mutual-aid agreements are also called _____?

Answer: *Emergency Management Assistance Compacts* (or *EMACS*).

8. How many command levels can NIMS utilize during an incident?
   a. 3
   b. 4
   c. 2
   d. 1

Answer: 2. NIMS utilize two levels of incident management structure, depending on the nature of the incident, which are: (1) Incident Command System (ICS); and (2) Multiagency Coordination System (MCS).

9. ICS is a management system designed to enable effective and efficient domestic incident management by integrating a combination of facilities, equipment, personnel, procedures, and communications operating within a common organizational structure. True or False?

Answer: *True*. A basic premise of ICS is that it is widely applicable. It is used to organize both near-term and long-term field-level operations for a broad spectrum of emergencies, from small to complex incidents, both natural and manmade.

10. ICS consists of how many functional areas?
   a. 5
   b. 6
   c. 4
   d. 7

Answer: 6. The functional areas of ICS are: (1) Command; (2) Operations; (3) Planning; (4) Logistics; (5) Finance; and (6) Administration.

11. The word _____ is a concern identified by employees and supervisors alike, particularly by those in organizations with broad spans of control or units in which employees perform work with traditionally high levels of quality control.

Answer: *Accountability*

12. The definition provides each individual involved within the incident operations, to be assigned to one and only one supervisor.
   a. Span of control
   b. Unity of Command
   c. Line of authority
   d. Accountability

Answer: *Unity of command*. Unless the span of control ratio is higher than anticipated, that individual may be reassigned to another supervisor, but still remains under the control of *only one supervisor.*

NOTES

1. Federal Emergency Management Agency, National Incident Management Systems (NIMS) Overview (March, 2004).
2. U.S. General Accounting Office, Homeland Security: Process for Reporting Lessons Learned from Seaport Exercises Needs Further Attention, GAO-05-170 (Washington, D.C., January 14, 2005).

3. Federal Emergency Management Agency, National Incident Management Systems (NIMS) Overview (March, 2004).
4. http://www.dhs.gov/dhspublic/interapp/editorial/editorial_0566.xml
5. Federal Emergency Management Agency, National Incident Management Systems (NIMS) Overview (March, 2004).
6. Federal Emergency Management Agency NIMS Compliance. http://www.fema.gov/nims/nims_compliance.shtm
7. Federal Emergency Management Agency, National Incident Management Systems (NIMS) Overview (March, 2004).
8. Whitehouse Homeland Security President Directive No. 5: Management of Domestic Incidents (February, 2003) (http://www.whitehouse.gov/news/releases/2003/02/20030228-9.html).
9. Federal Emergency Management Agency NIMS Compliance. http://www.fema.gov/nims/nims_compliance.shtm
10. Federal Emergency Management Agency, An Introduction to the National Incident Management Systems (NIMS) (IS-700), Self-Study Guide (August, 2004).
11. National Incident Management System (NIMS), State of Oregon Implementation and Compliance Guidance, First Edition, April 12, 2005. http://egov.oregon.gov/OOHS/SFM/docs/Emergency_Mobilization/NIMS_IS-700_DPWG_v3.doc
12. FEMA NIMS and the Incident Command System. http://www.fema.gov/txt/nims/nims_ics_position_paper.txt
13. FEMA Independent Study Program: IS-195 Basic Incident Command System. http://training.fema.gov/EMIWeb/IS/is195.asp
14. FEMA NIMS and the Incident Command System. http://www.fema.gov/txt/nims/nims_ics_position_paper.txt
15. Federal Emergency Management Agency, An Introduction to the National Incident Management Systems (NIMS) (IS-700), Self-Study Guide (August, 2004).
16. http://www.dhs.gov/dhspublic/interweb/assetlibrary/NIMS-90-web.pdf
17. Federal Emergency Management Agency, An Introduction to the National Incident Management Systems (NIMS) (IS-700), Self-Study Guide (August, 2004).
18. Federal Emergency Management Agency, An Introduction to the National Incident Management Systems (NIMS) (IS-700), Self-Study Guide (August, 2004).
19. Transit Safety and Security Executive Briefing, Federal Transit Administration, Office of Transit Safety and Security. http://transit-safety.volpe.dot.gov/security/SecurityInitiatives/Top20/1%20--%20Management%20and%20Accountability/3C%20--%20Incident%20Command%20System/Essential/ExecutiveSummary/ES-NIMS-90-web.asp
20. During interstate emergency use of an ESAR-VHP system, local jurisdictions rarely have the authority to invoke legislative and/or mutual-aid mechanisms such as Emergency Management Assistance Compacts (EMAC), which may only be activated by the state's highest executive, typically the Governor. Under EMAC and other similar state-level mutual-aid agreements, all resource requests, including health volunteers, are usually coordinated at the state level. Local jurisdictions might enter into mutual-aid agreements, but may not require state approval.
21. U.S. Department of Health and Human Services, Bioterrorism Hospital Preparedness, Emergency System for Advance Registration of Volunteer Health Care Personnel (ESAR-VHP) Interim Technical and Policy Guidelines, Standards, and Definitions, Section 9.0 Authorities and Emergency Operations, Subsection 9.1 Overview of Authorities and Emergency Operations. http://www.hrsa.gov/bioterrorism/esarvhp/guide_9-0.htm

22. Federal Emergency Management Agency, An Introduction to the National Incident Management Systems (NIMS) (IS-700), Self-Study Guide (August, 2004).

23. Federal Emergency Management Agency, An Introduction to the National Incident Management Systems (NIMS) (IS-700), Self-Study Guide (August, 2004).

24. Federal Emergency Management Agency, An Introduction to the National Incident Management Systems (NIMS) (IS-700), Self-Study Guide (August, 2004).

25. Federal Emergency Management Agency, An Introduction to the National Incident Management Systems (NIMS) (IS-700), Self-Study Guide (August, 2004).

26. Federal Emergency Management Agency, An Introduction to the National Incident Management Systems (NIMS) (IS-700), Self-Study Guide (August, 2004).

27. Federal Emergency Management Agency, An Introduction to the National Incident Management Systems (NIMS) (IS-700), Self-Study Guide (August, 2004).

28. Federal Emergency Management Agency, An Introduction to the National Incident Management Systems (NIMS) (IS-700), Self-Study Guide (August, 2004).

29. Federal Emergency Management Agency, An Introduction to the National Incident Management Systems (NIMS) (IS-700), Self-Study Guide (August, 2004).

30. Federal Emergency Management Agency, An Introduction to the National Incident Management Systems (NIMS) (IS-700), Self-Study Guide (August, 2004).

31. Federal Emergency Management Agency, An Introduction to the National Incident Management Systems (NIMS) (IS-700), Self-Study Guide (August, 2004).

32. Federal Emergency Management Agency, An Introduction to the National Incident Management Systems (NIMS) (IS-700), Self-Study Guide (August, 2004).

33. Meaning "plain text," or text that is unencrypted. http://www.its.bldrdoc.gov/projects/devglossary/_plain_text.html

34. http://www.its.bldrdoc.gov/projects/devglossary/_plain_text.html

35. http://www.its.bldrdoc.gov/projects/devglossary/_plain_text.html

36. http://www.its.bldrdoc.gov/projects/devglossary/_plain_text.html

37. U.S. Department of the Interior, Bureau of Land Management, Information Bulletin No. OR-98-003 (October, 1997).

38. The term refers to the total number of subordinates that a supervisor can effectively manage, with a guideline of somewhere between three and seven individuals per manager, optimally at five. http://teams.fema.gov/dmat/resource/ICS/sld010.htm

39. Federal Emergency Management Agency, ICS Concepts and Principles.

40. The property that ensures that the actions of an individual or an institution may be traced uniquely to that individual or institution. [After X9.57] 2. In information systems (IS), the process of tracing IS activities to a responsible source. [INFOSEC-99] 3. In COMSEC, this is a principle that an individual is entrusted to safeguard and control equipment, keying material, and information and is answerable to proper authority for the loss or misuse of that equipment or information [INFOSEC-99]. http://www.its.bldrdoc.gov/projects/devglossary/_accountability.html

41. U.S. Department of the Interior, Bureau of Land Management, Information Bulletin No. OR-98-003 (October, 1997).

42. Federal Emergency Management Agency, An Introduction to the National Incident Management Systems (NIMS) (IS-700), Self-Study Guide (August, 2004).

43. Federal Emergency Management Agency, An Introduction to the National Incident Management Systems (NIMS) (IS-700), Self-Study Guide (August, 2004).

44. Federal Emergency Management Agency, An Introduction to the National Incident Management Systems (NIMS) (IS-700), Self-Study Guide (August, 2004).

45. Federal Emergency Management Agency, An Introduction to the National Incident Management Systems (NIMS) (IS-700), Self-Study Guide (August, 2004).

46. Federal Emergency Management Agency, An Introduction to the National Incident Management Systems (NIMS) (IS-700), Self-Study Guide (August, 2004).
47. Federal Emergency Management Agency, An Introduction to the National Incident Management Systems (NIMS) (IS-700), Self-Study Guide (August, 2004).
48. Federal Emergency Management Agency, An Introduction to the National Incident Management Systems (NIMS) (IS-700), Self-Study Guide (August, 2004).
49. Federal Emergency Management Agency, An Introduction to the National Incident Management Systems (NIMS) (IS-700), Self-Study Guide (August, 2004).
50. Federal Emergency Management Agency, An Introduction to the National Incident Management Systems (NIMS) (IS-700), Self-Study Guide (August, 2004).
51. INCIDENT COMMAND SYSTEM, NATIONAL TRAINING CURRICULUM MODULE 16, MULTIAGENCY COORDINATION, October 1994, INSTRUCTOR GUIDE. http://www.nwcg.gov/pms/forms/ics_cours/i401/i401.pdf
52. National Wildfire Coordinating Group, Incident Command System, National Training Curriculum, Module 12, Command and General Staff (October, 1994).
53. http://www.fws.gov/contaminants/FWS_OSCP_05/fwscontingencyappendices/C-ICS/pps/CHAP16.ppt
54. http://www.fws.gov/contaminants/FWS_OSCP_05/fwscontingencyappendices/C-ICS/pps/CHAP16.ppt
55. National Wildfire Coordinating Group, Incident Command System, National Training Curriculum, Module 12, Command and General Staff (October, 1994).
56. National Wildfire Coordinating Group, Incident Command System, National Training Curriculum, Module 12, Command and General Staff (October, 1994).
57. Federal Emergency Management Agency, Principles of Emergency Management (IS 230) (March, 2003).
58. Multiagency Coordination Entities (MCE) typically consist of principals (or their designees) from organizations and agencies with direct incident management responsibility or with significant incident management support or resource responsibilities. These entities are sometimes referred to as crisis action teams, policy committees, incident management groups, executive teams, or other similar terms [e.g.; the wildland fire community has such an entity, the Multiagency Coordination Group (MAC Group)]. In some instances, EOCs may serve a dual function as a multiagency coordination entity; in others, the preparedness organizations discussed may fulfill this role. Regardless of the term or organizational structure used, these entities typically provide strategic coordination during domestic incidents. If constituted separately, multiagency coordination entities, preparedness organizations, and EOCs must coordinate and communicate with one another to provide uniform and consistent guidance to incident management personnel. http://www.fema.gov/txt/nims/nims_doc2.txt
59. Federal Emergency Management Agency, An Introduction to the National Incident Management Systems (NIMS) (IS-700), Self-Study Guide (August, 2004).
60. Federal Emergency Management Agency, An Introduction to the National Incident Management Systems (NIMS) (IS-700), Self-Study Guide (August, 2004).
61. Federal Emergency Management Agency, An Introduction to the National Incident Management Systems (NIMS) (IS-700), Self-Study Guide (August, 2004).
62. Federal Emergency Management Agency, An Introduction to the National Incident Management Systems (NIMS) (IS-700), Self-Study Guide (August, 2004).
63. Federal Emergency Management Agency, An Introduction to the National Incident Management Systems (NIMS) (IS-700), Self-Study Guide (August, 2004).
64. Federal Emergency Management Agency, An Introduction to the National Incident Management Systems (NIMS) (IS-700), Self-Study Guide (August, 2004).

65. Federal Emergency Management Agency, Public Information Training Curriculum: Basic Public Information Officers (G-290).

66. The JIC is designed to help emergency responders get accurate, complete, timely, understandable, and appropriate information to you, to your neighbors, and to the news media throughout the emergency. des.utah.gov/pdf/csepp/fs_Jic.pdf

67. To make sure information is received quickly, a Joint Information Center (JIC) often is established. The JIC helps different jurisdictions and agencies get accurate, complete, timely, understandable, and appropriate information to the public and media during an emergency. Trained specialists, such as public information officers, from all the groups involved can work in the same facility to gather, share, and process information. This approach means that abilities and resources of each responding organization are maximized during what some might consider an often confusing and emotional time, esp. during a regional-wide crisis, emergency or situation; the JIC's primary focus is protecting health and safety. http://www.dis.anl.gov/ep/rc/ep_rc_FS_ joint_information_center.html

68. Federal Emergency Management Agency, An Introduction to the National Incident Management Systems (NIMS) (IS-700), Self-Study Guide (August, 2004).

69. Federal Emergency Management Agency, An Introduction to the National Incident Management Systems (NIMS) (IS-700), Self-Study Guide (August, 2004).

70. When the JIC is activated, JIC management team, which includes the JIC Manager, a Public Information Officer (PIO), department/agency spokesperson, and outside agency representatives, should be located where it can most effectively share and coordinate information. These position titles may vary slightly from site to site, but the functions of information coordination, production, dissemination, and monitoring and analysis of media coverage and public perceptions should be incorporated into the JIC organization. Internal and external organizational relationships should be depicted with a defined emergency plan. www.directives.doe.gov/pdfs/doe/doetext/ neword/151/g1511-1v4-4.pdf

71. Federal Emergency Management Agency, An Introduction to the National Incident Management Systems (NIMS) (IS-700), Self-Study Guide (August, 2004).

72. Federal Emergency Management Agency, An Introduction to the National Incident Management Systems (NIMS) (IS-700), Self-Study Guide (August, 2004).

73. Responsible for overall management of the JIC, the timely release of clear and accurate information to the public and media; oversight of the JIC facility and JIC staff; and remains in direct communication with any representative from a public affairs affiliation, ensures coordination with, and among, local, state, tribal, and federal designated representatives at the JIC and other locations, and accommodates JIC administrative support needs. www.directives.doe.gov/pdfs/doe/doetext/neword/ 151/g1511-1v4-4.pdf

74. Federal Emergency Management Agency, Public Information Training Curriculum: Basic Public Information Officers (G-290).

75. Federal Emergency Management Agency, Preparedness Division (http://www.fema. gov/preparedness).

76. Essentially, the definition of "preparedness" means "activities, programs, and systems developed before a disaster or emergency designed to build individual organizational capabilities to support the response to and recovery from disasters or emergencies." http://www1.va.gov/emshg/apps/emp/emp/definitions.htm

77. Conversely, the definition "civil preparedness", in its broad meaning, is the methodology to carry out basic government functions of maintaining public peace, health, and safety during an emergency. This shall include plans and preparations, for protection from, and the relief of, as well as the recovery and rehabilitation from effects of an attack by the forces of an enemy group or nation or the agents thereof, and it shall

also include such activity in connection with disaster as defined herein; RESOLUTION/ ORDINANCE #3, Alleghany County Civil Preparedness Ordinance, Alleghany County, Civil Preparedness Agency, County of Alleghany, PA. http://www.alleghany-county-nc.gov/ordinances/1-49.pdf

78. Federal Emergency Management Agency, An Introduction to the National Incident Management Systems (NIMS) (IS-700), Self-Study Guide (August, 2004).
79. Federal Emergency Management Agency, An Introduction to the National Incident Management Systems (NIMS) (IS-700), Self-Study Guide (August, 2004).
80. Federal Emergency Management Agency, An Introduction to the National Incident Management Systems (NIMS) (IS-700), Self-Study Guide (August, 2004).
81. Federal Emergency Management Agency, An Introduction to the National Incident Management Systems (NIMS) (IS-700), Self-Study Guide (August, 2004).
82. Federal Emergency Management Agency, Emergency Planning (IS 235), Independent Study Guide (March, 2003).
83. An emergency operations plan identifies the necessary actions to provide a controlled response that will first protect human health and safety and second take the necessary steps to prevent further damage or loss to the resource and mitigate current damage.
84. U.S. Department of Interior, National Park Service, Emergency Management. http://www.nature.nps.gov/rm77/emergency.cfm
85. Federal Emergency Management Agency, Principles of Emergency Management (IS 230) (March, 2003).
86. Federal Emergency Management Agency, Principles of Emergency Management (IS 230) (March, 2003).
87. Federal Emergency Management Agency, Principles of Emergency Management (IS 230) (March, 2003).
88. The Nuclear Emergency Support Team (NEST) is a group of scientists and technicians that are part of a little-known agency inside the U.S. Department of Energy. The team is supported by helicopters forming the main assets of the program. The program is relatively small organization, consisting of (mostly) scientists, who number about 750, are all volunteers from the U.S. Department of Energy weapons laboratories, working on a rotating call. Their mission is to protect the countless bridges, tunnels, ports, skyscrapers, and monuments in American cities from a terrorist's nuclear strike. The task is almost unimaginable in this era of permanent alert. It is a task complicated by the bureaucratic thicket that has encircled the agency throughout its 28-year history. Rooted in the U.S. Department of Energy, NEST assists the FBI and reports to the Federal Emergency Management Agency as well as the Department of Defense Pentagon.
89. NEST was started in 1974 after an extortionist threatened to explode a nuclear bomb in Boston, MA if he didn't receive $200,000 USD. The threat turned out to be a hoax. Federal officials were horrified that they had no way of responding had it been real. NEST scientists have been deployed on occasional patrols in Washington, D.C., during the Bicentennial (1976) and in Atlanta and Salt Lake City during the Olympics.
90. ADVISORY COMMISSION ON RADIOACTIVE WASTE & DECOMMISSIONING NEWS, Department of Human Services MAINE RADIATION CONTROL PROGRAM, Volume 4, Issue 3 2002. http://www.maine.gov/dhhs/eng/rad/pdf-files/LLW/fall02news.pdf
91. The National Disaster Medical System (NDMS) is a section within the U.S. Department of Homeland Security, Federal Emergency Management Agency, Response Division, Operations Branch, and is responsible for supporting federal agencies in the management and coordination of the federal medical response to major emergencies

and federally declared disasters including: natural disasters, technological disasters, major transportation accidents, acts of terrorism including weapons of mass destruction events. It is the mission of the National Disaster Medical System to design, develop, and maintain a national capability to deliver quality medical care to the victims of, and responders to, a domestic disaster. NDMS provides state of the art medical care under any conditions at a disaster site, in transit from the impacted area, and into participating definitive care facilities. Under the Department of Homeland Security (DHS), through the National Disaster Medical System (NDMS) fosters the development of Disaster Medical Assistance Teams (DMATs). A DMAT is a group of professional and para-professional medical personnel (supported by a cadre of logistical and administrative staff) designed to provide medical care during a disaster or other event. Each team has a sponsoring organization, such as a major medical center, public health or safety agency, non-profit, public or private organization that signs a Memorandum of Agreement (MOA) with the DHS. The DMAT sponsor organizes the team and recruits members, arranges training, and coordinates the dispatch of the team. http://www.ndms.dhhs.gov/dmat.html

92. The National Urban Search and Rescue (US&R) Response System, established under the authority of the Federal Emergency Management Agency (FEMA) in 1989 is a framework for structuring local emergency services personnel into integrated disaster response task forces. These task forces, complete with necessary tools and equipment, and required skills and techniques, can be deployed by FEMA for the rescue of victims of structural collapse. http://www.fema.gov/usr/

93. Federal Emergency Management Agency, Principles of Emergency Management (IS 230) (March, 2003).

94. Federal Emergency Management Agency, An Introduction to the National Incident Management Systems (NIMS) (IS-700), Self-Study Guide (August, 2004).

95. The NIMS Integration Center is a multijurisdictional, multidisciplinary entity made up of federal stakeholders and over time state, local, and tribal incident management and first responder organizations. It is situated at the Department of Homeland Security's Federal Emergency Management Agency (FEMA). http://www.fema.gov/nims/nims.shtm

96. Federal Emergency Management Agency, An Introduction to the National Incident Management Systems (NIMS) (IS-700), Self-Study Guide (August, 2004).

97. Federal Emergency Management Agency, An Introduction to the National Incident Management Systems (NIMS) (IS-700), Self Study Guide (August, 2004).

98. The Emergency Management Assistance Compact (EMAC) is a mutual-aid agreement and partnership between states that exists because, from hurricanes to earthquakes and from wildfires to toxic waste spills or acts of terrorism, all states share a common enemy: the constant threat of disaster. Participating organizations join forces to help one another when they need it most or whenever disaster threatens the environment. http://emd.wa.gov/1-dir/emac/emac-idx.htm

99. Federal Emergency Management Agency, Principles of Emergency Management (IS 230) (March, 2003).

100. Federal Emergency Management Agency, An Introduction to the National Incident Management Systems (NIMS) (IS-700), Self-Study Guide (August, 2004).

101. Federal Emergency Management Agency, Principles of Emergency Management (IS 230) (March, 2003).

102. Federal Emergency Management Agency, An Introduction to the National Incident Management Systems (NIMS) (IS-700), Self-Study Guide (August, 2004).

103. Federal Emergency Management Agency, Principles of Emergency Management (IS 230) (March, 2003).

104. The National Mutual Aid and Resource Management System is a new initiative undertaken by FEMA within the U.S. Department of Homeland Security in support of the National Incident Management System (NIMS). FEMA received $5 million in FY02 supplemental appropriations and provided a grant of $2 million to the National Emergency Management Agency (NEMA) for mutual aid initiatives. Currently FEMA is working with NEMA to develop a comprehensive, integrated National Mutual Aid and Resource Management System that will allow for an efficient and effective response to all hazards, including terrorist attacks. This system will enhance emergency readiness and response at all levels of government through a comprehensive and integrated system that will allow a jurisdiction to augment needed resources to respond. The system will allow emergency management personnel to identify, locate, request, order, and track outside resources quickly and effectively as well as obtain information on specific resource capabilities, location, cost, and support requirements. http://www.fema.gov/preparedness/mutual_aid.shtm

105. Federal Emergency Management Agency, An Introduction to the National Incident Management Systems (NIMS) (IS-700), Self-Study Guide (August, 2004).

106. Federal Emergency Management Agency, An Introduction to the National Incident Management Systems (NIMS) (IS-700), Self-Study Guide (August, 2004).

107. Federal Emergency Management Agency, An Introduction to the National Incident Management Systems (NIMS) (IS-700), Self-Study Guide (August, 2004).

108. Federal Emergency Management Agency, An Introduction to the National Incident Management Systems (NIMS) (IS-700), Self-Study Guide (August, 2004).

109. On October 20, 2004, FEMA and the NIMS Integration Center (NIC) released the National Mutual Aid Glossary of Terms and Definitions and the Resource Typing Definitions for 120 different kinds of resources. Resource typing definitions are prepared by working groups consisting of subject matter experts and federal, state, and local responders who would be using the definitions to inventory their assets and to support mutual aid requests. In addition to the persons directly involved in the working groups, there were over 300 corresponding members who reviewed working drafts and participated in the formation of these definitions; recommended changes or additions are compiled and fed into the resource typing working groups for consideration on a quarterly basis. Working group membership will remain dynamic so that we can have leaders in these function areas either directly represented in the group or include a corresponding member(s). www.oes.ca.gov/Operational/ OESHome.nsf/PDF/Resource%20Typing%20Guidance/$file/NA005.05.pdf

110. http://www.fema.gov/pdf/preparedness/resource_typing_definitions.pdf

111. Federal Emergency Management Agency, Guide for All-Hazard Emergency Operations Planning (SLG 101), Attachment H: Resource Management (September, 1996).

112. Federal Emergency Management Agency, An Introduction to the National Incident Management Systems (NIMS) (IS-700), Self-Study Guide (August, 2004).

113. Federal Emergency Management Agency, An Introduction to the National Incident Management Systems (NIMS) (IS-700), Self-Study Guide (August, 2004).

114. Federal Emergency Management Agency, An Introduction to the National Incident Management Systems (NIMS) (IS-700), Self-Study Guide (August, 2004).

115. Federal Emergency Management Agency, An Introduction to the National Incident Management Systems (NIMS) (IS-700), Self-Study Guide (August, 2004).

116. Federal Emergency Management Agency, An Introduction to the National Incident Management Systems (NIMS) (IS-700), Self-Study Guide (August, 2004).

117. Federal Emergency Management Agency, An Introduction to the National Incident Management Systems (NIMS) (IS-700), Self-Study Guide (August, 2004).

118. Federal Emergency Management Agency, An Introduction to the National Incident Management Systems (NIMS) (IS-700), Self-Study Guide (August, 2004).

119. Federal Emergency Management Agency, An Introduction to the National Incident Management Systems (NIMS) (IS-700), Self-Study Guide (August, 2004).

120. With the explosion of telecommunications and information technologies has come a disturbing trend - a lack of interoperability among systems. This is demonstrated most dramatically primarily within the public safety community, as police and other agencies fail to communicate with each other during multijurisdictional events. Even when calamities do not occur, however, daily interoperability problems continue to plague public safety agencies nationwide. The federal government is conducting a technical program aimed at providing effective interoperability and information sharing among dissimilar public safety telecommunications and information technology systems. The key to the program is the identification and/or development of interoperability standards to allow local, state, and federal agencies to exchange information, without requiring substantial changes to internal systems or procedures. The program is sponsored by three federal agencies: the National Communications System (NCS), NTIA, and the National Institute of Justice (NIJ) (through its Advanced Generation of Interoperability for Law Enforcement (AGILE) Program). http://www.its.bldrdoc. gov/tpr/2000/its_p/pub_safe/pub_safe.html

121. By definition, communications interoperability refers to the ability of public safety agencies to talk across disciplines and jurisdictions via radio communications systems, to exchange voice and/or data with one another on demand, in real time, when needed, and as authorized. The federal program offices recognize that law enforcement, fire service, emergency medical service, and other emergency response personnel currently lack effective and modern communication systems within their respective organizations. The programs support the need to improve those systems so long as the improvement planning includes a vision for improved interoperability with other agencies. Additionally, the programs further encourage emergency response agencies developing systems to improve communications and interoperability to ensure that their solutions are compliant with the concepts, processes, and protocols set forth in the Department of Homeland Security's National Incident Management System (NIMS) document. www.safecomprogram.gov/ NR/rdonlyres/C8BCA065-EA73-477B-8AA0-0BFCFFF613DD/0/SAFECOMGrant-GuidanceFY05. pdf

122. http://www.dhs.gov/dhspublic/interapp/editorial/editorial_0566.xml

5 Incident Command Systems (ICS)

5.1 INTRODUCTION

This chapter summarizes the basic functionality of an Incident Command System (ICS), more specifically, the National Incident Management System (NIMS) ICS. The first sections of this chapter provide the historical background and significance behind ICS and how it has become so valuable and important over the past (almost) 30 years.

5.2 WHAT IS NIMS AND ICS?

NIMS provides a consistent, flexible, and adjustable national framework within which government and private entities at all levels can work together to manage domestic incidents, regardless of their cause, size, location, or complexity. This flexibility applies across all phases of incident management: prevention, preparedness, response, recovery, and mitigation.

NIMS provides a set of standardized organizational structures which include the ICS, multiagency coordination systems, and public information systems, as well as requirements for processes, procedures, and systems to improve interoperability among jurisdictions and disciplines in various areas. There will be circumstances in which responders from an incident management operation depend upon the involvement of emergency responders from other (sometimes multiple jurisdictions), as well as personnel and equipment from other government locations (other local governments, state governments, and federal), and it becomes necessary that (due to these circumstances) responders will also require effective and efficient coordination methodologies across a wide degree of involvement of organizations and their activities.[1]

Successful operations depend upon mobilization capabilities, effectively utilizing multiple external resources. These resources (when implemented) define an amalgamated organizational framework that is understood by everyone, often utilizing this framework as a common plan, specifying the framework of an incident action plan (IAP) throughout the entire process.

The U.S. Department of Homeland Security released NIMS on March 1, 2004. Secretary Tom Ridge and Under Secretary Michael Brown specifically highlighted compliance with the ICS in a relatively short time frame. Some of the caveats were that in some cities, fire and police departments have worked together using an ICS-like command structure for several years; for others, only fire departments used the ICS-like command structure. Although many departments were aware of the concept, those departments regarded ICS as a fire service system. The introduction of NIMS ended this discrepancy, as HSPD-5[2] required state and local adoption of NIMS as a condition for receiving federal preparedness funding. While ICS was first pioneered by a fire service, it was, at its core, a management system designed to integrate resources to effectively attack a common problem. This system was not exclusive to simply one discipline or set of circumstances; its most significant feature was its flexibility to accommodate all circumstances, from large-scaled circumstances (such as through multiagency assistance programs), to smaller, less-defined circumstances (multidepartment, but not without a single jurisdiction).

5.3 WHAT IS AN INCIDENT?

An incident is an occurrence caused by either human intervention or a national phenomenon which requires or may require action by emergency service personnel to prevent or minimize loss of life or damage to property and/or the environment. Some examples of incidents include the following:

- Fire (both structural and wildfire)
- Hazardous materials incidents
- Search and rescue missions
- Oil or chemical spills
- Natural disasters (such as hurricanes, tornadoes, or earthquakes)
- Terrorist/Weapons of Mass Destruction (WMD) events
- Planned events (such as parades, conventions, or political rallies)

5.4 WHAT IS AN INCIDENT COMMAND SYSTEM (ICS)?

Based on financial and budgetary constraints, along with limited staff and resources at all levels of the government, it may not be possible for any one group, department, or agency to handle all of the management and resource needs for the increasing numbers of incidents nationwide. As such, these government groups, departments, and agencies must work together to provide a fairly coordinated effort under a common management framework or system.

The ICS is an attempt at standardizing on-scene, all-hazard incident management, which allows its users to adopt an integrated organizational framework structure to match complexities and demands for single or multiple incidents without being hampered by any one jurisdictional boundary. ICS has considerable flexibility both within and between government groups, departments, and agencies; it can grow or shrink based on whatever needs are presented. Thus, this level of flexibility makes it very cost effective and provides an efficient management methodology approach for all sized organizations.

ICS is a proven management framework system based on several best practice methodologies implemented over several years, and it includes several decades of lessons learned in organization and management of emergency incidents. This system represents best practices and has become the standard for emergency management across the country.[3]

5.5 WHAT IS NIMS ICS?

With the exception of the way the intelligence function is handled, the principles and concepts of NIMS ICS are the same as the FIRESCOPE and NIIMS ICS.[4]

The NIMS ICS provides a common organizational structure for the immediate response to emergencies and involves the coordination of personnel and equipment that are on-site at an incident. One of the FY 2005 NIMS implementation requirements is that federal, state, local, and tribal governments institutionalize the use of ICS across their entire response systems. Although many agencies now use several forms of ICS, ultimately, the supported methodology is the one from the Department of Homeland Security (DHS). While the principles and concepts of the NIMS ICS are similar to FIRESCOPE[5] and NIIMS ICS,[6] it is important to note that the NIMS ICS pulls the most effective elements from the range of existing incident command system methodologies.

5.6 HISTORY OF ICS

The concept of ICS was developed more than thirty years ago in the aftermath of a devastating wildfire in California. During 13 days in 1970, 16 lives were lost, 700 structures were destroyed, and over one-half million acres burned. The overall cost and loss associated with these fires totaled $18 million per day. Although all of the responding agencies cooperated to the best of their ability, numerous problems with communication and coordination hampered their effectiveness. As a result, Congress mandated that the U.S. Forest Service design a system that would make a quantum jump in the capabilities of Southern California wildland fire protection agencies to effectively coordinate interagency action and to allocate suppression resources in dynamic, multiple-fire situations.

The California Department of Forestry and Fire Protection, the Governor's Office of Emergency Services; the Los Angeles, Ventura, and Santa Barbara County Fire Departments; and the Los Angeles City Fire Department joined with the U.S. Forest Service to develop the system. This system became known as FIRESCOPE (FIrefighting RESources of California Organized for Potential Emergencies).[7]

In 1973, the first FIRESCOPE Technical Team was established to guide the research and development design of a command structure. Two major components came out of this work: the ICS and the Multiagency Coordination System (MACS). The FIRESCOPE ICS is primarily a command and control system delineating job responsibilities and organizational structure for the purpose of managing day-to-day operations for all types of emergency incidents.[8] By the mid-1970s, the FIRESCOPE agencies had formally agreed upon an ICS-based commonly defined terminology and procedures and conducted limited field-testing of ICS. By 1980, parts of ICS had been used successfully on several major wildland and urban fire incidents.

It was formally adopted by the Los Angeles Fire Department, the California Department of Forestry and Fire Protection (CDF), the Governor's Office of Emergency Services (OES), and endorsed by the State Board of Fire Services. Also during the 1970s, the National Wildfire Coordinating Group (NWCG)[9] was chartered to coordinate fire management programs of the various participating federal and state agencies. By 1980, FIRESCOPE ICS training was under development. Recognizing that in addition to the local users for which it was designed, the FIRESCOPE training could satisfy the needs of other state and federal agencies, the NWCG conducted an analysis of FIRESCOPE ICS for possible national application.[10]

By 1981, ICS was widely used throughout Southern California by several fire agencies. In addition, the use of ICS in response to nonfire incidents was increasing. Although FIRESCOPE ICS was originally developed to assist in the response to wildland fires, it was quickly recognized as a system that could help public safety responders provide effective and coordinated incident management for a wide range of situations, including floods, hazardous materials accidents, earthquakes, and aircraft crashes. It was flexible enough to manage catastrophic incidents involving thousands of emergency response and management personnel. By introducing relatively minor terminology, organizational, and procedural modifications to FIRESCOPE ICS, the NIIMS ICS became adaptable to an all-hazards environment.[11]

While tactically each type of incident may be handled somewhat differently, the overall incident management approach still utilizes the major functions of the Incident Command System. The FIRESCOPE Board of Directors and the NWCG recommended a national application of ICS. In 1982, all FIRESCOPE ICS documentation was revised and was adopted as the National Interagency Incident Management System[12] (NIIMS).[13] In the years since FIRESCOPE and the NIIMS were blended, the FIRESCOPE agencies and the NWCG have worked together to update and maintain the Incident Command System Operational System Description (ICS 120-1).[14] This document would later serve as the basis for the NIMS ICS.

5.7 FIRESCOPE

The concept for an incident command system was developed in the aftermath of a devastating wildfire in California in 1970. The FIRESCOPE (FIrefighting RESources of California Organized for Potential Emergencies) ICS was the result of that effort.

Although FIRESCOPE ICS was developed for wildland fire response, many within the incident management community recognized that could be used by other public safety responders for a wide range of situations which include hurricanes, earthquakes, floods, and other natural disasters, as well as hazardous materials accidents. In 1982, as a result of collaboration between FIRESCOPE and the National Wildfire Coordinating Group[15] it was necessary to establish a national application for ICS, and as mentioned above, all FIRESCOPE ICS documentation was revised and adopted as the National Interagency Incident Management System (NIIMS).[16]

5.8 NATIONAL INTERAGENCY INCIDENT MANAGEMENT SYSTEM[17]

Not to be confused with NIMS, the National Interagency Incident Management System (NIIMS) is a system for responding to a wide range of emergencies, including fires, floods, earthquakes, hurricanes, tornados, tidal waves, riots, spilling of hazardous materials, and other natural or human-caused incidents. NIIMS includes five major subsystems, which together provide a comprehensive approach to incident management. The subsystems and their functions include:

1. *Incident Command System (ICS)*: This is an on-site management level structure of positions suitable for managing any crisis or incident.
2. *Training*: This is the development and delivery of training courses to personnel.
3. *Qualifications and Certification*: These are national standards for qualifications and certification for ICS positions.
4. *Publications Management*: This is the development, control, sources, and distribution of NIIMS documentation (provided by the National Wildfire Coordinating Group [NWCG]).
5. *Supporting Technology*: These are the technologies and systems used to support first responders of an emergency response.

5.9 WEAKNESSES ADDRESSED BY USING AN ICS

Weaknesses in incident management were often due to the following factors:

- Lack of accountability, including unclear chains of command and supervision
- Poor communication due to inefficient uses of available communications systems and conflicting codes and terminology
- Lack of an orderly, systematic planning process
- No common, flexible, predesigned management framework structure to enable delegation of responsibilities and manage workloads efficiently
- No predefined methods of integrating interagency requirements into the management framework structure and planning process efficiently

The ICS allows government groups, departments, and agencies to effectively manage their response efforts. ICS is a proven management framework system based on several successful business practices.[18]

5.10 BENEFITS OF USING AN ICS

The adoption of an ICS provides several advantages:

- Flexible, standardized response management systems that allow for the cultivation of response management expertise at all echelons within the command structure
- Provides an increased level of support of trained personnel during any given incident

- Allows unrestricted distribution by the command structure for improving the capabilities of and unifying local response communities into a more effective organization
- Applies to any response situation (as defined as being an "all hazard, all risk" incident)
- Provides for expansion and/or contraction capabilities that are segmented logically
- Maintains autonomy for each department and agency participating in the response

5.11 ICS FRAMEWORK

Designers of ICS recognized early that ICS must be interdisciplinary and organizationally flexible to meet the following management challenges[19]:

- Meet the needs of incident of any kind or size
- Allow personnel from a variety of agencies to merge rapidly into a common management framework structure
- Provide logistical and administrative support to operational staff
- Provide cost effective measure by avoiding duplication of any efforts

5.12 APPLICATIONS FOR THE USE OF ICS

Applications for the use of ICS include[20]:

- Routine or planned events (such as parades, concerts, or conventions)
- Fires, hazardous materials, and mass casualty incidents
- Multiple jurisdiction and agency cooperation resulting from natural disasters (such as floods, hurricanes, tornadoes, and earthquakes)
- Search and rescue missions
- Biological outbreaks and disease containment
- Acts of terrorism (includes Weapons of Mass Destruction)

5.13 ICS MANAGEMENT CHARACTERISTICS

ICS is based on proven management tools that contribute to the strength and efficiency of the overall system. The following ICS management characteristics are taught by DHS in its ICS training programs:

- Common terminology
- Modular organization
- Management by Objectives
- Reliance on an Incident Action Plan (IAP)
- Manageable span of control
- Predesignated Incident Mobilization Center locations and facilities
- Comprehensive resource management

- Integrated communications
- Establishment and transfer of command
- Chain-of-Command and Unity-of-Command
- Unified Command (UC)
- Accountability of resources and personnel
- Deployment
- Information and intelligence management

5.14 UNDERSTANDING THE ICS ORGANIZATION

There is no correlation between the ICS organization and the administrative structure of any one or single department or agency and its jurisdiction. Implementing the ICS organization is a deliberate measure, as confusion over different position titles and job requirements within the organizational structures have been a significant stumbling block to effective incident management, especially in recent years. Examples of this breakdown of the organizational structure might include the Incident Command role being filled by the County Sheriff, whereas the County Battalion Fire Chief serves as the Operations Section Chief.

Every incident or event requires that certain management functions are performed consistently, accurately, quickly, and efficiently. The problem must be identified and assessed — quickly — to develop and implement, and when necessary, deploy resources procured and paid for. Regardless of the size of the incident, these management functions still need to apply.[21]

5.15 ICS MANAGEMENT FUNCTIONS

There are five significant management functions (often referred to as "sections") that are the foundation upon which the ICS organization develops. These functions apply whether they are handling routine emergencies, organizing for a significant nonemergency event (such as a parade or protest), or managing a response to a significant disaster (such as train derailment, or chemical spill).[22] The five significant management functions are defined as follows:

1. Incident Command: Sets the incident objectives, strategies, and priorities; has overall responsibility at the incident or event.
2. Operations: Conducts tactical operations to carry out the incident plan. Develops the tactical objectives and organization, and directs all tactical resources.
3. Planning: Prepares and documents the Incident Action Plan (IAP) to accomplish the objectives, collecting and evaluating information, maintains resource status, and maintains documentation for incident records.
4. Logistics: Provides support, resources, and all other services needed to meet the operational objectives.
5. Finance/Administration: Monitors costs related to the incident. Provides accounting, procurement, time record keeping, and cost analysis management.

During smaller incidents and events, usually one person, the Incident Commander, may accomplish all five management functions. In many circumstances, the Incident Commander is the only position that is always staffed within any given ICS application. Larger incidents or events may require that the five management functions are set up to separate sections within the organization.[23]

5.16   ICS SECTIONS

Each of the primary ICS sections may be subdivided (as needed). The ICS organization has the capability to expand or contract to meet the needs of the incident. Basic ICS operating guidelines are that the individual at the top of the organization is responsible until the authority is delegated to another, more qualified individual. Thus, for smaller incidents, these individuals may not be required and the Incident Commander will oversee and manage all aspects of the incident organization.

5.17   WHAT IS SPAN OF CONTROL?

Another basic operating guideline concerns the supervisory capacity and structure of the organization. Defined as "span of control,"[24] this pertains to the number of individuals or resources that one supervisor can manage effectively during emergency response incidents or special events.[25] Maintaining an effective span of control is particularly important for incidents in which safety and accountability are considered a priority.[26]

Maintaining adequate span of control throughout the ICS organization is considerably important. Effective span of control for incident may vary from three to seven individuals, but a ratio of one supervisor for every five reporting elements is recommended.[27] If the number of reporting elements falls outside of this range, expansion or consolidation of the organization may be necessary. There are, however, exceptions, usually for lower risk assignments or where resources may work in close proximity with each other.[28]

5.18   ICS POSITION TITLES

To maintain span of control, the ICS organization may be divided into several levels of supervision. At each level, individuals with primary responsibility positions have distinct titles; using specific ICS position titles serves three very important purposes, which are as follows:

Titles provide a common standard for all users. If a department or agency were to use the title of "Branch Chief" with another using the title of "Branch Director," this lack of consistency can (oftentimes) cause confusion (as well as infighting) at the incident.

The use of distinct title for ICS positions allows for filling ICS positions with the most qualified individuals rather than based upon seniority.

Standardized position titles are useful when requesting qualified personnel such as with deployment of personnel, it is (usually) important to note if the positions are "Unit Leaders," "Clerk," and so forth.

5.19 ICS ORGANIZATIONAL COMPONENTS

The following definitions are representative of the ICS organization and its components[29]:

Section: The organizational levels with responsibility for a significant functional area of the incident (e.g., Operations, Planning, Logistics, Finance/Administration); the individual in charge of each section is designated as a "Chief."

Division: Used to divide an incident geographically; an individual in charge of each division is designated as a "Supervisor."

Group: Used to describe functional areas of operations; an individual in charge of each group is designated as a "Supervisor."

Branch: Used when the number of divisions or groups extends the span of control, and may be either geographically or functionally separated; an individual in charge of each branch is designated as a "Director."

Task Force: A combination of mixed resources with common communications operating under the direct supervision of the "Task Force Leader."

Strike Team: A set of number of resources of similar kind and type with common communications operating under the direct supervision of the "Strike Team Leader."

Single Resource: May be individuals, a piece of equipment and its personnel complement, or a crew or team of individuals with an identified supervisor that may be used at an incident.

5.20 UNIFIED COMMAND

Unified Command (UC) is an important element in multijurisdictional or multiagency domestic incident management. It provides guidelines to enable agencies with different legal, geographic, and functional responsibilities to coordinate, plan, and interact effectively. As a team, the Unified Command overcomes much of the inefficiency and duplication of effort that can occur when agencies from different functional and geographic jurisdictions, or agencies at different levels of government, operate without a common system or organizational framework.

The primary difference between the single command structure and the UC structure is that in a single command structure, the IC is solely responsible for establishing incident management objectives and strategies. In a UC structure, the individuals designated by their jurisdictional authorities jointly determine objectives, plans, and priorities and work together to execute them.

5.21 THE INCIDENT COMMANDER

The Incident Commander (IC) has overall responsibility for managing the incident. The IC must be fully briefed and should have written delegation of authority. Initially, assigning tactical resources and overseeing operations will be under the direct supervision of the Incident Commander.

Personnel assigned by the IC have the authority of their assigned positions and roles, even if it may not be the same (or similar) authority that they may have elsewhere. In addition to having the overall responsibility for managing the entire incident, the Incident Commander will conduct the following responsibilities[30]:

Has responsibility for ensuring incident safety, providing information services for internal and external stakeholders, and establishing and maintaining liaison communication capabilities with other groups, departments, or agencies that are participating in the incident.

May have one or more deputies from the same government group, department, or agency, or from other agencies or jurisdictions. The Deputy Incident Commander must be as qualified as the Incident Commander; henceforth, the Deputy Incident Commander is the "Backup Incident Commander."

As incidents expand in size, change in jurisdiction or disciplines, or incidents become more complex, command may change to a more experienced Incident Commander. Rank, grade, and seniority are *not* factors used to select the Incident Commander. Rather, the Incident Commander *should always* be a highly qualified individual who is trained to lead an incident response. Formal transfer of command at an incident always requires that there will be a full briefing for the incoming Incident Commander and notification to all personnel that a change in command is about to take place.[31]

As incidents expand, the Incident Command may delegate authority for performance considerations of specific activities to the Command Staff and the General Staff.

5.22 COMMAND STAFF

Command comprises the IC and Command Staff (CS). Command staff positions are established to assign responsibility for key activities not specifically identified in the General Staff functional elements. These positions may include the Public Information Officer (PIO), Safety Officer (SO), and the Liaison Officer (LNO), in addition to others, as required and assigned by the IC.[32]

Depending upon the size and type of the incident or event, it may be necessary for the Incident Command to designate personnel to provide information, safety, and liaison services for the entire organization. The ICS command positions are outlined as[33]:

Public Information Officer: Serves as the conduit for information to internal and external stakeholders, including the news media or other organization seeking information directly from the incident or event.

Safety Officer: Monitors safety conditions and develops measures for assuring the safety of all assigned personnel.

Liaison Officer: Serves as the primary contact for supporting departments and agencies assisting at an incident or event.

5.22.1 COMMAND STAFF: PUBLIC INFORMATION OFFICER

Some of the responsibilities of the Public Information Officer include[34]:

Advising the Incident Commander on issues related to information dissemination and news media relations.

Serving as the primary contact for anyone who wants information about the incident and the response for it.

Serving both an external audience through the news media and an internal audience, including both incident staff and agency personnel.

Coordinating with other public information staff to ensure that confusing or conflicting information is not issued.

Obtaining information from the Planning Section, since the Planning Section is gathering intelligence and other information pertinent to the incident.

Obtaining information from the community, the news media, and others, and providing that information to the Planning Section Chief and the Incident Commander.

5.22.2 COMMAND STAFF: SAFETY OFFICER

Some of the responsibilities of the Safety Officer include[35]:

Ensure that all personnel perform their jobs safely and arrive to the incident scene and back to their home or work office safely.

Advise the Incident Commander on issues regarding incident safety, also emphasizing safety awareness for all personnel staff.

Operate closely with operations staff in ensuring safety guidelines are adhered to throughout the incident, including wearing of appropriate protective equipment and safety gear (helmets, breathing apparatus, etc.) is utilized in areas not considered safe.

Conduct risk analysis and implement safety measures (where necessary), which is conducted through the planning process, but may also halt any activities deemed unsafe before, during, and after an incident.

Minimize personnel risk through the promotion of safe driving habits and providing safety training and awareness programs to personnel and staff.

5.22.3 COMMAND STAFF: LIAISON OFFICER

Some of the responsibilities of the Liaison Officer include[36]:

Assist the Incident Commander through the gathering of information regarding agencies that are supporting efforts at an incident.

Serve as a coordinator for all agencies at all levels of government that are not represented within the incident command structure, as well as acts as "go between" the Incident Commander and supporting agencies and their personnel.

Provide briefings to agency representatives that facilitates addressing any relevant questions or concerns about the operation of the incident.

Analyze restrictions on supporting agencies, and their resources, that may impact the operations of the incident, and how it may use them or special support requirements that might exist; this would include availability of any other specialized resources that may prove useful during an incident (for example, special equipment that may exist with another agency that may be lifesaving for personnel involved in an extremely hazardous materials incident).

5.23 GENERAL STAFF

The General Staff (GS) includes incident management personnel who represent the major functional elements of the ICS, including the Operations Section Chief, Planning Section Chief, Logistics Section Chief, and Finance/Administration Section Chief. Command Staff and General Staff must continually interact and share vital information and estimates of the current and future situation and develop recommended courses of action for consideration by the IC.

The individual in charge of each section is designated as a "Section Chief." Section Chiefs have the ability to expand their section to meet the needs of the situation. Each of the Section Chiefs may have a Deputy, or more than one, if necessary. The Deputy Section Chief has the following responsibilities[37]:

May assume responsibility for a specific portion of the primary position, work as relief, or be assigned other tasks.

Must be qualified to the same ICS level as the person for whom they work.

In larger incidents, especially where there are multiple disciplines or jurisdictions are involved, the use of Deputies from other organizations can greatly increase interagency coordination.

5.24 OPERATIONS SECTION

Until Operations is established as a separate section, the Incident Commander has direct control of tactical resources. The Incident Commander will determine the need for a separate Operations Section at an incident or event. When the Incident Commander activates the Operations Section, that individual will assign an individual to be the Operations Section Chief.[38]

The Operations Section Chief (OSC) will develop and manage the Operations Section to accomplish the incident objectives set by the Incident Commander. The Operations Section Chief is normally an individual with the greatest technical and tactical expertise in dealing with the current situation at hand, and includes the following responsibilities:

OSC is responsible for developing and implementing strategies and tactics to carry out the incident objectives.

OSC responsibilities include organizing, assigning, and supervising all tactical field resources assigned to an incident, including any air operations, as well as resources in staging areas.

OSC works very closely with other members of the Command and General Staff to coordinate activities.

Most incident resources are assigned to the Operations Section. Often, most hazardous activities are carried out within this section, and it is (usually) necessary to monitor carefully the number of resources that report to any one supervisor.

5.25 PLANNING SECTION

The Incident Commander will determine if there is a need for a Planning Section, designating the Planning Section Chief (PSC) as the section supervisor. If no Planning Section is established, the Incident Commander will perform all planning functions. It is left to the Planning Section Chief's decision to activate any needed additional staffing. Responsibilities of the PSC include[39]:

- Gathering and analyzing information
- Gathering, analyzing, and dissemination of intelligence and information
- Managing the planning process
- Compiling the Incident Action Plan (IAP)
- Developing a written IAP (usually conducted for larger incidents, and when the Incident Commander has directed to do so)
- Managing the activities of technical specialists
- Working closely with the Incident Commander and other members of the General Staff to ensure information is shared effectively and results in an efficient planning process to meet the needs of the Incident Commander and of operations objectives

Significant activities conducted within the Planning Section may include:

- Collecting, evaluating, and displaying incident intelligence and information
- Preparing and documenting Incident Action Plans
- Conducting long-range and/or contingency planning
- Develop plans for demobilization as the incident shuts or slows down
- Maintains incident documentation
- Tracking resources assigned for the incident or event

The Planning Section may be further staffed with Units, which include:

- Resources Unit
- Situation Unit
- Documentation Unit
- Demobilization Unit
- Technical Specialists (optional)

The Technical Specialists who provide specialist expertise useful in incident management and response may also be assigned to work in the Planning Section. Depending on the needs, Technical Specialists may also be assigned to other sections within the organization.

5.26 INCIDENT ACTION PLAN

The Incident Action Plan (IAP)[40] includes the overall incident objectives and strategies established by the IC or UC. The Planning Section is responsible for developing and documenting the IAP. In the case of UC, the IAP must adequately address the overall incident objectives, mission, operational assignments, and policy needs of each jurisdictional agency. This planning process is accomplished with productive interaction between jurisdictions, functional agencies, and private organizations. The IAP also addresses tactical objectives and support activities for one time frame called the "Operational Period," generally 12 to 24 hours. The IAP also contains provisions for continuous incorporation of "lessons learned" as identified by the Incident Safety Officer or incident management personnel as activities progress.

At the simplest level, all IAPs must have four elements through answering the following questions[41]:

- *What* do we want to do?
- *Who* is responsible for doing it?
- *How* do we communicate with each other?
- *What* is the procedure if someone is injured?

5.27 LOGISTICS SECTION

The Incident Commander will determine if there is a need for a Logistics Section at the incident and designate an individual to fill the position of Logistics Section Chief (LSC). If no Logistics Section is established, the Incident Commander will perform all logistical functions. The size of the incident, complexity of support needs, and the incident length will determine whether a separate Logistics Section is established. Additional staffing is the responsibility of the LSC.[42]

The LSC assists the Incident Commands by providing the resources and services required to support incident activities. This individual will coordinate activities very closely with other members from the Command and General Staff.

The Logistics Section develops several positions of the written IAP and forwards this to the Planning Section. Logistics and Finance have to work closely to contract and purchase good and services that might be needed at the incident.

The Logistics Section is responsible for all of the services and support needs, including:

- Obtaining, maintaining, and accounting for personnel, equipment, and supplies
- Providing communication planning and resource needs
- Setting up food services

- Setting up and maintaining incident facilities
- Providing support transportation
- Providing medical services to incident personnel

The Logistics Section may be further staffed by Branches and Units. The units under the Services Branch include:

- Communications Services
- Medical Services (for response personnel only)
- Food Services

The units under the Support Branch include:

- Supply Services
- Facilities Services and Management
- Ground Support

Not all of the units may be required; services will be established based on need.

5.28 FINANCE/ADMINISTRATION SECTION

The Incident Commander will determine if there is a need for a Finance/Administration Section at the incident and designate an individual to fill the position of the Finance/Administration Section Chief (FASC).[43]

The FASC is the individual who is concerned with paying for response efforts. This individual is responsible for all of the financial and cost analysis aspects of an incident. These include contract negotiation, tracking personnel and equipment time, documenting and processing claims for accidents and injuries occurring at the incident, and keeping a running tally of the costs associated with the incident.

The FASC will coordinate with all members of the Command and General Staff, but works closely with Logistics to be sure that all resources needed to manage the incident are contracted and procured. Because of the larger scope of some of incidents, the number of agencies involved, and the amount of financial activity it will generate, the FASC might need to activate all four units that report to them. These include: Time, Cost, Compensation and Claims, and Procurement Units.

The Finance/Administration Section is set up for an incident that requires incident-specific financial management. The Finance/Administration Section is responsible for the following:

- Personnel check-in and check-out at the incident
- Contract negotiations and monitoring
- Timekeeping
- Cost analysis
- Compensation for injury or damage to property

Larger incidents typically use a Finance/Administration Section to monitor costs. Smaller incidents may also require certain Finance/Administration support.[44]

5.29 ICS AREA COMMAND

Area Command (AC) is activated only if necessary, depending on the complexity of the incident and span of control considerations. An area command is established either to oversee the management of multiple incidents that are being handled by separate ICS organizations or to oversee the management of a very large incident that involves multiple ICS organizations. It is important to note that Area Command does not have operational responsibilities. For incidents under its authority, the Area Command[45]:

- Sets overall agency incident-related priorities
- Allocates critical resources according to established priorities
- Ensures that incidents are managed properly
- Ensures effective communications
- Ensures that incident management objectives are met and do not conflict with each other or with agency policies
- Identifies critical resource needs and reports them to the Emergency Operations Center(s)
- Ensures that short-term emergency recovery is coordinated to assist in the transition to full recovery operations
- Provides for personnel accountability and a safe operating environment

5.30 COMMUNICATIONS WITHIN THE ICS

One of the greatest strengths of ICS is the ability to expand or contract the organization as needed to fit the activity level at the incident. Deputies may be added as needed to maintain span of control, sections may be subdivided, and the organization can grow to include other agencies and jurisdictions as needed.[46]

The ability to communicate within ICS is absolutely critical. Using standard or common terminology is essential for ensuring efficient, clear communications. ICS requires the use of "common terminology," meaning that standard titled for facilities and positions within the organization. "Common terminology" includes the use of "clear text," that is, communications without the use of agency-specific codes or jargon, using plain, simple English.

NOTE: the term "clear text" also signifies that any communications method implemented is (usually) not encrypted.[47]

Every incident requires a Communications Plan, which includes the following:

- Hardware systems that transfer information (for example, cellular telephones, two-way "walkie-talkies," computers, and so on)
- Planning for the use of all available communications resources
- The procedures and processes for transferring information internally and externally

Communications needs for larger incidents may exceed available radio frequencies. In some cases, incidents are conducted entirely without any radio support. For those circumstances, other communications resources such as cellular telephones, alphanumeric or interactive pagers, electronic mail, and securing telephones may be the only communication methods used to coordinate communication and to transfer larger amounts of data efficiently.[48]

5.31 INCIDENT FACILITIES

Common terminology is also used to define incident facilities, help clarify the activities that may take place at a specific facility, and identify what members of the organization may be found there. Incident activities may be accomplished from a variety of facilities. Facilities will be established depending on the kind and complexity of the incident or event. ICS facilities are not fixed facilities and may change locations during an incident or event. It is important to know and understand the names and functions of the principal ICS facilities. Only those facilities needed for any given incident may be activated; some incidents may require facilities not included within the standard list.[49]

Only those facilities needed for any given incident will be activated. The standard ICS incident facilities include:

- Incident Command Post (ICP)
- Staging Areas
- Base (or Base Camp)
- Camps
- Helibase
- Helispot

5.31.1 INCIDENT FACILITIES: INCIDENT COMMAND POST

The Incident Command Post (ICP) location, from which the Incident Command oversees all incident operations, is generally only one facility for each incident or event; however, it may change locations during that incident or event. Every incident or event must have some form of an ICP. The ICP may be located within a vehicle, trailer, and tent or within a building. The ICP will be positioned outside of the present and potential hazard zone but close enough to the incident to maintain command.[50]

5.31.2 INCIDENT FACILITIES: STAGING AREA

These are temporary locations at an incident where personnel and equipment are kept while waiting for tactical assignments. Staging Areas should be located close enough to the incident for a timely response, but (again) far enough away to be out of the immediate impact zone. There may be more than one Staging Area at an incident. Each Staging Area should have a Staging Area Manager who reports to the Operations Section Chief or to the Incident Commander if an Operations Section has not been established.[51]

5.31.3 INCIDENT FACILITIES: BASE

This is the location from which primary logistics and administrative functions are coordinated and administered. The base may be colocated with the Incident Command Post; however, *there is only one Base per incident.*[52]

5.31.4 INCIDENT FACILITIES: CAMP

This is the location where resources may be kept to support incident operations if a Base is not accessible to all resources.[53] *Not all incidents will have Camps.*

5.31.5 INCIDENT FACILITIES: HELIBASE

This is the location from which helicopter-centered air operations are conducted. Helibase facilities are generally used on a more long-term basis and include such services as fueling and maintenance.[54]

5.31.6 INCIDENT FACILITIES: HELISPOT

These are more temporary facilities used for loading and unloading personnel and cargo. Oftentimes, larger incidents may require more than one Helibase and several Helispots.[55]

5.32 DIFFERENCES BETWEEN NIMS ICS AND FIRESCOPE/NIIMS ICS

The ICS organization has five major functions, including command, operations, planning, logistics, and finance and administration. In the NIMS ICS, a potential sixth functional area to cover the intelligence function may be established for gathering and sharing incident-related information and intelligence.

The Information and Intelligence functions provide analysis and sharing of information and intelligence during an incident. Intelligence can include national security or classified information but also can include operational information such as risk assessments, medical intelligence, weather information, structural designs of buildings, and toxic contaminant levels. Traditionally, information and intelligence functions are located in the Planning Section. In exceptional situations, however, the IC may need to assign this role to other parts of the ICS organization. Under the NIMS ICS, the intelligence and information function may be assigned in one of the following ways:

- Within the Command Staff
- As a unit within the Planning Section
- As a branch within the Operations Section
- As a separate General Staff Section

5.33 NIMS ICS TRAINING

The NIMS Integration Center is coordinating the development of a National Standard Curriculum for NIMS which will be built around available federal training opportunities and course offerings that support NIMS implementation. The curriculum also will serve to clarify training that is necessary for NIMS compliance and streamline the training-approval process for courses recognized by the curriculum.[56]

The NIMS Integration Center recognizes that many operational aspects of the NIMS, including ICS training, are available through state, local, and tribal training agencies and private training vendors. It is not necessary that the training requirements be met through a federal source. While some will be developing and providing stakeholders with an evaluation checklist for training content, it may be used to ensure that the ICS training offered through vendors meets the minimum standards outlined by DHS. The curriculum will be made up of NIMS awareness training and training to support the ICS. It expands upon the inclusion of all NIMS training requirements, including training established to meet national credentialing standards. Presently, the training site only lists NIMS-related course offerings available through Federal Emergency Management Agency (FEMA's) Emergency Management Institute (EMI), the U.S. Fire Administration (USFA), and the Noble Training Center.

5.34 HOW ICS INTEGRATES WITH CRITICAL INFRASTRUCTURE

Although one city in particular has captured attention regarding tensions, scuffling, mistrust, and miscommunication between its emergency uniformed services, there are indications that the "battle of the badges" is ongoing at many locations within the United States. This antagonistic relationship usually appears as a jurisdictional dispute at rescue operations, especially when no clear, formal protocols or guidelines exist to determine who should be in charge of the incident. Over a period of time, several municipalities developed frequent disagreements concerning legal, jurisdictional, functional, or geographic responsibilities of fire, police, and emergency medical personnel. This disparity was exacerbated occasionally by differing ideologies and competition for adequate funding to support department staffing and operations. These levels of discordances can potentially degrade critical infrastructure protection methodologies to practically a state of nonexistence. Such friction draws precious time and energy away from protecting human life, physical assets, and communication systems upon which their very survivability, continuity of operations, and procedural accomplishments are depended upon.[57]

To eliminate these levels of discordances that may have serious consequences for any given critical infrastructure and its ability to performan duties, numerous localities are preparing and applying an incident command system with a unified command component for an all-hazards response with the involvement and assistance of the appropriate office of emergency management. In most cases, these systems being developed or implemented contain practices and procedures for coordinating and harmonizing most responses to even minor incidents.

The USFA component of DHS/FEMA has adopted the FIRESCOPE ICS as its base for teaching the concepts of incident command. ICS is recognized by USFA as a system that is documented and successfully tested in managing resources during operations. Utilizing an ICS as an essential tool for protecting the critical infrastructures, as well as a coordination and collaboration tool, would assist in the streamlining of methodologies used with fire, police, and emergency medical services during emergency.[58]

5.35   QUESTIONS

1. The acronym IAP means Incident Action Procedure. True or False?

   Answer: *False.* The acronym means *Incident Action Plan.*

2. ICS is an attempt at standardizing on-scene, all-hazard incident management, which allows its users to adopt an integrated organizational framework structure to match complexities and demands for single or multiple incidents without being hampered by any one jurisdictional boundary. True or False?

   Answer: *True.* ICS has considerable flexibility both within and between government groups, departments, and agencies; it can grow or shrink based on whatever needs are presented. Thus, this level of flexibility makes it very cost effective and provides an efficient management methodology approach for all sized organizations.

3. The acronym FIRESCOPE means _____.

   Answer: *FIrefighting RESources of California Organized for Potential Emergencies.*

4. NIMS ICS is actually a blending of how many principles and concepts pertaining to incident management?
   a. 3
   b. 4
   c. 2
   d. 1

   Answer: *2.*

5. NIMSICS consists of FIRESCOPE and _____?

   Answer: *NIIMS ICS* (or *National Interagency Incident Management System*).

6. A command staff team consists of how many different areas of responsibility?
   a. 6
   b. 5
   c. 4
   d. 3

   Answer: *4.* They are: (1) *the Incident Commander*; (2) *the Public Information Officer*; (3) *the Safety Officer*; and (4) *the Liaison Officer.*

7. Incident Commanders are usually officers within the public safety group or emergency preparedness organization. True or False?

   Answer: *False*. Rank, grade, and seniority are *not* any factors used to select the Incident Commander. Rather, the Incident Commander *should always* be a highly qualified individual who is trained to lead an incident response. The Incident Commander is usually the first responder on the scene of an incident.

8. The Safety Officer is concerned about the safety and well-being of all staff serving at the incident. True or False?

   Answer: *True*. This individual ensures that all personnel perform their jobs safely and arrive to the incident scene and back to their home or work office safely.

9. The definition describing plain, simple English and no jargon is called

   _____.

   Answer: *Clear text*. This term also signifies communications that are unencrypted, but within ICS, this term means no use of "10" codes, no jargon terms that are department-specific, and can be easily understood by all who listen to the communications.

10. The term *base camp* refers to the base of operations. True or False?

   Answer: *True*. This is the location from which primary logistics and administrative functions are coordinated and administered.

NOTES

1. EMAC International, NIMS and the Incident Command System (November, 2004).
2. http://www.whitehouse.gov/news/releases/2003/02/20030228-9.html
3. U.S. Federal Emergency Management Agency, Introduction to the Incident Command System for Federal Workers (IS-100), Student Manual (August, 2004).
4. National Interagency Incident Management System (NIIMS) ICS is a standardized response management system. It is an "all hazard — all risk" approach to managing crisis response operations as well as noncrisis events. NIIMS was originally designed by a group of local, state, and federal agencies with wildland fire protection responsibilities and to improve the ability of fire forces to respond to any type of emergency. A new training curriculum was completed in 1994 to better reflect the "all hazard — all risk" capability of NIIMS (floods, earthquakes, oil spills, fires, planned events, and so on). It is organizationally flexible and capable of expanding and contracting to accommodate responses or events of varying size or complexity. http://www.uscg.mil/d7/units/mso-tampa/ics.html
5. http://www.firescope.org
6. http://www.uscg.mil/d7/units/mso-tampa/ics.html

7. http://www.firescope.org
8. EMAC International, NIMS and the Incident Command System (November, 2004).
9. http://www.nwcg.gov
10. EMAC International, NIMS and the Incident Command System (November, 2004).
11. National Wildfire Coordinating Group (NWCG), A History of the Incident Command System (ICS) (October, 1994).
12. U.S. Forest Service, Fire and Aviation Management, National Interagency Incident Management System. http://www.fs.fed.us/fire/operations/niims.shtml
13. NIIMS is a system for responding to a wide range of emergencies, including fires, floods, earthquakes, hurricanes, tornados, tidal waves, riots, spilling of hazardous materials, and other natural or human-caused incidents. NIIMS includes five major subsystems, which together provide a comprehensive approach to incident management: (1) Incident Command System (ICS); (2) training; (3) qualifications and certification; (4) publications management; and (5) supporting technology.
14. U.S. Fish and Wildlife Service, Fire Management Handbook (October, 2004).
15. http://www.nwcg.gov
16. Federal Emergency Management Agency News: NIMS Integration Center Discusses NIMS Incident Command System (ICS), HQ-04-246 (December, 2004) (http://www.fema.gov/news/newsrelease.fema?id=15556).
17. http://www.fs.fed.us/fire/operations/niims.shtml
18. U.S. Federal Emergency Management Agency, Introduction to the Incident Command System for Federal Workers (IS-100), Student Manual (August, 2004).
19. Federal Emergency Management Agency, Introduction to the Incident Command System for Federal Workers (IS-100), Student Manual (August, 2004).
20. Federal Emergency Management Agency, Introduction to the Incident Command System for Federal Workers (IS-100), Student Manual (August, 2004).
21. Federal Emergency Management Agency, Introduction to the Incident Command System for Federal Workers (IS-100), Student Manual (August, 2004).
22. Federal Emergency Management Agency, Introduction to the Incident Command System for Federal Workers (IS-100), Student Manual (August, 2004).
23. Federal Emergency Management Agency, Introduction to the Incident Command System for Federal Workers (IS-100), Student Manual (August, 2004).
24. The term "span of control" refers to the number of subordinates who report directly to a single manager, supervisor, or lead. A correlation generally exists between the span of control and the number of layers within an organization. A low span of control (i.e., few subordinates per manager, supervisor, or lead) leads to a "tall" organization (i.e., one with many layers) whereas a high span of control leads to a flat organization. There are two main schools of thought in organizational management theory regarding span of control: classical and contemporary. Classical (that is, before 1950) authors believed that supervisors needed to maintain close control over their subordinates, and they often specified the proper ratio as no more than six subordinates per supervisor. Contemporary management theory holds that such "command and control" organizations are inefficient and therefore advocates higher spans of control and flatter organizational structures. Although a consensus on the ideal ratio for span of control has not been reached, current authors advocate ratios ranging from 15 to 25 subordinates per supervisor. Several also recommend five organizational layers as the maximum for any large organization.
25. King County, Washington State, Auditor's Office, Span of Control, Report 94-1. http://www.metrokc.gov/auditor/1994/span.htm

26. Federal Emergency Management Agency, Introduction to the Incident Command System for Federal Workers (IS-100), Student Manual (August, 2004).

27. Federal Emergency Management Agency, Introduction to the Incident Command System for Federal Workers (IS-100), Student Manual (August, 2004).

28. Federal Emergency Management Agency, Introduction to the Incident Command System for Federal Workers (IS-100), Student Manual (August, 2004).

29. Federal Emergency Management Agency, Introduction to the Incident Command System for Federal Workers (IS-100), Student Manual (August, 2004).

30. Federal Emergency Management Agency, Introduction to the Incident Command System for Federal Workers (IS-100), Student Manual (August, 2004).

31. Federal Emergency Management Agency, Introduction to the Incident Command System for Federal Workers (IS-100), Student Manual (August, 2004).

32. (http://atiam.train.army.mil/soldierportal/atia/ad/sc/view/public/8447-1/fm/100-23-1/Apph.htm) and (http://oep.osophs.dhhs.gov/ccrf/roleinfo_9.htm).

33. Federal Emergency Management Agency, Introduction to the Incident Command System for Federal Workers (IS-100), Student Manual (August, 2004).

34. Federal Emergency Management Agency, Introduction to the Incident Command System for Federal Workers (IS-100), Student Manual (August, 2004).

35. Federal Emergency Management Agency, Introduction to the Incident Command System for Federal Workers (IS-100), Student Manual (August, 2004).

36. Federal Emergency Management Agency, Introduction to the Incident Command System for Federal Workers (IS-100), Student Manual (August, 2004).

37. Federal Emergency Management Agency, Introduction to the Incident Command System for Federal Workers (IS-100), Student Manual (August, 2004).

38. Federal Emergency Management Agency, Introduction to the Incident Command System for Federal Workers (IS-100), Student Manual (August, 2004).

39. Federal Emergency Management Agency, Introduction to the Incident Command System for Federal Workers (IS-100), Student Manual (August, 2004).

40. The Incident Action Plan (IAP) contains objectives reflecting the overall incident strategy and specific tactical actions and supporting information for the next operational period on an incident. The plan may be oral or written; when written, the plan may have a number of attachments, including incident objectives, organization assignment list, division assignment, incident radio communication plan, medical plan, traffic plan, safety plan, fire weather, and incident maps. http://www.fireplan.gov/resources/glossary/i.html

41. Federal Emergency Management Agency, Introduction to the Incident Command System for Federal Workers (IS-100), Student Manual (August, 2004).

42. Federal Emergency Management Agency, Introduction to the Incident Command System for Federal Workers (IS-100), Student Manual (August, 2004).

43. Federal Emergency Management Agency, Introduction to the Incident Command System for Federal Workers (IS-100), Student Manual (August, 2004).

44. Federal Emergency Management Agency, Introduction to the Incident Command System for Federal Workers (IS-100), Student Manual (August, 2004).

45. Federal Emergency Management Agency, Introduction to the Incident Command System for Federal Workers (IS-100), Student Manual (August, 2004).

46. Federal Emergency Management Agency, Introduction to the Incident Command System for Federal Workers (IS-100), Student Manual (August, 2004).

47. The definition "common terminology" can also refer to commonly used words or terms that may have a different meaning and understanding based upon their principle

and method of operation; thus, the definition applies also to the use of those words and terms that are mutually agreed upon. http://policy.lanl.gov/pods/home.nsf/Docs/DAPP-6BELNM?opendocument

48. Federal Emergency Management Agency, Introduction to the Incident Command System for Federal Workers (IS-100), Student Manual (August, 2004).
49. Federal Emergency Management Agency, Introduction to the Incident Command System for Federal Workers (IS-100), Student Manual (August, 2004).
50. Federal Emergency Management Agency, Introduction to the Incident Command System for Federal Workers (IS-100), Student Manual (August, 2004).
51. Federal Emergency Management Agency, Introduction to the Incident Command System for Federal Workers (IS-100), Student Manual (August, 2004).
52. Federal Emergency Management Agency, Introduction to the Incident Command System for Federal Workers (IS-100), Student Manual (August, 2004).
53. Federal Emergency Management Agency, Introduction to the Incident Command System for Federal Workers (IS-100), Student Manual (August, 2004).
54. Federal Emergency Management Agency, Introduction to the Incident Command System for Federal Workers (IS-100), Student Manual (August, 2004).
55. Federal Emergency Management Agency, Introduction to the Incident Command System for Federal Workers (IS-100), Student Manual (August, 2004).
56. Emergency Management Institute, National Incident Management System (NIMS) Training (December, 2004).
57. U.S. Fire Administration Infogram Article: Discord Can Degrade Infrastructure Protection (July, 2003) (http://www.usfa.fema.gov/subjects/emr-isac/infograms/ig2003/igjul1703.shtm).
58. U.S. Fire Administration Infogram Article: Discord Can Degrade Infrastructure Protection (July, 2003) (http://www.usfa.fema.gov/subjects/emr-isac/infograms/ig2003/igjul1703.shtm).

6 Emergency Preparedness and Readiness (EMR)

6.1 INTRODUCTION

This chapter introduces a structured methodology that defines "what to do" scenarios in case of a potential act of terrorism, resulting in a weapon of mass destruction (WMD) deployment, or a hazardous materials spill or contamination.

6.2 OFFICE FOR DOMESTIC PREPAREDNESS

The Office of Justice Programs (OJP) Office for Domestic Preparedness (ODP) is the Department of Justice (now part of the United States Department of Homeland Security's Office of State and Local Government Coordination and Preparedness [SLGCP])[1] component responsible for enhancing the capabilities of state and local jurisdictions to prepare for, and respond to, incidents of domestic terrorism involving chemical and biological agents and nuclear, radioactive, and explosive devices. ODP assistance to state and local jurisdictions includes providing grant funds to enable these jurisdictions to purchase specialized equipment for emergency response agencies, providing critical training to emergency response personnel, supporting state and local emergency response exercises, and providing technical assistance to state and local emergency response agencies and public officials. SLGCP is the federal government's lead agency responsible for preparing the nation against terrorism by assisting states, local, and tribal jurisdictions, and regional authorities as they prevent, deter, and respond to terrorist acts. SLGCP provides a broad array of assistance to America's first responders through funding, coordinated training, exercises, equipment acquisition, and technical assistance.[2]

Under the ODP domestic preparedness training program, training is developed and delivered to the nation's emergency response community through a number of mechanisms, including the Center for Domestic Preparedness (CDP) located at Anniston, Alabama. The CDP is a component of ODP and is a federal training facility dedicated to training state and local emergency response personnel.[3]

The following criteria have not been established as something other than guidelines and are offered not as definitive or official regulations but rather as informed advice insofar as to the subject matter specific to both public and private sectors. Concordantly, the guidelines are not official regulations, but were taken from documentation written in concert with existing codes and standards such as the National Fire Prevention Association (NFPA), and various federal regulatory agencies such as the United States Occupational Safety and Health Administration (OSHA). These guidelines are provided as an integrated compilation of responder skill sets, knowledge base, and capabilities before, during, and after a response to an emergency situation, environment, or hazardous condition.[4]

6.3 FIRST RESPONDER

The term *first responder* refers to those individuals who in the early stages of an incident are responsible for the protection and preservation of life, property, evidence, and the environment, including emergency response providers as defined within Section 2 of the Homeland Security Act of 2002 (6 U.S.C. 101), as well as emergency management, public health, clinical care, public works, and other skilled support personnel (such as equipment operators) that provide immediate support services during prevention, response, and recovery operations.[5]

6.4 FIRST RESPONDER CLASSIFICATIONS

Based upon the levels of whoever is tagged as the first responder to a given emergency situation, environment, or hazardous condition, the following groups are representative of how various governments might classify departments and agencies based upon their function:

- Law enforcement
- Fire services
- Emergency medical (or ambulatory) services
- Emergency management (including emergency preparedness)
- Hazardous materials (and containment) (HAZMAT)
- Public works

6.5 GUIDELINE CLASSIFICATIONS

Guidelines are broken into three definitive areas, which are:

1. Awareness level guidelines
2. Performance level guidelines
3. Planning and management level guidelines

These guidelines are intended for utilization by first responders, representing a step-by-step progression from awareness through performance to planning (and management); these guidelines require (slightly) more experience, specialized training, and depth of understanding (in their fields of application). The guidelines provide an integral compilation of responder skill sets, knowledge base, and capabilities, with each training level divided into specific response disciplines. The commonalities reflect the reality that effective response training must be built upon interoperability, with an understanding of how everything fits together; thus, the guidelines will help identify areas that are common to training and levels of understanding, which can be effectively accomplished.

6.6 *NORTH AMERICAN EMERGENCY RESPONSE GUIDEBOOK (NAERG)*

The Emergency Response Guidebook (ERG2004) was developed jointly by the U.S. Department of Transportation, Transport Canada, and the Secretariat of Communications and Transportation of Mexico (SCT) for use by firefighters, police, and other emergency services personnel who may be the first to arrive at the scene of a transportation incident involving a hazardous material[6]:

Quickly identifying specific or generic classifications of any material(s) involved

Protecting individuals, personnel, and the general public during the initial response phase of any given incident

NAERG is updated every 3 to 4 years specific to new products and technology available. *The next version is scheduled to be released sometime in 2008.*

6.7 AWARENESS LEVEL GUIDELINES

The awareness level guidelines address training requirements for personnel who are likely to witness or discover an incident or event involving acts of terrorism or criminal use of WMD or who may have been sent out initially to investigate reports of such an incident or event. Actions taken by personnel should be conducted from within a safety area; if personnel find themselves in a nonsafety area, personnel are suggested to move away from the nonsafety area and encourage others, if ambulatory, to move to either a safety area, or staging area, away from immediate threat and/or danger.

The awareness level guidelines are broken into six distinct classifications, with specific details for each one, which include:

1. Recognize hazardous materials incidents.
2. Know the protocols used to detect the potential presence of WMD agents or their materials.
3. Know/follow self-protection measures for WMD events and hazardous materials events.
4. Know procedures for protecting potential incident scenes.
5. Know and follow agency/organization's scene security and control procedures for WMD and hazardous materials events.
6. Possess and know how to properly use equipment to contact dispatcher or high authorities to report information collected at the scene and to request additional assistance or emergency response personnel.

6.7.1 RECOGNIZE HAZARDOUS MATERIALS INCIDENTS

Understand what hazardous materials are, as well as the risks associated with any materials for an emergency incident or event.

Identify if hazardous materials are present for an emergency incident or event.

Know how to use the *NAERG*, published by the U.S. Department of Transportation.[7]

Use the *NAERG* (and/or other resources that may be available) to identify any hazardous materials.

Understand the potential outcomes or consequences for an emergency due to the presence of any hazardous materials.

6.7.2 KNOW THE PROTOCOLS

Understand what WMD agents or materials are, and the risks associated with those materials for an emergency incident or event.

Know the indicators and effects of WMD upon human life and property.

Identify recognizable signs and symptoms common to initial victim responses pertaining to WMD-related incidents or events.

Know the physical characteristics and/or properties of WMD agents or materials that could be reported by victims or other individuals at the incident scene or event.

Be familiar with the potential use and means of delivery of WMD agents or materials.

Know locations or properties that could become targets for individuals using WMD agents or materials.

Recognize unusual trends or characteristics that may indicate an incident or event involving WMD agents or materials.

6.7.3 KNOW SELF-PROTECTION MEASURES

Understand the hazards and risks to human life and property associated with WMD agents or materials.

Recognize any signs and/or symptoms of exposure to WMD agents or materials.

Know how to use, inspect, and properly maintain protective equipment issues to the responder.

Understand limitations of any protective equipment issued to the responder in how to protect an individual exposed to any WMD agents or materials.

Understand the ambulatory individuals who should, or need, to be moved upwind or upgraded from the existing or danger area.

Know potential contaminated victims should be isolated from other victims that may have not been exposed to similar WMD agents or materials; victims exposed to such agents or materials should be advised of appropriate actions (if any) that are to be taken, or recommended courses of action insofar as to decontamination procedures, and methods of decontamination.

Maintain distances between those contaminated and those not contaminated; minimize contamination to adjacent areas as best as possible.

Understand the roles of first responder, any levels of response within the identified response plan, and methods or courses of action pursuant to whatever emergency incident, event, or hazardous situation is presented.

Be familiar with the department or agency emergency response plans and procedures.

Know defensive measures to be taken during a WMD or hazardous materials incident or event; measure taken will help ensure individual and community safety.

6.7.4 KNOW PROCEDURES FOR PROTECTING INCIDENT SCENES

Understand and implement procedures for protecting evidence, minimizing any disturbance of the incident scene, while protecting other individuals and team members.

Understand the roles, responsibilities, and jurisdictions of federal agencies related to any WMD incident or event.

Recognize the importance of incident scene preservation and initiate measures that would secure the incident scene.

Protect any physical evidence such as footprints, any relevant containers, papers, and so on.

Advise any witnesses and bystanders who may have information specific to the WMD incident or event to remain at the incident scene in a safe location until those individuals have been interviewed and released.

If the incident scene has a significant number of individuals going into and out of the incident scene, note license plate numbers and any other relevant data specific to those individuals, especially individuals who may not be a part of to the incident scene or any response team members.

6.7.5 KNOW SCENE SECURITY AND CONTROL PROCEDURES

Understand the department or agency site security and scene control procedures for awareness level trained personnel.

Follow those procedures outlined for ensuring scene security and for keeping unauthorized individuals or personnel away from the incident scene and/or adjacent hazardous areas; this includes cordoning off any such areas to prevent anyone from inadvertently entering the incident scene.

Maintain incident scene security and control until a higher authority arrives at the incident scene.

Be familiar with the department or agency incident command procedures.

Protect any physical evidence such as footprints, any relevant containers, papers, and so on.

Know the department or agency procedures for isolating individuals from danger areas.

Know to how deal with contaminated individuals until a higher authority arrives at the incident scene.

Recognize that the incident or event scene may be deemed as a criminal scene, and that evidence must be protected and left undisturbed until a higher authority arrives at the incident scene, taking control of the situation, incident, or event.

6.7.6 KNOW HOW TO USE EQUIPMENT PROPERLY

Know how to use communications equipment (two-way radio or cellular) to contact either dispatched communications or higher authorities that will apprise either party of the situation, incident, or event at the incident scene.

Request additional assistance, personnel, and/or equipment that will assist individuals in properly dealing with the incident or event.

Understand how to accurately describe a WMD incident or event, and be aware of any available response assets within the affected jurisdiction(s) that are nearest to the incident scene or event location.

Know when to request for additional assistance.

Follow the department or agency emergency response plan procedures for establishing an incident command.

Know how to notify the communications center (through dispatcher), and assess the degree or levels of hazards, in order to obtain additional resources.

6.8 PERFORMANCE LEVEL GUIDELINES

This level is divided into two sections, each with a separate set of training guidelines for each part. The training guidelines for the respondent at the performance level target personnel who will (more than) likely respond to the scene of a hazardous materials event, potential terrorist, or criminal use of WMD event. Personnel responding will conduct on-scene operations within a nonsafety area (if properly trained and equipped) that has been set up on the scene of a potential WMD or hazardous materials event to control and close out the incident. It is expected that those personnel trained for Level A performance levels will work within both nonsafety and safety areas, supporting personnel who are working in a nonsafety work area. Personnel trained for Level B performance levels will work within nonsafety areas, and in other areas set up on the incident scene or event (as needed).

6.9 OPERATIONAL LEVELS DEFINED

Level A is the *operations level*; Level B is the *technician level*. Section 6.10.1 through Section 6.10.3 are Level A; Section 6.11.1 through Section 6.11.8 is Level B; both levels are specific to the Performance Level (as outlined). Portions of these procedures may (or may not) have sections or pieces of their sections added or removed;

this was necessary to generalize the overall procedural efforts of on-scene crisis management.

6.10 LEVEL A: OPERATIONS LEVEL

6.10.1 HAVE SUCCESSFULLY COMPLETED AWARENESS LEVEL TRAINING

This training involves possible hazardous materials handling for WMD and other specialized training. The responder should:

Complete training in (or have an equivalent training and experience in) and understanding of the guidelines at the awareness level for the function specific to the respondent.

Understand terminology, classes of materials and agents, toxicology of hazardous materials, WMD agents or materials, and anything not previously mentioned that would be considered hazardous to human life or property.

Be aware of any potential targets for possible attack by any individual(s) having or using any WMD agents or materials.

Know preplans to be used within the department or agency emergency response plan for those locations listed (that is, know what to expect and do for a chemical storage facility, fuel depot, and so on, in case of an emergency).

Know how to collect and forward any intelligence gathered regarding potential terrorist or criminal activity or actions involving possible WMD agents or materials.

Be able to and capable of coordinating and gathering any relevant intelligence from any variety of sources, organizations, and so on, that may be at the incident scene or event.

Demonstrate skills and knowledge in preparation of any hazard and/or risk analysis of potential WMD target within the local community or target area.

Know how to assess the potential for different threats, as well as collateral damage effects resulting from the implementation and enactment of those threats.

Participate in joint training exercises or drills with other emergency response organizations, departments, or agencies, that are expected to participate within the response of potential WMD events within the target area.

6.10.2 KNOW INCIDENT COMMAND SYSTEM AWARENESS PROCEDURES

In this step, within this level, it is essential to know the Incident Command System and be able to follow the Unified Command System (UCS) procedures for integration and implementation methodologies of each system. The responder should:

Know how systems integrate with each other and provide support for the incident (as best as possible).

Be familiar with the operations of both command systems structures and methodologies and be able to (and capable of) assisting the UCS (if/where needed).

Know how to implement initial site management procedures following the department incident command system and emergency response plan; such procedures include:

1. Establishing communications with dispatched communications (or command center).
2. Establishing control zones for the incident scene or event.
3. Locating the command post.
4. Forwarding any intelligence gathered that has been collected at the incident scene or event.

Be able to (and capable of) implementing the ICS component of the department or agency emergency response plan for any given WMD situation or event.

Be aware of any assets available from the department or agency, as well as from local departments or agencies that could provide assistance specific to a potential WMD situation or event.

Know what procedures are required to be followed to get resources to the incident scene or event (if/when as needed).

Be familiar with any assets that could be made available from other emergency response organizations, local or otherwise.

Understand and follow department or agency procedures for accessing other organizations' help specific to a potential WMC situation or event.

Understand the purpose and function of UCS.

Know department or agency procedures for assisting in the implementation of the UCS for incident scene or event management specific to a potential WMD situation or event.

Be able to (and capable of) assisting the critique and review of actions taken before, during, and after the complete response specific to a potential WMD situation or event.

Assist with any documentation of lessons learned and activities from the critique or review as to how the lessons learned may be applied for future courses of actions specific to potential WMD situation or events.

Understand the importance of and know how to terminate documentation specific to a potential WMD situation or event, to be conducted relating to, or specific to, the areas of activities while conducted before, during, and after the specific potential WMD situation or event.

Know and follow department or agency guidelines specific to news media coverage.

Know how to develop an Incident Action Plan (IAP) specific to coordination activities with the on-scene incident command.

Ensure that the IAP is consistent with the department/agency emergency response plan.

6.10.3 KNOW SELF-PROTECTION AND RESCUE MEASURES

This includes following any self-protection measures and rescue and evacuation procedures for potential WMD situations or events. The responder should:

Know how and when to use appropriate personnel protective equipment (PPE) issued by the department or agency and to work within a nonsafety area that is on-scene specific to a potential WMD situation or event.

Follow department or agency policies for use, inspection, and maintenance of PPE.

Understand hazardous situations and risks associated with wearing protective garments or clothing or other protective clothing specific to a potential WMD situation or event.

Understand and follow rehabilitation methodologies to assist other responders to reduce any levels of heat-related stress.

Know precautionary measures necessary to protect responders who are on-scene.

Know how to determine the appropriate PPE for protecting officers who will be entering nonsafety areas on-scene specific to a potential WMD situation or event.

Know the protective measures that are necessary to protect individuals, other responders, and other department or agency personnel that are on scene specific to a potential WMD situation or event.

Know the department or agency and on-scene incident commanders' plan for evacuation of individuals within the nonsafety areas specific to a potential WMD situation or event.

Be able to (and capable of) rescuing and moving individuals specific to a potential WMD situation or event to a safety area for triage and treatment by emergency medical respondents.

Understand the roles of Level A performance level responders, and roles of other levels of respondents within the department or agency emergency response plan.

Know how to implement appropriate decontamination procedures for individuals, respondents, mass casualties, and equipment within, around, surrounding nonsafety areas.

Understand the importance of proper decontamination of any equipment reused.

Know and follow department or agency procedures or practices for handling and securing any suspicious packages, articles, or items.

6.11 LEVEL B: TECHNICIAN LEVEL

6.11.1 KNOW WEAPONS OF MASS DESTRUCTION (WMD) PROCEDURES

This is necessary in following procedures for working at on-scene situation specific to potential WMD situations or events. The responder should:

Know how to conduct any investigation and protect and collect evidence in conjunction with department or agency procedures for chain of custody, documentation, and any specific security measures necessary to store evidential information, articles, or items, regardless or whether or not contaminated, or however contaminated.

Implement the department or agency emergency response plan on-scene security measures and procedures; procedures should include:

1. Providing security for command post operations.
2. Controlling or monitoring activity into, or out of, on-scene areas (both safety and especially nonsafety areas) specific to a potential WMD situation or event.

Know how to implement appropriate on-scene decontamination procedures for protection of individuals, members of the public, emergency responders, or others who may have been contaminated on scene by agents or materials resulting specific to the potential WMD situation or event.

Know how to implement basic life saving and supporting procedures for protection and treatment of individuals, members of the public, emergency responders, or others on-scene specific to a potential WMD situation or event.

Know how to implement procedures and measures for minimizing the spread of contamination of hazardous agents or materials to other locations, individuals, or equipment not previously contaminated, either within, or surrounding nonsafety areas resulting from the contamination.

Be trained in recognizing any potential acts of, or threat of terrorism, or incident.

Be able to (and capable of) identifying possible agents or materials that be present at a WMD situation or event.

Understand the roles and jurisdictions of any federal departments or agencies specific to a potential WMD situation or event.

Be able to coordinate and assist in the overall investigative process specific to a potential WMD situation or event.

Be aware of any applicable laws (if any), as well as privacy and security related issues specific to the potential WMD situation or event.

6.11.2 HAVE SUCCESSFULLY COMPLETED AWARENESS AND PERFORMANCE LEVEL TRAINING

This involves possible hazardous materials handling for WMD and other specialized training. The responder should:

Complete training in (or have an equivalent training and experience in) and understanding of the guidelines at the awareness and performance levels for Level A training for the function specific to the respondent.

Know terminology that is used with and/or associated with/to WMD agents and with any equipment (mechanical or otherwise) that would be used in conjunction with any tasks or assignments specific to skill sets or knowledge base of the respondents.

Have knowledge of, and ability to utilize, any specialty equipment used in conjunction with decontamination procedures, containment, or transportation for evidential purposes.

Know how to conduct risk analysis and assessment for any hazardous materials of any WMD agents or materials for on-scene situations and for preplanned potential terrorist or criminal activities within any given area.

Have experience in (some) emergency medical basic life support treatment and rescue of individuals and responders, triage and decontamination of individuals and equipment, and transportation capabilities of individuals exposed to WMD agents or materials.

Participate with emergency response organizations in joint training exercises or drills involving specified tasks, mockup scenarios, or working with mock WMD agents or materials.

6.11.3 KNOW SELF-PROTECTION, RESCUE, AND EVACUATION PROCEDURES

This includes following any self-protection measures and rescue and evacuation procedures for potential WMD situations or events. The responder should:

Know how to select and use the (PPE)[8,9] needed to work safely within nonsafety or near nonsafety areas that are near on-scene specific to a potential WMD situation or event.

Understand the limitations of the PPE; follow department or agency policies and guidelines upon how to use, inspect, and maintain the PPE.

Follow department or agency safety procedures and practices for retrieving, handling, transporting, and disposing of any unknown or suspicious package, article, device, or item.

Understand the hazards and risks in using protective clothing.

Follow department or agency precautionary measures and safety practices to safeguard personnel against contamination (as best as possible).

Understand and implement rehabilitation measures to help responders reduce level of heat stress or frustration; take any other necessary precautions to protect on-scene responders and/or other individuals that are on-scene specific to a potential WMD situation or event.

Know how to develop site safety and a control plan initiative that coordinates activities with the incident commander (if qualified; that is, personnel conducting such tasks must be trained and experienced in these areas of safety and risk mitigation; otherwise, inexperienced personnel may cause further safety issues or concerns to those who are on-scene).

Assist (however possible) with the implementation of the IAP on scene, or if requested, develop an IAP per directive from the incident commander.

Be able to recognize types of WMD agents or materials.

Know how to use and read results from diagnostic and sampling equipment and instrumentation devices.

Understand the limitations of the detection and/or diagnostic instrumentation devices that are provided by the department or agency.

Have experience in (some) emergency medical basic life support treatment, rescue of individuals and responders, triage and decontamination of individuals and equipment, and transportation capabilities of individuals exposed to WMD agents or materials.

Assist (however possible) any emergency medical groups that are on scene with the incident commander coordinating efforts of this type of support.

Have experience to assist the incident commander in establishing any safety procedures for performing specialized tasks to lower the safety levels of the hazard from the potential WMD agent or hazardous material.

Be able to perform such tasks (if assigned).

Know how to plan for, and implement for, coordination efforts with any emergency medical group, medical monitoring procedures for those individuals entering or leaving nonsafety areas (as needed).

6.11.4 KNOW AND FOLLOW PROCEDURES FOR PERFORMING SPECIALIZED TASKS

This includes knowledge to perform specialized works or tasks at the scene of a potential WMD situation or event, in which the responder should:

Know how to select appropriate PPE for the specialized task to be performed on scene, and to establish safety procedures and practices to be followed as outlined within the procedures of the department or agency that is responding.

Use technical reference materials to assist in the selection process of the PPE that is appropriate for the tasks.

Recognize the activities that will be coordinated with the on-scene incident commander.

Follow procedures for operating any detection or sampling instrumentation devices or equipment.

Understand the limitations for collecting solid (which includes granular or particulate materials), liquid, and gaseous substances for detection, identification, and classification of potential WMD agents or materials, and for the verification of such materials (as needed).

Use technical reference materials to assist in the tasks outlined (as necessary or needed).

Know and follow procedures and best practices for retrieval of contaminated evidence and for the safe handling or transportation, storing, and securing of such evidence materials, items, articles, and so on.

Be able to mitigate any on-scene hazards and risks to responders and to members of the public.

Assist the on-scene incident commander in developing and implementing strategies and tactics that will reduce on-scene risks for any responders or members of the public.

Be able to recognize any special threats such as secondary incendiary or explosive devices that would otherwise be used to harm (or kill) any emergency responders, members of the public, any equipment used for the detection, decontamination, or removal of WMD agents or materials or the vehicles to be reused.

Follow procedures and best practices for safely searching for the suspected devices, and, if found, controlling or removing these types of threats from the scene and away from those individuals, members of the public, any responders or emergency personnel who might have otherwise been exposed, contaminated, or had some form of safety risk or threat posed upon them.

Coordinate decontamination procedures with the incident commander.

Be able to implement the department or agency emergency response plans as well as local/regional emergency response plans.

Know how to access local/regional assets to assist with any on-scene resolution or mitigation procedures specific to any potential WMD situation or event.

Coordinate the implementation of any necessary medical monitoring efforts with emergency medical group members and the incident command for those responders entering and leaving nonsafety areas.

Be able to assist in the implementation of rehabilitation assistance to those emergency responders that may have suffered from any heat-related stress or frustration, or other problems arising from protective clothing, or can be controlled or reduced on-scene.

6.11.5 KNOW INCIDENT COMMAND SYSTEM PERFORMANCE PROCEDURES

In this step, within this level, it is essential to know the Incident Command System and to be able to follow the UCS procedures for integration and implementation methodologies of each system. The responder should:

Know how to implement the Incident Command Systems (ICS) such that the department or agency has its emergency response plan.

Ensure that skill set and knowledge are available to serve the emergency operations officer for on-scene activities.

Be aware of any assets available from the department or agency and from local/regional emergency response organizations especially regarding handling hazards and/or threats that may happen on-scene specific to a potential WMD situation or event.

Know how to obtain desired assets for on-scene support (as necessary, or if needed).

Know and follow procedures for working with, and coordinating with, other departments or agencies under the UCS to handle specialized hazards and/or threats on-scene specific to potential WMD situations or events.

Understand and know how to implement termination procedures at the close of an emergency response incident.

Be able and capable to assist the incident commander in completing required documentation related to termination procedures, including appropriate measures for cost recovery and management.

Know how to conduct or assist in conducting critiques of any actions taken before, during, and after the response specific to a potential WMD situation or event.

Be able and capable to assist the incident commander in conducting incident critiques (as defined as a lessons learned capability, for future situations or events).

Assist in determining what improvements (if necessary, as needed) would be made for the next emergency response specific to a potential WMD situation or event, especially in areas regarding improvements specific to the tasks defined to those responders on scene and within special operations.

Know how to coordinate the development of an IAP with the on-scene incident commander that is consistent with the department or agency emergency response plan procedures and practices.

Be able and capable to implement IAP, including addressing special on-scene hazards.

Recognize coordination efforts with/between other department and agencies that are on-scene for gathering any evidence and/or intelligence data or information.

Understand the importance of developing and sharing of intelligence gathering techniques for on-scene data gathering, including information from any special operations activities.

Recognize that any intelligence information gathered should be shared with the on-scene incident commander (or incident commander designee), as well as any senior law enforcement leadership that may be on scene.

6.11.6 Planning and Management Level Guidelines

This section addresses training requirements for respondents who may be involved with hazard remediation efforts associated with potential terrorist/criminal use of WMD. Respondents will be involved in planning for and managing the emergency on-site scene and will help implement the on-scene command post. These individuals might be expected to manage specific tasks while on-scene, as well as other allied emergency responders, who will support the ongoing operations to mitigate and control the hazardous agents and materials, using any available resources to safely and sufficiently conclude the event. Actions to be taken by respondents should (initially) be conducted from a safety area. It is expected that respondents will be integrated into the overall command structure that is implemented for the management and supervision of resources and assets being deployed to mitigate and recover from the overall WMD situation or event.

6.11.7 Successfully Completed Awareness, Performance, and Management Training

Complete training in (or have an equivalent training and experience in) and understanding of the guidelines at the awareness and performance levels for Level A training for the function specific to the respondent.

Know how to implement the department or agency ICS and relevant portions of the department or agency emergency response plan.

Recognize the hazards, risks, and limitations associated with using protective clothing and equipment.

Be able and capable to implement local/regional emergency response plans specific to potential WMD situations or events or hazardous materials events.

Understand the roles of responder personnel within any given emergency response plan.

Be familiar with any assets available for implementing the emergency response plan specific to any potential WMD situation or event.

Know what additional assets and assistance may be available for assistance with handling WMD and/or hazardous materials events or situations.

Understand the importance of implementing appropriate decontamination procedures for any given hazardous materials and/or WMD situation or event.

Be able to implement those procedures to protect emergency responders, individuals, public safety personnel, and members of the public, and for equipment that could be reused.

6.11.8 Know Incident Command System Management Procedures

In this step, within this level, knowing the Incident Command System, and be able to follow the UCS procedures for integration and implementation methodologies of each system is essential, in which the responder should:

Know how to manage any one of the five basic functions for operating the department or agency ICS.

Be able and capable to assess needs for additional resources in obtaining those resources from the identified assets.

Understand Emergency Operations Center (EOC) responsibilities and roles.
Be able and capable of interfacing and coordinating with everyone involved.
Understand the applications and interfaces of the UCS with the ICS.
Know best practices and methodologies that are to be used and implemented within the UCS that are on-scene specific to a potential WMD or hazardous materials event.
Be able and capable to assist the incident command in the completion of all termination documentation for the situation or event and how specified tasks relate to respondents rendered at the scene.
Know how to conduct or assist in conducting critiques of any actions to be taken before, during, and after the completion of the response specific to the potential WMD situation or event.
Be able and capable of developing lesson learned scenarios for future situations/events.
Define and implement appropriate strategies and tactics that would assist in determining the types and levels of degree of improvements relevant to tasks performed by the various responders at the scene, which are/will be needed for the lessons learned documentation.
Know how to develop a media management plan specific to potential WMD situations or events, or hazardous materials events, in coordination with the on-scene incident commander.
Be capable of managing responder group activities under the UCS and ICS directives.
Be capable of assisting the on-scene incident commander (or designee) upon completion or conclusion of the WMD or hazardous situation or event.
Be able and capable of advising the incident commander and/or the management team of the respondents' roles and capabilities; share any intelligence data or information gathered, along with any modifications necessary (or needed) to the department or agency emergency response plans, procedures, and best practices.

6.12 KNOW PROTOCOLS TO SECURE, MITIGATE, AND REMOVE HAZARDOUS MATERIALS

Know how to assess agents or materials used in a potential WMD or hazardous materials event based on the signs and symptoms of any individuals exposed to the area.
Use appropriate methods in gathering of evidential data or information.
Follow emergency medical protocols for treating individuals.
Understand procedures and protocols for defining locations for the command post, staging areas, medical monitoring function areas, and proper isolation boundaries for the different areas at the emergency scene.
Know how to control entry within, into, and out of these areas.

Be able and capable of identifying hazards presented at the scene that will be implemented in the most effective methods; consider alternatives and especially consider safety concerns of any emergency responders at the scene.

Be familiar with environmental and public safety requirements for the removal of, handling of, transportation of, and storing of WMD and/or hazardous materials or agents found at the scene.

Understand the roles of the responders regarding any evidence gathering efforts, including chain of custody, and needs for the secure storage of contaminated/noncontaminated materials gathered at the scene.

Follow health and safety precautions and procedures for handling such materials.

6.13 ADDITIONAL PROTECTIVE MEASURES

Basically, a repeat of self-protection and protective measures that are to be implemented on-scene, with a few additions:

Recognize the special hazards to human life from any WMD or hazardous agent or material.

Be able and capable to assist in the caring for, and treatment of, individuals who may have been exposed to such agents or materials.

Know how to obtain resources for appropriate rescue, transportation, and emergency treatment of contaminated individuals and personnel.

Follow postevent rehabilitation best practices and procedures for emergency response and other on-scene personnel; procedures are inclusive to Critical Incident Street Management (CISM) and debriefing practices.

Be able and capable of coordinating programs outlined for department or agency personnel (if requested, usually by the incident commander or designee in charge).

Understand the importance of implementing medically prescribed and appropriate prophylactic treatments for those that may have become contaminated with a biological hazard.

Coordinate any treatments with health officials.

Understand the importance of the safety officer role in protecting on-scene emergency responders and personnel.

Be able and capable of assuming that role (if requested, again, by an incident commander or designee in charge).

6.14 UNDERSTAND DEVELOPMENT OF THE INCIDENT ACTION PLAN

This includes know assets available for controlling WMD and hazardous materials situations or events, in coordination with the on-scene incident commander:

In collaboration with the on-scene incident commander, be able to assist in planning management efforts, thus determining optional goals and objectives to bring the situation or event to successful conclusion.

Know what assets are available for addressing on-scene hazards.

Have the necessary communications equipment to request on-site assistance.

Coordinate activities with the on-scene incident commander.

Know how to draft an incident mitigation or action plan (referred to as IAP) to address any on-scene incidents, situations, or events, and to obtain assets to control or suppress any such hazards pertinent to any such situation or event.

Coordinate the development, implementation, and alteration of the plan with the on-scene incident commander.

Be able to advise the on-scene incident commander as well as other officials regarding site assessment and establishment of any zonal boundaries along with outer perimeter of respondents and emergency personnel that are on-scene, which include an appropriate location for establishment of a command post.

Follow procedures and methodologies outlined within the department or agency procedural or policy manuals for assessing any hazard and risk and for protecting the general public, as well as any emergency respondents.

Be able and capable of identifying any potential targets for what might be considered "terrorist attacks."[10]

Understand and comprehend tactical methods use by individuals who may be classified as "terrorists" and what they might use within the target area.

Be capable of developing preplans to mitigate any potential WMD of hazardous materials situation or event involving potential targets.

6.15   KNOW AND FOLLOW PROCEDURES FOR PROTECTING A POTENTIAL CRIME SCENE

Know appropriate procedures for protecting evidence and minimizing any disturbances of the crime scene to the maximum extent possible, while protecting any individuals at the potential scene.

Assist any individuals minimize adverse medical signs and symptoms (where possible).

Understand the importance of coordinating with law enforcement officials to ensure that any department or agency actions do not hinder with the gathering of any evidence by law enforcement officers.

Assist law enforcement officers in identifying and preserving evidence and sharing of intelligence.

Follow any protocols established that will help in minimizing any disturbances to the potential scene.

Understand the roles and jurisdictions of any federal or state department or agency pertaining specifically to any potential WMD or hazardous materials situation or event.

Know how to recognize an incident that may be defined as an "act of terrorism."

Be able and capable of identifying any evidence that could be useful to the investigation of the potential scene.

Share intelligence with law enforcement officials and the on-scene incident commander.

6.16 KNOW DEPARTMENT PROTOCOLS FOR MEDICAL RESPONSE PERSONNEL

Be able and capable of developing a medical action plan to protect any on-scene emergency responders.

Coordinate the implementation of the plan with the emergency medical manager and/or on-scene incident commander.

Know how to implement, in concert with the medical action plan, department or agency procedures for medical monitoring of all respondents of the emergency team members involved with, or working with/within, the non-safety areas.

Ensure that the plan includes the monitoring of baseline vital signs and physical assessments for all personnel either entering or leaving this area.

Ensure that any signs or symptoms of exposure to potential WMD or hazardous materials agents are included within the medical monitoring and physical assessments conducted of those responders who are entering or leaving nonsafety areas.

6.17 NATIONAL FIRE PREVENTION ASSOCIATION 472

For more definitive guidelines about emergency procedures, the National Fire Prevention Association Standard 472 (referred to as "NFPA 472"), entitled "Standard for Professional Competence of Responders to Hazardous Materials Incidents," identifies the levels of competence required of responders to hazardous materials incidents. It covers the competencies for first responders at the awareness level and the operational level, hazardous materials technicians, incident commanders, hazardous materials branch officers, hazardous materials branch safety officers, and other specialist employees. Guidance is provided for first responders on how to deal with terrorist activities and weapons of mass destruction. NFPA 472 specifically addresses this category of an individual who may be sent to a scene. NFPA 472 defines two categories of such responders: (a) Private Sector Specialist Employees B; and (b) Specialist Employees C. Competencies are listed for both categories based on the prerequisite that all such individuals receive first response awareness training. It should be noted that the distinction may be drawn such that any differences between category B and C (with respect to additional training for category C specialists, based on the assumption that these personnel) may be required to work in nonsafety areas.[11]

6.18 OCCUPATIONAL SAFETY AND HEALTH ADMINISTRATION HAZARDOUS WASTE OPERATIONS AND EMERGENCY RESPONSE

The Occupational Safety and Health Administration (OSHA) Hazardous Waste Operations and Emergency Response (HAZWOPER) standard already recognizes that these types of individuals may be called to the scene to assist in the mitigation, control, or other aspects to aid the incident commander, as necessary. HAZWOPER rules include provisions for skilled personnel who have expertise in particular activities that are needed in the response but that cannot be performed promptly by the responding units such as crane operators or tow truck drivers. These individuals are not expected to be trained emergency responders, nor are they expected to have prior training in accordance with HAZWOPER guidelines. Because it is likely that these individuals may be exposed to the hazards at the emergency response scene, they should receive appropriate on-scene briefing with respect to safety and health protections. Once emergency response operations are concluded and recovery and cleanup operations begin, those workers involved in these activities will not be considered emergency response workers and will be covered by other OSHA requirements. This section addresses only those workers called to the emergency scene to render some assistance to the incident commander, the Unified Command team and the response team that is on scene.[12]

Typically, skilled personnel are asked to fulfill a particular task. In doing so, they are oftentimes briefed on safety and health hazards which they may encounter, as well as are briefed on the types of control measures that any given incident commander may want them to follow. Typically, these persons understand the hazards they face in doing their job on a normal day. The briefing is intended to alert them about extraordinary or unusual hazards that they may face and procedures to help protect them or those around them. Thus, no one individual is asked to perform any given job or task in which that person cannot be reasonably protected from on-scene hazards, even though there may be some risks involved.

Specialist employees are those that may have knowledge or expertise specific to particular hazards, equipment, processes, or chemicals that may be present at the emergency incident scene. The incident commander may benefit from their wisdom on the given subject. These personnel are expected to provide technical advice and assistance to the incident commander and it is assumed that they generally will not be exposed to hazards on the scene. However, certain experts or specialist employees of railroad companies or chemical manufacturers may have been trained to work in Level A suits (if necessary). These personnel receive training each year, demonstrating their competency in their specialization area.

6.19 SKILLED SUPPORT PERSONNEL

Skilled support personnel may be called upon to perform some functions that are related to a WMD or hazardous materials emergency response, who are relied upon within the emergency response plan, and may receive (some) awareness training. It is suggested that these skilled support personnel receive the minimum training of the awareness level guidelines provided to public works agency employees before they have to respond to a WMD incident, situation, or event.[13]

6.20 SPECIALIST EMPLOYEE

Specialist employees may be called upon for a WMD or hazardous materials incident response to provide information and technical advice unique to their particular specialty, or they may be asked to perform some specific tasks that they are expert in performing that the incident commander needs to be undertaken at the scene. These specialist employees receive annual training in their area of expertise. They are also trained in how to work within an incident command system. Personnel are expected to wear chemical protective clothing, perform unique tasks in the nonsafety areas zone, and will need additional training (typically) beyond the awareness level guidelines.[14]

6.21 DEPARTMENT OF TRANSPORTATION (DOT) HAZARDOUS MATERIALS (HAZMAT) CLASSIFICATIONS

The United Nations (UN) and the U.S. Department of Transportation (DOT) have devised a method of classifying hazardous materials based on the chemical and physical properties of the product that is referred to as a hazard class. Each of these classes is then subdivided into specific subsets (such as gases that may be poisonous, flammable, or nonflammable). Oxygen and chlorine are gases that have their own individual labels. Each class has a symbol that suggests the primary type of hazard that it possesses. DOT has cataloged every known toxic substance within the Emergency Response Guidebook,[15] compiled by the DOT Research and Special Programs Administration (RSPA)[16] and published by the U.S. Government Printing Office and numerous distributors.[17]

6.21.1 DOT HAZMAT CLASS 1: EXPLOSIVES

This is a chemical that causes a sudden, almost instantaneous release of pressures, gas, and/or heat when subjected to sudden shock, pressure, or extreme temperatures. Explosives (usually) have thermal and mechanical impact potential.[18]

6.21.2 DOT HAZMAT CLASS 2: GASES

Gases are grouped into three types: (1) compressed, (2) liquefied, and (3) cryogenic. Gases can be flammable, nonflammable (sometimes called inflammable), or poisonous. Gases have the ability to vaporize, which could cause respiratory issues to human life and cause thermal-related injuries or cause frostbite due to exceedingly cold temperatures.[19]

6.21.3 DOT HAZMAT CLASS 3: FLAMMABLE LIQUIDS

This also includes combustible liquids. Flammable liquids are liquid substances with a flashpoint below 100° Fahrenheit (for example, alcohol or gasoline); combustible liquids are liquid substances with a flashpoint greater than 100° Fahrenheit, but below 200° Fahrenheit (such as various oils, such as household heating oil and solvents).[20]

6.21.4 DOT HAZMAT Class 4: Flammable Solids

This also includes solids that are reactive. Flammable solids are likely to cause fires through friction or retained heat from a manufacturing process that may be easy to ignite; reactive solids are solids that are unstable to environmental conditions and can produce (or intensify) sudden heat or explosive properties when exposed to other chemicals or come into contact with water or organic substances (such as potassium, sodium, aluminum or magnesium — all of these solid metals are highly combustible when exposed to water).[21]

6.21.5 DOT HAZMAT Class 5: Oxidizers

This class also includes peroxides. Oxidizers are materials that can be in any form (gas, liquid, or solid state) that have potential to readily yield oxygen, supporting combustion or explosive scenarios. This can include gases such as oxygen, ozone (definition: gaseous molecule that contains three oxygen atoms ($O3$); ground-level ozone is a product of reactions involving hydrocarbons and nitrogen oxides in the presence of sunlight, and is a potent irritant that can cause lung damage or respiratory problems[22]), or chlorine; liquids such as bromine, hydrogen peroxide, and nitric acid; and solids such as chlorates, iodine, nitrates, and peroxides.[23]

6.21.6 DOT HAZMAT Class 6: Toxic Materials

This also includes infectious substances, which include etiological or infectious organisms (for example, anthrax, botulism, polio). Toxic materials may be harmful to human life from inhalation, ingestion, or absorption through external layers of the skin; these substances can be in either liquid or solid form or may be produced through irritants, which are dangerous or harmful fumes when exposed to air or fire (for example, xylyl bromide).[24]

6.21.7 DOT HAZMAT 7: Radioactive Materials

Any material that spontaneously emits ionizing radiation that has specific activity greater than 0.02 microcuries per gram is considered harmful to human life. Depending on the exposure, it can be fatal or cause serious harm to internal organs, or cause long-term effect, resulting in cancer.[25]

6.21.8 DOT HAZMAT 8: Corrosive Materials

This refers to any liquid or solid material that can damage living tissue, steel, or glass on contact (for example, sulfuric acid, hydrochloric acid, ammonium hydroxide). Corrosive materials can also be classified as an irritant, as fumes from acids can have debilitating respiratory consequences upon humans if inhaled.[26]

6.22 IMPORTANCE OF IMPLEMENTING AN EMERGENCY RESPONSE PLAN

The effectiveness of responses during emergencies depends on the amount of planning and training performed. During hazardous materials incidents, many additional burdens may be placed on local environments. Stress effects resulting from hazardous materials incidents can cause increases of a plethora of various stress-related symptoms and can produce situations resulting in potentially fatal results such as cardiac arrest or further contagion to other individuals. When all incidents are compounded, the situation can get out of control — quickly — unless detailed procedures for handling such incidents are available and readily accessible. Additionally, simply having these procedures may not be enough. Periodical review of the procedures, establishing updates as they are needed, and ensuring that the procedures reflect current environmental conditions, is all necessary to ensure effectiveness of the utilization of these procedures and planning initiatives.[27]

6.23 QUESTIONS

1. The term "first responder" is defined within the Homeland Security Act of 2002. True or False?

   Answer: *True*. The term "first responder" refers to those individuals who in the early stages of an incident are responsible for the protection and preservation of life, property, evidence, and the environment, including emergency response providers as defined within Section 2 of the Homeland Security Act of 2002 (6 U.S.C. 101), as well as emergency management, public health, clinical care, public works, and other skilled support personnel (such as equipment operators) that provide immediate support services during prevention, response, and recovery operations.

2. How many classifications of "first responders" are there?
   a. 8
   b. 6
   c. 5
   d. 4

   Answer: *6*. The classifications which make up the definition "first responders" include: (1) law enforcement; (2) fire services; (3) emergency medical services; (4) emergency management; (5) hazardous materials management; and (6) public works.

3. There are _____ many guidelines within the Office for Domestic Preparedness emergency plan?

   Answer: *3*. The guidelines are: (1) awareness; (2) performance; and (3) planning/management.

4. The acronym *NAERG* means _____.

   Answer: *North American Emergency Response Guidebook.*

5. *NAERG* is coordinated between multiple countries. True or False?

   Answer: *True*. Those countries are adjoining countries Canada and Mexico.

6. *NAERG* is updated every _____ years.

   Answer: *4*.

7. The acronym HAZWOPER means _____.

   Answer: HAZardous Waster OPerations and Emergency Response.

8. HAZWOPER was implemented through which organization?
   a. DOE
   b. DHS
   c. OSHA
   d. DOT

   Answer: *OSHA*.

9. Individuals who may be called upon for a WMD or hazardous materials incident response to provide information and technical advice unique to their particular specialty or may be asked to perform some specific tasks in which they are expert in performing that the incident commander needs to be undertaken at the scene are called

   _____.

   Answer: *Specialist employee*.

10. The Department of Transportation recognizes and classifies how many dangerous materials categories?
    a. 9
    b. 7
    c. 8
    d. 6

    Answer: *8*. The classifications that the Department of Transportation recognizes are: (1) explosives; (2) gases; (3) flammable liquids; (4) flammable solids; (5) oxidizers; (6) toxic materials; (7) radioactive materials; and (8) corrosive materials.

NOTES

1. http://www.ojp.usdoj.gov/odp
2. http://www.ojp.usdoj.gov/odp

3. U.S. Department of Justice Office for Domestic Preparedness: Emergency Response Guidelines (August 1, 2002).
4. U.S. Department of Justice Office for Domestic Preparedness: Emergency Response Guidelines (August 1, 2002).
5. The Whitehouse: Homeland Security Presidential Directive/HSPD-8 (December 17, 2003), Section (2) (d) def. "first responder."
6. Pipeline and Hazardous Materials Safety Administration, Office of Hazardous Materials Safety, 2004 Emergency Response Guidebook (2004).
7. http://hazmat.dot.gov/pubs/erg2004/gydebook.htm; additional references taken from the U.S. Department of Transportation Office of Hazardous Materials Emergency Response Guidebook for 2004.
8. OSHA requires employers to use personal protective equipment (PPE) to reduce employee exposure to hazards when engineering and administrative controls are not feasible or effective. Employers are required to determine all exposures to hazards in their workplace and determine if PPE should be used to protect their workers. If PPE is to be used to reduce the exposure of employees to hazards, a PPE program should be initialized and maintained. This program should contain identification and evaluation of hazards in the workplace and if use of PPE is an appropriate control measure; if PPE is to be used, how it is selected, maintained, and its use evaluated; training of employees using the PPE; and vigilance of the program to determine its effectiveness in preventing employee injury or illness.
9. U.S. Department of Labor Occupational Safety and Health Administration, Safety and Health Topics: Personal Protective Equipment (PPE). http://www.osha.gov/SLTC/personalprotectiveequipment
10. Definition of the term "terrorist" is fluid in its very nature, signifying that the term "terrorist" may or may not be someone who enjoys to exhibit any form of terror or mayhem to specified targets, or in some aspects, even general public targets, sites, facilities, or events, results in the damage of, or the destruction of life and/or property. This definition is constantly changing, thus, the definition to its term is nonstandard.
11. National Fire Prevention Association, NFPA 472, Professional Competence of Responders to Hazardous Materials Incidents (2002).
12. U.S. Department of Justice Office for Domestic Preparedness: Emergency Response Guidelines (August 1, 2002).
13. U.S. Department of Justice Office for Domestic Preparedness: Emergency Response Guidelines (August 1, 2002).
14. U.S. Department of Justice Office for Domestic Preparedness: Emergency Response Guidelines (August 1, 2002).
15. Pipeline and Hazardous Materials Safety Administration, Office of Hazardous Materials Safety, 2004 Emergency Response Guidebook (2004).
16. http://www.rspa.dot.gov
17. Federal Emergency Management Agency, An orientation to Hazardous Materials for Medical Personnel, IS-346 (September, 1997).
18. Federal Emergency Management Agency, An orientation to Hazardous Materials for Medical Personnel, IS-346 (September, 1997).
19. Federal Emergency Management Agency, An orientation to Hazardous Materials for Medical Personnel, IS-346 (September, 1997).
20. Federal Emergency Management Agency, An orientation to Hazardous Materials for Medical Personnel, IS-346 (September, 1997).
21. Federal Emergency Management Agency, An orientation to Hazardous Materials for Medical Personnel, IS-346 (September, 1997).

22. U.S. Environmental Protection Agency, Mobile Source Emissions – Past, Present, Future – Definitions (March, 2005).
23. Federal Emergency Management Agency, An orientation to Hazardous Materials for Medical Personnel, IS-346 (September, 1997).
24. Federal Emergency Management Agency, An orientation to Hazardous Materials for Medical Personnel, IS-346 (September, 1997).
25. Federal Emergency Management Agency, An orientation to Hazardous Materials for Medical Personnel, IS-346 (September, 1997).
26. Federal Emergency Management Agency, An orientation to Hazardous Materials for Medical Personnel, IS-346 (September, 1997).
27. Federal Emergency Management Agency, An orientation to Hazardous Materials for Medical Personnel, IS-346 (September, 1997).

7 Security Vulnerability Assessment (SVA)

7.1 INTRODUCTION

This chapter outlines specifics on Security Vulnerability Assessments (SVA) for any given critical infrastructure or support organization responsible for a critical infrastructure. The chapter provides a summary of conditions, factors, and states of existence in which it may become necessary to provide levels of countermeasures for remediation efforts of any vulnerability discovered or known. This chapter is one of the more critical chapters outlined within this book, as any professional, specialist, or technician who is responsible for a critical infrastructure or any aspect of a critical infrastructure, should (at the very least) have a fundamental understanding of what is involved in securing an organization's or industrial sector's infrastructure.

7.2 WHAT IS A RISK ASSESSMENT?

The term *risk assessment*, whether it pertains to information security or other types of risk, provides decision makers with information necessary in determining and understanding factors that may negatively influence the operations and outcomes of an organization's operational success.[1] Through these assessments, decision makers may be able to make informed judgments concerning the extent of actions needed to reduce risk. As reliance upon computer-based systems and electronic data interchanges (such as the Internet) has steadily grown, information security risk has joined the ranks of the index of listed and identified risks that both governments and business organizations must manage (and perhaps, reduce or remove).

Regardless of the types of risks being considered, most risk assessments generally include the following elements:

Identify known (or obvious) threats: This step outlines those threats (or the risks resulting from the use of, exposure to, any threats discovered or known) that can potentially disrupt, disable, or adversely prevent/inhibit process operations from performing within, throughout, and between critical infrastructures. This may be within an enterprise of an organization, or between differing organizations. Nonetheless, threats have many different classifications, and routinely more newly discovered ones not yet classified are found regularly. Threats may be defined in several categories but are generally subcategorically based upon such factors as perimeter breaches from intruders, criminal activities, disabled processes or operations resulting from disgruntled employees, inhibited activities resulting from acts of terrorism, and (of course) service disruptions caused by natural disasters (such as severe weather, earthquakes, hurricanes, and so forth).

Estimate threat occurrences: That is, outline the number of times that a threat may occur, weighing other factors based on (perhaps) historical information from prior events (if any such events existed or were recorded; otherwise, information might be obtained through other, alternative external sources of similar occurrences from other organizations) and judgments or observational notations from knowledgeable individuals.

Identify and rank value, sensitivity, and criticality of operations affected: This steps represents a significant aspect of the risk assessment in that it identifies those risks initially identified as being labeled as a "risk," and ranks them based on (a) how they would affect operations and assets controlled or used with the organization's operations; (b) what would be affected; (c) where the risks could occur, pinpointing more precise locations such as facilities or processes at those facilities; and (d) possibly when it might occur (timed risk estimations are often difficult to effectively predict; however, range classifications can often give a "guesstimate" insofar as to states of the environment that could trigger or cause those risks to occur). Through the identification and ranking step, levels of value (are placed on those processes within the operation, and assets utilized), sensitivity (of the process and information contained within and produced from, are listed), and criticality of the operations and assets that could potentially be affected *if* a threat were to materialize, and determine which operations and assets are considered most important to the organization.

Estimate the losses should the threat occur: This step is probably the most significant step within the risk assessment process cycle in that it assigns a value to the processes, operations, and assets used within, throughout, and produced from (or by) those processes and operations listed earlier. To many organizations, this step is crucial in that it defines the potential losses or damage that could occur if a threat were to materialize, and this step would include recovery costs to restore service and operations to the organization. Essentially, this step determines (ahead of time that the actual threat were to occur) how much money the organization would need to continue to operate successfully.

Identify actions to mitigate (and if not remove) the risk: This step may include implementation of new organizational policies and procedures as well as be forward-thinking in technological, physical, and asset control implementations.

Document, document, document: Effective processes result only in good, well-thought, developed contingency plans. Without documentation of the results and developing action plans (or courses of action for remediation, removal, or reduction in risk), funding applied towards risk assessments will be wasted.

Equations of risk may be used to evaluate alternatives and to select the best available practices and procedures. Conditional risk reduction and/or mitigation methods may be comparably similar to like assets. As such, a risk analysis may be necessary to compare risk across diverse assets and its sectors.[2]

7.3 METHODS OF ASSESSING RISK

There are various models and methodologies available for assessing risk, the extent of an analysis, the resources expended (which can vary depending on the scope of the assessment), the availability of reliable data of risk factors, and the methods of analysis used. Availability of data used may affect the extent to which risk assessment results may be reliability quantified. Quantitative approaches (generally) estimate a monetary value/cost associated to a risk and its reduction based on several factors:

- Identifying the likelihood that a damaging event or occurrence will happen.
- Identifying costs resulting from potential losses from the event or occurrence.
- Identifying costs necessary for mitigating actions resulting from those losses.

The cost of implementing any countermeasures implemented is then compared to the cost of replacing lost assets and information to determine the cost-effectiveness of the countermeasure.[3] When reliable data and costs are not available, the qualitative approach may be taken by defining risk more subjectively in terms of "high," "medium," and "low" risks. Obviously, the definition of the words "high risk" has different meanings between organizations; thus, it is subjective to skewed perspectives of the organization conducting the assessment. Qualitative assessments rely upon the expertise, experience, and judgment of those conducting the assessment; however, it may be possible to combine both methodologies to form a hybrid quantitative/qualitative approach to any given assessment. Though this may not be practical, or might not apply, this method may be used when other methods fail.

Vulnerabilities are identified and are rated from high to low based on their potential impact to the (overall) operation. Based on analysis of these threats and vulnerabilities, risks are then identified. Risks with a higher probability of occurring and with the potential to have a serious impact or to incur serious damage to the operation are rated as high. Those with a lower probability of occurrence and with the potential to have only minimal impact on the operation are rated as low.[4]

7.4 THREAT RISK EQUATIONS

There are two basic equations that can determine the levels of risk. They are listed both below. *NOTE: Both formulas were taken from the American Society of Mechanical Engineers (AMSE) presentation.*[5]

$$R_{ai} = F_{ai} \times (\text{Vulnerability})_{ij} \times (\text{Consequences})_{ij}$$

Whereby the following symbols have significance such that:

R_{ai} = the annual economic risk for a given threat, i
F_{ai} = the annual frequency of an adversary attacking a critical asset using specific type of threat, i
Vulnerability = the conditional probability that a specific failure mode, j, will occur, assuming that the assumed potential threat, i, has occurred
Consequences = total measure of consequences of failure for threat, i, failing in mode, j

$$R_{ijk} = F_{ai}\ P_{fij}\ P_{cijk}\ C_{cijk}$$

Whereby the following symbols have significance such that:

R_{ijk} = the economic risk
F_{ai} = the annual frequency of an adversary attacking a critical asset using specific type of threat, i
P_{cijk} = the combination of the probability ranges at each node of the event starting at the node, after the node where P_{fij} is defined
P_{fij} = conditional probability of failure mode, j, due to threat, i

If F_{ai} is set to "1.0," then the calculated risk is termed as a "conditional threat risk" such that it may be used to evaluate alternatives and to calculate the probability of an occurrence or occurrences that will justify the cost of any countermeasures or mitigation strategies implemented. Conditional threat risks cannot be used to calculate for comparative purposes across diverse assets (and/or their sectors).

7.5   COMPARISON OF QUANTITATIVE VS. QUALITATIVE RISK ASSESSMENTS

Though quantitative security risk assessments were predominant several years ago, the increasing difficulty of accurately estimating asset values, especially data and information assets, has caused users to question the accuracy of their results. Many risk assessments conducted today are (usually) conducted (and their tools and utilities used) using the quantitative approach. These tools include optional features (not necessarily required, but is helpful when demonstrating levels of risk to senior management) which include elements such as a graphical outage (bar, line, combination charts and graphs), as well as other graphical representatives to demonstratively illustrate levels of risk.[6]

One issue that many of these automated reporting tools tend to produce are not-so-meaningful reports to management, primarily because they tend *not* to explain problematic issues and areas identified nor necessarily identify solutions for these problems. Though these tools do permit assessment teams to enhance their output and thus help in the explanation process by providing additional, explanatory text, which is (most often than) not done. Quantitative assessments are being looked upon more favorably once again in that insurance carriers are offering coverage against loss of data — in addition to loss of physical assets and property. Thus, having quantitative reports necessitates their method for determining value of data or for performing their own internally-conducted risk assessments (meaning, that the insurance carriers would bring their own auditor to assess the problematic issue or situation to the customer claiming loss of data and information).

Below is a comparison of ways to measure risk. There are pros and cons to each method.

	Quantitative	**Qualitative**
Process	Determine cost of assets. Estimate potential asset losses due to risk. Compare to mitigation costs.	Determine information criticality. Determine impacts to information and service delivery. Perform cost benefits analysis on mitigation costs vs. potential damage.
Advantages	Analysis is easy to follow and decisions are clearly justifiable.	Takes operations into account. Takes subjective issues into account. Pays more attention to information assets.
Disadvantages	Wide margin for error in results. Difficult to represent effects on service delivery and information. Assets as a number. Difficult to put cost on subjective assets such as reputation, and so on.	Can reflect personal biases. Dependent entirely on the skills of the assessor (or assessment team).

7.6 CHALLENGES ASSOCIATED WITH ASSESSING RISK

Reliably assessing security risks may be more difficult than assessing other forms of risks because data and cost information about threat likelihoods and costs associated with those risk factors may be more often limited because these factors are constantly changing. Such changes may be technologically related in that what was not considered a risk now is deemed as a risk as newer advances in technology have made the obsolete technology vulnerable to attacks. Publicly-available information through the Internet or other public forums of data interchange, have also made some factors more visible over the years as information is becomingly more and more available to the general public. Another challenge might be the costs of remediation such that what was once considered possible because of its low cost associated with its manufacturing, servicing, or its availability, now has a higher cost because of economic developments in other geographically separated locations or disruptions in operations, manufacturing, or servicing due to one of those threats previously outlined. Although the cost of manufacturing, operations, or servicing needed to strengthen costs may be known, it is often not possible to precisely estimate any related indirect costs such as possible loss of productivity resulting from the newly implemented controls.

7.7 OTHER FACTORS TO CONSIDER WHEN ASSESSING RISK

The lack of reliable information often precludes the ability to precisely determine which risks are considered as most significant insofar as to its comparative factors outlining which controls are most cost effective. As a result of these limiting factors, it is important that organizations properly identify and utilize such methods that will benefit from the use of those risk assessments while avoiding any costly attempts in developing resulting output that is of a questionable nature insofar its reliability and accuracy.

7.8 WHAT IS AN SVA?

The Security Vulnerability Assessment (or SVA) is a systematic examination of networks to determine the adequacy of security measures, identify security deficiencies, provide data from which to predict the effectiveness of proposed security measures, and confirm the adequacy of such measures after implementation.[8] SVA is another term used for assessing vulnerabilities and threats, and to (a) determine (first) if there are any that exist within the enterprise; (b) determine the level of risk upon discovery of the vulnerability or threat; (c) determine the level of remediation based upon the results; and (d) determine the method by which the results are communicated. The vulnerability assessment is oftentimes referred to as a "penetration test" (or its shortened term "pentest") in which one or more individuals attempts to penetrate through a given system, environment, or condition. There are many different kinds of assessments — each one has specific importance insofar as to its criticality levels:

Network-based vulnerability assessment: This test affirms (or reaffirms) the state or condition of the network enterprise and any device connected to, within, and throughout it. Essentially, any device connected to the Internet, or internally to the enterprise LAN or corporate network, is susceptible to discovered (and possibly exploited) vulnerabilities of those devices connected.

Computer-based vulnerability assessment: This test affirms that systems, not necessarily those connected with or throughout a network, are secured. If this test is being performed, it signifies that the computing device may not be connected to a network; if the device is connected to a network, this may be the control system device that is connected to a network-connected device, and so on. There are several scenarios which could be applied to this condition (sometimes referred to as a "host vulnerability assessment").

Software-based vulnerability assessment: This test affirms that whatever application is operating any given enterprise is secured. This ensures that whatever application (or suite of applications) tested does not suffer from buffer overflows, denial of service attacks, and so on, and that the application can accommodate for any nuance or circumstance.

Physical-based vulnerability assessment: This performs functions similar to that of the network-based assessment methodologies, except that its primary function is to breach physical perimeters, doorways, locks, and so on at its given target. This includes computer-based assessments as well.

Protocol assessment. Oftentimes this is called a "documentation assessment" or a "review assessment," in that this determines if any given target or system environment, more specifically, its processes within and throughout the enterprise, can account for security incidents, breach attempts, and penetrations. This includes any relevant documentation pertaining to standards, protocols, and procedures (strategic, tactical, and operational) for any given enterprise.

7.9 REASONS FOR HAVING AN SVA

President Decision Directive 63 (PDD-63) directs every department and agency of the federal government to have developed a plan by November 18, 1998, to protect its own critical infrastructure, including but not limited to, its computer-based and physical-based assets, information of or produced by those assets, and so on. While the departments or agencies implementing these plans may decide on alternative measures, the overall consideration of these initiatives should include any identification of those critical infrastructures supported and their vulnerabilities, including:

- Identify mission essential communications, information, and other systems.
- Identify significant vulnerabilities of organization minimum essential systems.
- Identify any external interdependencies.
- Assessments to determine vulnerabilities of department or agency minimum essential services to failures by private sector providers of their respective industrial sectors or other infrastructure services.

7.10 WHAT IS A THREAT?

A "threat" is any agent (person, activity, or event) with the potential to cause harm to a system or operational environment. All systems, regardless of their type and level of data processed, stored, and used, are subject to harm. The mere existence of the threat does not imply that the system will be harmed; however, the potential for harm can exist. Threats exist simply because the system exists. The probability that its occurrence will impact the system, however, is significantly lowered as a result of the type and degree of protection that is applied.

Threat entries are organized (primarily) into three distinct main threat categories:

1. Natural disasters
2. Accidental threats
3. Intentional or malicious threats

With "accidental" and "intentional" threat categories, threat occurrences or attacks may stem from two sources: (1) inside threats; or (2) outside threats. Inside threats (and their attacks) range from accidental file deletions by administrative staff to deliberate system reconfigurations or modifications of data resulting in impaired, degraded, or terminated operational functionalities.[9] As inside threats relate to individuals who have internal knowledge of the enterprise workings, they pose the most significant threat to security as opposed to outside threats, which might include hackers who access unauthorized systems through the Internet, former users and employers who still have active access to systems and their environments, or criminal activities for other, more hostile reasons.

7.11   WHAT IS VULNERABILITY?

The term "vulnerability" is an inherent weakness in a system or its operating environment that may be exploited to cause harm to the system. These weaknesses may be found in the system design, physical layout of the facility, procedures used, administration of the system, personnel within the system, management, hardware, software, and so on. As with threats, vulnerabilities indicate weaknesses or flaws with the potential for exploitation.[10]

Vulnerabilities are evaluated based on the impact after the countermeasure assumptions are applied. The "impact" of an environment is a rating of the amount of damage that could occur if a particular vulnerability were to be exploited. Impact ratings assigned to the vulnerabilities are qualitatively assigned and are based by assessment teams, as the participants' knowledge of those systems (and their processes) are being evaluated. The vulnerability of an asset may be modified (in some cases, practically removed) by using countermeasures that can reduce (if not remove) the probability that a particular or specific attack scenario's success is possible. Any consequences of failure resulting from the implementation for a particular or specific attack scenario may be reduced (again, if not removed) through the use of conventional mitigation strategies.[11]

7.12   COUNTERMEASURES

Countermeasures are active processes, procedures, and system features that serve to either detect, deflect, or reduce the probability of a threat, or the impact of vulnerability, thereby either reducing or (preferably) removing the system risk.

7.13   VULNERABILITY ASSESSMENT
FRAMEWORK (VAF)

The Vulnerability Assessment Framework (VAF) was designed to assist with whatever organization required a vulnerability determination, either resulting from prior knowledge issues, or even risks or vulnerability issues recently discovered. The VAF was produced under contract between KPMG Peat Marwick, LLP and the Critical Infrastructure Assurance Office (CIAO)[12] (now part of the U.S. Department of Homeland Security), with a review and evaluation process that is based on existing security requirements, standards, and principals, the VAF may be applied across all forms of government — federal, state, or local government, or even private sector industrial organizations and their infrastructures.

The VAF is a comprehensive and complete process,[13] consisting of a three-tiered set of processes; the VAF enables whatever organization is implementing it to:

- Define Minimum Essential Infrastructure (MEI) requirements.
- Identify and locate interdependencies and vulnerabilities of the MEI.
- Provide a basis and mechanism for development of any remediation plans.

The VAF was designed with scalability in mind such that it could be applicable to all levels of any given organization or government entity as well as the broad industrial sectors from the national infrastructures (as outlined from PDD-63).[14]

While some suggest conducting penetration testing and analysis techniques as an adequate methodology approach for assessing computer-based systems (and their potential vulnerabilities), the report recommends a more holistic approach, one which states that, although penetration testing and analysis is performed, it is simply a portion of a much larger process, one that encompasses the embodiment of penetration testing, and other methodologies that will produce a finished, more polished assessment of risks and vulnerabilities both found and encountered within and throughout the assessment process. Identification of those risks and vulnerabilities through root-cause analysis (essentially, what was the primary cause for the vulnerability or risk to occur, why does it exist, and how was it that it did not get fixed or patched) within the assessment process such that through this (and perhaps other) assessment criteria, established and enabled systemic remediation efforts that are effective, efficient, and time-affordable (as opposed to the opposite of time-prohibitive such that insufficient time was available to either permanently patch and/or remediate whatever risk or vulnerability was found or existed at the time of the assessment; in this case, time-affordable is productive such that whatever remediation efforts are offered are capable and allowable within the allotted time frame, either outlined, or permitted).

7.14 REASONS FOR USING THE VAF

Although there have been historical differences in whatever approaches were used to measure business risk and threats through assessment of an infrastructure, the importance of flexibility and capabilities of scalability were significant such that those methodologies were necessary in defining the VAF (and its framework). Though the framework emphasizes mostly on computer-based related aspects of critical infrastructure, the VAF methodologies defined may apply to physically-based related aspects and offer methods that are flexible enough in that, to the extent in which it may be possible to do so, the VAF may be applied in other contexts of requirements of security, risk assessment, and management, and so on.[15] The government has implemented a vast range of methodologies and documentation pertaining to these aspects for purposes of this or other related efforts specific to critical infrastructure protection.

In a world of growing dependencies on computer-based solutions, such threats might be construed as being nonconventional in their very nature, whereby both computer-based and physical-based threats may not be prudent to suppose that any given organization of entity will know in advance from where a threat may arise. Thus, assessments specific to any one infrastructure may or may not be suitable for utilization with other sectors (and their industries). For example, processes and methods used to assess computer-based, network-connected control systems that are interdependent and interconnected with each other within a power generation facility, may or may not apply to a petroleum distillation and refinement facility, as control mechanisms implemented may only apply specific to the power generation aspect of the energy industrial sector; conversely, the same may hold true and apply from the petroleum distillation and refinement facility towards the power generation facility.

This very critical aspect alone seriously complicates how "flat" (the term "flat process" or "flattened process" refers to an aspect of one particular process, such it may be easily and effectively duplicated either within the existing process family, or may be utilized in other process cycles elsewhere, outside of the scope of the initial process defined) an assessment methodology (and its processes) may be applied insofar as to cross-sector utilization.

The basis of experience for defining the assurance and auditing aspect of the KPMG VAF methodology was taken heavily from several different current process methodologies for measuring information technology (IT) system controls. These include aspects such as:

The April 1998 Control Objectives for Information Technology (COBIT™),[16] which is a defined process of the Information Systems Audit and Control Association (ISACA).

The May 1998 publication of the "Executive Guide for Information Security Management"[17] of the United States General Accounting Office (GAO).

Outlined standards, protocols, and procedures from the GAO's vast library of documentation pertaining to auditing of federal information systems, as outlined within the Federal Information Systems Control Auditing Manual (FISCAM).[18]

7.15 FEDERAL INFORMATION SYSTEMS CONTROL AUDITING MANUAL (FISCAM)

The Federal Information Systems Control Auditing Manual (FISCAM)[19] states that as computer technologies advance, government organizations have become increasingly dependent on computerized information systems to carry out their operations that process, maintain, and report essential information. The reliability of these systems that process, maintain, and report these data are a major concern to auditors of these government organizations. Auditors may need to evaluate the reliability of computer-generated data that supports financial statements or is used to analyze specific program costs and outcomes. Additionally, auditors may call on the evaluation of the adequacy of controls in systems to reduce risk of loss due to errors, fraud, or other illegal acts and disasters or other incidents that cause the systems to become unavailable.[20]

The FISCAM describes the computer-related controls that auditors should consider when assessing the integrity, confidentiality, and availability of computerized data. It is an applied guide by GAO primarily for support of statement audits and is available for use by other auditors.

It is not an audit standard; its purpose is to:

Inform auditors about computer-related controls and related audit issues so that they can better plan their work and integrate the work of information systems (IS) auditors with other aspects of the audit.[21]

Provide guidance to IS auditors regarding scope of issues that may be considered in review of computer-related controls over integrity, confidentiality, and availability of computerized data associated with those systems.[22]

The manual lists specific control techniques and related suggested audit procedures. However, the audit procedures are stated at a strategic level and assume that some expertise about the subject to be effectively performed. As a result, detailed audit steps specific to the organization conducting the audit should be developed by the IS auditor based on the specific software and control techniques employed by the audited party after consulting with the auditor about the auditing objectives. Many of the suggested audit procedures start with the word "review"; however, the manual stipulates that the auditor will do more than simply look at the subject to be reviewed. Rather, the auditor will perform a more critical evaluation, whereby the auditor utilizes professional judgment and experience, undertaking the task with a certain level of skepticism, critical thinking, and creativity.[23]

Although IS audit work, especially control testing, is generally performed by an IS auditor, financial auditors with appropriate training, expertise, and supervision may undertake specific tasks in this area of the audit. This is especially appropriate during financial statement audits where the work of financial auditors and IS auditors must be closely coordinated. Throughout this manual, the term "auditor" should generally be interpreted as either (a) an IS auditor, or (b) a financial auditor working in consultation with or under the supervision of an IS auditor.[24]

7.16 GENERAL METHODOLOGIES OF FISCAM AUDITING

A general methodology that should be used to assess computer-related controls involves evaluating[25]:

General controls at the organization or facility level.

General controls as they are being applied to their environment or the application that is being examined, such as the payroll or financial recording system, or the accounting system.

Application controls, which are controls over input, processing, and output of any data associated with specific applications.

7.17 WHAT ARE GENERAL CONTROLS?

The term "general controls" refers to policies and procedures that apply to all or a large segment of an organization's information systems, and thus, help ensure proper operation. Examples of primary objectives for general controls are to safeguard data, protect computer application programs, prevent system software from unauthorized access, and ensure continued computer operations in case of unexpected interruptions. The effectiveness of general controls is a significant factor in determining the effectiveness of application controls. Without effective general controls, application controls may be rendered ineffective by circumvention or modification. For example, edits designed to preclude users from entering unreasonably large dollar amounts in a payment processing system can be an effective application control. However, this control cannot be relied on if the general controls permit unauthorized program modifications that might allow some payments to be exempt from the edit.[26]

7.18 WHAT ARE APPLICATION CONTROLS?

Application controls are directly related to individual computerized applications. They help ensure that transactions are valid, properly authorized, and completely and accurately processed and reported. Application controls include (a) programmed control techniques, such as automated edits, and (b) manual follow-up of computer-generated reports such as reviews of reports identifying rejected or unusual items.[27]

Both general and application controls must be effective to help ensure the reliability, appropriate confidentiality, and availability of critical automated information.

7.19 CAVEATS WITH USING AN SVA

Considering that an assessment may find faults at the infrastructure level, or processes which surround or work within the infrastructure, assessors need to determine if the senior or executive management is cognitive of any of the security risks; as such, if those within management are cognitive of such risks, they are usually interested in taking preventative measures in understanding and managing those risks or threats found resulting from the assessments performed.[28] Having an interest at those levels within management ensures that necessary precautions are (or will be) taken considerably more seriously at lower organizational levels and ensures that security specialists have the necessary resources needed for implementing an effective countermeasure initiative. Thus, in a perfect world, this may be the case; however, in the real world, this is not always the case. Within a government office, department, or agency, senior or executive-level management might find obstacles or factors that would be inhibitive of their ability to effectively implement or execute management directives towards its remediation. Such factors (that are not limited to any one specific factor) include:

    Political motivation (or upheaval, depending upon the circumstance, how much funding is involved, and who is affected by/from the outcome resulting from the assessment).

    Government funding (what one manager or executive may find useful or important, another may not, again, probably based upon political motivations, funding, or all of the above).

    Motivation or influence from industrial private sectors.

    Influences from other offices, departments, or agencies, either similar to, or indirectly influenced by, the targeted organization.

The political undertows within an organization tend to be more subversive within private sectored industries rather than government organizations, as private sector organizations may or may not necessarily have reporting and accountability responsibilities, aside from the reporting of the financial health of a corporation (as required for publicly-traded companies with the Sarbanes-Oxley Act of 2002),[29] that are necessarily required. Many large corporations have a "don't ask, don't tell" approach insofar that if there is no acknowledgment of a security problem (or even worse, a security breach), then there is no problem. Having an SVA will shed light on most cracks and crevices of any organization, and if there are holes or leaks, it will find something.

7.20 HOW THE SVA IS USED

At a minimum, the (overall) recommendation is that first-discovery vulnerability assessment processes consist of a broadened, organizational-wide assessment of the organization's MEI, and the organization's relationship to, and in connection with (if applicable) national-level MEI standards. Once the area of scope and MEI(s) are defined, the assessment team can then target specific functions outlined within the SVA, focusing on core processes that are considered key components of a critical infrastructure.[30]

7.21 AUDIENCE OF AN SVA

The initial audiences for any given assessment consist of (mostly) the organizations that will be directly affected by whatever remediation efforts are practiced resulting from the outcome of the assessment. Its implementation with an assessment team should be formed, which includes members of management (or certainly those who are directly impacted or affected by the assessment). The team will consist of an internal auditing group (if one exists; if no internal auditing group exists, then an external auditing group may be required), the Chief Information Officer (CIO) and/or members of senior or executive management that report to the CIO, someone who is familiar with the audit process and oversees output produced throughout the assessment process, individuals responsible for information and data security, physical security, and personnel security (where applicable).[31]

7.22 INITIAL SVA PLAN

The initial plan is designed to be used by security professionals and auditors (internal and/or external, depending upon the size of scope, and whether or not internal auditors are involved), and will serve as a common language for facilitating communications, levels of expectations and cooperation among the varied groups. This plan will aid and guide team members in effectively working together as a team, while understanding the tasks to be accomplished, and achieving the common goal of minimizing any discovered or known vulnerabilities that may diminish the organization's ability to achieve operational success.[32]

If the organization is already conducting vulnerability assessments, or has conducted one recently, the assessment team should examine the processes currently in use against the VAF process and determine if any process gaps exist. The sole intention of the VAF process is to use, if available, existing data gathering and analysis techniques in the identification and documentation of discovered or known vulnerabilities within an infrastructure; additionally, these intentions are not meant to lay blame upon any one particular group or organization, merely that such efforts are to reduce the amount of time spent in the data gathering step of the assessment; that is, it is a time and cost saving measure.

7.23 NECESSARY STEPS OF AN SVA

The assessment team (generally) determines the level of detail to which it should be applied for any given enterprise environment and the analysis required to assess the MEI and its vulnerabilities. Each step of the VAF is outlined in a manner similar to what is shown below:

> *Goals and objectives*: This provides the basis or reason(s) for having the assessment performed. This step outlines the "why" an assessment is needed.
> *Critical Success Factors (CSF)*: Factors, principles, and elements performed within and throughout the assessment that will determine if the assessment was successful or not. This step outlines the "how" and determines the success of assessment or not.
> *Anticipated or expected outcomes*: This step identifies what are the anticipated or expected outcome(s) from its performance and what should be expected. This step outlines the "what" an assessment should expect given the scenario.
> *Activities performed*: This step outlines the "where" and "when" within an assessment, such that it outlines the detailed and summarized aspects of the assessment throughout its performance.

7.24 CRITICAL SUCCESS FACTORS

Critical Success Factors (CSF) are objectives and factors vital to the operational success of the assessment. The fact that if an assessment is initiated, and there are no vulnerabilities, risks, or threats found, may (or may not) signify if the assessment was considered successful (or not).[33] Some CSF aspects that might be necessary to take in consideration are:

VAF must apply to infrastructure vulnerabilities in both computer-based and physical-based areas.

VAF must be scalable; that is, the assessment process must be capable of being applied to larger, more sophisticated organizations, and then converge upon the small organization with little, or no, experience with infrastructure vulnerability issues.

VAF must be flexible, allowing individuals to give emphasis to areas of most significant to least significant importance to the targeted organization.

VAF should be capable of addressing multiple audiences; much depends upon whether the information is leaving the organization (or not), and if it is government-related (or not). Consequently, many private sector industrial infrastructures may define their assessments based upon previous defined assessments conducted by the government.

VAF should incorporate a delivery mechanism that is readily acceptable to all parties involved, and not one that would require government regulation or involvement.

VAF may be implemented by the auditing group, both within the context of a traditional business risk assessment and through the growing accountancy requirements that are necessary in assessing risk and adequacy of controls over any given system (and its processes).

VAF must be flexible enough to draw upon information and materials from other sources, for levels of understanding, levels of expertise, for updated applied information, either at the current organization, or at other similar organizations, within the industry.

VAF must be an integral part of long-term investment strategies of the organization; remediation costs might be more manageable if part of an information and comprehensive investment strategy.

VAF process must be repeatable; that is, similar tests conducted must be exercised again to ensure consistency with similar results, esp. if there are comparative analysis reports being produced between current and previously performed assessments.

Senior and/or executive management of the assessed organization must understand, comprehend, and accept the reasons for the assessments in order to ensure that the VAF process is successful.

VAF is not synonymous with penetration testing; penetration testing is one aspect of the overall assessment process cycle, and should not be considered a "sure fire" method for identifying and classifying vulnerabilities or threats.

7.25 VAF METHODOLOGY

The VAF consists of an almost cascading style of analysis such that information is isolated within each major step before proceeding to the next step, thus ensuring better accuracy. Each step consists of a series of activities, which are outlined within each section. Using these steps outlined, the assessment team will compile a list of vulnerabilities for the organization to evaluate and determine appropriate measures and countermeasures. Next steps include determining the order in which vulnerabilities might be addressed, resources applied in remediation, and the level of investment necessary to meet assessment objectives:

Step 1: Establish the Organization MEI — In Step 1, the assessment team defines the MEI requirements for the organization. The focus is on specific infrastructure components that support essential processes that are absolutely fundamental in achieving the organization's operational success.[34]

Step 2: Gather Data to Identify MEI Vulnerabilities — In Step 2, the VAF evaluation will review actions, devices, procedures, techniques, and other measures that can potentially place the organization at risk. The outcome will be the identification and reporting of flaws, omissions in control structures (such as vulnerabilities) which may affect the integrity, confidentiality, accountability, or even availability of resources utilized that are essential in achieving the organization's operational success.[35] This represents the intelligence gathering phase of the assessment, in which assessment team members attempt to gather as much data as possible about the organization, determine what information is available to the general public, what information is available within the organization, and determines whether any exposed information offered to potential intruders has provided an adequate view of the operational environment of the target facility, location, or enterprise.[36]

Step 3: Analyze, Classify, and Prioritize Vulnerabilities — In Step 3, the assessment team will define, analyze, and classify any discovered or known vulnerabilities identified within Step 2, as well as any external dependencies from Step 1, thus prioritizing either minimization or remediation efforts. The step will move processes from the vulnerability assessment phase into the first steps of the remediation process, with estimated costs necessary for remediation.[37] This step conducts active reconnaissance through the utilization of whatever tools and utilities are necessary in succeeding within the vulnerability assessment. The end result generates a partial list of services, facilities, and operations that are vulnerable.[38]

Step 4: Privileged Escalation — In Step 4, the assessment team determines if the assessment will become problematic; this step simulates privileged escalation as a preventative nature to determine just how far, and to the extent to which the vulnerability will extend without causing degradation of services or operational services failures. *This step is considered optional.*

7.26 INITIAL STEPS OF THE VAF

Throughout the process, the assessment team will gather information through a number of data gathering activities, which include:

Facilitated sessions: Also called "discovery sessions," this is similar to the interview process, targeted toward a group of individuals, and is specifically directed for defined input from group members.

On-site surveys: This method is passive in that, through observation while at the facility being assessed, is gathering information about process flow (or lack thereof), observed methods of attack, and so on.

Interviews: This step interrogates personnel and staff members of the facility being assessed. Usually interviews are conducted in one-on-one situations.

Documentation reviews: This step reviews documented procedures, protocols, and processes outlined, and makes comparative notes against what is stated versus what is actually being performed. Any variation in process flow is (usually) checked again.

Validation activities: Also called "process reviews," these include procedural checks, system and processing tests and simulations. This step determines if buffer overflows, application (or environmental) failure are possible; if this step demonstrates that a process can fail, provide recommended course of action for its remediation.

7.27 VAF STEP 1: ESTABLISH THE ORGANIZATION MINIMUM ESSENTIAL INFRASTRUCTURE (MEI)

The objective of this step is to define the MEI. There are two levels of MEI: (a) national-level MEI; and (b) organizational-level MEI, defined as follows:

(a) *National-level MEI* is defined as the framework of critical organizations, personnel, systems, and facilities that provide a flow of goods and services that are absolutely essential to the economic operational success, as well as national security of the United States. This definition of MEI is at a national level such that any interruption, slowdown, or shutdown of that infrastructure would have a cataclysmic effect upon other infrastructures that may be dependent upon the denied infrastructure. An example might be airline traffic control such that any severe effect at any metropolitan hub would have a detrimental effect nationwide, thus causing delays throughout the United States.

(b) *Organizational-level MEI* is defined as the framework of critical organizations, personnel, systems, and facilities that provide inputs and outputs necessary to support core processes essential in accomplishing an organization's operations, as they may relate to national security, national economic security, or continuity of government services. The functions factor in the operational success to each component that may make up the infrastructure such as one aspect of one organization that is part of an infrastructure (for example, computer components of the electrical power grid) rely upon one or more components to regulate power flow to itself; IT services provided by those private sector industries represents one aspect of the MEI, henceforth, it is at an organizational level, and may be strategic or tactical in nature, depending upon the circumstances.

In most cases, the MEI is intended to be the absolute core component of an organization's "mission critical elements" (MCE); oftentimes, businesses will refer to key computer servers and systems that represent revenue stream and collection services as "mission critical." This would be a prime example of that factorization. Essentially, the organization would cease to function if that element was inhibited or prevented from operating. Another example would be airline scheduling systems. Without these systems, ticketing agents would have to schedule passengers, their tickets, and the airplanes departing with those passengers — manually — something of which would severely cripple the airline affected. Most organizations have several key critical elements defined that are essential to that organization's continued operational success. The MCE are resources needed that are necessary in addressing each and every mission within or throughout the organization, regardless of its relevance to the core processes outlined.[39]

The assessment team must determine the scope of the assessment in order to decide whether a national-level MEI or organizational-level MEI, or both, need to be defined. Once the scope has been defined, the MEI(s) will allow the assessment team to target the next steps within the VAF methodology process, focusing on appropriate core processes that are considered components of the critical infrastructure.[40]

7.27.1 STRATEGIC-LEVEL MEI

This area consists of the following[41]:

Mission statements and high-level organization plans, goals, and attributes.
Organizational structure — essentially, who reports where to whom?
Governance insofar as to what is affected by which ordinance, public law, or act.
Critical components make up the very fabric of any given critical infrastructure; without this key item, part, or service, the infrastructure would grind to a halt.

7.27.2 TACTICAL-LEVEL MEI

This is also referred to as "resource elements" and is an area consisting of the following:

System specific functions that represent either individual or systematic functionalities of a given infrastructure; essentially, what aspect or system does this element perform?
Facility specific functions that represent functionalities of a given facility supporting a critical infrastructure (slightly more detailed, and is specific to facility issues).
Personnel specific functions that represent roles and functions of personnel supporting the critical infrastructure; this includes classification of those who are critical within the organization, which may include both management and nonmanagement personnel and staff members.

Process specific functions that represent the actual process of the control system of any given critical infrastructure (for example, electrical power flow regulation versus electrical power generation — both represent two distinctly different processes).

7.27.3 RESOURCE ELEMENTS THAT COMPRISE AN MEI

Once the strategic-level MEI is defined, the tactical-level MEI (or "resource elements") is examined; essential resource elements include the following factors:[42]

People: This includes the staff members, management, and executives needed to plan, organize, acquire, deliver, support, and monitor mission-critically related services, information systems, and their facilities. This also includes groups and individuals who are external to the immediate organization involved such as contractors or supporting vendors or critical equipment, software, or services provided that are required as part of the fulfillment process applied towards the organization's operational success.

Technology: All equipment, hardware and software, connectivity, countermeasures, and/or safeguards that are utilized in support of the core processes.

Applications: All application systems, internal or external, utilized in support of the core processes.

Data: All data (electronic and written form) and information required to support core processes; this includes numbers, characters, images, or other methods of recording, in a form which may be assessed by human intervention or (especially) input mechanisms for computer devices that are stored and processed there, or transmitted on some form of digital communications channel (such as the Internet or private area network).

Facilities: All facilities that are required to support the core processes, including the resources to house and support information technology resources, as well as other resource elements defined earlier.

7.27.4 DEFINING TEAM COMPOSITION

Within any organization, formation of a team framework is necessary for determining sizing, communications, and capabilities of each team member. It is recommended that *at least* two experts form a group, and the group should consist of the following types of individuals:

Project/Team Leader: Skilled in auditing (or perhaps forensics) methodologies.

Personnel Safety, Training, Awareness, and Education: Skilled in performing background investigations, training and awareness issues, dealing with personnel security issues. This person may be the Project/Team Leader.

Information Security: If government affiliated, this individual should be familiar with security protocols pertaining to government security (especially military-grade security and classification); if nongovernment affiliated, this individual should be familiar with the various security standards and guidelines for private sector industries, which include ISO 17799, COBIT, Sarbanes-Oxley, HIPAA, and so on. Also skilled in auditing and/or forensics management, project development life cycle, business continuity, and security administration.

For larger organizations requiring a more in-depth and detailed evaluation, it is recommended that at least five experts form the group, and the group should consist of the following types of individuals:

Project/Team Leader: Skilled in auditing (or perhaps forensics) methodologies.

Personnel Safety, Training, Awareness, and Education: Skilled in performing background investigations, training and awareness issues, dealing with personnel security issues.

Information Security: If government affiliated, this individual should be familiar with security protocols pertaining to government security (especially military-grade security and classification); if nongovernment affiliated, this individual should be familiar with the various security standards and guidelines for private sector industries, which include ISO 17799, COBIT, Sarbanes-Oxley, HIPAA, and so on. Also skilled in auditing and/or forensics management, project development life cycle, business continuity, and security administration.

Telecommunications and Networks: Skilled in WAN and LAN network design and architecture, as well as PBX systems.

Physical Security: Skilled in on-site assessment of perimeters, doors, entrances/exits, and skilled in surveillance systems.

7.27.5 IDENTIFYING THREAT AWARENESS

This includes any awareness by management staff of any threats or inherent risks that exist against their strategic mission(s) and goals, which may cause individuals, groups, or entire organizations to take appropriate actions that may threaten their implementation and continued operations. This level of awareness for any vulnerabilities identified are outlined within VAF Step 2. When considering threats in any environment for intentional acts, consideration should be given to defining potential threat sources and their motivations.[43]

7.27.6 POTENTIAL THREAT SOURCES

Some sources which might be considered a threat to an environment might include one of the following listed[44]:

*   Nations (hostile or otherwise)
*   Intelligence services/economic competition
*   Sub/transnational groups (such as terrorist factions or organized crime groups)

- Nontraditional threats (such as weapons of mass destruction or information warfare)
- Malicious computer code (intentionally transferred or otherwise)
- Threats to personal privacy
- Environmental (debris, smoke, water, heat, electrical)
- Unwitting/unknowing third-party (bystander)
- Disgruntled employee/contractor/vendor/service personnel
- Hackers/crackers/whacker/vandals
- Criminal (fraud, theft, etc.)

7.27.7 POTENTIAL THREAT MOTIVATION

From the list of potential threat sources, these sources need a specific reason as to why it is going to threaten an environment or organization, and as such, might include one of the following motivations[45]:

- Economic gain
- Revenge
- Political objectives (power)
- Extortion
- Competitive advantage (may tie with economic gain)
- Invasion of privacy (power)
- To meet a challenge or dare (just simply it was because it was there, or was fun)

7.28 VAF STEP 2: GATHER DATA TO IDENTIFY MEI VULNERABILITIES

The objective of this step is to identify the vulnerabilities within the organization relating specifically to the MEI identified throughout VAF Step 1. The VAF process defined will be much broader in its approach than some of the more traditional methods used to produce a comprehensive vulnerability identification framework. Although penetration testing may have its place within the traditional methodologies used elsewhere, several documents state that penetration testing may be inadequate or inappropriate for performing infrastructure vulnerability assessments. Reviews of root causes of infrastructure vulnerabilities may be necessary before any meaningful efforts to minimize those vulnerabilities may be undertaken.[46]

The criteria used to identify those vulnerabilities are categorized into three distinct groups,[47] as follows:

Areas of Control: Collectively, controls consist of policies, procedures, and best practices, along with organization structures and framework design to provide reasonable assurances that organizational success will be achieved, and that undesirable events or situations are detected (quickly) and corrected. These control areas are expanded from GAO's FISCAM definitions of control areas, and thus, may be incorporated into infrastructure vulnerability issues.

MEI Resource Elements: These are broad categories of resources, all or portion of which, constitutes the minimal essential infrastructure necessary for an organization to conduct its operations. These resource elements are similar to those outlined from the COBIT framework developed by ISACA, and have been expanded to incorporate physical infrastructure vulnerability areas as well.

Areas of Potential Compromise: These are also broad areas representing categories where losses that can occur will impact both the organization's MEI and its ability to conduct its operations.

7.28.1 Areas of Control

Entity-wide security: Planning and management that provides a framework and continuing cycle of activity for managing risk, developing security policies, assigning responsibilities, and monitoring an organization's security controls.

Access controls: Procedures and controls that limit or detect MEI resource elements, thereby protecting those resources against loss of integrity, confidentiality, accountability, and availability.

Segregation of duties: Policies, procedures, and organizational structure established such that no one individual can control key aspects of any part of the organization's operations and thereby conduct unauthorized actions or gain unauthorized access to MEI resource elements.

Continuity of service and operations: Controls that ensure that, when unexpected events occur, organizational MEI services and operations continue without interruption or are promptly resumed and critical and/or sensitive data is protected through adequate contingency and business recovery plans and exercises.

Change control and life cycle management: Procedures and controls that prevent unauthorized operations or modifications of operations from being implemented.

System controls: Controls that limit and monitor access to operations, as well as to areas that (a) control other aspects of operations, and (b) secure those environments supported by the operations systems.

7.28.2 Areas of Potential Compromise

If vulnerabilities are identified and are reviewed against the areas of control and the MEI resource elements, this would conclude that controls are not in place to ensure the following factors:

Integrity: This represents the accuracy, completeness, and reliability of transmission data, the reception of information, and its validity in accordance with business values and expectations; it is also the adequacy and reliability of processes assuring authorized access to and the safety of systems, and their facilities.

Confidentiality: This represents the protection of sensitive information from unauthorized disclosure and sensitive facilities from physical, technical, or electronic penetration and/or exploitation.

Availability: This represents the ability to have access to MEI resource elements as needed/necessary, both presently and for future use; essentially, this concerns the safeguarding of those resources and associated capabilities.

Accountability: This represents an explicit assignment of responsibilities for ownership or the overseeing of a process, system, and its input and outputs. Accountability may be assigned any level within a given organization to include executives, management, staff, system, information, or facilities owners, providers, and users of the MEI resource elements. These assignments are reviewed for effectiveness and appropriateness within the areas of control.

7.28.3 AREAS OF CONCERN USING THE FRAMEWORK

It is essential that the security program planning and management organization provides a framework and continuing cycle of activities for managing any risks, developing security policies, assigning responsibilities, and monitoring the adequacies of the organization's controls.[48]

The critical elements in developing and implementing an organizational-wide security program involve factors that are essential to several internal control components, including the control environment. These critical elements ensure that the effectiveness of the organizational overall internal controls are intact. The relevant factors include supportive attitudes and actions expressed and conveyed by senior management, ongoing assessments of risk and monitoring of related policies, along with effective communications between management and staff, are crucial. All internal control components should be present and functioning effectively to conclude that those internal controls implemented are effective and operational. As such, the control environment defines and sets the precedence for the rest of the organization. Specific control techniques, which include methodologies such as penetration testing, cannot be relied upon to be effective on an ongoing basis unless supported by strong control environments. For this reason, the auditor conducting the investigation should be aware of any (and all) control environmental factors throughout the audit, adjusting the audit procedures accordingly.[49]

7.28.4 CONTROL OBJECTIVES USED IN THE FRAMEWORK

Some of the objectives are more apparent than others, but almost all have equally significant importance to the success of the audit investigation conducted. The objectives are:

Risk management. Risk assessments should consider data sensitivity and the need for integrity and the range of risks that an organization's MEI resource elements may be subjected to, including those risks posed by authorized internal and external use, not to mention those outside of the organization attempting unauthorized access. Such analysis draws upon reviews conducted of systems, networks, and operations of existing security controls of those systems, as well as reviews and tests conducted of controls for other resource elements.

Organizational-wide security program plan: Entities should have a written, documented plan that clearly describes the organization's security program, policies, and procedures. At the very least, the plan and any related policy should cover all MEI resource elements, outlining duties and responsibilities for overseeing security and the organization's resources.

Security management structure: Senior management should establish a structure to implement a security program throughout the organization. The structure generally consists of a core of personnel who are designated as security resources. This staff will then serve in a crucial role in developing, communicating, and monitoring compliance with security policies, reporting activities periodically to management. The security resources also provide roles in evaluating the effectiveness of security controls for daily operations, which include program managers who rely on those systems, administrators, and its user base.

Security personnel policies: Policies relating to personnel action such as hiring and terminating staff members and employee expertise are important factors for security staff. If personnel policies are not adequate, an organization runs the risk of: (a) hiring unqualified or untrustworthy individuals; (b) providing terminated employees with opportunities for sabotage or operational impairment, disablement, or rendering the organization inoperative; (c) failing to detect continuing unauthorized employee actions; (d) lowered employee morale; and (e) allowing staff expertise to decline.

Outsourcing: A rather sensitive area of discussion, but nonetheless, necessary. Vendor management controls involve the definition of procedures or services to be provided, adherence to agreements and services levels, and qualifications of personnel.

Electronic commerce (or e-commerce): Electronic commerce controls involve the management of contractual standards for transactional security and minimum standards requirements for authentication using certificate authorities.

Interdependencies: Important considerations in managing organizational-wide security are the resulting risks to organizational entities from interdependencies of forces internal and external to the organization. A good example of internal and external interdependencies might be a labor strike from outsourced service providers or contractual difficulties by service providers — in either circumstance, neither situation is controllable as it is beyond the control of the organization, yet is interdependent upon them.

7.28.5 DATA CLASSIFICATION

Resource owners should determine the level of protection that is most appropriate for the resources that are their responsibility. These determinations should flow directly from the results of the risk assessments that identify threats, vulnerabilities, and possible negative effects that could result from disclosure of confidential or sensitive data or failing to protect the integrity of data supporting mission critical environments.[50]

All resource classifications should be reviewed and approved by senior management, maintained on file, and periodically reviewed to ensure that they reflect current conditions. Implementing adequate access controls involves determining the level and type of protection, what is appropriate for resources, and who needs access to those resources. Resource owners typically perform and assign these tasks.

Policies specifying classification categories and criteria assist resource owners in classifying their resources according to need for protective controls. The Computer Security Act of 1987 requires federal government departments and agencies to identify systems that process "sensitive data." The term "sensitive data" is defined as "any information, the loss, misuse, or unauthorized access to or modification of which could adversely affect the national interest or the conduct of federal programs, or the privacy to which individuals are entitled under the Privacy Act." OMB Circular A-130, under Appendix III, directs federal agencies to assume that all major systems contain some sensitive information that needs to be protected, but focus extra security controls on a limited number of systems considered "high risk."[51]

7.29 VAF STEP 3: ANALYZE, CLASSIFY, AND PRIORITIZE VULNERABILITIES

The major objective of this step is to define and analyze the vulnerabilities identified within the VAF process, most notably Step 2 and the MEI external dependencies outlined from Step 1, thereby enabling the first order of prioritization for purposes of remediation and minimization of any threats. This step will move the process from the vulnerability assessment phase into the first steps of the remediation phase, with accompanying funding and resource estimates and timelines.[52] For areas of potential compromise involving aspects of integrity, confidentiality, and/or availability, the assessment team will assign a color-coded value to indicate the impact if the vulnerability were executed and exploited. Color-coding demonstrates graphically (overall) just how vulnerable an operational system is in terms of its levels of exposures and risks to those threats. Most assessment color-code mechanisms weigh the risks (and their threats) using red, yellow, and green colors — signifying extremely risky (red), moderately risky (yellow), not risky at all (green); these threat matrices vary from organization to organization.[53]

7.30 QUESTIONS

1. Risk can be assessed through quantitative and qualitative approaches. True or False?

   Answer: *True.*

2. If the risk factor of a calculated risk is set to 1.0, then it is called a
   _____.

   Answer: *Conditional threat risk.*

3. The acronym SVA means _____.

Answer: *Security Vulnerability Assessment*. This is a systematic examination of networks to determine the adequacy of security measures,
identify security deficiencies, provide data from which to predict the
effectiveness of proposed security measures, and confirm the adequacy
of such measures after implementation.

4. SVA's may be called by another term. What is that term?
   a. Penetration test
   b. Vulnerability assessment
   c. Risk assessment
   d. Threat assessment

Answer: *Penetration test.*

5. Any agent with the potential to cause harm to a system or operational
environment is called a _____.

Answer: *Threat*. All systems, regardless of their type and level of data processed, stored, and used, are subject to harm. The mere existence of the
threat does not imply that the system will be harmed; however, the potential
for harm can exist. Threats exist simply because the system exists.

6. How many types of threats exist?
   a. 5
   b. 4
   c. 3
   d. 2

Answer: *3*. There are 3 types of threats: (1) natural disasters; (2) accidental
(or unintentional) threats; and (3) intentional threats.

7. This represents an inherent weakness in a system or its operating environment that may be exploited to cause harm to a system.
   a. Risk
   b. Threat
   c. Vulnerability
   d. Flaw

Answer: *Vulnerability*. Weaknesses may be found in the system design,
physical layout of the facility, procedures used, administration of the
system, personnel within the system, management, hardware, software,
and so on. As with threats, vulnerabilities indicate weaknesses or flaws
with the potential for exploitation.

8. Methods of reducing, removing, or deflecting the probability of a threat, or the impact of its vulnerability are called _____.

Answer: *Countermeasures.*

9. A _____ refers to an aspect of one particular process, such that it may be easily and effectively duplicated either within the existing process family, or utilized elsewhere.

Answer: *Flat process.*

10. Policies and procedures that apply to all or a large segment of an organization's information system is called the _____.

Answer: *General controls.*

NOTES

1. U.S. General Accounting Office, Information Security Risk Assessment: Practices of Leading Organizations, GAO/AIMD-00-33 (Washington, D.C., November, 1999).
2. ASME Critical Assets Protection Initiative, ASME Homeland Security, Risk Analysis and Management for Critical Assets Protection (RAMCAP) Methodology Document, PS&S Interagency Working Group (September 17, 2004).
3. ITSC UI Security Risk Assessment Guidebook (September, 2001).
4. ITSC UI Security Risk Assessment Guidebook (September, 2001).
5. ASME Critical Assets Protection Initiative, ASME Homeland Security, Risk Analysis and Management for Critical Assets Protection (RAMCAP) Methodology Document, PS&S Interagency Working Group (September 17, 2004).
6. ITSC UI Security Risk Assessment Guidebook (September, 2001).
7. ITSC UI Security Risk Assessment Guidebook (September, 2001).
8. http://www.bitpipe.com/tlist/Vulnerability-Assessments.html
9. ITSC UI Security Risk Assessment Guidebook (September, 2001).
10. ITSC UI Security Risk Assessment Guidebook (September, 2001).
11. ASME Critical Assets Protection Initiative, ASME Homeland Security, Risk Analysis and Management for Critical Assets Protection (RAMCAP) Methodology Document, PS&S Interagency Working Group (September 17, 2004).
12. *Vulnerability Assessment Framework 1.1,* U.S. Critical Infrastructure Assurance Office, Washington, D.C. (October, 1998).
13. *Vulnerability Assessment Framework 1.1,* U.S. Critical Infrastructure Assurance Office, Washington, D.C. (October, 1998).
14. http://www.fas.org/irp/offdocs/pdd/pdd-63.htm
15. *Vulnerability Assessment Framework 1.1,* U.S. Critical Infrastructure Assurance Office, Washington, D.C. (October, 1998).
16. http:// www.isaca.org/cobit.htm
17. U.S. General Accounting Office, 2010 Census: Basic Design Has Potential, but Remaining Challenges Need Prompt Resolution, GAO/-05-9 (Washington, D.C., January, 2005).

18. U.S. General Accounting Office, Federal Information Systems Controls and Auditing Manual: Volume I: Financial Statement Audits, GAO/AIMD-12.19.6 (Washington, D.C., January, 1999).

19. U.S. General Accounting Office, Federal Information Systems Controls and Auditing Manual: Volume I: Financial Statement Audits, GAO/AIMD-12.19.6 (Washington, D.C., January, 1999).

20. U.S. General Accounting Office, Federal Information Systems Controls and Auditing Manual: Volume I: Financial Statement Audits, GAO/AIMD-12.19.6 (Washington, D.C., January, 1999).

21. U.S. General Accounting Office, Federal Information Systems Controls and Auditing Manual: Volume I: Financial Statement Audits, GAO/AIMD-12.19.6 (Washington, D.C., January, 1999).

22. U.S. General Accounting Office, Federal Information Systems Controls and Auditing Manual: Volume I: Financial Statement Audits, GAO/AIMD-12.19.6 (Washington, D.C., January, 1999).

23. U.S. General Accounting Office, Federal Information Systems Controls and Auditing Manual: Volume I: Financial Statement Audits, GAO/AIMD-12.19.6 (Washington, D.C., January, 1999).

24. U.S. General Accounting Office, Federal Information Systems Controls and Auditing Manual: Volume I: Financial Statement Audits, GAO/AIMD-12.19.6 (Washington, D.C., January, 1999).

25. U.S. General Accounting Office, Federal Information Systems Controls and Auditing Manual: Volume I: Financial Statement Audits, GAO/AIMD-12.19.6 (Washington, D.C., January, 1999).

26. U.S. General Accounting Office, Federal Information Systems Controls and Auditing Manual: Volume I: Financial Statement Audits, GAO/AIMD-12.19.6 (Washington, D.C., January, 1999).

27. U.S. General Accounting Office, Federal Information Systems Controls and Auditing Manual: Volume I: Financial Statement Audits, GAO/AIMD-12.19.6 (Washington, D.C., January, 1999).

28. *Vulnerability Assessment Framework 1.1,* U.S. Critical Infrastructure Assurance Office, Washington, D.C. (October, 1998).

29. http://www.sec.gov/divisions/corpfin/faqs/soxact2002.htm

30. U.S. General Accounting Office, Federal Information Systems Controls and Auditing Manual: Volume I: Financial Statement Audits, GAO/AIMD-12.19.6 (Washington, D.C., January, 1999).

31. U.S. General Accounting Office, Federal Information Systems Controls and Auditing Manual: Volume I: Financial Statement Audits, GAO/AIMD-12.19.6 (Washington, D.C., January, 1999).

32. U.S. General Accounting Office, Federal Information Systems Controls and Auditing Manual: Volume I: Financial Statement Audits, GAO/AIMD-12.19.6 (Washington, D.C., January, 1999).

33. *Vulnerability Assessment Framework 1.1,* U.S. Critical Infrastructure Assurance Office, Washington, D.C. (October, 1998).

34. *Vulnerability Assessment Framework 1.1,* U.S. Critical Infrastructure Assurance Office, Washington, D.C. (October, 1998).

35. *Vulnerability Assessment Framework 1.1,* U.S. Critical Infrastructure Assurance Office, Washington, D.C. (October, 1998).

36. State of North Carolina, Information Security Vulnerability Assessment, Preliminary Statewide Assessment, Office of the State Auditor (December, 2002).

37. *Vulnerability Assessment Framework 1.1,* U.S. Critical Infrastructure Assurance Office, Washington, D.C. (October, 1998).
38. State of North Carolina, Information Security Vulnerability Assessment, Preliminary Statewide Assessment, Office of the State Auditor (December, 2002).
39. *Vulnerability Assessment Framework 1.1,* U.S. Critical Infrastructure Assurance Office, Washington, D.C. (October, 1998).
40. *Vulnerability Assessment Framework 1.1,* U.S. Critical Infrastructure Assurance Office, Washington, D.C. (October, 1998).
41. *Vulnerability Assessment Framework 1.1,* U.S. Critical Infrastructure Assurance Office, Washington, D.C. (October, 1998).
42. *Vulnerability Assessment Framework 1.1,* U.S. Critical Infrastructure Assurance Office, Washington, D.C. (October, 1998).
43. *Vulnerability Assessment Framework 1.1,* U.S. Critical Infrastructure Assurance Office, Washington, D.C. (October, 1998).
44. *Vulnerability Assessment Framework 1.1,* U.S. Critical Infrastructure Assurance Office, Washington, D.C. (October, 1998).
45. *Vulnerability Assessment Framework 1.1,* U.S. Critical Infrastructure Assurance Office, Washington, D.C. (October, 1998).
46. *Vulnerability Assessment Framework 1.1,* U.S. Critical Infrastructure Assurance Office, Washington, D.C. (October, 1998).
47. *Guide for Developing Security Plans for Information Technology Systems*, NIST Special Publication 800-18, National Institute of Standards and Technology: Washington, D.C., 1998.
48. *Vulnerability Assessment Framework 1.1,* U.S. Critical Infrastructure Assurance Office, Washington, D.C. (October, 1998).
49. *Vulnerability Assessment Framework 1.1,* U.S. Critical Infrastructure Assurance Office, Washington, D.C. (October, 1998).
50. *Practices for Securing Critical Information Assets*, The Critical Infrastructure Assurance Office, Washington, D.C., 2000.
51. *Vulnerability Assessment Framework 1.1,* U.S. Critical Infrastructure Assurance Office, Washington, D.C. (October, 1998).
52. *Vulnerability Assessment Framework 1.1,* U.S. Critical Infrastructure Assurance Office, Washington, D.C. (October, 1998).
53. *Vulnerability Assessment Framework 1.1,* U.S. Critical Infrastructure Assurance Office, Washington, D.C. (October, 1998).

8 Standards and Guidelines

8.1 INTRODUCTION

This chapter outlines some standards, guidelines, and protocols that have been, or are currently, defined in terms of security and personal safety. Standards and guidelines outlined are provided as reference materials since we feel that they are pertinent to setting security or safety standards for critical infrastructure and emergency response methods. Overall, most standards and compliance protocols are directly governed within each representative sector, except for a few (maintained by International Organization for Standardization [ISO] and/or the American National Standards Institute [ANSI]) — *NOTE: Not ALL sectors have established (or are developing) standards of compliance protocols.*

8.2 ABOUT THE NATIONAL FIRE PREVENTION ASSOCIATION (NFPA)

The mission of the international nonprofit organization the National Fire Prevention Association (NFPA) is to reduce the worldwide burden of fire and other hazards on the quality of life by providing and advocating scientifically-based consensus codes and standards, research, training, and education. NFPA membership exceeds more than 75,000 individuals from around the world and more than 80 national trade and professional organizations worldwide.

Established in 1896, NFPA serves as the world's leading advocate of fire prevention and is an authoritative source on public safety. In fact, NFPA's 300 codes and standards influence every building, process, service, design, and installation in the United States, as well as many of those used in other countries. NFPA's focus on true consensus has helped the association's code-development process earn accreditation from the ANSI.[1]

8.2.1 NFPA 730 AND NFPA 731

The security industry provides protection to company assets and/or people, but what defines protection for the security industry insofar as to providing consistent results? The answer lies with an establishment of standards and guidelines that are industry-wide, ranging from personal security and safety, to defining how circuitry should be configured for a close-circuit television (CCTV). Several organizations have taken initiatives to develop several (rather) comprehensive sets of security standards and guidelines.

Some aspects of the security industry, pertaining partially to the manufacturing aspect of the security industry, are standardized and regulated; these organizations are controlled and their operations are dictated by organizations such as the Underwriters Laboratories Inc. (UL) and ANSI, which offer hundreds of standards and operating protocols for manufactured products, components, and services which may utilize these products and many of which emphasize fire safety and electrical system specifications. The NFPA offers more than 300 technical standards and code protocol definition guidebooks, which are predominantly related to life safety and fire prevention. Consequently, the Security Industry Association (SIA) has produced more than 20 technology standards of varying natures.

The NFPA (at the time of writing this book) is developing several standards documents in the form of NFPA 730, entitled "Guide for Premises Security," and NFPA 731, entitled "Standard for the Installation of Electronic Premises Security Systems."

NFPA 730 offers information and recommendations for protecting various types of facilities, from one- and two-family dwellings to industrial complexes. The document covers exterior and interior security devices and systems, physical security devices, security personnel, and security planning, detailing various aspects ranging from the recommended components of intrusion detection systems to suggested duties of security personnel.

NFPA 731 provides specifications for installing electronic security systems in the included types of facilities.

At the time of publishing their book this document was still under development.

8.2.2 NFPA 472

This standard identifies the levels of competency required of responders to hazardous materials incidents. It defines four different levels of first responders, including the awareness level, operational level, technician level, and incident commander level as well as the types of competencies expected at each of these first responder levels. A wide array of experts from fire fighting and related professions across the country meet as expert committees to carry out this voluntary, industry-based, consensus-based effort. Development of the standard, NFPA 472, is entitled "Standard on Professional Competence of Responders to Hazardous Materials Incidents" which began in 1986; and the current standard was issued in 1997. This document sets out the knowledge and skills (known as "competencies") that should be achieved through emergency response training. These competencies were established for the various levels of emergency response training contained in Occupational Health and Safety Act (OSHA) 29 C.F.R. 1910.120 (q)(6), although the Hazardous Materials Specialist level has been deleted and replaced with various specialty levels of training. Changes in the standard resulted because NFPA technical committees review their standards for currency and update them at least every 5 years. NPFA 472 specifies minimum competencies for those who will respond to hazardous materials incidents and is not intended to restrict any jurisdiction from exceeding these minimum competencies.[2]

Employees of state and local governments in states that do not have OSHA approved health and safety plans are subject to Environmental Protection Agency (EPA) 40 C.F.R. 311. Section 126(f) of the Superfund Amendments Reauthorization Act of 1986 required the EPA to promulgate standards identical to those contained in 29 C.F.R. 1910.120. As a result, state and local government emergency responders enjoy the health and safety protections provided to all workers and are subject to the training requirements detailed in the OSHA regulation. While this regulation cites specific training requirements, it provides limited detail on the wide array of hazardous material emergency response knowledge, known as competencies, needed by emergency response personnel. These competencies were detailed in the National Fire Protection Association's standard NFPA 472.[3]

8.2.3 NFPA 1600

This standard establishes the minimum criteria for disaster/emergency management. It provides common program elements, techniques, and processes for disaster/emergency management planning and operations in the private and public sectors.[4] The Emergency Management Accreditation Program is a voluntary accreditation process for state and local programs responsible for disaster mitigation, preparedness, response, and recovery. An independent team of emergency managers assesses states and local communities to determine whether their emergency response programs meet national standards. These standards are based on NFPA 1600, which is entitled for emergency management and business continuity programs and adapts them specifically for state and local use.

8.3 NORTH AMERICAN ELECTRIC RELIABILITY COUNCIL (NERC)

The North American Electric Reliability Council (NERC) is a not-for-profit organization representing industry-wide organizations that generate, supply, and transmit electrical power throughout the entire United States power grid, and has been operational since 1968. NERC represents ten regional reliability councils, whose members come from all segments of the electric industry: investor-owned utilities; federal power agencies; rural electric cooperatives; state, municipal, and provincial utilities; independent power producers; power marketers; and end-use customers. These entities account for virtually all the electricity supplied and used in the United States, Canada, and a portion of Baja California Norte, Mexico.[5]

8.3.1 NERC STANDARDS

NERC has defined reliability standards that have been developed through an ANSI-accredited process that utilizes a weighted-segment voting structure, in which members of the following nine industry segments vote to approve or reject proposed reliability standards:

- Transmission owners (transmission lines)
- Regional transmission organizations
- Operator and regional reliability councils

- Load-serving entities
- Transmission-dependent utilities
- Electricity producers (generators)
- Brokers, aggregators, marketers
- End-use customers
- Federal, state, and provincial government agencies

NERC works with the North American Energy Standards Board (NAESB) and the Independent System Operator/Regional Transmission Organization Council to ensure that the development of reliability standards and wholesale electric business practices are coordinated and harmonized.

8.3.2 NERC 1200

NERC 1200 were preliminary standards established by NERC several years ago, pertaining mostly to perimeter security. This standard expired in September 2005 and has been superseded by NERC 1300 (now NERC Critical Infrastructure Protection [CIP]).[6]

8.3.3 NERC 1300

Since the power blackout in August 2003 in the northeastern United States, changes have been implemented within the electric industry that have altered many of the traditional mechanisms, incentives, and responsibilities for maintaining reliability to the point that the voluntary systems compliance with reliability standards are no longer adequate. In response to these changes, NERC is promoting the development of a new mandatory system of reliability standards and compliance that would be backstopped in the United States by the Federal Energy Regulatory Commission (FERC).

This will require federal legislation in the United States to provide for the creation of an electric reliability organization with the statutory authority to enforce compliance with reliability standards among all market participants. Legislation has been introduced in Congress that will enable NERC to apply to become that electric reliability organization. In the meantime, NERC encourages compliance with its reliability standards through agreements with its members and through peer pressure among industry participants.[7]

8.3.4 NERC CRITICAL INFRASTRUCTURE PROTECTION

"NERC 1300" was renamed "NERC Critical Infrastructure Protection (CIP)" standard as its intent of the proposed NERC cyber security standards is to ensure that all entities responsible for the reliability of the bulk electric systems in North America identify and protect critical cyber assets that control or could impact the reliability of the bulk electric systems. The implementation plan is based on the following assumptions[8]:

- Cyber Security Standards CIP-002-1 through CIP-009-1 is to be approved by the ballot body and NERC Board of Trustees *no later than November 1, 2005*.
- Responsible entities have registered.

- Cyber Security Standards CIP-002-1 through CIP-009-1 became effective November 1, 2005, and will allow sufficient time for the responsible entities to examine their policies and procedures, assemble the necessary documentation, and meet the requirements of these standards; compliance assessments will commence beginning Q1-2006.

8.3.5 SUBSECTIONS OF NERC CIP

Each document pertains to a different aspect of the NERC Cyber Security Standards which include the following documents[9]:

- CIP-002-1: Critical Cyber Assets
- CIP-003-1: Security Management Controls
- CIP-004-1: Personnel and Training
- CIP-005-1: Electronic Security
- CIP-006-1: Physical Security
- CIP-007-1: Systems Security Management
- CIP-008-1: Incident Reporting and Response Planning
- CIP-009-1: Recovery Plans

8.4 AMERICAN GAS ASSOCIATION (AGA)

The American Gas Association (AGA) represents approximately 200 local energy utility companies that deliver natural gas to more than 60 million homes, businesses, and industries throughout the United States. AGA member companies account for roughly 85% of all natural gas delivered by the nation's local natural gas distribution companies. AGA is an advocate for local natural gas utility companies and provides a broad range of programs and services for member natural gas pipelines, marketers, gatherers, international gas companies, and industry associates. Natural gas meets π of the United States' energy needs.[10] These utilities are part of the critical infrastructure and rely on distributed control systems (System Control and Data Acquisition [SCADA]) networks to control its operations. AGA, in conjunction with Gas Technology Institute (GTI), as well as other industrial groups, has developed AGA 12 in response to the growing need for cyber security standards and protocols for the industry.[11]

8.4.1 AGA 12

This standard represents a partnership between the AGA, the GTI, the Institute of Electrical and Electronics Engineers (IEEE), National Institute of Standards and Technology (NIST), gas and electric utilities operators, control systems (SCADA) along with encryption vendors and security industry experts.[12] The standard establishes best practices in implementing cryptographic protection on control systems (SCADA) communication links. Cryptographic modules implementing this practice will provide the functions, features, and performance specified, and should introduce only minimal interference with normal SCADA communications. Cryptographic system developers should use AGA 12 to design and develop cryptographic solutions. End users should use this report to define requirements for purchasing, installing, commissioning, and operating cryptographic solutions to protect infrastructure against cyber attack.[13]

AGA 12-1 is a draft version of AGA 12 and represents the early standardization stages from an overall system standpoint. Key management has been saved for later standard development.

8.4.2 SUBSECTIONS OF AGA 12

The standards development team recently revised the document structure by splitting it into four distinct sections:

- Part 1 provides guidelines for general cyber security, including threat assessments, security goals, and some encryption *(currently in development)*.
- Part 2 was taken from ISA-SP99 TR1: Technical Report for Field Bus Data Link Layer,[14] covering the more technical aspects of how encryption will work with asynchronous communications.
- Part 3 covers protection of networked systems.
- Part 4 covers protection of embedded components.

8.5 INSTRUMENTATION, SYSTEMS, AND AUTOMATION SOCIETY (ISA)

Founded in 1945, the Instrumentation, Systems, and Automation Society (ISA) is a global, not-for-profit organization that defines and implements standards for automation systems. Based in Research Triangle Park, North Carolina, ISA develops standards; certifies industry professionals; provides education and training; publishes books and technical articles; and hosts the largest conference and exhibition for automation professionals in the Western Hemisphere.[15]

8.5.1 ISA-SP99

The ISA-SP99 establishes standards, recommended practices, technical reports, and related information that defines procedures for implementing electronically secure manufacturing and control systems and security practices and assessing electronic security performance. Guidance is directed towards those responsible for designing, implementing, or managing manufacturing and control systems and shall also apply to users, system integrators, security practitioners, and control systems manufacturers and vendors. ISA SP99 addresses manufacturing and control systems whose compromise could result in any or all of the following situations[16]:

- Endangerment of public and/or personnel safety
- Loss of confidence in the eyes of the public
- Violation of regulatory requirements
- Loss of proprietary and/or confidential information
- Economic and financial loss
- Impacts (overall) to national security, and may have devastating consequences upon other sectors

The concept of manufacturing and control systems electronic security is applied in the broadest possible sense, encompassing all types of facilities and financial systems in all industries. Manufacturing and control systems include, but are not limited to[17]:

- Hardware and software based systems that include Distributed Control Systems (DCS), Programmable Logic Circuits (PLC) and SCADA, networked electronic sensors, and monitoring and diagnostics systems.
- Associated internal, human, network and/or machine interfaces used to provide control, safety, and manufacturing operations functionality to continuous, batch, discrete, and other processes.

ISA-SP99 was completed using the first editions of two key ISA technical reports in 2004. The first technical report is ANSI/ISA-TR99.00.01-2004: Security Technologies for Manufacturing and Control Systems.[18] The second technical report is ANSI/ISA-TR99.00.02-2004: Integrating Electronic Security into the Manufacturing and Control Systems Environment.[19]

8.6   AMERICAN PETROLEUM INSTITUTE (API)

The American Petroleum Institute (API) represents more than 400 members involved in all aspects of the petroleum and natural gas industry.[20]

8.6.1   API 1164

This standard on control systems security provides guidance to the operators of petroleum and natural gas pipeline systems for managing control systems integrity and security. The use of the standards document is not limited to pipelines regulated under Title 49 CFR 195.1, but should be viewed as a listing of best practices to be employed when reviewing and developing standards for control systems. This document embodies the API Security Guidelines for the Petroleum Industry. This guideline is specifically designed to provide the operators with a description of industry practices in control systems security, providing a framework needed to develop sound security practices within the operator's individual companies.[21]

API 1164 was written for the small to medium sized pipeline operator, requiring fairly easy to understand information on securing their control systems. API has no plans at this time for any third-party certifications or to require members to self-certify. Documents from ISA, PCSRF, and other various technical papers will provide better information for the control systems security professional.[22]

8.7   CHEMICAL INDUSTRY DATA EXCHANGE

The Chemical Industry Data Exchange (CIDX) has developed a document titled "Guidance for Addressing Cybersecurity in the Chemicals Sector."[23] This document provides a broad, general guidance and ties in with the American Chemistry Council's (ACC) Responsible Care Program.[24] The Responsible Care Program includes management practices such as "prioritization and periodic analysis of potential security threats, vulnerabilities, and consequences using accepted methodologies."[25] The CIDX document explains how each management practice is applicable to cybersecurity activities and how to apply best practices. Similar to the NERC standards program for the electric industrial sector, this document provides a slight increase in security even though it may never achieve uniform and/or acceptable levels of security across the chemical industrial sector.[26]

8.8   ISO 15408

Formerly referred to as the "Common Criteria" (CC), it was initially published as Version 2.1 in 1999.[27] CC and the associated Common Evaluation Methodology (CEM) have been used by several nations (of which the United States, National Institute of Standards and Technology, and the National Security Agency are members) that are involved in the development of the Common Criteria Recognition Arrangement (CCRA) to gain assurance in products, protection profiles, and so on and evaluated under various circumstances.[28] CC/CEM has been adopted and renamed as ISO 15408, and it works conjunctively with ISO 17799 (another standard) used to reduce and mitigate risk.

CC was initially developed to eliminate redundant evaluation activities; reduce or eliminate activities which contributed little to the final assurance of a product; clarify CC terminology to reduce misunderstandings; restructure and refocus the evaluation activities to those areas where security assurance would truly be gained; and add new CC requirements (as needed).[29] CC defines a common set of security requirements, divided into several functional and assurance requirements which defines two kinds of documents that are built using this common set:

- Protection Profiles (PP): A PP is a document created by a user or user community, and it identifies user security requirements.[30]
- Security Targets (ST): An ST is a document typically created by a system developer that identifies the security capabilities of a particular product. An ST may claim to implement zero or more PPs.[31]

CC originated from three security standards:

- Information Technology Security Evaluation Criteria (ITSEC)
- Trusted Computer System Security Evaluation System (TCSEC) (formerly referred to as "Orange Book")
- Canadian Trusted Computer Product Evaluation Criteria (CTCPEC)

CC was produced by unifying preexisting standards such that companies selling computer products or offering services for defense or intelligence related projects would only need to have them evaluated against one set of standards. The resulting CC/CEM standard was developed through cooperative efforts between the governments from the U.K., France, the Netherlands, Germany, the United States, and Canada.[32]

8.8.1 ISO 17799

ISO/IEC 17799 was an information security standard introduced in December 2000 by the ISO and the International Electrotechnical Commission (IEC) in 2000 entitled: "Information technology — Code of practice for information security management." ISO 17799 was revised and reissued in June 2005.[33]

ISO/IEC 17799 provides best practice methods specific to information security management for use by those who are responsible for initiating, implementing, or maintaining information security management systems. ISO/IEC 17799 contains the following ten main category sections[34]:

- Security Policy
- Security Organization
- Asset Classification and Control
- Personnel Security
- Physical and Environmental Security
- Communications and Operations Management
- Access Control
- Systems Development and Maintenance
- Business Continuity Management
- Compliance

8.9 NIST PCSRF

The National Institute of Standards and Technology (NIST) Process Control Security Requirements Forum (PCSRF) has applied the ISO 15408 Common Criteria and Common Evaluation Methodology to develop security requirements for industrial process control systems. The first draft of the System Protection Profile for Industrial Control Systems (SPP-ICS)[35] was designed to present a cohesive, cross-industry, baseline set of security requirements for new industrial control systems. The SPP-ICS was designed to be an industry voice to the industrial control system vendors and system integrators, defining the security capabilities that are desired in new products and systems. It is a consensus-based specification, not a NIST specification. These security requirements could be specified in procurement Request For Proposals (RFPs) for new industrial control systems. *NOTE: There is no intent to suggest or imply that the federal government will enforce the adaptation of these requirements.*[36]

8.10 HEALTH INSURANCE PORTABILITY AND ACCOUNTABILITY ACT (HIPAA)

In 1996, the federal government instituted the Health Insurance Portability and Accountability Act (HIPAA) to regulate and protect the confidentiality, integrity, and availability of personal health information.[37] The HIPAA was passed by Congress to reform the insurance market and to simplify health care administrative processes. The administrative simplification portion of HIPAA was aimed at reducing administrative costs and any burdens imposed upon the health care industry by adopting and requiring the use of standardized, electronic transmissions of administrative and financial data. HIPAA will most likely have a significant impact on the health care industry over the next several years. The HIPAA rulings require that the Department of Health and Human Services (HHS) adopt a national uniform standard for the electronic transmission of patient health information.[38]

8.10.1 SUBSECTIONS OF HIPAA

There are four primary elements of the HIPAA rulings that are broken down into subcomponents of HIPAA, which are as follows:

1. Privacy standards
2. Transaction Code Sets (TCS) standards
3. Identifier standards
4. Security standards

Security is usually considered to be the technical method by which privacy requirements are enforced and risks posed by increased online transactions through TCS. While this may hold true, analysis of the security rule standards indicated that the authors of the HIPAA Security Rule understood having effective security requires a comprehensive security program addressing administrative, physical, and technical security.

Compliance with the HIPAA Security Rule will require the following prerogatives:

- Security risk assessments to find any issues resulting from noncompliance
- Remediation efforts to improve or adhere to security requirements
- Implementation efforts
- Evaluation of security implementations
- Performance improvements, either resulting from remediation or ongoing compliance activities to ensure continuity of the overall systems

The HIPAA Security Rule standards went into effect on April 21, 2005.

8.11 PATIENT SAFETY AND QUALITY IMPROVEMENT ACT (PSQIA)

Signed into law by President Bush on July 29, 2005, the Patient Safety and Quality Improvement Act (PSQIA)[39] of 2005 is intended to encourage the reporting and analysis of medical errors by providing peer review protection of information reported to patient safety organizations for the purposes of quality improvement and patient safety. These protections will facilitate an environment in which health care providers are able to discuss errors openly and learn from them.[40] The protections apply to certain categories of documents and communications termed "patient safety work product" that are developed in connection with newly created "patient safety organizations." The definition for the term "patient safety organization"[41] is represented "as an organization certified by the Secretary of Health and Human Services that conducts efforts to improve patient safety and the quality of health care delivery through the collection and analysis of patient safety data."[42] This patient safety work product is considered privileged and, therefore, cannot be subject to civil or administrative proceedings, disclosed pursuant to the Freedom of Information Act, or utilized to carry out an adverse personnel action. Patient safety organizations will analyze information reported from providers and disseminate information back to providers in effort to improve quality and patient safety. It is intended that providers, with the assistance of patient safety organizations, will determine the causes of these errors, identify what changes need to be made in the health care delivery system in order to prevent these errors, and then implement these changes.[43]

These new protections *do not*, however, prevent a health care provider from complying with authorized requests for information that has been developed, maintained, or which exists separately from patient safety work product. Providers can also voluntarily disclose nonidentifiable information, and upon authorized request, they can also disclose identifiable information for purposes of improving safety and quality to entities required to comply with the HIPAA. Violations of these provisions are subject to existing penalties under the Public Health Service Act, including a civil monetary penalty or penalties under HIPAA for violations related to individually identifiable health information.[44]

8.11.1 Subsections of PSQIA

The law *does* provide for the following provisions, it[45]:

- Creates/establishes a system for voluntary reporting of medical errors to promote the development of interventions and solutions that will ensure that such errors are not repeated.
- Defines a confidential reporting mechanism to the Patient Safety Organization (PSO), health care providers would be given the opportunity to report any medical errors, incidents of "near misses" and enhanced health care quality practices to PSOs.
- Develops recommendations, interventions, and best practices of PSOs; PSOs may be either private or public organizations or a component of such an organization, and are tasked with analyzing reported patient safety data and developing strategic guidance to give back to health care providers on how to improve patient safety and quality of care.
- Allows PSOs and health care providers to disseminate methods and strategies; PSOs and health care providers may disseminate information on recommended interventions and best practices to other PSOs, health care providers, and consumers, to improve quality of care and enhance patient safety.
- Establishes a federal evidentiary privilege and confidentiality protections mechanism to promote the reporting of all medical errors.
- Grants privileges for data and reports being collected and developed by health care providers, as well as data and reports sent to PSOs.

- Provides that health care providers may report and analyze medical errors without fear of being sued and without compromising patient's legal rights; this nonpunitive environment fosters the sharing of medical error information.
- Preserves current opportunities for discovery such as medical records that exist separately from the patient safety process, and would remain discoverable under state or federal law.
- Promotes the development of national standards to integrate health care technology information systems.

The law *does not* provide for the following provisions[46]:

- Alter existing rights or remedies available to injured patients.
- Compromise patient's privacy rights concerning their medical information.
- *Does not* mandate any punitive reporting system.

8.12 GRAMM-LEACH-BLILEY ACT (GLBA)

The Financial Modernization Act of 1999, also known as the Gramm-Leach-Bliley Act (GLBA), includes provisions to protect consumers' personal financial information held by financial institutions. There are three principal parts to the privacy requirements: the Financial Privacy Rule, Safeguards Rule, and pretexting provisions.[47]

The GLBA gives authority to eight federal agencies and the states to administer and enforce the Financial Privacy Rule and the Safeguards Rule. These two regulations apply to financial institutions, which include banks, securities firms, and insurance companies, but also companies providing many other types of financial products and services to consumers. Among those services are:

- Lending
- Brokering
- Servicing any type of consumer loan
- Transferring or safeguarding money
- Preparing tax returns
- Providing financial advice or credit counseling
- Providing real estate settlement services
- Collecting any consumer debts

Such nontraditional financial institutions are regulated by the Federal Trade Commission (FTC).[48]

8.12.1 Subsections of GLBA

There are two significant rulings which provide the governance of the GLBA:

1. *Financial Privacy Rule* governs the collection and disclosure of customers' personal financial information by financial institutions. It also applies to companies, whether or not they are financial institutions, which receive such information.[49]

2. *Safeguards Rule* requires all financial institutions to design, implement, and maintain safeguards to protect customer information. The Safeguards Rule applies not only to financial institutions that collect information from their own customers, but also to financial institutions — such as credit reporting agencies — that receive customer information from other financial institutions.[50]

The pretexting provisions of the GLBA protect consumers from individuals and companies that obtain their personal financial information under false pretenses, a practice known as pretexting.

8.13 SARBANES-OXLEY ACT

The Sarbanes-Oxley Act of 2002 (SOX) includes provisions that address audits, financial reporting, and disclosure, conflicts of interest, and corporate governance at public companies. The act also establishes new supervisory mechanisms, including the new Public Company Accounting Oversight Board, for accountants and accounting firms that conduct external audits of public companies. The most important provisions of the act that examiners should be aware of are those concerning conducting examinations and inspections of public organizations that are subject to the act and are supervised by the Federal Reserve. It also provides a general overview of the act for affected domestic and foreign banking organizations.[51]

In general, the Sarbanes-Oxley Act applies to public companies, that is, companies (including banks and bank holding companies) that have a class of securities registered under section 12 of the Securities Exchange Act of 1934 (the 1934 Act), or are otherwise required to file periodic reports (for example, 10-Ks and 10-Qs) under section 15(d) of the 1934 Act. Bank holding companies, state member banks, and foreign banks that meet these qualifications (referred to herein as public banking organizations) are subject to the requirements of the Act, as well as any rules and regulations that the Security Exchange Commission (SEC) may adopt to implement the Act. Some of the act's provisions are currently effective, while others will become effective on a specified future date or upon the issuance of implementing rules by the SEC.[52] Security provisions are found under auditing controls under the control of Section 404 of the Sarbanes-Oxley Act.[53]

8.14 THE AMERICAN NATIONAL STANDARDS INSTITUTE (ANSI)-HOMELAND SECURITY STANDARDS DATABASE (HSSD)

The American National Standards Institute (ANSI) announced on June 24, 2005, the operational status of their online Homeland Security Standards Database (HSSD),[54] which is now available. ANSI and the Homeland Security Standards Panel (ANSI-HSSP) undertook the project on behalf of the U.S. Department of Homeland Security (DHS).[55] The database provides a single access portal to homeland security standards critical to jobs of emergency preparedness first responders, code officials, and others charged with keeping the United States and its critical infrastructures secured. The standards in the database are distributed under the following categories:

- Threats
- Emergency Preparedness and Response
- Borders and Transportation
- Information Analysis and Infrastructure Protection
- DHS Adopted Standards

The database provides a catalog number, title of the standard, a brief description or summary of its functionalities, which area it pertains to, and how to obtain a copy of it.

8.15 FEDERAL INFORMATION PROCESSING STANDARDS (FIPS)

Under the Information Technology Management Reform Act (Public Law 104-106), the Secretary of Commerce approves standards and guidelines that are developed by NIST for federal computer systems. These standards and guidelines are issued by NIST as Federal Information Processing Standards (FIPS) for use government-wide. NIST develops FIPS when there are compelling federal government require-ments such as for security and interoperability and there are no acceptable industry standards or solutions.[56]

The Federal Information Security Management Act (FISMA) does not include a statutory provision allowing agencies to waive the provisions of mandatory FIPS. Waivers approved by the head of agencies had been allowed under the Computer Security Act, which was superseded by FISMA. Therefore, the waiver procedures included in many FIPS are no longer in effect.[57]

The applicability sections of each FIPS should be reviewed to determine if the FIPS is mandatory for agency use. FIPS do not apply to national security systems (as defined in Title III, Information Security, of FISMA).[58]

The major focus of NIST activities in information technology is developing tests, measurements, and proof of concept, reference data, and other technical tools to support the development of pivotal, forward-looking technology.[59]

Under Section 5131 of the Information Technology Management Reform Act of 1996 and the Federal Information Security Management Act of 2002 (Public Law 107-347), NIST develops standards, guidelines, and associated methods and tech-niques for federal computer systems.[60] This includes information that is/are:

Needed to assure the cost-effective security and privacy of sensitive informa-tion in federal computer systems.
Needed when there are compelling federal requirements and there are no existing voluntary industry standards.

In accordance with the National Technology Transfer and Advancement Act of 1995 (Public Law 104-113) and administrative policies, NIST supports the devel-opment of voluntary industry standards both nationally and internationally as the preferred source of standards to be used by the federal government. The use of voluntary industry standards eliminates the cost to the government of developing its own standards and furthers the policy of reliance upon the private sector to supply goods and services to the government. NIST collaborates with national and international standards committees, users, industry groups, consortia, and research and trade organizations to get needed standards developed.[61]

Thus, FIPS are developed only when there are no existing voluntary standards to address federal requirements for the interoperability of different systems, for the portability of data and software, and/or for computer security.[62]

8.15.1 FIPS 113

FIPS 113 specifies a Data Authentication Algorithm (DAA) which, when applied to computer data, automatically and accurately detects unauthorized modifications, both intentional and accidental. Based on FIPS PUB 46, this standard is compatible with requirements adopted by the Department of Treasury and the banking community to protect electronic fund transfer transactions.[63]

8.15.2 FIPS 140-1

FIPS 140-2 superseded this standard on May 25, 2001 (see Section 8.15.3).

8.15.3 FIPS 140-2

FIPS 140-2 was approved by the Secretary of Commerce on May 25, 2001, and supersedes FIPS 140-1. It specifies the security requirements that will be satisfied by a cryptographic module, providing four increasing, qualitative levels intended to cover a wide range of potential applications and environments. The areas covered, related to the secure design and implementation of a cryptographic module, include specification; ports and interfaces; roles, services, and authentication; finite state model; physical security; operational environment; cryptographic key management; electromagnetic interference and electromagnetic compatibility (EMI/EMC); self-tests; design assurance; and mitigation of other attacks.[64]

If the operational environment is a modifiable operational environment, the operating system requirements of the Common Criteria are applicable at Security Levels 2 and above. FIPS 140-1 required evaluated operating systems that referenced the TCSEC classes C2, B1, and B2.[65] However, TCSEC is no longer in use and has been replaced by the Common Criteria. Consequently, FIPS 140-2 now references the Common Criteria for Information Technology Security Evaluation, under the standard ISO/IEC 15408:1999, which has replaced the TCSEC methodology.[66]

The CC and FIPS 140-2 are different in the abstractness and focus of tests. FIPS 140-2 testing is against a defined cryptographic module and provides a suite of conformance tests to four security levels. FIPS 140-2 describes the requirements for cryptographic modules and includes such areas as physical security, key management, self tests, roles and services, and so on. The standard was initially developed in 1994, which was prior to the development of the Common Criteria. Conversely, CC is an evaluation against a created protection profile (PP) or security target (ST).

Typically, a PP covers a broad range of products. CC evaluations do not supersede or replace a validation to both FIPS 140-1 or FIPS 140-2 standards and guidelines. The four security levels identified in FIPS 140-1 and FIPS 140-2 do not map directly to specific CC EAL or to CC functional requirements. A CC certificate cannot be a substitute for a FIPS 140-1 or FIPS 140-2 certificate.[67]

8.15.4   FIPS 180-1

FIPS 180-2 superseded this standard on August 1, 2002 (see Section 8.15.5).

8.15.5   FIPS 180-2

The FIPS 180-2 standard specifies a secured hashing algorithm that is to be used by both the transmitter and intended receiver of a message in computing and verifying a digital signature.[68]

8.15.6   FIPS 186-1

FIPS 186-2 superseded this standard on January 27, 2002 (see Section 8.15.7).

8.15.7   FIPS 186-2

This standard specifies algorithms appropriate for applications requiring a digital, rather than written, signature. A digital signature is represented in a computer as a string of binary digits, and is computed using a set of rules and a set of parameters such that the identity of the signatory and integrity of the data can be verified. An algorithm provides the capability to generate and verify signatures. Signature generation makes use of a private key to generate a digital signature. Signature verification makes use of a public key, which corresponds to, but is not the same as, the private key. Each user possesses a private and public key pair. Private keys are kept secret; public keys may be shared. Anyone can verify the signature of a user by employing that user's public key. Signature generation can be performed only by the possessor of the user's private key. *This revision supersedes FIPS 186-1 in its entirety.*[69]

8.15.8   FIPS 190

FIPS 190 describes the primary alternative methods for verifying the identities of computer system users and provides recommendations to federal agencies and departments for the acquisition and use of technology which supports these methods.[70]

8.15.9   FIPS 191

This guideline discusses threats and vulnerabilities and considers technical security services and security mechanisms. The use of risk management is presented to help the reader to determine Local Area Network (LAN) assets, to identify threats and vulnerabilities, to determine the risk of those threats to the LAN, and to determine the possible security services and mechanisms that may be used to help reduce the risk to the LAN. [71]

8.15.10 FIPS 197

FIPS 197 introduced the Advanced Encryption Standard (AES), which specifies a FIPS-approved cryptographic algorithm that can be used to protect electronic data. The AES algorithm is a symmetrical block cipher that encrypts (encipher) and decrypts (decipher) information. Encryption converts data to an unintelligible form called ciphertext[72]; decrypting the ciphertext converts the data back into its original form, called plaintext.[73] The AES algorithm is capable of using cryptographic keys of 128, 192, and 256 bits to encrypt and decrypt data in blocks of 128 bits.[74]

8.15.11 FIPS 199

FIPS 199 addresses one of the requirements specified in the FISMA of 2002 which requires all federal agencies to develop, document, and implement agency-wide information security programs for the information and information systems that support the operations and the assets of the agency, including those provided or managed by another agency, contractor, or other source. FIPS 199 provides security categorization standards for information and information systems. Security categorization standards make available a common framework and method for expressing security. They promote the effective management and oversight of information security programs, including the coordination of information security efforts throughout the civilian, national security, emergency preparedness, homeland security, and law enforcement communities. Such standards also enable consistent reporting to Office of Management and Budgeting (OMB) and Congress on the adequacy and effectiveness of information security policies, procedures, and practices.[75]

8.15.12 FIPS 201

This standard specifies the architectural and technical requirements for common identification standards for federal employees and contractors. The overall goal is to achieve appropriate security assurance for multiple applications by efficiently verifying the claimed identity of individuals seeking physical access to federally controlled government facilities and electronic access to government information systems.[76] *This standard is currently being developed for HSPD 12.*

8.16 NATIONAL STANDARDS SYSTEMS NETWORK

When first named, the National Standards Systems Network (NSSN) was originally defined as the National Standards Systems Network; however, as global organizations began to contribute data and to develop standards and guidelines, the scope of NSSN went beyond national standards as the service now contains information from over 600 national, foreign, regional, and international standards, compliance, and governance bodies.[77]

8.17 BSR/ASCE/AEI XX-2006

Defined by ASCE, this standard is the recommended electrical installation practices for Control, Communication, and Power (C2P) for critical facilities.[78] This standard addresses hardening techniques and methods for electric power, communications, and control systems for critical infrastructure facilities. Upon its completion it is expected that this standard will provide design professionals with guidance to provide for the continuity of these vital services for buildings and facilities tasked with providing critical infrastructure functions.[79] *This standard is currently under development.*

8.18 BSR T1M1-27-200X

Defined by the Alliance For Telecommunications Industry Solutions (ATIS), this represents a project currently in progress in which it provides a project plan for OAM&P (Operations, Administration, Maintenance and Provisioning) work in T1M1[80] for supporting international and national emergency telecommunications service (ETS) used during recovery operations to restore critical community infrastructure and restore the population to normal living conditions after serious disaster events such as earthquakes, hurricanes, floods, and terrorist attacks.[81] *This standard is currently under development.*

8.19 BSR X9.49-200X

Defined by the Accredited Standards Committee X9, Inc. (ASC X9), this standard provides for secure remote access to financial services: credential management and infrastructure processes.[82] The need for secure remote access to financial services is more critical today than ever, such that X9.49 will [83]:

- Incorporate stronger front-end authentication requirements and methods for online web, wireless, and mobile environments.
- Address the impact of integrating front and back-end management and its security of authentication credentials.
- Address management and security methods of the system infrastructure and application processes.
- Provide compliance control objectives and evaluation criteria suitable for use by practitioners.

This standard is currently under development.

8.20 ASTM F1756-97A (2002)

Defined by ASTM International, this guide provides an overview and guide for the selection and implementation by ship owners and operators of a Fleet Management System (FMS) network of computer services in client/server architectures.[84] The FMS is based upon a wide area enterprise network consisting of an unspecified number of Shipboard Information Technology Platforms (SITP) and one or more shore side Land-Based Information Technology Platforms (LITP), which provides management services for the shipping enterprise. FMS can be understood as a computer system comprised of one or more LITPs and one or more SITPs.[85] This standard was approved and documented into the ANSI library on May 10, 2002.

8.21 QUESTIONS

1. The acronym NFPA means _____ and has what significance?

    Answer: *National Fire Prevention Association.* This is a nonprofit organization that was established more than 100 years ago and is the leading advocate in fire prevention worldwide.

2. NFPA 731 deals with on-site premise security. True or False?

    Answer: *False.* NFPA 731 provides specifications for installing electronic security systems in the included types of facilities.

3. NFPA 472 deals primarily with what aspect?
    a. Emergency preparedness
    b. Hazardous materials spills and containment
    c. Public safety
    d. Identifies levels of compctency of first responders

    Answer: *Identifies levels of competency of first responders* especially during HAZMAT operations.

4. NERC can be simply thought of as what?
    a. Controlling the U.S. power grid
    b. Determining the levels of responsibility of the utilities
    c. Managing incidents power blackouts
    d. Providing methods for backup power during disasters

    Answer: *Controls the U.S. power grid.* Essentially, NERC does the entire set of functions above, but simplistically, they can be thought of as the controlling organization over the entire U.S. power grid.

5. NERC 1300 and NERC CIP are one and the same. True or False?

    Answer: *True.*

6. Which standard defines security controls for gas pipelines?
    a. AGA 12
    b. API 1164
    c. CIDX
    d. ISO 15408

Answer: *API 1164*, which was defined by the American Petroleum Institute. This standard defines security guidance for the operators of petroleum and natural gas pipeline systems for managing control systems integrity and security.

7. Which standard is the development standard for SCADA?
   a. NIST PCSRF
   b. ISO 15408
   c. ISA-SP99
   d. AGA 12

   Answer: *NISC PCSRF*, which means "Process Control Security Requirements Forum" applying the ISO 15408 Common Criteria and Common Evaluation Methodology to develop security requirements for industrial process control systems.

8. In 2005, the federal government aligned itself with another organization to define a standards development area for Homeland Security. What is it?

   Answer: *ANSI-HSSP*. The American National Standards Institute (ANSI) announced on June 24, 2005, the operational status of their online Homeland Security Standards Database (HSSD),[86] which is now available. ANSI and the Homeland Security Standards Panel (ANSI-HSSP) undertook the project on behalf of the U.S. Department of Homeland Security (DHS).[87]

9. The acronym FIPS means

   _____.

   Answer: *Federal Information Processing Standards.*

10. FIPS is controlled by NIST. True or False?

    Answer: *True*.

NOTES

1. http://www.nfpa.org
2. U.S. General Accounting Office, Hazardous Materials Training: DOT and Private Sector Initiatives Generally Complement Each Other, GAO/RCED-00-190 (Washington, D.C., July, 2000).
3. U.S. General Accounting Office, Hazardous Materials Training: DOT and Private Sector Initiatives Generally Complement Each Other, GAO/RCED-00-190 (Washington, D.C., July, 2000).
4. U.S. General Accounting Office, Rail Safety and Security: Some Actions Already Taken to Enhance Rail Security, but Risk-based Plan Needed, GAO-03-435 (Washington, D.C., April, 2003).

5. http://www.nerc.com/about
6. http://www.nerc.com
7. http://www.nerc.com/about
8. NERC Implementation Plan for Cyber Security Standards CIP-002-1 through CIP-009-1 (May 9, 2005).
9. NERC Implementation Plan for Cyber Security Standards CIP-002-1 through CIP-009-1 (May 9, 2005).
10. http://www.aga.org/Content/NavigationMenu/Membership_Services/About_AGA/About_AGA.htm
11. http://www.digitalbond.com/SCADA_security/AGA%2012.htm
12. Cryptographic Protection of SCADA Communications **DRAFT 5**, AGA Report No. 12-1 (April 14, 2005) [AGA 12 Working Group].
13. Cryptographic Protection of SCADA Communications **DRAFT 5**, AGA Report No. 12-1 (April 14, 2005) [AGA 12 Working Group].
14. Digitalbond A Review: ISA-SP99 TR1 Security Technologies for Manufacturing and Control Systems (January 23, 2004).
15. http://www.isa.org
16. ISA-SP99: Manufacturing and Control Systems Security (overview).
17. ISA-SP99: Manufacturing and Control Systems Security (overview).
18. http://www.isa.org/Template.cfmSection=____&Template=/Ecommerce/ProductDisplay.cfm&ProductID=7372
19. http://www.isa.org/Template.cfmSection=____&Template=/Ecommerce/ProductDisplay.cfm&ProductID=7382
20. http://www.digitalbond.com/SCADA_security/API.htm.
21. SCADA Security, First Edition (September 1, 2004) [http://www.techstreet.com/cgi-bin/detail?product_id=1175186]
22. http://www.digitalbond.com/SCADA_security/API.htm
23. CIDX Guidance for Addressing Cybersecurity in the Chemical Sector, Version 2.1 (May 2005).
24. http://www.digitalbond.com/SCADA_security/CIDX.htm
25. CIDX Guidance for Addressing Cybersecurity in the Chemical Sector, Version 2.1 (May 2005).
26. CIDX Guidance for Addressing Cybersecurity in the Chemical Sector, Version 2.1 (May 2005).
27. http://niap.nist.gov/cc-scheme/index.html
28. Common Criteria for Information Technology Security Evaluation, Part 1: Introduction and general model, Version 3.0, Revision 2 (June 2005).
29. Common Criteria for Information Technology Security Evaluation, Part 1: Introduction and general model, Version 3.0, Revision 2 (June 2005).
30. http://en.wikipedia.org/wiki/Common_Criteria
31. http://en.wikipedia.org/wiki/Common_Criteria
32. http://en.wikipedia.org/wiki/Common_Criteria
33. http://en.wikipedia.org/wiki/ISO_17799
34. The Information Systems and Internet Security (ISIS) Laboratory ISO 17799: Infosec: Can you dig it?
35. NIST System Protection Profile - Industrial Control Systems, Version 1.0 (April 14, 2004).
36. http://www.isd.mel.nist.gov/projects/processcontrol
37. http://www.hhs.gov/ocr/hipaa
38. http://www.hhs.gov/ocr/hipaa

39. http://thomas.loc.gov/cgi-bin/bdquery/z?d109:s.00544:
40. http://www.gop.gov/Committeecentral/bills/s544.asp
41. http://thomas.loc.gov/cgi-bin/bdquery/z?d109:SN00544:@@@D&summ2=m&
42. http://thomas.loc.gov/cgi-bin/bdquery/z?d109:SN00544:@@@D&summ2=m&
43. http://www.gop.gov/Committeecentral/bills/s544.asp
44. http://www.gop.gov/Committeecentral/bills/s544.asp
45. http://jeffords.senate.gov/~jeffords/press/05/07/072205patientsafety.html
46. http://jeffords.senate.gov/~jeffords/press/05/07/072205patientsafety.html
47. http://www.ftc.gov/privacy/glbact
48. http://www.ftc.gov/privacy/glbact
49. http://www.ftc.gov/privacy/glbact
50. http://www.ftc.gov/privacy/glbact
51. Board of Governors, Federal Reserve System Memo SR 02-20 (October 29, 2002).
52. Board of Governors, Federal Reserve System Memo SR 02-20 (October 29, 2002).
53. http://www.oalj.dol.gov/public/wblower/refrnc/Sarbanes_Oxley_Act_of_2002.htm
54. http://www.hssd.us
55. http://www.securityinfowatch.com/online/Standards-and-Legislation/4516SIW320
56. http://www.itl.nist.gov/fipspubs/geninfo.htm
57. http://www.itl.nist.gov/fipspubs/geninfo.htm
58. http://www.itl.nist.gov/fipspubs/geninfo.htm
59. http://www.itl.nist.gov/fipspubs/geninfo.htm
60. http://www.itl.nist.gov/fipspubs/geninfo.htm
61. http://www.itl.nist.gov/fipspubs/geninfo.htm
62. http://www.itl.nist.gov/fipspubs/geninfo.htm
63. FEDERAL INFORMATION PROCESSING STANDARDS PUBLICATION FIPS 113, COMPUTER DATA AUTHENTICATION. http://www.itl.nist.gov/fipspubs/fip113.htm
64. FEDERAL INFORMATION PROCESSING STANDARDS PUBLICATION FIPS 140-2 (Supersedes FIPS PUB 140-1, January 11, 1994), SECURITY REQUIREMENTS FOR CRYPTOGRAPHIC MODULES. http://csrc.nist.gov/publications/fips/fips140-2/fips1402.pdf
65. http://csrc.nist.gov/cryptval
66. National Institute of Standards and Technology Communications Security Establishment, Frequently Asked Questions for the Cryptographic Module Validation Program. http://csrc.nist.gov/cryptval/140-1/CMVPFAQ.pdf
67. National Institute of Standards and Technology Communications Security Establishment, Frequently Asked Questions for the Cryptographic Module Validation Program. http://csrc.nist.gov/cryptval/140-1/CMVPFAQ.pdf
68. FEDERAL INFORMATION PROCESSING STANDARDS PUBLICATION FIPS 180-2 (Supersedes FIPS PUB 180-1, 2002 August 1), SECURE HASH STANDARD. http://csrc.nist.gov/publications/fips/fips180-2/fips180-2.pdf
69. FEDERAL INFORMATION PROCESSING STANDARDS PUBLICATION FIPS 186-2 (Supersedes FIPS PUB 186-1, 2000 January 27), DIGITAL SIGNATURE STANDARD(DSS). http://csrc.nist.gov/publications/fips/fips186-2/fips186-2-change1.pdf
70. FEDERAL INFORMATION PROCESSING STANDARDS PUBLICATION FIPS 190, GUIDELINE FOR THE USE OF ADVANCED AUTHENTICATION TECHNOLOGY ALTERNATIVES. http://www.itl.nist.gov/fipspubs/fip190.htm
71. FEDERAL INFORMATION PROCESSING STANDARDS PUBLICATION FIPS 191, GUIDELINE FOR THE ANALYSIS OF LOCAL AREA NETWORK SECURITY. http://www.itl.nist.gov/fipspubs/fip191.htm

72. Ciphertext is encrypted text. The term "plaintext" is unencrypted text as ciphertext is the encrypted result. The term "cipher" sometimes is used interchangeably as a synonym for the term "ciphertext" but more properly refers to the method of encryption rather than its result.

73. Ciphertext is encrypted text. The term "plaintext" is unencrypted text as ciphertext is the encrypted result. The term "cipher" sometimes is used interchangeably as a synonym for the term "ciphertext" but more properly refers to the method of encryption rather than its result.

74. FEDERAL INFORMATION PROCESSING STANDARDS PUBLICATION FIPS 197, Advanced Encryption Standard (AES). http://csrc.nist.gov/publications/fips/fips197/FIPS-PUB-197-final.pdf

75. FEDERAL INFORMATION PROCESSING STANDARDS PUBLICATION FIPS 199, Standards for Security Categorization of Federal Information and Information Systems. http://csrc.nist.gov/publications/fips/fips199/FIPS-PUB-199-final.pdf

76. FEDERAL INFORMATION PROCESSING STANDARDS PUBLICATION FIPS 201. http://csrc.nist.gov/publications/fips/fips201/FIPS-201-022505.pdf

77. http://www.nssn.org/about.html

78. http://www.nssn.org/NssnSearch/DisplayRecord.asp?RecordNo=961976

79. http://www.nssn.org/NssnSearch/DisplayRecord.asp?RecordNo=961976

80. The acronym "T1M1" is itself a communications standard (CMISE/T1M1.5) developed by ANSI; it established telecommunications and operational standards for how all communications would operate.

81. http://www.nssn.org/NssnSearch/DisplayRecord.asp?RecordNo=961516

82. http://www.nssn.org/NssnSearch/DisplayRecord.asp?RecordNo=961747

83. http://www.nssn.org/NssnSearch/DisplayRecord.asp?RecordNo=961747

84. http://www.nssn.org/NssnSearch/DisplayRecord.asp?RecordNo=566925

85. http://www.nssn.org/NssnSearch/DisplayRecord.asp?RecordNo=566925

86. http://www.hssd.us

87. http://www.securityinfowatch.com/online/Standards-and-Legislation/4516SIW320

9 Information Sharing and Analysis Centers (ISAC)

9.1 INTRODUCTION

This chapter outlines all Information Sharing and Analysis Centers (ISAC) established throughout the United States for various critical infrastructure sectors. Not all sectors have ISAC organizations, and as such, may be conglomerated or associated with other sectors' ISAC organizations.

> Editor's Note: At the time of writing this book, there were additional ISAC organizations found or established. Not all ISAC organizations may be listed within this book, and as such, may be revised for future releases.

9.2 WHAT IS A CRITICAL INFRASTRUCTURE ASSET?

A "critical infrastructure asset"[1] is an asset (both physical and logical), which is so vital that its disruption, infiltration, incapacitation, destruction, or misuse would have a debilitating impact on the health, safety, welfare, or economic security of citizens and businesses. Critical infrastructures shall include human, physical, and cyber assets.[2] An example might be a Business Master File (BMF) identified within the Internal Revenue Service (IRS),[3] which is labeled as an IRS critical infrastructure asset; all tax data and related information pertaining to individual business income taxpayers is posted to the BMF so that the file reflects a continuously updated and current record of each taxpayer's account. All settlements with taxpayers are effected through computer processing of the BMF account and the data therein is used for accounting records, for issuance of refund checks, bills or notices, answering inquiries, classifying returns for audit, preparing reports and other matters concerned with the processing and enforcement activities of the Internal Revenue Service.[4]

9.3 WHAT IS AN ISAC?

An Information Sharing and Analysis Center (or ISAC) provides several services that are key-specific to whatever sector (as outlined within Presidential Decision Directive [PDD]-63 and/or Homeland Security Presidential Decision Directive [HSPD]-7) is specified; that is, an ISAC provides the following functions:

- Provides a 24×7 (early) threat and detection warning system, and incident reporting and response processes.
- Provides a "members area" that ensures the protection of member, proprietary, and sensitive information, specific to one (or more) sector(s) (and the companies that they represent).

- Provides an open forum community to all relating members within the sector being serviced by the ISAC (usually limited to only membership).
- Provides tailored/customized-alerting mechanisms based on membership physical and IT-based profiles.
- Information sharing among members; membership decides and determines methods of dissemination.
- Information reports from sources, which include educational institutions, government, law enforcement (along with public safety), vendors supporting the sector; information is consolidated and vetted based upon the criteria established by the membership.
- Information that is facilitated and distributed is sanitized of any classified or proprietary information for general distribution and dissemination to the membership of the ISAC.

9.4 ADVANTAGES OF BELONGING TO AN ISAC

An ISAC is a one-stop clearinghouse for information relating to information technology (IT) threats, physical threats, risks, vulnerabilities, and their solutions. The member company (individual or agency) will better understand the threats and vulnerabilities for that sector to take any appropriate action, when and where necessary. Members may submit information anonymously and receive near-time updates, receiving information, patches, and updates from the 24 × 7 incident response center(s) from sector experts.

9.5 ACCESS TO ISAC INFORMATION

Access to industry-specific sources of information includes the following:

- U.S. and foreign government information (not necessarily publicly released or available through public communications channels).
- National and international Computer Emergency Response Team (CERT) information (also, not necessarily publicly available through public communications channels).
- Law enforcement/public safety agencies, departments and related information.
- Hardware and software vendors and manufacturing information.
- Independent research and analysis information from sector experts.
- Geo-spatial analysis of threats to membership assets within the sector.

9.6 EXPANDED ISAC SERVICES

Expanded membership services allow for the immediate availability of additional services and products at discounted prices, which includes the following:

- Network vulnerability assessments and information obtained from those assessments (recent and historical information is often available).
- On-site incident reporting and response support mechanisms.

- Intrusion investigation and IT/data forensics capabilities (where applicable).
- Remote monitoring of intrusion attempts for either/both physical and/or IT-related intrusions.
- Risk management, mitigation, and its analysis, along with any/all data produced resulting from the investigation process.

9.7 SURFACE TRANSPORTATION ISAC (ST-ISAC)

At the request of the U.S. Department of Transportation (DOT), the Surface Transportation ISAC (ST-ISAC) was formed, which includes the Public Transportation ISAC (PT-ISAC) (as referred to as an "ISAC within an ISAC"), taking advantage of the overarching capabilities of the ST-ISAC to realize economies of scale. The ST-ISAC provides a secure physical and IT-related security capability for owners, operators, and users of the transportation infrastructure(s). Security and threat information is collected from worldwide resources, analyzed, and distributed to members to help protect vital systems from any potential attack (physical or IT-related). The ST-ISAC is owned by the EWA Information and Infrastructure Technologies, Inc. (EWA/IIT), http://www.ewa-iit.com, and coowned by the Association of American Railroads (AAR), http://www.aar.org, and the American Public Transportation Association (APTA), http://www.apta.com.[5]

The ST-ISAC is a natural extension of the railroad industry's "Terrorism Risk Analysis and Security Management Plan"[6] and will work in conjunction with the DOT's Transportation Information Operations Center (TIOC), which will rely on industry resources, receiving information from the AAR/Railinc ST-ISAC, for physical and cyber-related information and to serve as a link with industry.[7]

9.8 PUBLIC TRANSPORTATION ISAC (PT-ISAC)

Through the APTA Executive Committee's Security Task Force, the transit industry identified a nationwide need for sharing security intelligence information. In January 2003, the APTA was designated as the sector coordinator by the DOT in creation of the Public Transit ISAC (PT-ISAC) to further promote security for the public transportation industry. As the designated sector coordinator, APTA serves as the primary contact to organize and bring the public transportation community together to work cooperatively on physical and IT-related security issues. The PT-ISAC collects, analyzes, and distributes critical security and threat-related information from government and private information resources, and is an "ISAC within an ISAC," signifying that it has taken advantage of the already existing support structure mechanisms currently supported by the ST-ISAC, which is sponsored and coordinated by AAR. The PT-ISAC has specialists with security clearances working at government-cleared facilities with secured communications; advantages of being underneath the ST-ISAC are the viability of reporting and support is greatly increased, enhanced, and economies of scale are more easily realized.[8] Best security practices and plans to eliminate threats, attacks, vulnerabilities, and countermeasures are drawn upon to protect the sector's cyber and physical infrastructures.[9]

The PT-ISAC collects, analyzes, and distributes critical cyber and physical security and threat information from various sources such as law enforcement, government operations centers, the intelligence community, the U.S. military, academia, and IT vendors on a 24-hour basis, seven days a week. The PT-ISAC has government-experienced analysts with TOP SECRET and higher clearances working in government-cleared facilities with secure communications focusing on transit-specific information requirements.[10]

There is no cost to the organization for the initial two years of service. Through a two-year grant from the Federal Transit Administration (FTA)[11], APTA has retained a private sector contractor, EWA IIT. EWA IIT, counterterrorism and intelligence community experts, currently operates both the Surface Transportation and Water ISACs.[12]

9.9 AMERICAN PUBLIC TRANSPORTATION ASSOCIATION (APTA)

APTA is a nonprofit international association of over 1500 public and private member organizations including transit systems, commuter rail operators; planning, design, construction, and finance firms; product and service providers; academic institutions; transit associations; and state departments of transportation. APTA members service the public interest by providing safe, efficient, and economical transit services and products. Roughly 90% of all public transportation systems within the United States and Canada are served by APTA members.[13]

9.10 ASSOCIATION OF AMERICAN RAILROADS (AAR)

AAR members include the major freight railroads in the United States, Canada, and Mexico, as well as Amtrak. Based in Washington, D.C., the AAR is committed to keeping the railroads of North America safe, fast, efficient, clean, and technologically advanced, which includes involvement in programs to improve efficiency, safety, and servicing capabilities of the railroad industry. Two subsidiaries of AAR, the Transportation Technology Center, Inc. and Railinc, ensure that railroads remain on the up-to-date on transportation and information technologies.[14]

9.11 TRANSPORTATION TECHNOLOGY CENTER, INC. (TTCI)

The Transportation Technology Center, Inc. (TTCI) is one of two wholly owned subsidiaries of AAR. Located in Pueblo, Colorado, TTCI provides intermodal research and test center information used in both passenger and freight operations. TTCI focuses on programs that will enhance railroad safety, reliability, and productivity, and operates a 24×7 training facility for emergency response personnel responding to transportation accidents involving hazardous materials. The facilities that may conduct any testing are owned by the Federal Railroad Administration but are operated by TTCI.[15]

9.12 RAILINC

Railinc is one of two wholly owned subsidiaries of AAR. Located in Cary, North Carolina, Railinc is the leading provider of information technology and related services to North America's railroads. It has extensive databases that include information such as all rail freight inventories within North America. It also supports one of the world's largest Electronic Data Interchange (EDI) networks, over which approximately 5.8 million messages and transactions are transmitted and processed daily. Railinc also operates a Web-based service in which rail customers can track shipments, receive estimated time of arrival information, order equipment, discover shipping options, and find out pricing information.[16]

9.13 WATER ISAC

Approximately 170,000 public water systems provide water for more than 250 million people in the United States. The Safe Drinking Water Act[17] defines public water system as "a system for the provision to the public of water for human consumption through pipes or other constructed conveyances, if such system has at least 15 service connections or regularly serves at least 25 individuals ... and includes collection, treatment, storage, and distribution facilities used primarily in connection with the system."[18] Environmental Protection Agency (EPA) regulations recognize two primary types of such systems: (1) "community water systems," which provide drinking water to the same people year-round; and (2) "noncommunity water systems," which serve people on a less than year-round basis at such places as schools, factories, or gas stations.[19]

There are approximately 16,000 municipal sewage treatment works, servicing 73% of the U.S. population. Privately owned treatment systems, including septic tanks, serve the remaining population. The Federal Water Pollution Control Act[20] (also known as the Clean Water Act)[21] defines treatment works as "any devices and systems used in the storage, treatment, recycling, and reclamation of municipal sewage or industrial wastes of a liquid nature ... including intercepting sewers, outfall sewers, sewage collection systems ... and any works that will be an integral part of the treatment process."[22]

Physical threats to drinking water systems include chemical, biological, and radiological contaminants and disruption of flow through explosions or other destructive actions. In recent years, much attention has been focused on threats to drinking water systems, particularly in regards to water storage reservoirs. Similar to sewage treatment plants, drinking water facilities may have stockpiles of chemicals that could create fire, explosion, or other hazards. Cyber threats are an increasing concern, given the automated, remote control nature of most drinking water treatment and distribution systems. Systems are also dependent on other critical infrastructure systems such as energy, telecommunications, and transportation. An example might be a water treatment plant that depends on daily deliveries by truck of aluminum sulfate, chlorine, or other chemicals needs an emergency operations plan, if such deliveries are interrupted.

Wastewater treatment facilities have received increasing attention after the September 11, 2001, attacks. Like drinking water plants, they face physical and cyber threats and the vulnerability of dependence on other critical infrastructures. Particular attention has also focused on the large volume of liquid chlorine, sulfur dioxide, and other toxic chemicals that may be stored or in use at sewage and waste remediation facilities and the potential for an explosion to create a toxic cloud that could threaten employees and communities. Some research has occurred with respect to alternative treatment systems and chemicals (such as chlorine bleach or sodium hypochlorite in lieu of liquid chlorine). As such, the importance of establishing the Water ISAC provides a communications continuity between all water districts, organizations, and affiliates.

The Water ISAC provides America's drinking water and wastewater system managers with a forum for sharing and discussing sensitive information via secure electronic bulletin boards. It is a repository for water security data, a resource for education on water security topics, a contact point for resources beyond the world of utilities, and a secure library tailored to the needs of the water sector. The Water ISAC offers a secure database, expert analysis, information gathering, and the rapid distribution of reports and government alerts about threats to America's drinking water and wastewater utilities. It is the most comprehensive and readily available resource about water system vulnerabilities, incidents, and solutions, and provides subscribers with Internet access to exhaustive research for improving the security of their utilities, planning for emergencies, and responding to physical and environmental threats of any kind. A Board of Managers, comprised of appointed water utility managers, consisting of several national drinking water and wastewater organizations, governs the Water ISAC.[23]

9.14 ASSOCIATION OF STATE DRINKING WATER ADMINISTRATORS (ASDWA)

The Association of State Drinking Water Administrators (ASDWA) is a professional association serving state drinking water programs. Formed in 1984 to address a growing need for state administrators to have national representation, ASDWA has become a respected voice for state agents with Congress, EPA, and other professional organizations. ASDWA's principal activities include:

- Representing states' Safe Drinking Water Act (SDWA) implementation issues.
- Keeping Congress informed on key issues related to drinking water, including appropriations, new legislation, contaminants of concern, and program efficiency and effectiveness.
- Informing states about federal and state activities and initiatives through regular communications channels which include newsletters, annual conferences, annual membership meetings, electronic mail, periodical mailings, and facsimiles.
- Providing technical training opportunities to state agencies and water departments.

ASDWA is governed by a Board of Directors consisting of a state program administrator from each of the ten federal regions, the President, the President-Elect (who may also represent a region), and the Past President. The ASDWA Executive Director serves on the Board as an *ex officio* member, with staff personnel located in Washington, D.C., managing the daily activities of the association.[24]

9.15 WATER ENVIRONMENT RESEARCH FOUNDATION (WERF)

The Water Environment Research Foundation (WERF) is a subscriber-based organization consisting of utilities and municipalities, environmental engineering and consulting firms, government agencies, equipment manufacturers, and industrial organizations, all with a common interest in promoting research and development in water quality science and technology. WERF personnel consist of volunteers of environmental professionals who work with subscribers and staff to help select, fund, and coordinate hundreds of research projects specific to water. Investigations from WERF-related research projects include individuals and organizations from municipal agencies, academia, government laboratories, and various industrial and consulting firms specific to the research and development of water collection and treatment systems, watersheds and ecosystems, human and environmental health, and stormwater collection and dispersal. WERF helps its subscribers improve the water environment and protect human health by providing sound, reliable science and innovative, effective, cost-saving technologies for improved management of water resources.[25] It provides information related to advancing science and technology to address water quality issues as they impact water resources, the atmosphere, the lands, and quality of life.[26]

9.16 ASSOCIATION OF METROPOLITAN WATER AGENCIES (AMWA)

The Association of Metropolitan Water Agencies' (AMWA) primary objective is to be the unified and definitive voice for the largest publicly-owned drinking water systems on regulatory, legislative, and security issues. To this end, the association works with Congress and federal agencies to ensure safe and cost-effective federal drinking water laws and regulations and to develop federal-local partnerships to protect water systems and consumers against acts of terrorism. AMWA provides collection and exchange of management, scientific, and technical information to support competitive utility operations, effective utility leadership, safe and secure water supplies, and effective public communication on drinking water quality.[27]

9.17 ASSOCIATION OF METROPOLITAN SEWAGE AGENCIES (AMSA)

The Association of Metropolitan Sewage Agencies (AMSA) represents the interests of the country's wastewater treatment agencies, true environmental practitioners that serve the majority of the sewer population in the United States, and collectively treatment and reclamation of more than 18 billion gallons of wastewater daily. AMSA maintains key roles in the development of environmental legislation, and it works closely with federal regulatory agencies in the implementation of environmental programs. AMSA is a dynamic national organization, involved in all facets of water quality protection. Viewed as a key stakeholder in both the legislative and regulatory arenas, AMSA has built credible, collaborative relationships with members of Congress, presidential administrations, and the EPA. Recent years have reflected heightened involvement in a broadening array of environmental laws and regulations that include the entire scope of ecosystem issues encompassed under the umbrella of watershed management, among them nonpoint source pollution control and the protection of air quality and endangered species.[28]

9.18 NATIONAL ASSOCIATION OF WATER COMPANIES (NAWC)

The National Association of Water Companies (NAWC) is the only national trade association that exclusively represents the private and investor-owned water utility industry. Its members provide safe, reliable drinking water to 22 million Americans across the country. The NAWC seeks to strengthen America's investor-owned drinking water supply industry by affording its members the means to develop responses to federal legislative and state regulatory initiatives having broad impacts on the industry. The association's relations with federal legislators and agency directors, as well as with public service commissions and staff, improve its members' effectiveness in addressing common concerns of the industry; concerns range from federal legislation and water quality regulations to state regulatory decisions having broad implications. NAWC will continue to pursue[29]:

- Favorable amendments to the SDWA.
- Favorable tax legislation.
- Involvement in state regulatory decisions that may set national precedents.
- Education of public utility companies concerning economic realities for investor-owned utilities.
- Sharing of information, through NAWC, its affiliates, and any information provided through publication.

9.19 AMERICAN WATER WORKS ASSOCIATION (AWWA)

The American Water Works Association (AWWA) is a powerful advocate for meeting public health needs of water quality and supply. AWWA serves as the voice of the drinking water community, building and bridging gaps with regulators, legislators, and special interest groups, as well as the general public in its stead as a vital resource to its subscriber-based membership, the water profession, and the public.[30]

9.20 AWWA RESEARCH FOUNDATION (AWWARF)

The AWWA Research Foundation's (AWWARF) mission is the advancement of science of water to improve the quality of life. AWWARF personnel serve as a coordinating group for various research functions. The research agendas are developed utilizing the consultation from subscriber-based membership, drinking water community experts, working professionals, and technical advisor groups. With its member base, hundreds of suggestions are examined to identify high priority projects that are crucial to the drinking water community. The final research agenda is then approved by a Board of Trustees, in which information is disseminated to its member base.[31]

9.21 FINANCIAL SERVICES ISAC (FS-ISAC)

The Financial Services ISAC (FS-ISAC), under the auspices of the President's Commission on Critical Infrastructure Protection, is a private partnership of major banks, brokerages, insurance companies, and utilities and is managed by a board of managers elected by the FS/ISAC membership,[32] and is exclusively for, and designed by, professionals in the banking, securities, and insurance industries. No federal government agency, regulator, or law enforcement agency may access the FS-ISAC incident database. The mission of the FS-ISAC is to disseminate trusted and timely information to increase sector wide knowledge about physical and IT-related security operating risks faced by and within the financial services sector. The FS-ISAC has access to a secure database, analytic tools, and information-gathering and distribution facilities designed to allow authorized people to submit either anonymous or attributed reports about cyber and physical security threats, vulnerabilities, incidents, and recommended solutions. Members have access to information and analysis relating to information provided by other members and obtained from other sources such as federal law enforcement agencies, technology providers, and security associations.[33]

Through the FS-ISAC, some of the nation's leading experts in the financial services sector share and assess threat intelligence provided by its membership and by the National Infrastructure Protection Center (NIPC), an arm of the Department of Homeland Security (DHS), and other public and commercial sources, and assist the NIPC to prepare warnings of threats against the financial services infrastructure. Through the FS-ISAC, the financial service companies pass and receive incident information to and from the federal agencies that are responsible for seeking patterns that may indicate pending threats. The secure FS-ISAC Web site offers security information on the latest physical and cyber vulnerabilities, threats, and incidents related to the banking and finance industries. Physical security, such as regional intelligence, travel advisories, benchmarking, and best practices, are also addressed. In December 2003, the FS-ISAC began devoting a $2 million award from the U.S. Department of the Treasury to programs designed to enhance security awareness for all financial institutions, including providing members with secure collaboration, additional feeds for threats and vulnerabilities, confirmation of alerts, and new analytical capabilities.[34]

Science Applications International Corporation (SAIC) is the service provider for the FS-ISAC.[35]

9.22 SCIENCE APPLICATIONS INTERNATIONAL CORPORATION (SAIC)

Science Applications International Corporation (SAIC) is the nation's largest employee-owned research and engineering company, providing information technology, systems integration, and e-solutions to commercial and government customers.

SAIC engineers and scientists work to solve complex technical problems in national and homeland security, energy, the environment, space, telecommunications, health care, transportation, and logistics.[36]

9.23 ELECTRICITY SECTOR ISAC (ES-ISAC)

The North American Electric Reliability Council (NERC)[37] is the Electricity Sector ISAC (ES-ISAC)that performs essentially the same functions that have been required of NERC for physical sabotage and terrorism, and it coordinates all activities between the NIPC[38] and the Critical Infrastructure Protection Advisory Group (CIPAG).[39] NERC created CIPAG to evaluate sharing cyber and physical incident data affecting the bulk electric systems throughout North America. This advisory group, which reports to NERC's Board of Trustees, has Regional Reliability Council and industry sector representation as well as participation by the Critical Infrastructure Assurance Office in the Department of Commerce (CIAO) (which is now part of the Department of Homeland Security)[40], U.S. Department of Energy (DOE), NIPC (also assimilated into the Department of Homeland Security)[41], and the Federal Energy Regulatory Commission (FERC).[42] CIPAG activities are conducted so as to reduce the vulnerability of the North American bulk electric system to the effects of physical and cyber terrorism. The advisory group's activities include developing recommendations and practices related to monitoring, detection, protection, restoration, training, and exercises.[43]

For electricity sector segments to be represented within any given Critical Infrastructure Protection (CIP) development process, participants must include dedicated personnel from the electricity sector who represent physical, cyber, and operations security. NERC is recognized as a representative organization of the electricity sector for this coordination function, as demonstrated by NERC's performance as project coordinator for the electricity sector for the Year 2000 transition.[44] The security committees and communities associated with industry organizations (American Public Power Association, Canadian Electricity Association, Edison Electric Institute, and National Rural Electric Cooperative Association) provide the expertise for physical security in the electricity sector to complement NERC's existing operational and cyber security expertise.

The advisory group relies on small self-directed working teams, which appeared to be an effective method for developing detailed processes, and practices by subject matter experts, concluded with peer review in forum environments.[45]

After CIPAG established its relationship with the Sector Liaison, the U.S. DOE, the advisory group and representatives of the DOE met with the NIPC.[46] From this has emerged a close security working relationship that resulted in the development of the electricity sector's NIPC Indications, Analysis, and Warning Program (IAWP).[47,48]

The IAWP provides several reporting mechanisms that enable reliable and secure communications between electricity sector entities and the NIPC; the IAWP operating procedures contain several event criteria and thresholds with report timing for nine physical/operational and six cyber/social engineering event types. Those events to be reported include those occurrences to an electricity sector entity that are either of known malicious intent or are of unknown origin. Events include such things as the loss of a key element of an electric power system or telecommunications critical to system operations, announced threats, intelligence gathering (surveillance), and computer system intrusion detection (each event type contains specificity as to level of actual or potential impact on operations of the reporting electric entity).[49] The IAWP evolved from this work, and implemented in July 2000; initial emphasis was on reporting mechanisms established by NERC Reliability Coordinators and utility control areas. Individual electric utilities, marketers, and other electricity supply and delivery entities have been encouraged to participate by submitting incident data and receiving the various types of NIPC warnings and related materials.[50]

With board approval, NERC announced the ES-ISAC in October 2000. This function has grown in capability and support since then and is staffed by NERC personnel who consult with particular subject matter experts throughout the electricity sector.[51]

The CIPAG provides oversight to the ES-ISAC with regular reviews at each meeting.[52]

Essentially, the CIPAG oversees just about everything, with several security and critical infrastructure protection reliability groups reporting or communicating with it, with the ES-ISAC collecting, analyzing, and disseminating critical information to ES-ISAC participants.[53]

The mission of the ES-ISAC is to disseminate and establish communications channels with an ISAC to communicate with its members, its government partners, and other ISACs about threat indications, vulnerabilities, and protective strategies.[54] ISACs work together to better understand cross-industry dependencies and to account for them in emergency response planning. All entities within the electricity sector are participants with the ES-ISAC.[55]

The ES-ISAC and CIPAG coordinate with many organizations, including[56]:

- American Gas Association
- American Petroleum Institute
- American Public Power Association
- Canadian Electricity Association
- Critical Infrastructure Assurance Office (now part of DHS)
- Department of Defense
- Department of Energy (including several national laboratories)
- Department of the Interior
- Edison Electric Institute
- Electric Power Supply Association
- Electricity Consumers Council
- Federal Energy Regulatory Commission
- National Infrastructure Protection Center (now part of DHS)
- National Rural Electric Cooperative Association
- Nuclear Energy Institute
- Nuclear Regulatory Commission
- Oil and Gas Sector Partnership for Critical Infrastructure
- Rural Utility Services

The ES-ISAC is funded as part of the NERC budget, which is approved by an independent Board of Trustees. There are no fees to those participating from any electricity sector entities.[57]

9.24 EMERGENCY MANAGEMENT AND RESPONSE ISAC (EMR-ISAC)

The mission of the Emergency Management and Response-Information Sharing and Analysis Center (EMR-ISAC) is to promote critical infrastructure protection and the deterrence or mitigation of "all-hazards" attacks by providing timely and consequential information to the Emergency Services Sector (ESS) of the nation. In October 2000, the United States Fire Administration (now part of the Federal Emergency Management Agency [FEMA], which is part of the Department of Homeland Security [DHS]), http://www.usfa.fema.gov, established the EMR-ISAC to develop and manage the CIP program in support of federal government initiatives. On the local level, community leaders, including emergency response organizations, have the responsibility to determine which infrastructures must be protected from attacks by people, nature, or hazardous materials (HAZMAT) accidents. The EMR-ISAC performs the following major tasks to accomplish this mission and assist community and agency leadership[58]:

- Conducts daily research for current CIP issues.
- Facilitates CIP information sharing between the DHS and ESS.
- Publishes weekly *INFOGRAM Newsletters* and periodic *CIP Bulletins*.
- Disseminates CIP notices "For Official Use Only" (FOUO).
- Develops instructional materials for CIP implementation or training needs.
- Provides technical CIP assistance to the ESS leadership.

Primarily, the EMR-ISAC offers no-cost CIP consultation services to ESS leaders by a variety of convenient methods. To assist the implementation of CIP, the EMR-ISAC also published a CIP Process Job Aid and Homeland Security Advisory System Guide, which are posted on the USFA Web site. Additionally, the EMR-ISAC offers quick and user-friendly CIP portals on the DISASTERHELP.GOV Web site. By using the Internet-based, nonsecure portals, registered and verified users of DISASTERHELP.GOV will receive the following:

- *INFOGRAM Newsletters*: Contain four very short articles about the protection of the critical infrastructures of communities and their emergency responders, issued weekly.[59]
- *CIP Bulletins*: Contain timely, consequential homeland security information affecting the CIP of emergency response agencies, published as needed.[60]

Furthermore, the EMR-ISAC disseminates DHS CIP information (FOUO) to the ESS key leaders through the secure portals of DISASTERHELP.GOV, http://www.disasterhelp.gov. These CIP (FOUO) notices contain emergent, action-able information regarding threats and vulnerabilities to support effective advanced preparedness, protection, and mitigation activities.[61] To receive electronic CIP (FOUO) notifications, senior emergency managers, fire, EMS, and police department chief and deputy chief officers, and fire marshals must subscribe to receive the INFOGRAM newsletters and complete the online application.[62] Only senior leadership positions will receive CIP (FOUO) notices after their identity has been validated.[63]

9.25 INFORMATION TECHNOLOGY ISAC (IT-ISAC)

CSC helped found the IT-ISAC in January 2001 in response to PDD-63. PDD-63 called for increased cooperation and partnership between the federal government and the private sector to address critical cyber and physical infrastructure vulnera-bilities. IT-ISAC and other ISACs formed in other industries became even more important following the events of September 11, 2001, and again with the formation of the DHS. IT-ISAC is a coalition of leading IT companies that provides members with real-time and historical information about urgent alerts, security news, vulner-abilities, viruses, and other threats, thus providing a comprehensive picture of current Internet threats. It provides a forum for information sharing, joint analysis, and incident response coordination with the other sector ISAC and the federal govern-ment to protect critical infrastructure.[64]

9.26 NATIONAL COORDINATING CENTER FOR TELECOMMUNICATIONS (NCC-ISAC)

In January 2000, the National Coordinator for Security, Infrastructure Protection, and Counterterrorism designated the National Coordinating Center for Telecommunica-tions (NCC)-ISAC as the ISAC for telecommunications. On March 1, 2000, the NCC-ISAC commenced operations. The initial NCC-ISAC membership is based on NCC membership, which is evolving to reflect a broader base of technologies comprising the telecommunications infrastructure. NCC-ISAC will support the mission assigned by Executive Order 12472 and the national critical infrastructure protection goals of government and industry. The NCC-ISAC will facilitate voluntary collaboration and information sharing among its participants gathering information on vulnerabilities, threats, intrusions, and anomalies from telecommunications industry, government, and other sources. The NCC-ISAC will analyze the data with the goal of averting or mitigating impact upon the telecommunications infrastructure.[65] Additionally, data will be used to establish baseline statistics and patterns and maintained to provide a library of historical data. Results are sanitized and disseminated in accordance with sharing agreements established for that purpose by the NCC-ISAC participants. In October 1999, the Network Reliability and Interoperability Council (NRIC) IV recommended a voluntary outage reporting trial by commercial mobile radio, satellite, cable, data networking, and Internet service providers. Participants are to alert the NCC of outages likely to have significant public impact.[66]

9.27   COMMUNICATIONS RESOURCE INFORMATION SHARING (CRIS)

Many federal departments and agencies possess telecommunications assets, services, and capabilities, which could be made available to other federal departments and agencies during emergency situations. The National Communications System (NCS) Communications Resource Information Sharing (CRIS) initiative established an information source, which identifies transportable communications equipment, over-the-counter services, and fixed communications networks of the federal government, which could be used on a shared basis with other federal organizations to support national security and emergency preparedness (NS/EP) requirements. NCS Directive 3-9, CRIS Initiative, approved by the Executive Office of the President in February 1996, established the program. CRIS further implements Executive Order No. 12472, "Assignment of National Security and Emergency Preparedness Telecommunications Functions,"[67] dated April 3, 1984. Participation in the CRIS initiative is open to all NCS member organizations and their affiliates on a voluntary basis. Identification of telecommunications resources for use in CRIS is also on a voluntary basis, and the sharing of such resources is not to interfere with the organization's mission. Twenty-six federal and industrial organizations currently contribute resources to CRIS. Telecommunications resources identified for use in CRIS consist of agency points of contact, associated communications resources, and supporting information. CRIS resources are listed as source data in NCSH 3-9-1, CRIS Directory, which is processed and maintained as an NCS Issuance System document. Guidance and direction for the CRIS initiative is the responsibility of the NCS CRIS Working Group. Made up of representatives from the NCS member organizations, the CRIS Working Group is a formally established standing committee under the NCS Council of Representatives (COR). The NCS Committee of Principals (COP) in accordance with NCS Issuance System procedures establishes policy for the CRIS initiative. Day-to-day administration of CRIS is provided by the Chief Operations Division (N3), and NCS.[68]

9.28   GOVERNMENT EMERGENCY TELECOMMUNICATIONS SERVICE (GETS)

The Government Emergency Telecommunications Service (GETS) is a White House-directed emergency phone service provided by the NCS in the Information Analysis and Infrastructure Protection Division of the Department of Homeland Security. GETS supports federal, state, local, and tribal government, industry, and nongovernmental organization (NGO) personnel performing their NS/EP objectives.

GETS provides emergency access and priority processing in the local and long distance segments of the Public Switched Telephone Network (PSTN). It is intended for use in an emergency or crisis situation when the PSTN is congested and the probability of completing a call over normal or other alternate telecommunication means has significantly decreased. GETS is necessary because of the increasing reliance on telecommunications. The economic viability and technical feasibility of such advances as nationwide fiber optic networks, high-speed digital switching, and intelligent features have revolutionized the way we communicate. This growth has been accompanied by an increased vulnerability to network congestion and system failures.

Although backup systems are in place, disruptions in service can still occur. Recent events have shown that natural disasters, power outages, fiber cable cuts, and software problems can cripple the telephone services of entire regions. Additionally, congestion in the PSTN, such as the well-documented "Mother's Day phenomenon," can prevent access to circuits. However, during times of emergency, crisis, or war, personnel with NS/EP missions need to know that their calls will go through. GETS addresses this need.

Using enhancements based on existing commercial technology, GETS allows the NS/EP community to communicate over existing PSTN paths with a high likelihood of call completion during the most severe conditions of high-traffic congestion and disruption. The result is a cost-effective, easy-to-use emergency telephone service that is accessed through a simple dialing plan and Personal Identification Number (PIN) card verification methodology. It is maintained in a constant state of readiness as a means to overcome network outages through such methods as enhanced routing and priority treatment.

To provide guidance to financial organizations seeking sponsorship for NCS services, the Financial and Banking Information Infrastructure Committee (FBIIC)[69,70] developed policies on the sponsorship of priority telecommunications access for private sector entities through the NCS. The goal of the policies was two-fold: (1) to make financial organizations aware of NCS programs and, (2) to provide a consistent set of guidance regarding qualification criteria and the appropriate process for interested organizations.[71]

As a first step, on July 22, 2002, the FBIIC established a policy and process to sponsor qualifying financial sector institutions for GETS. GETS was designed to help assure communication between key public and private sector personnel during times of crisis.[72]

On December 11, 2002, the FBIIC established a policy and process to sponsor qualifying financial sector organizations for the NCS Telecommunications Service Priority (TSP) Program.[73] The TSP Program was developed to ensure priority treatment for the nation's most important telecommunications services.[74]

On July 22, 2002, the GETS policy was updated to include the NCS Wireless Priority Services (WPS). Both GETS and WPS are designed to help assure communication between key public and private sector personnel during times of crisis.[75] GETS uses these major types of networks[76]:

- The local networks provided by Local Exchange Carriers (LECs) and wireless providers such as cellular carriers and personal communications services (PCS).
- The major long-distance networks provided by Interexchange Carriers (IXCs) which include AT&T, MCI Nextel, and Sprint (now owned by Verizon), including their international services.
- Government-leased networks such as the Federal Technology Service (FTS) and the Defense Switched Network (DSN).

GETS is accessed through a universal access number using common telephone equipment such as a standard desk set, STU-III, facsimile, modem, or wireless phone. A prompt will direct the entry of your PIN and the telephone number. Once authenticated as a valid user, the call is identified as an "NS/EP call," receiving priority treatment.[77]

There are five broad categories that serve as guidelines for determining who may qualify as a GETS user:[78]

1. National security leadership.
2. National security posture and U.S. population attack warning.
3. Public health, safety, and maintenance of law and order.
4. Public welfare and maintenance of national economic posture.
5. Disaster recovery.

The FBIIC agencies have determined that to qualify for GETS sponsorship, organizations must support the performance of NS/EP functions necessary to maintain the national economic posture during any national or regional emergency. In particular, the FBIIC agencies view maintenance of the national economic posture as the minimization of systemic disruption to the financial system directly related to the operation of critical financial markets and related essential services and systems.[79]

Essential services and systems are those that have no easily accessible substitute and that are necessary to support one of three critical NS/EP functions in key financial markets and payment mechanisms: necessary crisis response and coordination activities; resumption and maintenance of economic activity; and the orderly completion of outstanding financial transactions and necessary offsetting transactions. Essential services and systems include[80]:

- Critical funds transfers systems (wholesale/large-value payment systems).
- Securities and derivatives clearing and settlement systems.
- Supporting communication systems and service providers.
- Key financial market trading systems and exchanges.

Private sector financial organizations and their service providers may qualify for GETS sponsorship if they play a significant role in one or more financial markets or essential services or systems. In determination of whether an individual organization plays a significant role, the appropriate FBIIC member agency may consider whether the organization[81]:

- Is a registered securities or futures exchange, self-regulatory organization, registered securities clearing agency/depository and futures clearinghouse, and their critical service providers and utilities.
- Acts as a market utility for effecting payments or clearance and settlement of transactions.
- Processes a large aggregate value of daily payments.
- Provides critical services or systems to financial institutions.

- Has a national or large regional presence in one or more product lines.
- Demonstrates other facts or circumstances that suggest facilitating the organization's access to the GETS priority service in times of national emergency would serve to maintain the national economic posture.

The FBIIC agencies may contact those organizations that clearly qualify under these criteria and inform them of the availability of GETS sponsorship.[82,83]

9.29 TELECOMMUNICATIONS SERVICE PRIORITY (TSP)

The Telecommunications Service Priority (TSP) Program provides NS/EP users' priority authorization of telecommunications services that are vital to coordinating and responding to crises. Telecommunications services are defined as the transmission, emission, or reception of intelligence of any nature, by wire, cable, satellite, fiber optics, laser, radio visual, or other electronic, electric, electromagnetic, or acoustically coupled means, or any combination thereof. As a result of hurricanes, floods, earthquakes, and other natural or man-made disasters, telecommunications service vendors may become overwhelmed with requests for new telecommunications services and requirements to restore existing telecommunications services. The TSP Program provides service vendors with a Federal Communications Commission (FCC) mandate for prioritizing service requests by identifying those services critical to NS/EP. A telecommunications service with a TSP assignment is assured of receiving full attention by the service vendor before a service that is not TSP. The procedures identified here are applicable to the Manager, NCS; NCS member organizations; and other federal executive entities participating in the TSP Program. All other telecommunications service users (for example, state, local, foreign governments, or private industry) who request and obtain a TSP assignment agree to its application by their use of the TSP Program.[84] The TSP system replaced the Restoration Priority (RP) system effective September 1990.[85]

9.30 SHARED RESOURCES HIGH FREQUENCY RADIO PROGRAM (SHARES)

The NCS, in its role of planning and preparing for NS/EP, has undertaken a number of initiatives to provide communications to support all hazardous situations. One of these initiatives, developed through the combined efforts of the 23 NCS member organizations, is the SHAred RESources (SHARES) High Frequency (HF) Radio Program. The purpose of SHARES is to provide a single, interagency emergency message handling system by bringing together existing HF radio resources of federal, state, and industry organizations when normal communications are destroyed or unavailable for the transmission of national security and emergency preparedness information. SHARES further implements Executive Order No. 12472, Assignment of National Security and Emergency Preparedness Telecommunications Functions,[86] dated April 3, 1984.

As of July 2004, over 1000 HF radio stations, representing 93 federal, state, and industry entities are resource contributors to the SHARES HF Radio Program. SHARES stations are located in every state and at 20 overseas locations. Roughly 194 emergency planning and response personnel also participate in SHARES. Over 90 HF frequencies have been authorized for use in SHARES. A SHARES Bulletin is published periodically to keep members updated on program activities.

SHARES provide the federal community a forum for addressing issues affecting HF radio interoperability. The SHARES HF Interoperability Working Group (IWG), established as a permanent standing committee under the NCS Council of Representatives, is responsible for providing guidance and direction for the SHARES radio network, and for fostering interoperability of federal HF radio systems through examination of regulatory, procedural, and technical issues.[87]

The SHARES HF Interoperability Working Group currently consists of 91 members and 105 participating entities vice organizations. Overall support for the SHARES HF Radio Program is the responsibility of the Manager, National Communications System. The Chief, Operations Division, Office of the Manager, NCS, is responsible for administering the SHARES program. The Manager, National Coordinating Center for Telecommunications, is responsible for day-to-day operations of SHARES.[88]

9.31 NETWORK RELIABILITY AND INTEROPERABILITY COUNCIL (NRIC)

In October 1999, the Network Reliability and Interoperability Council (NRIC) IV recommended a voluntary outage reporting trial by commercial mobile radio, satellite, cable, data networking, and Internet service providers. Trial participants were alerted to contact the NCC of any outages likely to have a significant public impact.[89]

9.32 NATIONAL SECURITY TELECOMMUNICATIONS ADVISORY COMMITTEE (NSTAC)

President Ronald Reagan created the National Security Telecommunications Advisory Committee (NSTAC) by Executive Order 12382 in September 1982. Since then, the NSTAC has served four presidents.[90]

Composed of up to thirty industry chief executives representing the major communications and network service providers and information technology, finance, and aerospace companies, the NSTAC provides industry-based advice and expertise to the president on issues and problems related to implementing NS/EP communications policy. Since its inception, the NSTAC has addressed a wide range of policy and technical issues regarding communications, information systems, information assurance, critical infrastructure protection, and other NS/EP communications concerns.

NS/EP communications enable the government to make an immediate and coordinated response to all emergencies, whether caused by a natural disaster such as a hurricane, an act of domestic terrorism such as the Oklahoma City bombing and the September 11th attacks, a man-made disaster, or a cyber attack.

NS/EP communications allow the President of the United States and other senior administration officials to be continually accessible, even under stressed conditions. The impact of today's dynamic technological and regulatory environment is profound: new technologies and the increasingly competitive marketplace combine to bring both new opportunities and new vulnerabilities to the information infrastructure.

The NSTAC is strongly positioned to offer advice to the President on how to:

- Leverage this dynamic environment to enrich NS/EP communications capabilities and ensure that new architectures fulfill requirements to support NS/EP operations.
- Avoid introducing vulnerabilities into the information infrastructure that could adversely affect NS/EP communications services.

For almost two decades, industry chief executives from communications and information technology companies have offered their expertise to give the president NSTAC's independent, private sector, nonpartisan, provider-based perspective. By virtue of its mandate to address NS/EP communications issues, the NSTAC's partnership with government through the NCS is unique in two ways — direct industry involvement with both the defense agencies and the civil agencies comprising the NCS; and regular, sustained interaction between industry and the NCS member departments and agencies through the NCC-ISAC, and the Network Security Information Exchange (NSIE) process.[91] The NSTAC's perspective and its experiences with a broad range of federal departments and agencies make the NSTAC a key strategic resource for the president and his national security team in their efforts to protect our nation's critical infrastructures in today's dynamic environment. The NSTAC's current work plan includes initiatives that intersect with several programs set forth in the National Plan for Information Systems Protection, that is, information sharing, the security and reliability of converged networks, and research and development (R&D) issues related to converged networks. Thirty years ago, NS/EP communications services were provided by a communications infrastructure based on a discrete, monolithic, domestic, terrestrial, circuit-switched voice network, supported primarily by mechanical controls.[92]

Today's communications infrastructure is composed of interdependent, diverse, circuit and packet switched networks using terrestrial, satellite, and wireless transmissions systems to support voice, data, image, and video communications, supported primarily by software-based controls. Globalization introduces another element of diversity and interdependence, as domestic service providers establish joint ventures, or merge, with foreign-service providers.[93] Communications networks and information systems have inextricably converged into an information infrastructure in which neither communications nor information processing can fully function without the other. This growth and convergence have offered capabilities and applications that have profoundly changed how both the public and private sectors conduct business, increasing their dependence on the technologies comprising the information infrastructure.[94]

Although it is critical to the government, the information infrastructure is owned and operated by the private sector. Consequently, the government is unable to fully address NS/EP communications issues associated with the information infrastructure without a government-industry partnership, such as that offered by NSTAC.[95]

As the strategic and technological environments have changed, NSTAC's work has kept pace with these changes and has evolved from an initial emphasis on NS/EP communications to a broader scope that encompasses the information infrastructure. Today NSTAC offers advice to the president on policy issues affecting not only the government's ability to leverage the information infrastructure to better support NS/EP operations but also the government's ability to protect the information infrastructure itself from threats and vulnerabilities that might ultimately jeopardize the country's national and economic security.[96]

The NSTAC has addressed numerous issues in the past 18 years. Three accomplishments best illustrate NSTAC's capabilities to address NS/EP communications issues in today's environment: the establishment of the NCC and its ISAC; the implementation of the government and NSTAC NSIE process; and the examination of the NS/EP implications of Internet technologies and the vulnerabilities of converged networks. These accomplishments are briefly described below. The NCC was established in 1984 as a result of an NSTAC recommendation to develop a joint government-industry national coordinating mechanism to respond to the federal government's NS/EP communications service requirements. The NCC's mission is to assist in the initiation, coordination, restoration, and reconstitution of NS/EP communications services or facilities. Currently 13 NSTAC member companies are represented in the NCC.[97]

The NSTAC was instrumental in expanding the NCC's responsibilities to include functioning as an ISAC for the telecommunications infrastructure. Established in January 2000, the NCC-ISAC was the second ISAC to be formed following the promulgation of PDD-63 and the first ISAC with both industry and government membership.[98] The NCC-ISAC gathers information about vulnerabilities, threats, intrusions, and anomalies from telecommunications industry, government, and other sources, and then analyzes the data with the goal of averting or mitigating effects on the communications infrastructure.[99] Results are sanitized and disseminated in accordance with sharing agreements established by the NCC-ISAC participants. In 1991, the NSTAC, working with the NCS, recommended establishing a government-industry partnership to reduce the vulnerability of the nation's telecommunications systems to electronic intrusion.[100] The NSIE process was established as a forum in which government and industry could share information in a trusted and confidential environment.[101] The NSIE process continues to function today, demonstrating that industry and government will share sensitive security information if they find value in doing so.[102]

In 1998, PDD-63 called for the establishment of similar information exchange forums to reduce vulnerabilities in all critical infrastructures.[103] In 1999, the NSTAC identified the need for the government to consider how the convergence of traditional circuit switched telecommunications systems with the Internet might affect the government's existing priority communications systems. The NSTAC also recommended that the government determine how it could obtain priority services in the next generation packet-based networks.[104]

9.33 WIRELESS PRIORITY SERVICES (WPS)

In the early 1990s, the OMNCS[105,106] initiated efforts to develop and implement a nationwide cellular priority access capability in support of NS/EP telecommunications and pursued a number of activities to improve cellular call completion during times of network congestion. Subsequently, as a result of a petition filed by the NCS in October 1995, the FCC released a Second Report and Order (FCC-00-242, July 13, 2000) (R&O) on wireless Priority Access Service (PAS). The R&O offers federal liability relief for NS/EP wireless carriers if the service is implemented in accordance with uniform operating procedures. The FCC made PAS voluntary, found it to be in the public interest, and defined five priority levels for NS/EP wireless calls. Wireless Priority Service (WPS), the NCS program implementation of the FCC PAS, is the wireless complement to the wireline GETS.[107]

GETS utilizes the PSTN to provide enhanced wireline priority service to qualified NS/EP personnel. WPS users are authorized and encouraged to use GETS to better their probability of completing their NS/EP call during periods of wireless and wireline network congestion. Wireless network congestion was widespread on September 11, 2001. With wireless traffic demand estimated at up to ten times normal in the affected areas and double nationwide, the need for wireless priority service became a critical and urgent national requirement.[108]

Reacting to the events of September 11, 2001, the National Security Council issued the following guidance to the NCS:

- NCS will move forward on implementing an immediate solution (target: within 60 days) using channel reservation capabilities from one vendor for the Washington, D.C. area, and based on lessons learned in Washington, D.C., the NCS will make a recommendation on whether to expand the immediate solution to other metropolitan areas.
- In parallel, the NCS will proceed with deploying a priority access queuing system for wireless nationwide (target: within 1 year).

This triggered the development of two WPS efforts to overcome the wireless priority access problem:

- *Immediate solution*: A solution using commercially available and readily implemented technology for limited geographic areas.
- *Nationwide solution*: This solution is aimed towards the development of a long-term, nationally available solution.

With the White House guidance in October 2001, the NCS began immediate acquisition of service for the Washington metropolitan area and recommended and proceeded with services for New York City as well. The NCS entered into subcontracts with the Immediate WPS service providers, T-Mobile (previously VoiceStream) and Globalstar.[109]

The NCS provided Globalstar satellite phones to quickly field the Immediate WPS in the Salt Lake City area during the Olympics for over 600 users. Globalstar increased satellite capacity and redirected Utah calls directly to a U.S.-based Earth station. Globalstar also increased landline trunking at the Earth station for Government Emergency Telecommunications Service calls. T-Mobile uses the Global System for Mobile communications (GSM) technology and has capitalized on an existing GSM feature called enhanced Multi-Level Precedence and Preemption (eMLPP).

During congestion, this feature allows the emergency call to queue for the next available radio channel, without preempting any calls in progress.

This immediate capability required an FCC waiver for T-Mobile because it did not initially conform to the R&O requirement to invoke the priority service on a call-by-call basis. This means that all calls using authorized Immediate WPS phones receive priority service when the radio channels are congested. T-Mobile's implementation of the Immediate Solution became operational during May 2002 in Washington and New York. By November 2002, T-Mobile supported 2084 WPS users in Washington and 725 in New York, for a total of 2809 WPS cellular users. Globalstar also supported 906 customers as well.

Due to the requirement for nationwide WPS coverage, multiple carriers and multiple access technologies are needed. WPS is based on the two digital access technologies most widely available in the United States, GSM (that is, AT&T Wireless, Cingular, Nextel [Sprint], and T-Mobile) and Code Division Multiple Access (CDMA) (that is, Sprint PCS and Verizon Wireless). Nationwide WPS is provided in two major phases, Initial Operating Capability (IOC) and Full Operating Capability (FOC).

IOC is a GSM-based solution only, consisting of priority radio channel access at call origination. IOC began December 31, 2002, and it satisfied the requirements of the FCC Second R&O for invocation of the service on a call-by-call basis by dialing the WPS prefix (*272) at the start of each NS/EP WPS call. FOC provides a full, end-to-end capability, beginning with the NS/EP wireless caller, through the wireless networks, through the IntereXchange Carrier (IXC) and/or Local Exchange Carrier (LEC) wireline networks, and to the wireless or wireline called party.

T-Mobile began deploying WPS FOC in December 2003. AT&T Wireless and Cingular began deploying WPS FOC in July 2004. Nextel (now part of Sprint) also deployed WPS in July 2004, and will upgrade to FOC beginning in April 2005.

As of December 2004, there were over 11,000 WPS users. It is the objective of NCS to provide the WPS capability to an estimated NS/EP wireless user population of 200,000 GSM users and 90,000 CDMA users.

Congestion occurs when the network becomes overloaded and is unable to respond to additional requests for service. The PSTN has hundreds of millions of customers, all of whom may try to make a call at the same time. However, it can only accommodate a much smaller percentage of these potential calls simultaneously. When that design threshold is exceeded, congestion occurs. In some cases, this is first recognized by a user being unable to complete calls (slow busy tone), followed by the user's inability to even access the network (fast/rapid busy tone), that can be further followed by the complete loss of dial tone. This can occur as a result of a natural or man-made disaster when the network is being heavily used and needed the most. WPS and GETS are designed to mitigate this situation by providing users with NS/EP missions a higher probability of completion for their emergency calls.

The Nationwide WPS capability is based on wireless standards with Industry Requirements (IR) documents defining specific WPS requirements. The active and cooperative participation of all stakeholders, including major wireless equipment vendors and service providers, successfully produced these IR documents. Definitions of the FOC requirements were initiated in the Fall of 2002 to allow the switch vendors to include WPS capabilities in the next software development cycle.

The NCS has also taken steps to ensure that the use of the nation's cellular telecommunication networks by NS/EP personnel does not hinder public use during emergency events. The FCC issued guidelines for NS/EP use of wireless networks, and only NS/EP leadership and key personnel will be approved to use WPS. For those critical individuals who require the priority service, WPS will be a powerful new emergency communications asset and an important national resource.[110]

WPS works also with SAFECOM. SAFECOM[111] is managed by the DHS Science and Technology (S&T) Directorate's Office for Interoperability and Compatibility (OIC). Its mission is to serve as the umbrella program within the federal government to help local, state, tribal, and federal public safety agencies improve public safety response through more effective and efficient interoperable wireless communications, allowing public safety agencies to talk across disciplines and jurisdictions via radio communications systems, exchanging voice and/or data with one another on demand, in real time, when needed as authorized.[112]

SAFECOM is the first national program designed by public safety for public safety. As a public safety driven program, SAFECOM works with existing federal communications initiatives and key public safety stakeholders to address the need to develop better technologies and processes for the cross-jurisdictional and cross-disciplinary coordination of existing systems and future networks. SAFECOM harnesses diverse federal resources in service of the public safety community.[113]

9.34 ALERTING AND COORDINATION NETWORK (ACN)

The Alerting and Coordination Network (ACN) is an emergency voice communications network for communications service providers.[114]

The network supports NS/EP communications restoration coordination when the public switched network (PSN) is inoperable or congested. It is engineered to provide a reliable and survivable network capability, and has no logical dependency on the PSN. As a result, if the PSN is congested, the ACN will not be affected. ACN members include all of the major telecommunications companies in the United States as well as some federal agencies. Currently, the ACN connects 32 users and the NCC–ISAC. The ACN is one of a number of initiatives sponsored by the NCS in its role of planning and preparing for NS/EP communications within the Department of Homeland Security.

The ACN is operational 24 × 7 to support the NCC–ISAC during normal and emergency operations. The ACN is an emergency communications (voice) network connecting the communications service providers' network operations and/or emergency operation centers to support restoration coordination, transmission of telecommunications requirements and priorities, and incident reporting when the public switched network is inoperable or congested.[115]

9.35 ENERGY ISAC

The Energy ISAC is exclusively for, and designed by, professionals in the energy industries. No federal government agency, regulator, or law enforcement agency can access the Energy ISAC. Other critical industries such as finance and telecommunications have ISACs in place. The threats and vulnerabilities to the energy industry are increasing. The events of September 11, 2001, introduced heightened physical security measures. The energy infrastructure also depends on information technology and telecommunications security. Critical systems include supervisory control and data acquisition (SCADA), trading, Internet-based transactions, and e-commerce. The Energy ISAC is the one-stop clearinghouse for information on threats, vulnerabilities, solutions, and best practices. Members can submit information anonymously and receive near-real-time updates.[116]

9.36 CHEMICAL SECTOR ISAC (CHEM-ISAC)

In 2002, the Chemical Transportation Emergency Center (CHEMTREC®), in conjunction with the former NIPC, created the Chemical Sector ISAC (CHEM-ISAC). The purpose of the CHEM-ISAC was to provide a means for security-related information to move between the multiagency NIPC and the chemical sector. In March 2004, the NIPC was dissolved and the DHS assumed its responsibilities. The CHEM-ISAC now receives information from several divisions within DHS, including the Information Analysis and Infrastructure Protection Division. The goal of the CHEM-ISAC is to enable the chemical sector to receive fast and cost-effective access to sensitive information about cyber, physical, and contamination issues. It accomplishes this by providing a venue for DHS to disseminate assessments, advisories, and alerts to the private sector when such incidents are deemed to have possible serious national security, economic, or social consequences. Since 9/11, CHEMTREC and other elements of the American Chemistry Council (ACC) have worked closely with the DHS and the FBI to provide information to assist federal law enforcement and intelligence agencies better understand the potential threats that might be of concern to the business of chemistry and to provide actionable and timely threat information to industry. This relationship led ACC and CHEMTREC to establish the Chemical Sector ISAC. A primary goal of the Chemical Sector ISAC is to enable DHS, to disseminate timely and actionable assessment, advisories, and alerts to appropriate government and private sector entities when such incidents are deemed to have possible serious national security, economic, or social consequences. The Chemical Sector ISAC is intended for those companies or other organizations involved in the production, storage, transportation, and delivery of chemicals.[117]

Participation by the chemical industry is intended to be inclusive to maximize the value and utility of the ISAC. The Chemical Sector ISAC utilizes CHEMTREC, the chemical industry's 24-hour emergency communication center as the communication link between the DHS and CHEM-ISAC participants. When CHEMTREC receives information from the DHS, that information is immediately transmitted, on an around-the-clock basis, to Chemical Sector ISAC participants utilizing electronic mail and a secure Web site. The Chemical Sector ISAC includes the following key elements:

- A 24-hour, electronic communication network to provide chemical facilities and chemical transportation systems with timely, accurate, and actionable warning for both physical and IT-related threats.
- An electronic communication system that will allow for voluntary and secure electronic reporting to DNS of any malicious, unexplained, or suspicious incidents involving chemical facilities or chemicals in commerce to allow federal intelligence and law enforcement agencies to identify and analyze incidents.[118]

9.37 CHEMICAL TRANSPORTATION EMERGENCY CENTER (CHEMTREC)

CHEMTREC is a 24-hour emergency communications center operated as a public service by the ACC. Since its creation in 1971, CHEMTREC has provided critical emergency communications services to emergency first responders and to shippers of hazardous materials.[119]

9.38 HEALTHCARE SERVICES ISAC (HCISAC)

The health care sector requires a framework through which it can protect the industry from cyber and physical infrastructure threats. Industry collaboration, the adoption of best practices, the development of security standards, and the establishment of a governance structure for the inclusion of new IT systems and communication networks are vital for the industry's future viability. A Healthcare Information Sharing and Analysis Center (HCISAC) must serve as a first responder to such threats and provide a framework to achieve fundamental and vital cyber security objectives for the industry. The purpose of the HCISAC is to protect the components of the health care industry's cyber and physical infrastructure that are essential to patient care delivery. It is the industry's steadfast commitment as a critical sector to act in response to the National Strategy to Secure Cyberspace. The mission of the HCISAC is to gather, analyze, and disseminate to its members an integrated view of cyber and physical threats and vulnerabilities of the health care industry, in partnership with our national Homeland Security activities. HCISAC members will have access to information analyses derived from information provided by several sources, including other HCISAC members, the U.S. government and law enforcement agencies, technology providers, and security associations, and from the private health care sector as a whole. Data collected will be used to provide alerts and develop awareness and responses based on the state of the health care infrastructures and the national threat environment. Through the HCISAC, information such as industry best practices will be shared among HCISAC members and exchanged with the government through the DHS.[120]

9.39 HIGHWAY ISAC

The Highway ISAC is operated by the American Trucking Associations (ATA), in partnership with the state and national trucking associations and conferences of the ATA Federation, numerous other national highway transportation organizations in the HighwayWatch Coalition in cooperation with the Department of Homeland Security, for the benefit of the entire Highway Transportation Sector. This page contains public bulletins and advisories, both national, as well as specific alerts for the highway sector and industry subsectors.[121]

Transportation professionals can observe things such as trucks parked under bridges, routes that make no sense, abandoned rigs, frontline participants who don't really know their business, shipping practices which make no sense, or any of a thousand items that an experienced professional is well suited to discern. Currently operated by the ATA in cooperation with the Transportation Security Administration (TSA) and supported by the HighwayWatch Coalition and Anti-Terrorism Working Group and the National Infrastructure Protection Center of the Department of Homeland Security, the Highway ISAC benefits the entire transportation industry. Its mission is to serve as an alert system, leveraging the Internet and other communication channels to provide the transportation industry with incident, threat, and vulnerability information. By compiling industry and government intelligence in one location, the Highway ISAC assists both the private and public sectors in creating security measures, planning for emergencies, and protecting our nation's citizens and infrastructure.[122]

9.40 CARGO THEFT INFORMATION PROCESSING SYSTEMS (CARGOTIPS)

The Cargo Theft Information Processing System (CargoTIPS) was developed in response to the need for a national cargo theft database. The system was designed as a result of a partnership with law enforcement and the transportation industry to turn the tide on this escalating crime. With cargo theft information ascertained, development of a comprehensive assessment of the problem to begin a counterattack may be formulated.[123]

9.41 AMERICAN TRUCKING ASSOCIATIONS (ATA)

The mission of American Trucking Associations, Inc. is to serve and represent the interests of the trucking industry with one united voice; to positively influence federal and state governmental actions; to advance the trucking industry's image, efficiency, competitiveness, and profitability; to provide educational programs and industry research; to promote highway and driver safety; and to strive for a healthy business environment.[124]

9.42 HIGHWAYWATCH®

HighwayWatch is the roadway sector's national safety and security program that utilizes the skills, experiences, and "road smarts" of America's transportation workers to help protect the nation's critical infrastructure and the transportation of goods, services, and people. HighwayWatch participants are transportation infrastructure workers, commercial and public truck and bus drivers, and other highway sector professionals, and are specially trained to recognize potential safety and security threats and avoid becoming a target of terrorists. The HighwayWatch effort seeks to prevent terrorists from using large vehicles or hazardous cargoes as weapons. HighwayWatch training provides HighwayWatch participants with the observational tools and the opportunity to exercise their expert understanding of the transportation environment to report safety and security concerns rapidly and accurately to the authorities. In addition to matters of homeland security, stranded vehicles or accidents, unsafe road conditions, and other safety-related situations are reported eliciting the appropriate emergence responders. HighwayWatch reports are combined with other information sources and shared both with federal agencies and the roadway transportation sector by the Highway ISAC. After completing the HighwayWatch training, transportation professionals use cellular telephones and other telecommunications equipment to contact emergency personnel through a special HighwayWatch hotline, providing emergency responders with precise location and incident information. A trained operator at the HighwayWatch Call Center verifies the highway professional's identity (each participant has a unique HighwayWatch ID number) and location and then routes the call to the appropriate law enforcement authorities in that area.

The HighwayWatch Call Center correlates the location information and routes the call to the proper response agency in that area or to the proper state or regional emergency dispatch center. Additionally, HighwayWatch training instructs all participants to use 911 for life threatening emergencies.[125]

9.43 FOOD AND AGRICULTURE ISAC

On February 9, 2002, a public/private sector partnership known as the Food and Agriculture ISAC was created. The objectives of the Food and Agriculture ISAC include:

- Making the food industry a difficult and undesirable target for terrorist attacks.
- Bringing the industry's talents together to deal with preventing terrorism and deliberately malicious attacks.
- Providing a rapid means of communicating and disseminating information relevant to those tasks.
- In the event of an attack, providing a means for a coordinated industry-wide response to limit the effect and enable the food system to recover as rapidly as possible.
- To work directly with the NIPC and the FBI's Weapons of Mass Destruction Unit to identify credible threats and craft specific warning messages for the food industry.
- To facilitate the development of, and serve as a central repository for, best practice recommendations and countermeasures for preventing and recovering from malicious attacks; these would include bioterrorism attacks, attacks on physical assets, and cyber attacks on the industry's computer or financial networks.

The Food Marketing Institute (FMI), located in Washington, D.C., coordinates this voluntary industry network. For information on FMI, see the Institute's Web site at www.fmi.org. Because the food supply is a critical national resource, the Food Industry ISAC is supported by FMI at no additional charge to those food industry companies that participate.[126]

9.44 FOOD MARKETING INSTITUTE (FMI)

As the representative of one of the largest single business categories in the world, the Food Marketing Institute will:

- Provide its retail and wholesale membership with a forum to work effectively with government, suppliers, employees, and customers and their communities.
- Promote the principles of free enterprise to ensure a vigorous, competitive, economically healthy food industry.
- Program its efforts and energies in five primary areas: (1) research and development; (2) education; (3) public information and its dissemination; (4) government relations; and, (5) industrial relations.

By pursuing these activities, the FMI will provide leadership and support for the role of the grocery retailer and wholesaler as purchasing agent for our consumers.[127]

9.45 MULTI-STATE ISAC (MS-ISAC)

Recognizing the need for collaboration, a Multi-State (MS-ISAC) was established in January 2003. The MS-ISAC began with the Northeast states and quickly expanded. Currently, there are 49 states and the District of Columbia participating. The goal is to have this MS-ISAC include all fifty states, which would provide a valuable centrally-coordinated mechanism for sharing important security intelligence and information between the states. The MS-ISAC can serve as a critical point of contact between the state and the federal government. A primary goal of the MS-ISAC is to eliminate duplicative efforts. The MS-ISAC member states meet monthly by teleconference to discuss issues and share information relating to each state's cyber security readiness and resilience.

The MS-ISAC has moved quickly since its inception and has been recognized by the Department of Homeland Security for its proactive role in bringing the states together. It is only through collaboration and communication that we can be successful in helping to protect and secure the critical infrastructure that supports all of our citizens and businesses.[128]

9.46 ISAC COUNCIL (ISAC-ISAC)

The mission of the Information Sharing and Analysis Centers Council (ISAC Council) is to advance the physical and cyber security of the critical infrastructures of North America by establishing and maintaining a framework for valuable interaction between and among the ISACs and with government.[129]

9.47 WORLD WIDE ISAC (WW-ISAC)

The World Wide ISAC (WW-ISAC) offers a confidential venue for sharing security vulnerabilities and solutions. It facilitates trust among its participants. Members benefit from the World Wide ISAC organization's means of mitigating cyber-security risks.[130]

9.48 REAL ESTATE ISAC (RE-ISAC)

The Real Estate (RE-ISAC), a not-for-profit organized by The Real Estate Roundtable, was announced in February 2003. The organization represents both coordinated and elevated response efforts towards security-related issues. RE-ISAC is a public-private partnership between the U.S. real estate industry and federal homeland security officials.[131]

Principally, RE-ISAC serves three roles:

1. Disseminate information from the federal government, including terrorist alerts and advisories, to real estate industry participants, and bring government officials and building owners and operators together to assess and evaluate the information so it is more useful and actionable for real estate. With the latest validated intelligence, building owners and operators are better prepared to develop and activate their own counterterrorism activities, including steps to protect people and property.
2. Facilitate the industry's reporting to government authorities of credible threats to real estate assets and enable analysis of the information to detect patterns or trends, and to develop potentially coordinated action steps.
3. Bring private- and public-sector experts together to share useful information, and discuss and develop best practices and solutions on subsector specific issues (such as matters affecting retail or office property owners) or cross-sector issues such as risk assessment, asset fortification/hardening, building security, and emergency-response planning.[132]

9.49 THE REAL ESTATE ROUNDTABLE

The Real Estate Roundtable is the organization that brings together leaders of the nation's top public and privately-held real estate ownership, development, lending, and management firms with the leaders of major national real estate trade associations to jointly address key national policy issues relating to real estate and the overall economy. [133]

9.50 RESEARCH AND EDUCATIONAL NETWORKING ISAC (REN-ISAC)

The Research and Educational Networking (REN-ISAC) supports higher education and the research community by providing advanced security services to national supporting networks, and supports efforts to protect the national cyber infrastructure by participating in the formal sector ISAC infrastructure.[134]

9.51 BIOTECHNOLOGY AND PHARMACEUTICAL ISAC (BIOPHARMA ISAC)

The Biotechnology and Pharmaceutical (BioPharma ISAC) is being established to enhance the security of its members and the nation's critical infrastructure by developing and sharing information on cyber and physical security threats, vulnerabilities, countermeasures, and best practices in the biotechnology and pharmaceutical industry sector.[135]

9.52 MARITIME ISAC (M-ISAC)

The Maritime (M-ISAC) was established specifically to collect, analyze, and disseminate maritime threat information in coordination with the federal government intelligence and security agencies. By its charter, the M-ISAC also works in close cooperation with the U.S. and international port and shipping industries. M-ISAC is intended to serve as the principal means by which the maritime industry communicates security and intelligence concerns with appropriate government agencies. Industry representatives are drawn from strategic seaports and multinational shipping companies. Such information sharing has been made essential in light of the International Ship & Port Facility Security (ISPS) Code, which was adopted by the International Maritime Organization, an arm of the UN. M-ISAC is a not-for-profit Florida corporation and is sponsored by the Maritime Security Council.[136]

For reasons not stated, the Port and Maritime Sector never really created their own ISAC. As such, the United States Coast Guard (USCG) appears to have taken the leadership role, in which sometime in February 2003, the USCG signed a Memorandum of Understanding with the National Response Center (NRC) as well as the FBI's National Infrastructure Protection Center, now part of the DHS Information Analysis and Infrastructure Protectorate (IAIP). The USCG is responsible for the collection of reports of any suspicious activities or behavior within the maritime environments throughout the United States (and its ports), and for the distribution of any threat-related information.[137]

For threat information relating to the Port and Maritime Sector, DHS sends a copy of threat-related information to the USCG Headquarters, located in Washington, D.C., where it is further distributed to the Coast Guard Captains of the Port as well as other command staff. The Captains of the Port, as the Federal Maritime Security Coordinators (defined within the Maritime Transportation Security Act of 2002), distribute threat-related information to their responsible security committee members, other stakeholders for their representative ports, and their affiliates. Currently, the USCG distributes threat-related information to approximately 50 national maritime affiliated associations and their organizations.[138]

Other maritime affiliated organizations now include[139]:

- The meta association responsible for various trade associations.
- The Marine Transportation System National Advisory Council.
- Various harbor operations and/or harbor safety committees.
- Various area maritime security committees.
- Various maritime associations and/or maritime exchanges.
- The Maritime Security Council (MSC).

9.53 MARITIME SECURITY COUNCIL (MSC)

In addition to being the principal clearinghouse for the exchange of information between its carrier members, the Maritime Security Council (MSC) also acts as a liaison with regulators and governments, offering vital intelligence on crimes at sea and information to U.S. Customs to assist with their antidrug efforts. As a consequence of this role, the

MSC assisted in the development of the Sea Carrier Initiative and Super Carrier Programs and actively participates in international activities with the U.S. Drug Control Program, World Customs Organization, and the Baltic and International Maritime Council. Because of its successful assistance to the government, the MSC was the proud recipient of the U.S. Vice President's National Performance Review (or Hammer Award), and has been a maritime security advisor to the White House, National Security Council, U.S. Customs, U.S. Department of Transportation, and the U.S. Coast Guard. In 2000, the Maritime Security Council was appointed as the Technical Advisor to the U.S. State Department's Overseas Security Advisory Council on maritime security issues. The MSC is also an advisor to INTERPOL, the international police organization.[140]

9.54 MARINE TRANSPORTATION SYSTEM NATIONAL ADVISORY COUNCIL

The Marine Transportation System (MTS) consists of waterways, ports, and inter-modal land-based connections, allowing for the various modes of transportation moving both people and goods to, from, and on the water. The MTS National Advisory Council (MTSNAC) is a chartered, nonfederal body, whose sole purpose is to advise the Secretary of Transportation pertaining to MTS issues. Its membership is comprised of leadership members from more than 30 commercial transportation firms, trade associations, state and local public entities, recreational boating interests, academics, and environmental groups. MTSNAC exists to assist policy and decision makers, and also provides general public information that will help the public understand security-related issues, thus permitting greater flexibility and participation pertaining to the development of possible solutions to their issues.[141] Member organizations affiliated with and supporting the MTSNAC include[142]:

- American Association of Port Authorities
- American Great Lakes Ports Association
- American Maritime Congress
- American Trucking Associations
- Association of Metropolitan Planning Organization
- Boat Owners Association of the United States
- Coastwise Coalition
- Gulf of Mexico States Partnership, Inc.
- I-95 Corridor Coalition
- Intermodal Association of North America
- International Longshore and Warehouse Union
- International Longshoreman's Association
- Lake Carriers' Association
- Maritime Information Services of North America
- Maritime Security Council
- National Association of Counties
- National Association of Waterfront Employers
- National Governor's Association
- National Industrial Transportation League

- National Waterways Conference
- Pacific Maritime Association
- Propeller Club of the United States
- Shipbuilders Council of America
- Society of Naval Architects and Marine Engineers
- The Waterfront Coalition
- U.S. Chamber of Commerce
- United States Maritime Alliance, Ltd.
- World Shipping Council

9.55 QUESTIONS

1. The _____ represents an asset that is so vital that its disruption, infiltration, incapacitation, destruction, or misuse would have a debilitating impact on the health, safety, welfare, or economic security of citizens and businesses.

   Answer: *Critical infrastructure asset.* Critical infrastructures shall include human, physical, and cyber assets.[143]

2. The acronym ISAC means _____ .

   Answer: *Information Sharing and Analysis Center.*

3. An ISAC may also be thought of as a _____ .

   Answer: *Information clearinghouse* (or *Clearinghouse*).

4. Access to industrial-specific sources of information includes how many sources?
   a. 5
   b. 7
   c. 6
   d. 8

   Answer: *6.* Those sources include: (1) U.S. and foreign government information; (2) U.S. and foreign emergency response team information; (3) law enforcement information; (4) hardware/software vendor information; (5) independent research and analysis information from sector experts; and (6) geospatial analysis of threats.

5. How many ISACs are there?
   a. 20
   b. 15
   c. 16
   d. 17

Answer: *17*. Including one for each sector, there is an ISAC for each and every ISAC as well as a worldwide ISAC for foreign involvement.

6. ISACs are defined under which Presidential Directive?
   a. HSPD-5
   b. HSPD-6
   c. HSPD-7
   d. HSPD-8

   Answer: *HSPD-7*. As part of the definition of the Department of Homeland Security, the definition of the ISACs is also outlined under the same directive.

7. The Financial Services ISAC (FS-ISAC) is operated by _____.

   Answer: *SAIC*. The Science Applications International Corporation is the service provider for the FS-ISAC.

8. The Emergency Management and Response ISAC (EMR-ISAC) is operated and maintained by the Federal Emergency Management Agency (or FEMA). True or False?

   Answer: *True*. In October, 2000, the United States Fire Administration (now part of the Federal Emergency Management Agency [FEMA], which is part of the DHS), http://www.usfa.fema.gov, established the Emergency Management and Response-Information Sharing and Analysis Center (EMR-ISAC) to develop and manage the critical infrastructure protection (CIP) program in support of federal government initiatives.

9. The acronym PSTN stands for _____ .

   Answer: *Public Switched Telephone Network*

10. GETS allows key government personnel priority calling over standard switched calling. True or False?

    Answer: *True*. It is intended for use in an emergency or crisis situation when the PSTN is congested and the probability of completing a call over normal or other alternate telecommunication means has significantly decreased.

NOTES

1. https://disasterhelp.gov/portal/jhtml/general/about_msisac.jhtml
2. https://disasterhelp.gov/portal/jhtml/general/about_msisac.jhtml
3. http://www.irs.gov/privacy/article/0,,id=130752,00.html

4. Internal Revenue Service, Privacy Impact Assessment-Business Master File (BMF). http://www.irs.gov/privacy/article/0,,id=130752,00.html

5. http://www.surfacetransportationisac.org

6. The "Terrorism Risk Analysis and Security Management Plan" represents a security task force composed of railroad representatives with expertise in areas such as operations, legal issues, railroad police activities, hazardous materials transportation, and information technology; outside consultants with expertise in intelligence and counter-terrorism were retained to provide advice on best practices.

7. U.S. Department of Transportation Applauds Association of American Railroads' Initiative to Create a Center to Enhance Security. (http://www.dot.gov/affairs/dot 4502.htm) (http://commerce.senate.gov/hearings/071002hamberger.pdf).

8. http://www.surfacetransportationisac.org/APTA.asp

9. U.S. DOT State Safety Oversight Newsletter-Issue 12, Summer 2004. http://transit-safety.volpe.dot.gov/Safety/sso/newsletters/Issue12/PDF/Issue12.pdf

10. U.S. DOT State Safety Oversight Newsletter-Issue 12, Summer 2004. http://transit-safety.volpe.dot.gov/Safety/sso/newsletters/Issue12/PDF/Issue12.pdf

11. http://www.fta.dot.gov

12. U.S. DOT State Safety Oversight Newsletter-Issue 12, Summer 2004. http://transit-safety.volpe.dot.gov/Safety/sso/newsletters/Issue12/PDF/Issue12.pdf

13. http://www.apta.com

14. http://www.aar.org

15. http://www.aar.com/ttci/index.htm

16. http://www.railinc.com

17. http://www.epa.gov/safewater/sdwa/index.html

18. U.S. Environmental Protection Agency, Information for the Public on Preparing Capacity Development Strategies, EPA 8916-R-98-009, July, 1998. http://www.epa.gov/OGWDW/smallsys/cdguid/nfo-pub.html

19. http://www.house.gov/science/full/nov14/full_charter_111401.htm

20. Growing public awareness and concern for controlling water pollution led to enactment of the Federal Water Pollution Control Act Amendments of 1972. As amended in 1977, this law became commonly known as the Clean Water Act. The Act established the basic structure for regulating discharges of pollutants into the waters of the United States. http://www.epa.gov/region5/water/cwa.htm

21. http://www.epa.gov/region5/water/cwa.htm

22. http://www.epa.gov/region5/water/cwa.htm

23. http://www.waterisac.org

24. http://www.asdwa.org

25. http://www.werf.org

26. http://www.cdc.gov/nceh/ehhe/water/links.htm

27. http://www.amwa.net

28. http://www.amsa-cleanwater.org

29. http://www.nawc.org

30. http://www.awwa.org

31. http://www.awwarf.org

32. The President's Commission on Critical Infrastructure Protection was created on July 15, 1996, by Executive Order 13010 to bring the public and private sectors together to assess and develop strategies to address infrastructure vulnerabilities. The banking and finance sector was identified as one of eight critical infrastructures requiring review and assurance strategies, and in 1999, the banking and finance sector established FS/ISAC.

33. FDIC, Putting an End to Account-Hijacking Identity Theft. http://www.fdic.gov/consumers/consumer/idtheftstudy/industry.html
34. http://www.fdic.gov/consumers/consumer/idtheftstudy/industry.html
35. http://www.fsisac.com
36. http://www.saic.com
37. http://www.nerc.com
38. U.S. Department of Homeland Security integrated legacy operations of the NIPC, CIAO, NCS and Energy Assurance Office, and developed the functional organizational components of the Infrastructure Assurance (IA) and Infrastructure Protectorate (IP) directorates. http://www.dhs.gov/dhspublic/display?theme=87&content = 4123& print=true
39. The CIPAG brings together the generation and transmission providers, public and investor-owned utilities, power marketers, regional transmission organizations and independent system operators, electric power associations, and government agencies. Both Canadian and United States entities participate.
40. U.S. Department of Homeland Security integrated legacy operations of the NIPC, CIAO, NCS and Energy Assurance Office, and developed the functional organizational components of Information Analysis (IA) and Infrastructure Protection (IP) directorates (IAIP). http://www.dhs.gov/dhspublic/display?theme=87&content=4123 &print=true
41. http://www.dhs.gov/dhspublic/display?theme=87&content=4123&print=true
42. http://www.ferc.gov
43. http://www.senate.gov/~gov_affairs/050802gent.pdf
44. Testimony to The United States House of Representatives Committee on Government Reform Subcommittee on Government Efficiency, Financial Management and Intergovernmental Relations Discussing Activities Undertaken by the Electricity Sector to Address Physical and Cyber Security with Emphasis on the Electricity Sector – Information Sharing and Analysis Center (ES-ISAC), Louis G. Leffler, Manager-Projects North American Electric Reliability Council July 24, 2002. http://esisac.com/publicdocs/HouseCommitteeonGovtReform072402.pdf
45. Testimony to The United States House of Representatives Committee on Government Reform Subcommittee on Government Efficiency, Financial Management and Intergovernmental Relations Discussing Activities Undertaken by the Electricity Sector to Address Physical and Cyber Security with Emphasis on the Electricity Sector – Information Sharing and Analysis Center (ES-ISAC), Louis G. Leffler, Manager-Projects North American Electric Reliability Council July 24, 2002. http://esisac.com/publicdocs/HouseCommitteeonGovtReform072402.pdf
46. U.S. Department of Homeland Security integrated legacy operations of the NIPC, CIAO, NCS and Energy Assurance Office, and developed the functional organizational components of Information Analysis (IA) and Infrastructure Protection (IP) directorates (IAIP). http://www.dhs.gov/dhspublic/display?theme=87&content=4123 &print=true
47. Testimony of Michehl R. Gent, President and Chief Executive Officer North American Electric Reliability Council Hearing Before the United States Senate Committee on Governmental Affairs, May 8, 2002, SECURING OUR INFRASTRUCTURE: PRIVATE/PUBLIC INFORMATION SHARING. http://www.senate.gov/~gov_affairs/050802gent.pdf
48. Testimony to The United States House of Representatives Committee on Government Reform Subcommittee on Government Efficiency, Financial Management and Intergovernmental Relations Discussing Activities Undertaken by the Electricity Sector to Address Physical and Cyber Security with Emphasis on the Electricity Sector – Information Sharing and Analysis Center (ES-ISAC), Louis G. Leffler, Manager-

Projects North American Electric Reliability Council July 24, 2002. http://esisac.com/publicdocs/HouseCommitteeonGovtReform072402.pdf

49. http://esisac.com/publicdocs/HouseCommitteeonGovtReform072402.pdf
50. http://esisac.com/publicdocs/HouseCommitteeonGovtReform072402.pdf
51. http://esisac.com/publicdocs/HouseCommitteeonGovtReform072402.pdf
52. http://esisac.com/publicdocs/HouseCommitteeonGovtReform072402.pdf
53. http://esisac.com/publicdocs/HouseCommitteeonGovtReform072402.pdf
54. http://www.esisac.com
55. http://www.esisac.com
56. Testimony to The United States House of Representatives Committee on Government Reform Subcommittee on Government Efficiency, Financial Management and Intergovernmental Relations Discussing Activities Undertaken by the Electricity Sector to Address Physical and Cyber Security with Emphasis on the Electricity Sector – Information Sharing and Analysis Center (ES-ISAC), Louis G. Leffler, Manager-Projects North American Electric Reliability Council July 24, 2002. http://esisac.com/publicdocs/HouseCommitteeonGovtReform072402.pdf
57. http://esisac.com/publicdocs/HouseCommitteeonGovtReform072402.pdf
58. U.S. Fire Administration, Federal Emergency Management Agency, Critical Infrastructure Protection (EMR-ISAC), http://www.usfa.fema.gov/subjects/emr-isac
59. http://www.usfa.fema.gov/subjects/emr-isac
60. http://www.usfa.fema.gov/subjects/emr-isac
61. http://www.usfa.fema.gov/subjects/emr-isac
62. http://www.usfa.fema.gov/subjects/emr-isac
63. U.S. Fire Administration, Federal Emergency Management Agency, CIP/EMR-ISAC Factsheet, March, 2005. http://www.usfa.fema.gov/subjects/emr-isac/factsheet.shtm
64. http://www.it-isac.com
65. http://www.ncs.gov/informationportal/portal.html
66. http://www.ncs.gov/ncc
67. Federal Register Vol. 49. No. 67 Thursday, April 5, 1984. http://www.au.af.mil/au/awc/awcgate/execordr/eo12472.htm
68. http://www.ncs.gov/n3/cris/cris.htm
69. The Financial and Banking Information Infrastructure Committee, Sponsorship of Priority Telecommunications Access for Private Sector Entities through the National Communications System Government Emergency Telecommunications Service (GETS) and Wireless Priority Service (WPS). http://www.fbiic.gov/policies/ GETS_policy.htm
70. The Financial and Banking Information Infrastructure Committee (FBIIC) is chartered under the President's Working Group on Financial Markets, and is charged with improving coordination and communication among financial regulators, enhancing the resiliency of the financial sector, and promoting the public/private partnership. Treasury's Assistant Secretary for Financial Institutions chairs the committee. Members of the FBIIC include representatives of the Commodity Futures Trading Commission, the Conference of State Bank Supervisors, the Farm Credit Administration, the Federal Deposit Insurance Corporation, the Federal Housing Finance Board, the Federal Reserve Bank of New York, the Federal Reserve Board, the Homeland Security Council, the National Association of Insurance Commissioners, the National Credit Union Administration, the North American Securities Administrators Association, the Office of the Comptroller of the Currency, the Office of Federal Housing Enterprise Oversight, the Office of Thrift Supervision, the Securities and Exchange Commission, and the Securities Investor Protection Corporation. http://www.fbiic.gov
71. http://www.fbiic.gov

72. http://www.fbiic.gov
73. Refer to Section 9.28, Telecommunications Service Priority (TSP).
74. The Financial and Banking Information Infrastructure Committee, Sponsorship of Priority Telecommunications Access for Private Sector Entities through the National Communications System Government Emergency Telecommunications Service (GETS) and Wireless Priority Service (WPS). http://www.fbiic.gov/policies/GETS_policy. htm
75. http://www.fbiic.gov/policies/GETS_policy.htm
76. http://gets.ncs.gov
77. http://gets.ncs.gov
78. The Financial and Banking Information Infrastructure Committee, Sponsorship of Priority Telecommunications Access for Private Sector Entities through the National Communications System Government Emergency Telecommunications Service (GETS) and Wireless Priority Service (WPS). http://www.fbiic.gov/policies/GETS_ policy.htm
79. http://www.fbiic.gov/policies/GETS_policy.htm
80. http://www.fbiic.gov/policies/GETS_policy.htm
81. http://www.fbiic.gov/policies/GETS_policy.htm
82. The Financial and Banking Information Infrastructure Committee, Sponsorship of Priority Telecommunications Access for Private Sector Entities through the National Communications System Government Emergency Telecommunications Service (GETS) and Wireless Priority Service (WPS). http://www.fbiic.gov/policies/GETS_ policy.htm
83. In its role as a payments system operator, the Federal Reserve has traditionally sponsored significant participants in the payments system for NCS services. The Federal Reserve therefore intends to contact those organizations that clearly qualify under the criteria and ask them to provide the names of individuals who should receive GETS cards. The Federal Reserve will notify the other FBIIC agencies of institutions they have contacted.
84. http://tsp.ncs.gov
85. http://www.its.bldrdoc.gov/projects/devglossary/_telecommunications_service_prior ity_system.html
86. Federal Register Vol. 49. No. 67 Thursday, April 5, 1984. http://www.au.af.mil/au/ awc/awcgate/execordr/eo12472.htm
87. http://www.ncs.gov/n3/shares/shares.htm
88. http://www.ncs.gov/n3/shares/shares.htm
89. NRIC Network Interoperability: The Key to Competition, July 15, 1997.
90. http://www.ncs.gov/nstac/nstac_publications.html
91. http://www.ncs.gov/nstac/nstac.html
92. http://www.ncs.gov/nstac/nstac.html
93. http://www.ncs.gov/nstac/nstac.html
94. http://www.ncs.gov/nstac/nstac.html
95. http://www.ncs.gov/nstac/nstac.html
96. http://www.ncs.gov/nstac/nstac.html
97. http://www.ncs.gov/nstac/nstac.html
98. http://www.ncs.gov/nstac/nstac.html
99. http://www.ncs.gov/nstac/nstac.html
100. http://www.ncs.gov/nstac/nstac.html
101. http://www.ncs.gov/nstac/nstac.html
102. http://www.ncs.gov/nstac/nstac.html
103. http://www.ncs.gov/nstac/nstac.html
104. http://www.ncs.gov/nstac/nstac.html
105. The Priority Access Service (PAS) program was developed by the Federal Communications Commission (FCC), and is managed by the Office of the Manager National

Communication System (OMNCS). OMNCS is a federal government organization established to perform NS/EP telecommunications functions among its 23 member organizations. OMNCS' primary mission is to develop a responsive, survivable, and enduring national telecommunication infrastructure to support the NS/EP telecommunication needs of the federal government. As a first step in satisfying the mission requirements, OMNCS developed and deployed GETS. GETS is designed and maintained in a state of readiness that makes use of available PSTN resources, should outages occur during an emergency or crisis. In general PAS is intended to provide authorized personnel priority access to telecommunications (both wireless and wireline). For the purposes of this article, PAS will be used to refer to all priority access, particularly the wireless component of PAS.

106. U.S. Department of Homeland Security SAFECOM Emerging Wireless Technologies Priority Access Services in the Mobile Environment. www.safecomprogram. gov/.../emerging_wireless_technologies_priority_access.pdf
107. http://www.get.ncs.gov
108. http://wps.ncs.gov
109. http://wps.ncs.gov
110. http://wps.ncs.gov
111. http://www.safecomprogram.gov
112. http://www.safecomprogram.gov/SAFECOM
113. http://www.safecomprogram.gov/SAFECOM
114. http://www.ncs.gov/acn
115. http://www.ncs.gov/acn
116. http://www.energyisac.com/index.cfm
117. http://chemicalisac.chemtrec.com
118. http://chemicalisac.chemtrec.com
119. http://www.chemtrec.com
120. http://www.hcisac.org
121. http://www.highwayisac.com
122. http://www.highwayisac.com
123. http://www.cargotips.org
124. http://www.truckline.com
125. http://www.highwatch.com
126. http://www.fmi.org/isac
127. http://www.fmi.org
128. http://www.cscic.state.ny.us/msisac
129. http://www.isaccouncil.org
130. http://www.wwisac.com
131. http://www.reisac.org
132. http://www.reisac.org/about.html
133. http://www.rer.org
134. http://ren-isac.net
135. http://www.biotech-isac.org
136. http://72.14.207.104/search?q=cache:7w03gjeHQiYJW: www.seasecure.com/m-isac.htmtm-isac.htm&hl-en&gl-us&ct-clnk&cd-1
137. http://www.wagner.nyu.edu/transportation/files/summer04.pdf
138. http://www.wagner.nyu.edu/transportation/files/summer04.pdf
139. (http://www.wagner.nyu.edu/transportation/files/summer04.pdf). The Marine Transportation System National Advisory Council (http://www.mtsnac.org). The Maritime Security Council (http://www.maritimesecurity.org).
140. http://www.maritimesecurity.org/background_info.htm

141. Marine Transportation System National Advisory Council. http://www.mtsnac.org
142. Marine Transportation System National Advisory Council (http://www.mtsnac.org/member.htm). American Association of Port Authorities (http://http://www.aapaports.org). American Maritime Congress (http://www.usflag.org). American Trucking Associations (http://www.truckline.com). Association of Metropolitan Planning Organization (http://www.ampo.org). Boat Owners Association of the United States (http://www.boatus.com). Gulf of Mexico States Partnership, Inc. (http://www.gomsa.org). I-95 Corridor Coalition (http://www.i95.org). Intermodal Association of North America (http://www.intermodal.org). International Longshore and Warehouse Union (http://www.ilwu.org). International Longshoreman's Association (http://www.ilaunion.org). Lake Carriers' Association (http://www.lcaships.com). Maritime Information Services of North America (http://www.misnadata.org). Maritime Security Council (http ://www.maritimesecurity.org). National Association of Counties (http://www.naco.org). National Governor's Association (http://www.nga.org). National Industrial Transportation League (http://www.nitl.org). National Waterways Conference (http://www.waterways.org). Pacific Maritime Association (http://www. pmanet. org). Propeller Club of the United States (http://www.propellerclubhq.com). Shipbuilders Council of America (http://www.shipbuilders.org). Society of Naval Architects and Marine Engineers (http://www.sname.org). The Waterfront Coalition (http://www.portmod.org). U.S. Chamber of Commerce (http://www.chamber.org). United States Maritime Alliance, Ltd. (http://www.usmx.com). World Shipping Council (http://www.worldshipping.org).
143. https://disasterhelp.gov/portal/jhtml/general/about_msisac.jhtml

10 Supervisory Control and Data Acquisition (SCADA)

10.1 INTRODUCTION

This chapter introduces terms and concepts that are associated with automated control systems, of which Supervisory Control and Data Acquisition (SCADA) is a part of the system. Some of the terms introduced involve information technology (IT) related security methodologies and what methods would be used to breach security controls and their mechanisms.

10.2 WHAT ARE CONTROL SYSTEMS?

Essentially, *control systems* are computer-based systems that are used by many infrastructures and industries to monitor and control sensitive processes and physical functions. Typically, control systems collect sensor measurements and operational data from the field, process and display this information, and relay control commands to local or remote equipment. In the electric power industry they can manage and control the transmission and delivery of electric power, for example, by opening and closing circuit breakers and setting thresholds for preventive shutdowns. Employing integrated control systems, the oil and gas industry can control the refining operations on a plant site as well as remotely monitor the pressure and flow of gas pipelines and control the flow and pathways of gas transmission. With water utilities, control systems can remotely monitor well levels, control the wells' pumps, monitor water flows, tank levels, or water pressure in storage tanks; monitor water quality characteristics such as pH, turbidity, and chlorine residual; and control the addition of chemicals. Control system functions vary from simple to complex; they may be used to simply monitor processes running. For example, environmental conditions within a small office building being the simplest form of site monitoring, to managing most (or in most cases, all) activities for a municipal water system, or even a nuclear power plant. Within certain industries such as chemical and power generation, safety systems are typically implemented to mitigate a disastrous event if control and other systems fail.

In addition to guarding against both physical attack and system failure, organizations may establish backup control centers that include uninterruptible power supplies and backup generators.[1]

10.3 TYPES OF CONTROL SYSTEMS

There are two primary types of control systems:

1. *Distributed Control Systems (DCS)*, are typically used within a single processes or generating plant or utilized over a smaller geographic area or even a single site location.
2. *Supervisory Control and Data Acquisition (SCADA)* systems are typically used for larger-scaled environments that may be geographically dispersed in an enterprise-wide distribution operation.

A utility company may use a DCS to generate power, and utilize a SCADA system to distribute it.[2]

10.4 COMPONENTS OF CONTROL SYSTEMS

A control system typically consists of a *master control system* or central supervisory control and monitoring station, consisting of one or more human-machine interfaces in which an operator may view displayed information about the remote sites and/or issue commands directly to the system. Typically, this is a device or station that is located at a site in which application servers and production control workstations that are used to configure and troubleshoot other control system components. The central supervisory control and monitoring station is generally connected to local controller stations through a hard-wired network or to remote controller stations through a communications network which may be communicated through the Internet, a public switched telephone network (POTS), or a cable or wireless (such as radio, microwave, or wireless) network.

Each controller station has a Remote Terminal Unit (RTU), a Programmable Logic Controller (PLC), a DCS controller, and/or other controllers that communicate with the supervisory control and monitoring station. The controller stations include sensors and control equipment that connects directly with the working components of the infrastructure (for example, pipelines, water towers, and power lines). Sensors take readings from infrastructure equipment such as water or pressure levels, electrical voltage, and so on, sending messages to the controller. The controller may be programmed to determine a course of action, sending a message to the control equipment instructing it what to do (for example, to turn off a valve or dispense a chemical). If the controller is not programmed to determine a course of action, the controller communicates with the supervisory control and monitoring station before sending a command back to the control equipment. The control system may also be programmed to issue alarms back to the control operator when certain conditions are detected. Handheld devices such as personal digital assistants (PDA) may be used to locally monitor controller stations. Controller station technologies are becoming more intelligent and automated and can communicate with the supervisory central monitoring and control station less frequently, requiring less human intervention. Historically, security concerns about control stations have been less frequent, requiring less human intervention.

10.5 VULNERABILITY CONCERNS ABOUT CONTROL SYSTEMS

Historically, security concerns about control systems were related primarily to protecting against physical attacks or the misuse of refining and processing sites or distribution and holding facilities. However, more recently there has been a growing recognition that control systems are now vulnerable to cyber attacks from numerous sources, including hostile governments, terrorist groups, disgruntled employees, and other malicious intruders.

In October 1997, the President's Commission on Critical Infrastructure Protection specifically discussed the potential damaging effects on the electric power and oil and gas industries of successful attacks on control systems.[3] Sometime in 2002, the National Research Council identified "the potential for attack on control systems" as requiring "urgent attention."[4] And, in February 2003, President Bush outlined his concerns over "the threat of organized cyber attacks capable of causing debilitating disruption to our nation's critical infrastructures, economy, or national security," noting that "disruption of these systems can have significant consequences for public health and safety" and emphasizing that the protection of control systems has become "a national priority."[5]

Several factors have contributed to the escalation of risk of these control systems which included the following concerns:

- The adoption of standardized technologies with known vulnerabilities.
- The connectivity of many control systems via, through, within, or exposed to unsecured networks, networked portals, or mechanisms connected to unsecured networks.
- Implementation constraints of existing security technologies and practices within the existing control systems infrastructure (and its architectures).
- The connectivity of insecure remote devices in their connections to control systems.
- The widespread availability of technical information about control systems, most notably via publicly available and/or shared networked resources such as the Internet.

10.6 ADOPTION OF STANDARDIZED TECHNOLOGIES WITH KNOWN VULNERABILITIES

Historically, proprietary hardware, software, and network protocols made it rather difficult to understand how control systems operated as information wasn't commonly or publicly known, was considered proprietary (in nature), and was therefore, not susceptible to hacker attacks. Today, however, to reduce costs and improve performance, organizations have begun transitioning from proprietary systems to less expensive, standardized technologies which utilize and operate under platforms that run operating systems such as Microsoft Windows, UNIX and/or LINUX systems, along with the common networking protocols used by the Internet. These widely used standardized technologies have commonly known vulnerabilities such that more sophisticated and effective exploitation tools are widely available and relatively easy to use. As a consequence, both the number of people with the knowledge to wage attacks and the number of systems subject to attack has increased.

10.7   CONNECTIVITY OF CONTROL SYSTEMS TO UNSECURED NETWORKS

Corporate enterprises often integrate their control systems within their enterprise networks. This increased connectivity has significant advantages, including providing decision makers with access to real-time information allowing site engineers and production control managers to monitor and control the process flow and its control of the entire system from within different points of the enterprise network. Enterprise networks are often connected to networks of strategic partners, as well as to the Internet. Control systems are increasingly using wide area networks and the Internet to transmit data to their remote or local stations and individual devices. This convergence of control networks with public and enterprise networks potentially exposes the control systems to additional security vulnerabilities. Unless appropriate security controls are deployed within and throughout the enterprise and control system network, breaches in enterprise security may affect operations.

10.8   IMPLEMENTATION CONSTRAINTS OF EXISTING SECURITY TECHNOLOGIES

The uses of existing security technologies, as well as use of strong user authentication and patch management practices, are typically not implemented in control systems as control systems operate in real time; control systems are typically not designed with security in mind and usually have limited processing capabilities to accommodate or handle security measures or countermeasures.

Existing security technologies such as authorization, authentication, encryption, intrusion detection, and filtering of network traffic and communications require significantly increased bandwidth, processing power, and memory; much more than control system components typically have or are capable of sustaining. The entire concept behind control systems was integrated systems technologies, which were small, compact, and relatively easy to use and configure. Because controller stations are generally designed to perform specific tasks, they use low-cost, resource-constrained microprocessors. In fact, some devices within the electrical industry still use the Intel 8088 processor, introduced in 1978. Consequently, it is difficult to install existing security technologies without seriously degrading the performance of the control systems, thus requiring the need for a complete overhaul of the entire control system infrastructure and its environment.

Furthermore, complex password controlling mechanisms may not always be used to prevent unauthorized access to control systems, partially because this could hinder a rapid response to safety procedures during an emergency, or could affect the performance of the overall environment. As a result, according to experts, weak passwords that are easy to guess, are shared, and infrequently changed are reportedly common in control systems, including the use of default passwords or even no password at all.

Current control systems are based upon standard operating systems as they are typically customized to support control system applications. Consequently, vendor-provided software patches are generally either incompatible or cannot be implemented without compromising service by shutting down "always-on" systems or affecting interdependent operations.

10.9 INSECURE CONNECTIVITY TO CONTROL SYSTEMS

Potential vulnerabilities in control systems are exacerbated by insecure connections, either within the corporate enterprise network or external to the enterprise or controlling station. Organizations often leave access links (such as dial-up modems to equipment and control information) open for remote diagnostics, maintenance, and examination of system status. Such links may not be protected with authentication or encryption which increases the risk that an attempted external penetration could use these insecure connections to break into remotely controlled systems. Some control systems use wireless communications systems, which are especially vulnerable to attack, or leased lines that pass through commercial telecommunications facilities; in either situation, neither method of communication performs any security methodologies whatsoever, and if there are any security measures implemented, are capable of being easily compromised. Without encryption to protect data as it flows through these insecure connections or authentication mechanisms to limit access, there is limited protection for the integrity of the information being transmitted, and may be subjected to interception, monitoring of data from interception, and (eventually) penetration.

10.10 PUBLICLY AVAILABLE INFORMATION ABOUT CONTROL SYSTEMS

Public information about critical infrastructures and control systems is available through widely available general publicly available networks such as the Internet. The risks associated with the availability of critical infrastructure information poses a serious threat to those critical infrastructures being served as demonstrated by a George Mason University graduate student whose dissertation reportedly mapped every industrial sector connected via computer networks utilizing tools and materials that were publicly available on the Internet, and none of the data, site maps, or tools used were classified nor sanitized. A prime example of publicly available information is with regard to the electric power industry, in which open sources of information such as product data, educational materials, maps (even though outdated), are still available showing line locations and interconnections that are currently being used; additional information includes filings of the Federal Energy Regulation Commission (FERC), industrial publications on various subject matters pertaining to the electric power industry, and other materials — all of which are publicly available via the Internet.

10.11 CONTROL SYSTEMS MAY BE VULNERABLE TO ATTACK

Entities or individuals with intent to disrupt service may take one or more of the following methods that may be successful in their attack(s) of control systems[6]:

Disrupt the operations of control systems by delaying or blocking the flow of information through the networks supporting the control systems, thereby denying availability of the networks to control systems' operators and production control managers.

Attempt at, or succeed at, making unauthorized changes to programmed instructions within PLCs, RTUs, or DCS controllers, change alarm thresholds, or issue unauthorized commands to control station equipment which could potentially result in damage to equipment (if tolerances have been exceeded), premature shutdown of processes (shutting down transmission lines or causing cascading termination of service to the electrical grid), or rendering disablement of control station equipment.

Send falsified information to control system operators either to disguise unauthorized changes or to initiate inappropriate actions to be taken by system operators; that is, falsified information is sent or displayed back to systems operators thinking that an alarmed condition has been triggered, resulting in system operators acting upon this falsified information, thus potentially causing the actual event.

Modify or alter control system software or firmware such that the net effect produces unpredictable results (such as introducing a computer *time bomb* to go off at 12 midnight every night, thus partially shutting down some of the control systems, causing a temporary brownout condition; a *time bomb* is a forcibly-introduced piece of computer logic or source code that causes certain courses of action to be taken when either an event or triggered state has been activated).

Interfere with the operation and processing of safety systems (for example, tampering with, or denial of service of control systems which regulate processing control rods within a nuclear power generation facility).

Many remote locations containing control systems (as part of an enterprise DCS environment) are often unstaffed and may not be physically monitored through surveillance; the risk of threat remains and may be higher if the remote facility is physically penetrated at its perimeter and intrusion attempts are then made to the control systems' networks from within.

Many control systems are vulnerable to attacks of varying degrees; these attack attempts range from telephone line sweeps (a.k.a. *wardialing*), to wireless network sniffing (*wardriving*), to physical network port scanning, and to physical monitoring and intrusion.

10.12 CONSEQUENCES RESULTING FROM CONTROL SYSTEM COMPROMISES

Some consequences resulting from control system compromises are:

While computer network security is undeniably important, unlike enterprise network security, a control system compromised can have significant impacts within real-world life. These impacts can have far-reaching consequences not previously thought, or in areas that could affect other industrial sectors (and their infrastructures).

Enterprise network security breaches can have financial consequences, customer privacy becomes compromised, computer systems need to be rebuilt, and so forth.

A breach of security of a control system can have a cascade effect upon other systems, either directly or indirectly connected to those control systems that have been compromised; however, not only can property be destroyed, but people can be hurt, or even worse, people can get killed.[7]

10.13 WARDIALING

Before there was AOL or AT&T Yahoo DSL, or any popular Internet Service Provider (ISP) of today, many people directly connected with remote computer systems via modems. Instead of dialing up the ISP and surfing a Web site or downloading email, users would access bulletin board systems (*BBS*) to do their personal business; in many cases, these BBSs would have features specific to those sites and locations. Some of these features included: interactive chat rooms (quite similar to many of the instant messaging services provided by AOL, Yahoo, and MSN), electronic mail (*email*), file up/download areas, and so on. Many nationwide corporate enterprises made use of BBS services for internal employees of the company. Companies would set up specific numbers for employees to access while on the road to access corporate servers for email or private phone lines to make telephone calls billed back to the sponsoring company. Phone companies would (and still do) use special numbers to perform diagnostics, trouble shoot, and configure their networks remotely. Special tones, or the sequencing of these tones, could be sent through telephone lines to activate or deactivate specific services.

Not soon after these services became available, individuals with less-than-honorable intentions or motives (often stating that they were merely "curious") began seeking out these special or private telephone numbers, or the tones associated with the diagnostic functions of the various telephone companies. Thus, the method of *phreaking* was born. A *phreaker* is an individual who specializes in unauthorized penetration and access of telephone systems. One of the easiest methods of determining the existence of these special or private telephone numbers is by calling each telephone number within a range or block of suffixed numbers within a given prefix or area code. Each telephone number dialed is checked for a modem carrier tone that uniquely identifies that the telephone number may be associated with a computer or network-connected device. Many of the dialup blocks were performed manually, and it wasn't long before those individuals found faster, more efficient methods of dialing the telephone numbered blocks through custom written software. The software applications would dial up each and every telephone number that was included within a list of telephone number to dial, going through the list number by number, dialing and recording its findings until something interesting would show. This method of sequential dialing with the intent of either exploiting the service connected to, and associated with, the telephone number found is called *wardialing*.

10.13.1 GOALS OF WARDIALING

The main goal of wardialing is simple: access. Access to a specific company's system, access to free long distance, access to an anonymous connection to anonymously access another computer system or entire network, access to a place to hide illegal or contraband software, data, or information, or access with an intent to steal data, information, or software without payment. Whatever the case may be, those that are wardialing a remote location, or attempting to find a remote location, are attempting to find access into the remote telephone system, computers, and its network.

10.13.2 THREATS RESULTING FROM WARDIALING

The combination of loosely controlled telephone infrastructures (compared to a typical Internet perimeter location) and the ubiquity of modems, means that it is prudent to understand and manage telephone-based vulnerabilities. Some of the information or outcome of information obtained from wardialing includes:

- *Carrier detection*: Determination through several methods of whether carrier is modem or facsimile, and may be capable of determining manufacturer of device that is answering.
- *Banner logging and identification*: Many systems identify not only the name of the organization that is using or sponsoring the carrier-answering device but may also identify basic functionalities of the device that answered based upon its name or a brief description.
- *System identification*: Once connected, individuals may determine the type of system through a series of scanning attempts which would identify the computer manufacturer type, model, operating system running on the computer system.
- *Network identification*: It may be possible to scan other computing devices if the device has been compromised and may be capable of traversing within and throughout the enterprise network.

10.14 WARDRIVING

Similar to wardialing efforts, the principle and primary goal of wardriving remains the same: access via wireless connectivity. This method of scanning is a form of wireless network sniffing from a stationary, sometimes remote location to the target point.[8] Many control systems are, or have, implemented wireless connectivity at remote locations. This may be for several reasons, but some of the more obvious reasons stand out: (a) access at a remote facility without having to enter the facility, or site location;

(b) use of PDA devices to access critical control stations within and throughout the remote facility without being tethered to a cable; or (c) remote distribution of telemetry data and information back to a centralized monitoring facility.

10.15 WARWALKING

Similar to wardriving, the warwalking method of wireless network sniffing is performed at (or near) the target point and is performed by a pedestrian, meaning that instead of a person being in an automotive vehicle, the potential intruder may be sniffing the network for weaknesses or vulnerabilities on foot, posing as a person walking, but they may have a handheld PDA device or laptop computer.[9]

10.16 THREATS RESULTING FROM CONTROL SYSTEM ATTACKS

There have been a number of reported exploitations of several control systems throughout the country. Resulting from the penetration attempts, intruders were successful at several locations:

> Sometime in 1998, during a two-week military exercise, codenamed *Eligible Receiver*, staff from the National Security Agency (NSA) used widely available tools and software to simulate how sections of the United States' electrical power grid's control systems' networks could be disabled through computer-based attacks. Their attempts were successful, demonstrating how within several days, portions of (or the entire) the country's national power grid could have been rendered useless. The attacks also demonstrated the impotency capabilities of command-and-control elements within the United States Pacific Command (USPACOM).[10]

> In spring of 2000, a former employee of an Australian company that develops manufacturing software applied for a job within the local government but was rejected. The disgruntled former employee reportedly used a radio transmitter device on numerous occasions to remotely access control systems of a sewage treatment system, releasing an estimated 264,000 gallons of untreated, raw sewage into nearby waterways.[11]

10.17 ISSUES IN SECURING CONTROL SYSTEMS

A significant challenge in effectively securing control systems is based upon several criteria which may (or may not) prevent capabilities of properly securing control systems' environments and their networks. Some of the issues surmounting from securification efforts include:

- Lack of, or unavailability of, specialized security technologies and their implementation.
- Computing resources within control systems that are needed to perform some security functions may be limiting in their capabilities, and thus, may be ineffective against attack.

- Control systems' architectures may prevent any security implementation such that: (a) configuration and layout of implementation may prohibit any such implementation; (b) performance considerations (again possibly due to configuration or the layout of implementation) may be prohibitive such that redesign of, or reimplementation of, may be cost-prohibitive or time-prohibitive; (c) additional security mechanisms may be ineffective completely, and would require a redesign of, or reimplementation of, the entire control systems' architecture.
- Criticality of specific control systems may not allow for outages without significant cost to the enterprise or customers resulting from lack of service.
- Many organizations are reluctant to spend more money to secure a control system. Hardening security of control systems would require industries to expend more resources, including acquiring more personnel to safeguard the secured control systems, provide additional training for personnel, and potentially prematurely replacing control systems that typically have an average lifespan of about 20 years.
- Political and legal entanglements insofar as to who controls and maintains control systems' infrastructure and who has responsibility for securing those environments. Conflicting priorities, lack of concern, lack of interest due to an expansive financial burden to harden those environments, perpetuate the lack of IT strategies that could be deployed to mitigate any potentially exposed vulnerability of control systems without affecting performance or significant cost involved.
- Industrial plants and the instrumentation they include tend to be long-life cycle projects that are upwards to 20-year project cycles, and are by no means uncommon. As a result, the devices that were deployed as part of that construction may be virtual antiques by the time the facility is finally decommissioned, and there's no provision for refreshing those devices in any manner similar to that of computer workstation upgrades.
- Similarly, if security upgrades were probable and capable, the life cycles of the projects for implementation would be considerably longer than standard, conventional computer system implementations. One of the caveats might be that by the time the security upgrade was completed, there would be a vulnerability or exploit available that could jeopardize continued upgrade implementations, thus cause disruptions in the life cycle process of the upgrade project.
- Many antiviral software packages have little or no affect upon the control systems architectures as these architectures often predate initial computer-based viruses.
- Remote devices (RTUs and PLCs) may be difficult to upgrade; these devices might utilize a hardware-based operating system that was burned into a read-only memory (ROM) chip. ROM chips are not rewritable, and some of the chips may no longer be manufactured.
- Remote devices may be physically sealed and not be upgraded or may be located in a difficult-to-reach location, or have no removable media.

- Worst-case scenario might be that the manufacturer of the remote devices may no longer be in business, not producing upgrades, or may not be allowing (or be allowed for legal reasons) the upgrades.
- If the remote devices are capable of being upgraded and have some security capabilities added, the shear number of devices (maybe in the thousands, even tens of thousands of devices) poses serious issues with password aging and retention.
- Because of the shear volume of devices, many control systems operators may have a unitary password for all remote devices or find common methods of maintaining passwords remotely (which might be capable of compromise).

10.18 METHODS OF SECURING CONTROL SYSTEMS

Several steps may be taken to address potential threats to control systems:

- Research and develop new security techniques to protect or enhance control systems; there are currently some open systems development efforts involving the IEC 1131-3 protocol.[12]
- Develop security policies, standards, and/or procedures that are implemented on, for, or with control systems' security in mind. Use of consensus standardization would have encouragement within the industry for investing in stronger securification methods of control systems.
- If developing independent security policies, standards, and/or procedures are not applicable, and then implement similar security policies, standards, and/or procedures taken from the plethora of widely available IT security practices. A good example might be the segmentation of control systems' networks with firewall (and possibly) network-based intrusion detection systems technologies, along with strong authentication practices.
- Define and implement a security awareness program to employees, contractors, and (especially) customers.
- Define and implement information sharing capabilities that promote and encourage the further development of more secure architectures and security technology capabilities and enhancements. Organization can benefit from the education and distribution of corporate-wide information about security and the risks related to control systems, best practices, and methods.[13]
- Define and implement effective security management programs and practices that include or take (highly) into consideration of control systems' security and its management.
- Periodic audits conducted that test and ensure security technologies integrity is at expected levels of security. Review information with all necessary parties involved, mitigating potential risk issues. Audit should be based upon standard risk assessment practices for mission-critical business units (and its functional subunits).[14]
- Define and implement mission-critical business continuity strategies and continuity plans within organizations and industries, which ensure safe

and continued operation in the event of an unexpected interruption or attack. Elements of continuity planning typically include: (a) assessments performed against the target mission-critical business unit for criticality of operations and identifying supporting resources to mitigate (if any); (b) developing methods that will prevent and minimize potential damage and interruption of service; (c) develop and document comprehensive continuity plans; (d) periodic testing and evaluation of the continuity plans (similar to performing security audits, but are specialized against disaster recovery and/or business continuity efforts of the control systems' environments), making adjustments where necessary (or as needed).[15]

10.19 TECHNOLOGY RESEARCH INITIATIVES OF CONTROL SYSTEMS

Research and development of newer technologies is a constant process, providing additional security options in efforts of protecting control systems. Several federally funded entities have ongoing efforts to research, develop, and test new technologies. Those entities are as follows:

- *Sandia National Laboratories*: Current development of improved SCADA technologies at the Sandia SCADA Development Laboratory, in which industry representatives can test, improve, and enhance security of its SCADA architectures, systems, and components.
- *Idaho National Engineering and Environmental Laboratory*: Current development of the National SCADA Test Bed, which is a full-scale infrastructure testing facility that will allow for large-scaled testing of SCADA systems before exposing those architectures and technologies to production networks, and for testing newer standards and protocols before implementation.
- *Los Alamos National Laboratory*: Cojointly working together, both Sandia and Los Alamos are cooperatively developing critical infrastructure modeling, simulation, and analysis centers known as the National Infrastructure Simulation and Analysis Center. The center provides modeling and simulation capabilities for the analysis of all critical infrastructures, particularly the electricity, oil, and gas industrial sectors.

10.20 SECURITY AWARENESS AND INFORMATION SHARING INITIATIVES

Several efforts to develop and disseminate security awareness about control systems' vulnerabilities and take proactive measures/countermeasures are being coordinated between government agencies (mostly), with some industrial sector participation. Some of those initiatives are as follows:

Department of Homeland Security: The Department of Homeland Security created a National Cyber Security Division to identify, analyze, and reduce cyber threats and vulnerabilities, disseminate threat warning information, coordinate incident response, and provide technical assistance in continuity of operations and recovery planning. The Critical Infrastructure Assurance Office (now part of the Department of Homeland Security) within the Department coordinates the federal government's initiatives on critical infrastructure assurance and promotes national outreach and awareness campaigns about critical infrastructure protection.

Sandia National Laboratories, Environmental Protection Agency, and industrial groups: Sandia National Laboratories has collaborated with the Environmental Protection Agency and industry groups to develop a risk assessment methodology for assessing the vulnerability of water systems in major U.S. cities. Sandia has also conducted vulnerability assessments of control systems within the electric power, oil and gas, transportation, and manufacturing industries. Sandia is involved with various activities to address the security of our critical infrastructures, including developing best practices, providing security training, demonstrating threat scenarios, and furthering standards efforts.

North American Energy Reliability Council: Designated by the Department of Energy as the electricity sector's Information Sharing and Analysis Center coordinator for critical infrastructure protection, the North American Energy Reliability Council facilitates communication between the electricity sector, the federal government, and other critical infrastructure sectors. The council has formed the Critical Infrastructure Protection Advisory Group which guides computer security activities and conducts security workshops to raise awareness of cyber and physical security in the electricity sector. The council also formed a Process Controls subcommittee within the Critical Infrastructure Protection Advisory Group to specifically address control systems.

Federal Energy Regulatory Commission: The Federal Energy Regulatory Commission regulates interstate commerce in oil, natural gas, and electricity. The commission has published a rule to promote the capturing of critical energy infrastructure information, which may lead to increased information sharing capabilities between industry and the federal government.

Process Control Systems Cyber Security Forum: The Process Control Systems Cyber Security Forum is a joint effort between Kema Consulting and LogOn Consulting, Inc. The forum studies the computer security issues surrounding the effective operation of control systems and focuses on issues, challenges, threats, vulnerabilities, best practices/lessons learned, solutions, and related topical areas for control systems. It currently holds workshops on control system computer security.

Chemical Sector Cyber Security Program: The Chemical Sector Cyber Security Program is a forum of 13 trade associations and serves as the Information Sharing and Analysis Center for the chemical sector. The Chemical Industry Data Exchange is part of the Chemical Sector Cyber Security Program and is working to establish a common security vulnerability assessment methodology and to align the chemical industry with the ongoing initiatives at the Instrumentation Systems and Automation Society, the National Institute of Standards and Technology, and the American Chemistry Council.

The President's Critical Infrastructure Protection Board and Department of Energy. The President's Critical Infrastructure Protection Board and the Department of Energy developed 21 Steps to Improve the Cyber Security of SCADA Networks. These steps provide guidance for improving implementation and establishing underlying management processes and policies to help organizations improve the security of their control networks.

Joint Program Office for Special Technology Countermeasures. The Joint Program Office has performed vulnerability assessments on control systems, including the areas of awareness, integration, physical testing, analytic testing, and analysis.

10.21 PROCESS AND SECURITY CONTROL INITIATIVES

Several efforts to develop policies, standards, and/or procedures that will assist in the securification of control systems are being coordinated between government and industry to identify and prevent potential threats, assess infrastructure vulnerabilities, and develop guidelines and standards for mitigating risks through protective measures. Some of those initiatives have already begun, while others are still being considered and developed:

The President's Critical Infrastructure Protection Board. In February 2003, the board released the National Strategy to Secure Cyberspace.[16] The Protection Board document provides a general strategic picture, specific recommendations and policies, and the rationale for these initiatives. The strategy ranks control network security as a national priority and designates the Department of Homeland Security to be responsible for developing best practices and new technologies to increase control system security.[17]

Instrumentation, Systems, and Automation Society. The Instrumentation, Systems, and Automation Society is composed of users, vendors, government, and academic participants representing the electric utilities, water, chemical, petrochemical, oil and gas, food and beverage, and pharmaceutical industries. It has been working on a proposed standard since October 2002. The new standard addresses the security of manufacturing and control systems. It is to provide users with the tools necessary to integrate a comprehensive security process. One report, ISA-TR99.00.01, Security Technologies for Manufacturing and Control Systems, will describe electronic security technologies and discuss specific types of applications within each category, the vulnerabilities addressed by each type, suggestions for deployment, and known strengths and weaknesses. The other report, ISA-TR99.00.02, Integrating Electronic Security into the Manufacturing and Control Systems Environment, will provide a framework for developing an electronic security program for manufacturing and control systems, as well as a recommended organization and structure for the security plan.[18]

Gas Technology Institute and Technical Support Working Group: Sponsored by the federal government's Technical Support Working Group, the Gas Support Working Group Technology Institute has researched a number of potential encryption methods to prevent hackers from accessing natural gas company control systems. This research has led to the development of an industry standard for encryption. The standard would incorporate encryption algorithms to be added to both new and existing control systems to control a wide variety of operations. This standard is outlined in the American Gas Association's report, numbered 12-1.

National Institute of Standards and Technology and the National Security Agency: The National Institute of Standards and Technology and the National Security Agency have organized the Process Controls Security Requirements Forum to establish security specifications that can be used in procurement, development, and retrofit of industrial control systems. NIST and NSA (both) have developed a set of security standards and certification processes.

North American Energy Reliability Council (NERC): The North American Energy Reliability Council has established a computer security standard for the electricity industry. The council requires members of the electricity industry to self-certify that they are meeting the computer-security standards. It should be noted, however, that at the time of writing, the standard does not apply to control systems.

Electric Power Research Institute: The Electric Power Research Institute has developed the Utility Communications Architecture, a set of standardized guidelines that provides interconnectivity and interoperability for utility data communication systems for real-time information exchange.

10.22 SECURING CONTROL SYSTEMS

As part of methodologies or securing critical infrastructure control systems, here are some suggested recommendations insofar as to implementation of a more secured environment involving control systems:

- Implement auditing controls over process systems; systems are periodically audited.
- Develop policies, standards, and/or procedures that are managed and updated periodically.
- Assist in the development of secured architectures that can integrate with computer technologies today and 10 years from now.
- Implement segments networks that are protected with firewalls and intrusion detection technology; periodically test intrusion attempts to ensure that security countermeasures operate correctly.
- Develop a method for exception tracking.
- Develop and implement company-wide Incident Response Plans (IRP); IRP documentation should work with existing DRP and BCP documentation, just in case of an outage.

10.23 IMPLEMENT AUDITING CONTROLS

Develop methodologies of understanding with levels of awareness for corporate management such that stateful computer-based security mechanisms are implemented for process control systems.

Control systems' auditing is not the same focus as computer-based security auditing; audits conducted have a far-reaching impact on all aspects involved; thus, control systems utilized must take into consideration real-life scenarios involving loss of life, loss of financial or capital gain or monetary loss, and loss of property.

Testing and evaluation of control systems during an auditing routine is not without risk. Although the audits may be similar in nature to their counterparts from other industrial sectors, it is important to note that technical audits must be performed following a carefully outlined guideline or plan and performed by certified or licensed technical professionals that are knowledgeable in the areas of control systems operation.

10.24 DEVELOP POLICY MANAGEMENT AND CONTROL MECHANISMS

Develop security policies, standards, and/or procedures for the control systems that: (a) set and define a statement of goals and objectives for the control system device, responsibilities broken down based on department, group, and individual for supporting and responding to emergency or disaster conditions or situations, and acceptable responses, as part of the Incident Response Planning Team, that will be an overseeing group or committee in its implementation.

Define within the policies, standards, and/or procedures sections in which all documentation is subject to change at any time, and should be periodically revisited for validity, content, and functionality.

Define within the policies, standards, and/or procedures verbiage outlining that the documentation is representative of goals and objectives in terms of achievement, not specifically as to how, or the method of, performing any security task; essentially, security policies should be at a strategically, possibly tactical, level.

10.25 CONTROL SYSTEMS ARCHITECTURE DEVELOPMENT

Develop and implement a multiple-leveled network infrastructure, segmenting the control systems architecture from that of the remainder of the corporate enterprise network; use firewalls and intrusion detection technologies to provide this level of protection.

Simpler architectures could be divided within a facility into two distinctive levels: (a) all inter-networking and interlayer network traffic flows through firewall and intrusion detection systems areas; and (b) provide a single point of control to oversee, manage, and maintain control of all network traffic in and out of areas involving control systems.

10.26 SEGMENT NETWORKS BETWEEN CONTROL SYSTEMS AND CORPORATE ENTERPRISE

Implementing the use of firewall and intrusion detection technologies is not required; however, implementing these two very important technologies would reduce risk but would not completely remove the risk (if any):

Essentially, the firewall is the lock on the door; the firewall is not the "burglar alarm." This is where an intrusion detection system would be useful.

Require network intrusion detection systems to monitor any and all network traffic, and identify any unintended and/or malicious activity on, within, or through the network.

Control systems network traffic patterns tend to be very repetitive and consistent based upon their simplicity such that definition of network traffic matrices may be enough to determine what is accessing the control systems' networks.

10.27 DEVELOP METHODOLOGIES FOR EXCEPTION TRACKING

This area essentially identifies any exceptions for any rule insofar that if the device or environment were to be secured tightly, it would be unable to operate properly; therefore, defining an exception listing makes good sense[19]:

A layered security model is very strong (if implemented properly) as designed without exception; however, as with any system, there may be circumstances in which exceptions might have to be made. If one or more exceptions are to be made, identify those exceptions within a list and keep it with the rest of the security documentation as part of the auditing process (for example, support vendor may require the use of dial-in capabilities utilizing computer modems for technical support-related issues).

Require that any recordkeeping of exceptions listed are kept safe, and that, by any other means, any other method of access or communications remains secured.

10.28 DEFINE AN INCIDENT RESPONSE PLAN

With any critical infrastructure environment, the continued operation of the business unit is crucial to the success of the business; therefore, a "what if" scenario is highly recommended. This document (or suite of documents) should coincide with any business continuity planning documentation and/or disaster recovery planning documentation. Develop an incident response plan for security incidents, in that: (a) there is definition of a process to deal with incidents in advance (if applicable); and (b) establish a Security Response Team (SRT). The SRT is a central resource that provides testing, guidance, and solutions in the event of an incident (or a serious nature) is reported.

10.29 SIMILARITIES BETWEEN SECTORS

Not all industrial sectors have specialized or proprietary policies, standards, and/or procedures related to their specific industrial sector; however, it should be noted that (overall), best security practices should be coordinated between the various sectors, thus reinforcing their availability, capabilities, enhancements, and encouraging the dissemination of useful and worthwhile information that would be of great significance to (possibly) more than one industrial sector.

10.30 QUESTIONS

1. Control systems are used to reproduce processes and functions of any given system. True or False?

   Answer: *False*. Control systems are computer-based systems that are used by many infrastructures and industries to monitor and control sensitive processes and physical functions.

2. How many types of control systems are there?
   a. 4
   b. 3
   c. 2
   d. 5

   Answer: *2*. There are two primary types of control systems: (1) Distributed Control Systems; and (2) Supervisory Control and Data Acquisition Systems.

3. The central supervisory control and monitoring station is called a
   _____.

   Answer: *Master control system*. This is a device or station that is located at a site in which application servers and production control workstations that are used to configure and troubleshoot other control system components

4. The controller stations have how many components?
   a. 5
   b. 4
   c. 3
   d. 2

Answer: *3.* There are three components of a controller station: (1) Remote Terminal Unit; (2) Programmable Logic Controller; and (3) a DCS controller.

5. Control systems are increasingly using wide area networks and the Internet to transmit data to their remote or local stations and individual devices. True or False?

    Answer: *True.* This convergence of control networks with public and enterprise networks potentially exposes the control systems to additional security vulnerabilities. Unless appropriate security controls are deployed within and throughout the enterprise and control system network, breaches in enterprise security may affect operations.

6. A "time bomb" is defined as:
    a. A ticking bomb or explosive device
    b. Countdown to an event
    c. A condition or state once encountered will become activated
    d. Programmable logic flaws or failures

    Answer: *A condition or state once encountered will become activated.* A "time bomb" is a triggered event that is activated once a logical flag or state within the computer-based system is encountered. Think of it as the fuse being lit on an actual bomb when a situation or circumstance is encountered or triggered.

7. Wardialing and wardriving are exactly the same. True or False?

    Answer: *False.* The method of sequential dialing with the intent of either exploiting the service connected to, and associated with, the telephone number found is called *wardialing*. With *wardriving*, the principle and primary goal remains the same: access via wireless connectivity. This method of scanning is a form of wireless network sniffing from a stationary, sometimes remote location to the target point.[20] So, one is hardwired-connected switched telephone systems, the other is wireless networked.

8. Control systems can be secured using similar techniques from existing networked-based technologies. True or False?

    Answer: *True.* Control systems are simply computerized environments connected to computer workstations or servers. These workstations or servers have operating systems that need to be periodically patched, checked, and validated periodically.

9. How many organizations have developed security standards and guidelines for securing control system environments?
    a. 5
    b. 4
    c. 3
    d. 2

Answer: *4.* Those organizations are: (1) AGA (AGA 12); (2) ISA (ISA-
SP99-TR1); (3) NIST (NIST PCSRF); and (4) NERC (NERC CIP).

10. The only development standard in place for control systems is offered by
_____.

Answer: *NIST.*

NOTES

1. The Library of Congress, CRS Report for Congress: "Critical Infrastructure: Control Systems and the Terrorist Threat," CRS-RL31534 (February 21, 2003).
2. The Library of Congress, CRS Report for Congress: "Critical Infrastructure: Control Systems and the Terrorist Threat," CRS-RL31534 (February 21, 2003).
3. President's Commission on Critical Infrastructure Protection, Critical Foundations: Protecting America's Infrastructures (Washington, D.C., October 1997).
4. The National Research Council, Making the Nation Safer: the Role of Science and Technology in Countering Terrorism (Washington, D.C., December 2002).
5. The White House, the National Strategy to Secure Cyberspace (Washington, D.C., February 2003).
6. U.S. General Accounting Office, Critical Infrastructure Protection: Challenges and Efforts to Secure Control Systems, GAO-04-354 (Washington, D.C., March 15, 2004).
7. NLANR/Internet2 Joint Techs Meeting: SCADA Security, Joe St. Sauver, Ph.D., University of Oregon (Columbus, OH, July 21, 2004).
8. http://www.wardriving.com
9. http://wiki.personaltelco.net/index.cgi/WarDriving
10. http://www.fas.org/irp/news/1998/08/98082502_ppo.html
11. http://www.fas.org/irp/news/1998/08/98082502_ppo.html
12. http://www.ncbi.nlm.nih.gov/entrez/query.fcgi?cmd=Retrieve&db=PubMed&list_uids=11005165&dopt=Abstract
13. U.S. General Accounting Office, Homeland Security: Information Sharing Responsibilities, Challenges, and Key Management Issues, GAO-03-1105T (Washington, D.C., September 17, 2003).
14. U.S. General Accounting Office, Federal Information System Controls Audit Manual, GAO/AIMD-12.19.6 (Washington, D.C., January 1999).
15. U.S. General Accounting Office, Critical Infrastructure Protection: Challenges for Selected Agencies and Industry Sectors, GAO-03-233 (Washington, D.C.: February 28, 2003) and U.S. General Accounting Office, Critical Infrastructure Protection: Efforts of the Financial Services Sector to Address Cyber Threats, GAO-03-173 (Washington, D.C., January 30, 2003).

16. U.S. Department of State, The National Strategy to Secure Cyberspace (November, 2003) (http://usinfo.state.gov/journals/itgic/1103/ijge/gj11.htm).
17. U.S. General Accounting Office, Critical Infrastructure Protection: Significant Challenges Need to Be Addressed, GAO-02-961T (Washington, D.C., July 24, 2002).
18. U.S. General Accounting Office, Critical Infrastructure Protection: Challenges in Securing Control Systems, GAO-04-140T (Washington, D.C., October 1, 2003).
19. BCIT: Myths and Facts Behind Cyber Security of Industrial Control (April, 2003).
20. http://www.wardriving.com

11 Critical Infrastructure Information (CII)

11.1 INTRODUCTION

This chapter introduces concepts surrounding the reclassification of information and provides some introspective views as to how both industry and government are altering how information is perceived. With publicly available information unsecured and providing demographical, financial, security-related information, as well as critical infrastructure information that pertains to the operation, description, geographic/geospatial mapping data, system or access information about a critical infrastructure (or its sectors) — has and is currently being reviewed; this is a continuous process undergoing some serious reconsideration of information classification.

11.2 WHAT IS CRITICAL INFRASTRUCTURE INFORMATION?

The definition of "critical infrastructure information"[1] (CII)[2] represents a type of designation of data or information that is representative of a critical infrastructure, or its sector, and is considered sensitive in nature but remains unclassified (*this implies the federal government's "Sensitive, But Unclassified" designation, as discussed later within this chapter*). In some regards, CII is information[3] that is a form of metadata[4]; that is, it is data[5] about data, or more appropriately, data containing additional data. Some have stipulated that CII is another redefinition of the term "information." As defined by more than one credible source, the definition of the term "information" represents data that has been transformed through analysis and interpretation into a form useful for drawing conclusions and making decisions. Thus, CII is clearly *not* the same as "information."

Therefore, CII is specifically defined consisting of any of the five criteria such that it:

1. Represents information directly relating to specific data, tasks, or information relating to any given critical infrastructure (or its sector).
2. Represents information generated by, produced by, or indirectly related to such information that results from or is resulting from daily operations of any given critical infrastructure (or its sector).
3. Represents geographical or geospatial information pertaining to locations, access-points, methods of access to or from a site, facility, or area that is representative of a critical infrastructure (or its sector).

4. Represents any other information that may be indirectly related to or from any given critical infrastructure that is deemed, labeled, or marked as "protected critical infrastructure information" (as defined within the Critical Infrastructure Information Act of 2002), or as accepted by the U.S. Department of Homeland Security.

5. Represents any recently defined or newly found or discovered information that could be utilized to destroy, dismantle, render useless or inoperative, incapacitate, or lessen the usefulness of any given critical infrastructure, or any impacts resulting from said methods against, to, from, or within any given critical infrastructure (or its sector).

To translate (without sounding too circular), in a nutshell, "critical infrastructure information"[6] is loosely defined as consisting of any of the five criteria such that it:

Relates to information about critical infrastructures (or its sectors).

Relates to information produced from the operations of those critical infrastructures (such as patient information, financial records, transaction logs).

Relates to mapping information about locations and/or directions to any critical infrastructure site, facility, or work area.

Relates to information that the government considers "protected critical infrastructure information."

Relates to any newly found or discovered information about a critical infrastructure (such as exploit information and/or "How-To FAQs" that would explain how to disable, dismantle, or destroy (say) a high-energy electrical transmission tower).

A few additional criteria may hold true to the refined definition of CII, which might include the following alternative criteria:

Relates to information about future developments of critical infrastructures (such as maps and/or architectural drawings or designs of power generation facilities).

Relates to information about discontinued or dismantled critical infrastructures that are no longer in use (such as dismantled nuclear power generation facilities, or long-term nuclear material storage facilities).

Relates to geological information about locations to any critical infrastructure (such as earthquake-prone sites, facilities, or areas of critical infrastructures that would show possible weaknesses of that location)[7] (not to rule out other locations throughout the United States, but this would be more prevalent in the Western region of the United States, such as the states of California, Oregon, and Washington where earthquakes occur more frequently and are more predominate than elsewhere throughout the United States).

Relates to any meteorological information about locations to any critical infrastructure.

CII was implemented, through regulation, through the Critical Infrastructure Information Act of 2002 in February 2004. As of March 2, 2004, a U.S. Department of Justice report stated that the CII designation would apply only to documents that were/are in the possession of the U.S. Department of Homeland Security.

11.3 HOW DOES THE GOVERNMENT INTERPRET CII?

Exemption 1 of the Freedom of Information Act (FOIA) protects data owners from disclosure of national security information concerning national defense or foreign policy, provided that it has been properly classified in accordance with the substantive and procedural requirements of an executive order.[8] As of October 14, 1995, the executive order in effect was Executive Order 12958 issued by President Clinton (and amended in 1999 by Executive Order 13142).[9,10]

Section 1.5 of the order specifies the types of information that may be considered for classification: military plans, weapons systems, or operations; foreign government information; intelligence activities, sources or methods, or cryptology; foreign relations or foreign activities, including confidential sources; scientific, technological, or economic matters relating to national security; federal government programs for safeguarding nuclear materials and facilities; or vulnerabilities or capabilities of systems, installations, projects, or plans relating to national security.[11] The categories of information that may be classified seemingly appear broad enough to include homeland security information concerning critical infrastructures. Under Executive Order (E.O.) 12958, information may not be classified unless "its disclosure reasonably could be expected to cause damage to the national security."[12]

On March 19, 2002, the White House Chief of Staff issued a directive to the heads of all federal agencies addressing the need to protect information concerning weapons of mass destruction as well as other sensitive homeland security-related information.[13]

The implementing guidance for the directive concerned sensitive homeland security information that was currently classified, as well as previously unclassified or declassified information.[14] The guidance stipulated that if information was currently classified, that its classified status should be maintained in compliance to E.O. 12958. This included extending the duration of classification as well as exempting such information from automatic declassification (as appropriate).

For previously unclassified or declassified information concerning weapons of mass destruction and other sensitive homeland security-related information, the implementing guidelines stipulated that, if it has never been publicly disclosed under proper authority, it may be classified or reclassified as outlined within E.O. 12958.

If the information was subject to a previous request for access such as a FOIA request, classification, or reclassification, then it is subject to the special requirements of that executive order.[15]

11.4 EXEMPTION 3 OF THE FREEDOM OF INFORMATION ACT

As outlined under Exemption 3 of the FOIA, information protected from disclosure under other statutes is also exempt from public disclosure.[16]

Exemption 3 allows the withholding of information prohibited from disclosure by another statute if and only if the other statute meets one of three criteria:

1. Requires that records are to be withheld (with no agency discretion).
2. Grants discretion on whether to withhold information, but provides specific criteria outlining the exercise of that discretion.
3. Describes the types of records to be withheld.

To support an Exemption 3 claim, the information requested must fit within a category of information that the statute authorizes to be withheld (as circular as this may sound, essentially, if the information does not fit the criteria established, it cannot be acted upon).[17] As with all FOIA exemptions, the government bears the burden of proving that requested records are properly withheld.[18] Numerous statutes have been held to qualify as Exemption 3 statutes under the exemption's first subpart, in which those statutes that require information to be withheld leave the agency, no discretion.[19]

Several statutes have failed to qualify under Exemption 3 because too much discretion was vested in the agency or because the statute lacked specificity regarding the records to be withheld.[20] Unlike other FOIA exemptions, if the information requested under FOIA meets the withholding criteria of Exemption 3, the information must be withheld.[21]

Congress has considered a number of proposals that address the disclosure under FOIA of cyber security information, of information maintained by the Department of Homeland Security, and of critical infrastructure information voluntarily submitted to the Department of Homeland Security.[22] Generally, legislation has specifically exempted the covered information from disclosure under FOIA, in effect creating an Exemption 3 statute for purposes of FOIA.[23]

11.5 EXEMPTION 4 OF THE FREEDOM OF INFORMATION ACT

Exemption 4 of the FOIA exempts from disclosure "trade secrets and commercial or financial information obtained from a person and privileged or confidential."[24] The latter category of information (commercial information that is privileged or confidential) is relevant to the issue of the federal government's protection of private sector critical infrastructure information.[25]

To fall within this second category of Exemption 4, the information must satisfy three criteria. It must be[26]:

1. Considered to be commercial or financial.
2. Obtained from an individual.
3. Labeled or classified as confidential or privileged.

The Washington, D.C. circuit court held that the terms "commercial or financial" should be given their ordinary meaning, and that records are commercial if the submitter has a "commercial interest" in them.[27] The second criteria, "obtained from a person," refers to a wide range of entities.[28] However, information generated by the federal government is not "obtained from a person," and as a result is excluded from Exemption 4's coverage.[29] Most Exemption 4 cases involved in a dispute are generally over whether the information was considered as "confidential."[30]

11.6 SECTION 214 OF THE HOMELAND SECURITY ACT

After extensive deliberation (which still appears to be continuing today), and no small amount of controversy involved, the U.S. Department of Homeland Security (DHS) has regulations defining the "Protected Critical Infrastructure Program" within the implementation of Section 214 of the Homeland Security Act of 2002, 6 U.S.C.A. §133 (West Supp. 2003).[31] Section 214 of the Homeland Security Act, enacted in November 2002, contains a series of provisions aimed at promoting the flow of sensitive information specifically relating to the national critical infrastructures (of which, approximately 85% are located within private sectors) to the federal government for homeland security purposes.[32]

This section established a new category defined as "critical infrastructure information" (referred to as "CII").

Section 214 of the Homeland Security Act of 2002 (P.L. 107-269) exempted from disclosure under FOIA for Exemption 3[33] protection such that "critical infrastructure information (including the identity of the submitting person or entity) that is voluntarily submitted to a covered agency for use by that agency regarding the security of critical infrastructure (as defined in the USA PATRIOT Act) ...,[34] when accompanied by an express statement ...."[35] The new Exemption 3 statute for CII, which now applies to information held by DHS only, is one of "a growing trend [of] statutes enacted in recent years [that] contain disclosure prohibitions that are not general in nature but rather are specifically directed toward disclosure under the FOIA in particular."[36]

The Homeland Security Act defines "critical infrastructure information" to be representative of "information not customarily in the public domain and related to the security of critical infrastructure or protected systems":

A. Actual, potential, or threatened interference with, attack on, compromise of, or incapacitation of critical infrastructure or protected systems by either physical or computer-based attack or other similar conduct (including misuse of or unauthorized access to all types of communications and data transmission systems) that violates federal, state, or local law, harms interstate commerce of the United States, or threatens public health and safety.

B. The ability of critical infrastructures or protected systems to resist such interference, compromise, or incapacitation, including any planned or past assessment, projection or estimate of the vulnerability of critical infrastructure or a protected system, including security testing, risk evaluation thereto, risk management planning, or risk audit.

C. Any planned or past operational problem or solution regarding critical infrastructure ... including repair, recovery, reconstruction, insurance, or continuity to the extent it relates to such interference, compromise, or incapacitation."[37]

A "covered agency" is defined as the U.S. Department of Homeland Security.[38] The submission of critical infrastructure information is considered voluntary if done in the absence of the DHS exercising its legal authority to compel access to or submission of such information.[39] Information submitted to the Securities and Exchange Commission pursuant to Section 12(i) of the Securities and Exchange Act of 1934 is explicitly not protected by this provision.[40]

Besides exempting from FOIA, critical infrastructure information which has been submitted voluntarily with the appropriate express statement to the DHS, the Homeland Security Act also states that the information shall not be subject to any agency rules or judicial doctrine regarding "ex parte" communications with decision-making officials.[41]

The act also prohibits such information without the written consent of the person or entity submitting such information in good faith from being used directly by the DHS, any other federal, state, or local authority or any third party, in any civil action.[42]

Nor may the information, without the written consent of the person or entity submitting such information be used or disclosed by any officer or employee of the United States for any purpose other than the purposes of the subtitle except in the furtherance of a criminal investigation or prosecution, or when disclosed to either House of Congress, or to the Comptroller General or other authorized General Accounting Office official, in the conduct of official business.[43]

11.7 ENFORCEMENT OF SECTION 214 OF THE HOMELAND SECURITY ACT

Any federal official or employee who knowingly publishes, divulges, discloses, or makes known in any manner or to any extent not authorized by law, any protected information, is subject to removal, imprisonment up to one year, and fines.[44] If the information is disclosed to state or local officials, it may not be used for any purpose other than the protection of critical infrastructures, and it may not be disclosed under state disclosure laws.[45]

The protections afforded protected information *do not* result in waiver of any privileges or protections provided elsewhere in law.[46] Finally, no communication of critical infrastructure information to the DHS shall be considered to be an action subject to the requirements of the Federal Advisory Committee Act.[47]

For information to be considered protected, it must be accompanied with a written statement to the effect that "This information is voluntarily submitted to the federal government in expectation of protection from disclosure as provided by the Critical Infrastructure Information Act of 2002 (the name given to Subtitle B)." The Secretary of the Department of Homeland Security is to establish procedures for handling the information once it is received. Only those agency components or bureaus designated by the President or the Secretary of Homeland Security, as having a Critical Infrastructure Program may receive critical infrastructure information from the department.

The above protections for information voluntarily submitted by a person or entity to the Department of Homeland Security do not limit or otherwise affect the ability of a state, local, or federal government entity, agency or authority, or any third party, under applicable law, to obtain critical infrastructure information (including any information lawfully and properly disclosed generally and broadly to the public) and to use that information in any manner permitted by law.[48]

Submittal to the government of information or records that are protected from disclosure is not to be construed as compliance with any requirement to submit such information to a federal agency under any other provision of law.[49] Finally, the Act does not expressly create a private right of action for enforcement of any provision of the Act.[50]

11.8 WHAT DOES "SENSITIVE, BUT UNCLASSIFIED" MEAN?

In recent years, more reports and information contained on Web sites have introduced a new data classification referred to as "sensitive, but unclassified" especially when dealing with information pertaining to a critical infrastructure such as the national power grid. The term "sensitive, but unclassified" (also referred to as "SBU")[51] is an informal designation applicable to all types and forms of information that, by law or regulation, require some form of protection, but are outside the formal system for classifying national security information.[52]

As a general rule, information may be exempt from release to the public under the Freedom of Information Act.[53,54] This section reviews the most common types of sensitive unclassified information.[55]

The U.S. Department of Defense (DoD) also uses the term "Controlled Unclassified Information" (CUI)[56] to refer to certain types of sensitive information within DoD that required controls and protective measures.[57] CUI includes "For Official Use Only" and information with comparable designations that is received from other agencies, DoD Unclassified Controlled Nuclear Information, "Sensitive Information" as defined in the Computer Security Act of 1987, and DoD technical data.[58]

Some information that is not formally designated as sensitive is nonetheless inappropriate for putting on a public, *unsecured* Internet Web site.[59] Federal law defines most categories of sensitive unclassified information; while others such as the "For Official Use Only" classification are defined by organization policy and several government organizations use different names for this category of information.[60]

Most legislative authorities are very specific in identifying the protected category of information, while others are general and leave much discretion to the agency or company.[61] Procedures for safeguarding sensitive unclassified information depend on the category of information and, in some cases, vary from one agency or company to another.[62]

Generally speaking, the law provides protection for established categories of protected information only when the owners of the information have taken reasonable or required steps to protect it.[63] These steps are sometimes stated in the law or regulation; however, they are often left up to the information owner to develop internally.[64] Legal history shows that the following elements are the key to successful enforcement of an information protection program.

The organization must have[65]:

- An established information security policy.
- A system or mechanism to identify specific information that is to be protected (this includes periodic reviews of the need for continued protection).
- Procedures for safeguarding and controlling protected information such that any risk of exposure is only to those who have specific need for knowledge of the information, as well as a duty to protect its safety.
- Duty to protect and safeguard information may be imposed or regulated by law (for some categories), or established by a confidential agreement.
- A system or mechanism of warnings and markings advising of the sensitivity and/or handling requirements of the information.

11.9 INFORMATION HANDLING PROCEDURES

Procedures for handling the various categories of sensitive unclassified information vary from one agency or company to another.[66] This is due to different legal and/or regulatory requirements for each category and the agency or organization's implementation of those requirements.[67] Factors affecting the implementation are the degree of sensitivity of the information, nature of the threat to the information, vulnerability of the information, options that are available for protecting the information, and organizational facilities/capabilities for secure handling, storage, and transmission.[68]

11.10 FREEDOM OF INFORMATION ACT

The public has a right to information concerning the activities of its government. The Freedom of Information Act (FOIA) requires all government organizations (mostly federally related) to conduct their activities in an open manner and to have a system for providing the public with the maximum amount of accurate and timely information allowed by law.[69] Agencies commonly have an FOIA office for processing public requests for information.[70]

The FOIA allows nine exemptions from this mandatory release policy.[71] The purpose of the exemptions is to preclude the unauthorized disclosure of information that requires protection.

These exemption categories reflect laws, executive orders, regulations, or court decisions that either require or permit protection of certain classes of information.[72] The exemption categories, in turn, also help define information that may be protected.[73] For example, the U.S. Department of Defense Regulation 5200.1-R defines "For Official Use Only" information as "unclassified information that may be exempt from mandatory release to the public under the Freedom of Information Act (FOIA)."[74]

DoD Regulation 5200.1-R, Appendix C, describes the nine FOIA exemptions as written below.[75] The wording reflects the history of court decisions interpreting the Freedom of Information Act and, therefore, differs from the language of the act itself.[76]

To be exempt from mandatory release, information must fit into one of the following categories, and there must be a legitimate government purpose served by withholding it[77]:

Exemption #1: Information which is currently and properly classified.

Exemption #2: Information that pertains solely to the internal rules and practices of the agency. This exemption has two profiles, high and low. The high profile permits withholding of a document that, if released, would allow circumvention of an agency rule, policy, or statute, thereby impeding the agency in the conduct of its mission. The low profile permits withholding if there is no public interest in the document, and it would be an administrative burden to process the request.

Exemption #3: Information specifically exempted by statute establishing particular criteria for withholding. The language of the statute must clearly state that the information will not be disclosed.

Exemption #4: Information such as trade secrets and commercial or financial information obtained from a company on a privileged or confidential basis that, if released, would result in competitive harm to the company, impair the government's ability to obtain like information in the future or to protect the government's interest in compliance with program effectiveness.

Exemption #5: Interagency memoranda that are deliberative in nature; this exemption is appropriate for internal documents that are part of the decision making process and contain subjective evaluations, opinions, and recommendations.

Exemption #6: Information the release of which could reasonably be expected to constitute a clearly unwarranted invasion of the personal privacy of individuals.

Exemption #7: Records or information compiled for law enforcement purposes that (a) could reasonably be expected to interfere with law enforcement proceedings; (b) would deprive a person of a right to a fair trial or impartial adjudication; (c) could reasonably be expected to constitute an unwarranted invasion of the personal privacy of others; (d) disclose the identify of a confidential source; (e) disclose investigative techniques or procedures; or (f) could reasonably be expected to endanger the life or physical safety of any individual.

Exemption #8: Certain records of agencies responsible for supervision of financial institutions.

Exemption #9: Geological and geophysical information concerning wells.

FOIA requires agencies to promulgate policies to implement the requirements of the act and to publish these policies in the Federal Register.[78] Each agency is responsible for establishing an appropriate administrative system to manage the FOIA.[79]

The act has no requirements for protection of information. It only permits withholding information from disclosure, when appropriate.[80]

When an FOIA request seeks public release of information held under Exemption #4 (commercial information provided to the government on a confidential basis), the responsible government agency must determine whether the public right to know outweighs the companies' right to protection of proprietary information.[81] If the agency determines that the information should be released under FOIA, Executive Order 12600 requires that the company be advised and be given an opportunity to present its arguments for continued protection before the information is released.[82]

11.11   NEED-TO-KNOW

Not all critical infrastructure information is defined as "protected critical infrastructure information" and may be defined or categorized as something other than CII; one of those designations may be "need-to-know." Need-to-know is one of the most fundamental security principles.[83] The practice of need-to-know limits the damage that can be done by a trusted insider who might betray one's trust. Failures in implementing a need-to-know principle may cause serious damage to an organization.[84]

Need-to-know imposes a dual responsibility on whomever as well as all other authorized holders of protected information[85]:

When performing their job, one is expected to limit their requests for information to that which is a need-to-know. Under some circumstances, an individual may be expected to explain and justify their need-to-know when asking others for information.

Ensure that anyone to whom is given protected information has a legitimate need to know that information. In some cases, one may need to ask the other person for sufficient information to enable that person to make an informed decision about their need-to-know status.

Refrain from discussing protected information in hallways, cafeterias, elevators, rest rooms, or smoking areas where persons who do not have a need-to-know the subject of conversation may overhear the discussion.

A caveat of the need-to-know classification is that need-to-know is difficult to implement as it conflicts with our natural desire to be friendly and helpful.[86] It also requires a level of personal responsibility that many of us find difficult to accept. The importance of limiting sensitive information to those who have a need to know is underscored, however, every time a trusted insider is found to have betrayed that trust.[87] Although every individual with access to a particular computer network is approved for that system, they may not have a need to know all of the information coming across the system.[88]

11.12   "FOR OFFICIAL USE ONLY" (FOUO)

For Official Use Only (FOUO) is a document designation, not a classification.[89] This designation is used by the U.S. Department of Defense and a number of other federal agencies to identify information or material which, although unclassified, may not be appropriate for public release.[90]

There is no national policy governing use of the For Official Use Only designation.[91] DoD Directive 5400.7 defines For Official Use Only information as "unclassified information that may be exempt from mandatory release to the public under the Freedom of Information Act (FOIA)."[92,93] The policy is implemented by DoD Regulations 5400.7-R and 5200.1-R.[94]

> NOTE: The For Official Use Only designation is also used by the CIA as well as a number of other federal agencies, but each agency is responsible for determining how it shall be used. The categories of protected information may be quite different from one agency to another, although in every case the protected information must be covered by one of the nine categories of information that are exempt from public release under FOIA.[95]

Some agencies use different terminology for the same types of information. For example, the U.S. Department of Energy uses "Official Use Only" (OUO).[96] The U.S. Department of State uses "Sensitive, But Unclassified" (SBU) (formerly called "Limited Official Use" [LOU]).[97] The U.S. Drug Enforcement Administration uses "DEA Sensitive." In all cases, the designations refer to unclassified, potentially sensitive information that is or may be exempt from public release under the Freedom of Information Act.[98]

The fact that information is marked FOUO *does not* mean it is automatically exempt from public release under FOIA.[99] If a request for the information is received, it must be reviewed to see if it meets the FOIA dual test[100]:

1. If it fits into one of the nine FOIA exemption categories.
2. If there is a legitimate government purpose served by withholding the data.

Consequently, on the other hand, the absence of the FOUO or other marking does not automatically mean the information must be released in response to a FOIA request.[101]

11.13 ENFORCEMENT OF FOUO INFORMATION

Administrative penalties may be imposed for misuse of FOUO information.[102] Criminal penalties may be imposed depending on the actual content of the information (privacy, export control, and so on).[103,104]

11.14 REVIEWING WEB SITE CONTENT

With all its many benefits, the Internet can also do a great deal of harm if not used properly.[105] Information on the Internet that may be intended for a limited audience is actually available to a worldwide audience.[106] The World Wide Web was not designed with security in mind, and unencrypted information is at high risk of compromise to any interested adversary or competitor.[107] It is very easy to search the web and put together related pieces of information from different sites. For example, the search engine [www.searchmil.com specializes] in indexing sites with a .mil domain name. It claims (as of August 2001) to have indexed over 1 million pages of military sites, with the number of pages still growing rapidly.[108]

The DoD has been among the first government departments to take the lead in spelling out rules for what should and should not go on a Web site and how information should .be reviewed before it is posted on a Web site.[109] The DoD policy should be reviewed prior to posting DoD or DoD-controlled information to a Web site.[110]

The DoD policy applies to all unclassified DoD Web sites, requiring a review and approval process of requests received from DoD contractors and subcontractors as well as other government agencies to post DoD information on their Web sites.[111]

DoD guidelines take into account what security access controls, if any, are in effect for the site, the sensitivity of the information, and the target audience for which the information is intended.[112] Briefly, most types of sensitive, unclassified information discussed (usually) are not permitted for public viewing, and thus, should not be displayed on a Web site unless that site is protected by encryption.[113]

In other words, DoD Technical Information, "For Official Use Only" information, export-controlled information, Unclassified Nuclear Information, and Privacy Act information may not be posted on an unencrypted Web site.[114] Decisions on the handling of proprietary or trade secret information in the private sector are made by the owners of that information.[115]

DoD guidelines also require that judgments about the sensitivity of information take into account the potential consequences of "aggregation." The term "sensitive by aggregation" refers to the fact that information on one site may seem unimportant, but when combined with information from other Web sites it may form a much larger and more complete picture that was neither intended nor desired.[116] In other words, the combination of information from multiple Web sites may amount to more than the sum of its parts. Similarly, the compilation of large amounts of information together from simply one Web site may increase the sensitivity of that information and make it more likely that that Web site will be accessed by those seeking information that might be used against the United States.[117]

Table 11.1 from the DoD guidance on reviewing Web sites[118] has been modified to fit into a smaller space. It is a guide to determining an acceptable level of risk, but the listed types of access controls are not necessarily the only options available for protecting information.

There are several common mistakes that people make when deciding what to put on a Web site. One is to ignore the danger associated with personal data on the Internet. Another is to assume that information is not sensitive just because it is not marked with any sensitivity indicator. A third is that people underestimate the ease and potential significance of "point-and-click aggregation" of information.

"For Official Use Only" information and other sensitive information are normally marked with a sensitivity indicator at the time of creation. However, the absence of any sensitivity marking is not a valid basis for assuming that information is nonsensitive. Before putting unmarked information on a Web site, it must be examined for the presence of information that requires protection and qualifies as exempt from public release.

People who have not themselves developed strong skills at searching the Internet generally underestimate the amount and nature of the information that can be found

TABLE 11.1

If access control is:	the vulnerability is:	and information can be:
Open — no access limitations, plain text, unencrypted.	Extremely high. Subject to worldwide dissemination and access by everyone on the Internet.	Nonsensitive, of general interest to the public, cleared and authorized for public release. Worldwide dissemination must pose limited risk even if information is combined with other information reasonably expected to be in the public domain.
Limited by Internet domain (e.g., military, government) or IP address. Plain text, unencrypted.	Very high. This limitation is not difficult to circumvent.	Nonsensitive, not of general interest to the public although approved and authorized for public release. Intended for DoD or other specifically-targeted audiences.
Limited by requirement for User ID and password. Plain text, unencrypted.	High. Still vulnerable to hackers, as User IDs and passwords can be compromised if encryption is not used.	Nonsensitive information that is appropriate only for a specifically-targeted audience.
User certificate-based (software). Requires PKI encryption through use of secure sockets layer.	Moderate. This provides a moderate level of secure access control.	Sensitive unclassified information, and information that is "sensitive by aggregation."
User certificate-based (hardware). Requires PKI encryption.	Very low vulnerability.	Sensitive unclassified information and information that is "sensitive by aggregation" where extra security is required.

there and the ease with which it can be located. The vast quantity of information on the Internet, combined with powerful computer search engines, has spawned sophisticated "data mining" techniques for the rapid collection and combination of information from many different Web sites. Very little know-how is needed, as the tools of the Internet have been designed to do this. A single user sitting at a computer in a foreign country can now identify, aggregate, and interpret information available on the Internet in ways that sometimes provide insights into classified or sensitive unclassified programs or activities.

Information relevant to operations security (OPSEC) is a particular concern. Commanders and program managers responsible for OPSEC need to identify what needs to be protected and then take a "red team" approach to how outsiders might obtain unauthorized knowledge. As a double check, military reserve units have been tasked to conduct ongoing operations security and threat assessments of DoD Web sites.

One useful tool is to conduct keyword searches on the Internet to learn what related information may already be out there that others might use to deduce information about any sensitive activities. As sites are visited or newsgroup messages are read, personnel should determine if information that could be used in conjunction with the information in question, or with information from some other site, to deduce if it is considered sensitive information.

11.15 EXPORT-CONTROLLED INFORMATION

There may be some CII that is related to a device or information that may be shared outside of the United States. If the device contains cryptographic information or is a protected cryptographic mechanism, it may be protected as an export-controlled device, as well as its information.

Export-controlled information[119] or material is any information or material that cannot be released to foreign nationals or representatives of a foreign entity without first obtaining approval or license from the Department of State for items controlled by the International Traffic in Arms Regulations (ITAR) or the Department of Commerce for items controlled by the Export Administration Regulations (EAR).[120] Export-controlled information is controlled as sensitive information and marked accordingly.[121]

One objective of ITAR and EAR is to prevent foreign citizens, industry, or governments, or their representatives, from obtaining information that is contrary to the national security interests of the United States.[122]

Different laws and regulations use different definitions of a U.S. person, U.S. national, and foreign national. This is a source of considerable confusion when implementing international security programs.[123]

The rules are especially confusing when dealing with an immigrant alien who possesses a green card for permanent residence in the U.S.[124] For the purpose of export control regulations, such an individual is a "U.S. person" and may be allowed access to export-controlled information without an export license.[125] If the export-controlled information is classified, however, the regulations for release of classified information apply. According to the National Industrial Security Program Operating Manual, a permanent resident with a green card is still a foreign national and not a "U.S. person." Therefore, such an individual cannot have access to classified export-controlled information.[126]

11.16 ENFORCEMENT OF EXPORT-CONTROLLED INFORMATION

The penalty for unlawful export of items or information controlled under the ITAR is up to two years imprisonment, or a fine of $100,000, or both.[127] The penalty for unlawful export of items or information controlled under the EAR is a fine of up to $1,000,000 or five times the value of the exports, whichever is greater;

or for an individual, imprisonment of up to ten years or a fine of up to $250,000 or both.[128]

11.17 SOURCE SELECTION DATA

Source Selection Data[129] is information related to the decision making process (including the decision itself) for an award of a contract to industry.[130] Information in this category is generally only sensitive until after a formal award of the contract. Such information must be protected from disclosure outside the government and limited within the government to individuals with a need to know that information.[131]

Federal Acquisition Regulations[132] (FAR)[133] specify procedures to be followed to protect source selection data.[134] Bids may not be disclosed except on a need-to-know basis and only to government employees (FAR Part 14.401[135] — Receipt and safeguarding of bids [48 CFR]).[136]

Proprietary and source selection information may only be disclosed to individuals authorized by the head of an agency (FAR Part 3.104-5[137] — Disclosure, Protection, and Marking of Proprietary and Source Selection Information). For contracts over $100,000, the names of individuals having access to the file shall be listed with the contract file.[138]

11.18 ENFORCEMENT OF SOURCE SELECTION DATA

For knowing disclosure of nongovernment information to which a government agency has gained access in connection with a procurement action, Title 41 U.S.C. 423 — Procurement Integrity, provides both civil and criminal penalties.[139] The criminal penalty is up to five years imprisonment. The civil penalty is a fine up to $100,000.[140]

This applies mainly to government employees who receive nongovernment information, but it also applies to nongovernment personnel who receive sensitive procurement information from government (for example, if government gives industry a bid package containing information from a potential subcontractor).[141] This procurement integrity law applies only prior to the award of a contract. Once a contract has been awarded, other laws with lesser penalties may apply.[142]

Title 18 U.S.C. 1905 applies to disclosure by a government employee of any information provided to the government by a company or other nongovernment organization, if the provider of the information identified it as proprietary or as being provided to the government in confidence.[143] The penalty is mandatory removal from office (termination of employment), and the offender may be fined not more than $1,000 and imprisoned not more than one year.[144]

11.19 PRIVACY INFORMATION

Privacy information is information about an individual including, but not limited to, personal identifying information, social security number, payroll number, and information on education, financial transactions, medical history, including results of drug testing and criminal or employment history.[145]

The Privacy Act addresses information contained in a "federal system of records."[146] A system of records is a collection of information on individuals in which the information is retrievable by the individual's name, identifying number, symbol, or other identifying particular.[147] An "individual" is defined in the act as "a citizen of the U.S. or an alien lawfully admitted for permanent residence."[148]

The Privacy Act requires that privacy information in the custody of the federal government be protected from unauthorized disclosure and provides for both civil and criminal penalties for violation of the act.[149]

Privacy information in the custody of government contractors is not covered by the Privacy Act unless the contractor is performing on a contract under which the contractor is provided access to or custody of such information by the federal government.[150] Under this condition, the law would apply to contractor personnel the same as it applies to government personnel.[151]

11.20 ENFORCEMENT OF PRIVACY INFORMATION

Title 5 U.S.C. 552a, allows civil remedies against the United States for noncompliance, criminal penalties for individual acts of noncompliance, and criminal penalties for maintaining a system of records without meeting the reporting requirements of the Privacy Act.[152]

Title 12 U.S.C. 3417 of the Right to Financial Privacy Act allows civil penalties to agencies and requires an investigation by the Office of Personnel Management and appropriate disciplinary action for federal employees disclosing financial information.[153]

Title 18 U.S.C. 1905 applies to disclosure by a government employee of any information provided to the government by a company or other nongovernment organization, if the provider of the information identified it as proprietary or as being provided to the government in confidence.[154]

The penalty is mandatory removal from office (termination of employment), and the offender may be fined not more than $1,000 and imprisoned not more than one year.[155]

Additionally, several recent acts of legislation have been implemented which protect and safeguard private information of the general public, specifically in the financial and health care sectors. Those pieces of legislation are: (1) the "Gramm-Leach-Bliley Act" (GLBA), which includes provisions to protect consumers' personal financial information held by financial institutions. There are three principal parts to the privacy requirements: the Financial Privacy Rule, Safeguards Rule and pretexting provisions[156]; and (2) the "Health Insurance Portability and Accountability Act" (HIPAA), which regulates and protects the confidentiality, integrity, and availability of personal health information.[157]

11.21 UNCLASSIFIED CONTROLLED NUCLEAR INFORMATION (UCNI)

Unclassified Controlled Nuclear Information (UCNI)[158] is regulated and governed under the jurisdiction of the U.S. Department of Energy which includes unclassified facility design information, operational information concerning the production, processing, or utilization of nuclear material for atomic energy defense programs, safeguards and security information, nuclear material, and declassified or controlled nuclear weapon information once classified as Restricted Data (RD).[159]

Conversely, Department of Defense Unclassified Controlled Nuclear Information (DoD UCNI) is unclassified information on security measures (including security plans, procedures, and equipment) for the physical protection of DoD Special Nuclear Material, equipment, or its facilities.[160]

Information is designated UCNI only when it is determined that its unauthorized disclosure could reasonably be expected to have a significant adverse effect on the health and safety of the public or the common defense and security by increasing significantly the likelihood of the illegal production of nuclear weapons or the theft, diversion, or sabotage of Special Nuclear Material, equipment, or facilities.[161]

11.22 ENFORCEMENT OF UCNI

Violation of Section 148 of the Atomic Energy Act[162] carries a civil fine not to exceed $110,000. In addition, the individual may be subject to a criminal penalty under Section 223 of the act.

11.23 CRITICAL ENERGY INFRASTRUCTURE INFORMATION (CEII)

The Critical Energy Infrastructure Information (CEII) was defined by the Federal Energy Regulatory Commission (FERC) as information concerning proposed or existing critical infrastructure (physical or virtual) that[163]:

Relates to the production, generation, transmission, and distribution of energy.
Is potentially useful for planning an attack on a critical infrastructure from the energy sector.
Is exempt from mandatory disclosure under the Freedom of Information Act.
Provides strategic information beyond specific locations of energy sector critical infrastructures.

FERC established procedures for gaining access to CEII that would otherwise not be available under the FOIA[164]:

CEII is defined as infrastructure explicitly covering proposed facilities, and does not distinguish among projects or portions of projects.
Procedures detailing geospatial or geographical location information is excluded from the definition of CEII and which is included.
CEII rules address some issues that are specific to state agencies, and clarifies that energy market consultants should be able to get access to the CEII when they need it.
CEII rules modify the proposed CEII process and delegates the responsibility to the CEII Coordinator to process requests for CEII and to determine what information qualifies as CEII.

11.24 ENFORCEMENT OF CEII

Non-Internet Public (NIP) documents (documents that are not for disclosure to the general public and are subject to CEII restrictions) are the direct result of FERC Order 630, issued on February 21, 2003. FERC's Order 630 established CEII regulations.[165] Public may file a CEII request under 18 C.F.R. §388.113 or a FOIA request under 18 C.F.R. §388.108.[166] Absent a waiver from the Commission, natural gas pipelines and public utilities are still required to comply with the Commission regulations that may require that CEII be available in county public reading rooms or from companies upon request, as appropriate.[167]

11.25 LESSONS LEARNED PROGRAM

The Lessons Learned programs are part of the national network of lessons learned and best practices for whatever subject matter that the department, agency, or organization is responsible for. The Lessons Learned programs are general, unclassified information that is shared in order to improve operational safety by benefiting from the experience of others.

Information is prepared and distributed whenever there is an opportunity to share a valuable new work practice or warn others of an adverse practice, experience, or product. Information also constitutes archived information provided or contributed by its membership base, which may include whitepapers written by member constituents, or articles taken from third-party news or reference sources.[168]

11.26 INFRAGARD

INFRAGARD is a Federal Bureau of Investigation (FBI) program that began at their Cleveland Field Office in 1996.[169] It was a local effort to gain support from the information technology industry and academia for the FBI's investigative efforts in the cyber arena.[170] The program expanded to other FBI field offices, and in 1998 the FBI assigned national program responsibility for INFRAGARD to the former National Infrastructure Protection Center (NIPC) and to the FBI Cyber Division in 2003.[171] INFRAGARD and the FBI have developed a relationship of trust and credibility in the exchange of information concerning various terrorism, intelligence, criminal, and security matters.[172]

INFRAGARD is an information sharing and analysis effort serving the interests and combining the knowledge base of a wide range of members.[173] At its most basic level, INFRAGARD is a partnership between the FBI and the private sector, and is an association of businesses, academic institutions, state and local law enforcement agencies, and other participants dedicated to sharing information and intelligence to prevent hostile acts against the United States.[174] Its local chapters are geographically linked with FBI field office territories, and each chapter has an FBI Special Agent Coordinator assigned to it; the FBI Coordinator works closely with Supervisory Special Agent Program Managers in the Cyber Division at FBI Headquarters in Washington, D.C.[175]

While under the direction of NIPC, the focus of INFRAGARD was (originally) cyber infrastructure protection.[176] After September 11, 2001, however, NIPC expanded its efforts to include physical and cyber threats to critical infrastructures; consequently, INFRAGARD's mission expanded accordingly.[177]

In March 2003, NIPC was transferred to the DHS, which has responsibility for Critical Infrastructure Protection (CIP) matters.[178] The FBI retained INFRAGARD as an FBI sponsored program and works with DHS in support of its CIP mission, facilitates INFRAGARD's continuing role in CIP activities, and its further development of INFRAGARD's ability to support the FBI's investigative mission, especially as it pertains to counterterrorism and cyber crimes.[179]

11.27 QUESTIONS

1. Critical infrastructure information (CII) is "metadata." True or False?

   Answer: *True*. CII is a form of metadata or "data about data."

2. CII has how many defined categories?
   a. 7
   b. 5
   c. 6
   d. 4

   Answer: *5*.

3. Mapping information is considered CII. Yes or No?

   Answer: *Yes*. CII includes representations of geographical or geospatial information pertaining to locations, access-points, methods of access to or from a site, facility, or area that is representative of a critical infrastructure (or its sector).

4. The CII designation only applies to documents that were/are in the possession of the U.S. Department of Homeland Security (DHS). True or False?

   Answer: *True*. Refer to the Critical Infrastructure Information Act of 2002.

5. What is a "covered agency?"
   a. The U.S. Department of Homeland Security
   b. Controlling or regulating department
   c. Organization in charge of maintaining the CII
   d. Submitting organization or agency

   Answer: This was a trick question. The answer can be either the *a. U.S. Department of Homeland Security* or *c. Organization in charge of maintaining the CII*. Effectively the DHS is the organization responsible for maintaining the CII documentation once it has been submitted as being CII documentation from the critical infrastructure organization, public or private sector.

6. The acronym SBU means "Sensitive, But Unclassified." True or False?

    Answer: *True*. The term "Sensitive, But Unclassified" (also referred to as SBU)[180] is an informal designation applicable to all types and forms of information that, by law or regulation, require some form of protection, but are outside the formal system for classifying national security information.[181]

7. The U.S. Department of Defense (DoD) refers to SBU as _____.

    Answer: *Controlled Unclassified Information (CUI)*.

8. Does CUI include "For Official Use Only?" Yes or No?

    Answer: *Yes*. CUI includes "For Official Use Only" and information with comparable designations that is received from other agencies, DoD Unclassified Controlled Nuclear Information, "Sensitive Information" as defined in the Computer Security Act of 1987, and DoD technical data.[182] Federal law defines most categories of sensitive unclassified information while others such as the "For Official Use Only" classification are defined by organization policy and several government organizations use different names for this category of information.[183] Some agencies use different terminology for the same types of information. For example, the U.S. Department of Energy uses "Official Use Only" (OUO).[184] The U.S. Department of State uses "Sensitive, But Unclassified" (SBU) (formerly called "Limited Official Use" [LOU]).[185] The U.S. Drug Enforcement Administration uses "DEA Sensitive." In all cases, the designations refer to unclassified, potentially sensitive information that is or may be exempt from public release under the Freedom of Information Act.[186]

9. There are _____ exemptions within the Freedom of Information Act (FOIA) that pertain to CII.

    Answer: *9*.

10. Combined sensitive data from several sources, which may seem unimportant, but when combined, are considered sensitive information is referred to as _____.

    Answer: *Sensitive by aggregation*. The combination of information from multiple Web sites may amount to more than the sum of its parts. Thus, the compilation of large amounts of information together from simply one Web site may increase the sensitivity of that information and make it more likely that that Web site will be accessed by those seeking information that might be used against the United States.[187]

11. The organization that the U.S. Federal Bureau of Investigation (FBI) started in 1996 is named _____.

   Answer: *INFRAGARD*.

NOTES

1. Though there appears to be several references, both government and industry, which give regards to the definition of the term "critical infrastructure information," there does not appear to be any contextual data provided which demonstrates a defined term. All in all, all interested involved appear to be more concerned insofar as to what to do with the information, rather than defining it; if it is defined, it consumes numerous volumes of text outlining an overtly detailed explanation, which (simply put) might be explained with but a few bulleted items. Therefore, this definition is, by no means, perfect; however, it is an attempt at defining what it means and signifies.
2. This definition represents a consensus of observed statements, as well as online and printed materials, that were reviewed from both government and industry alike; it is an attempted abbreviated version to what was observed; the shortest/smallest definition of the term "critical infrastructure information" consumed approximately 34 pages of material.
3. def: information: Data that has been transformed through analysis and interpretation into a form useful for drawing conclusions and making decisions. See also "data"; http://www.merrea.org/glossary%20i.htm.
4. def: metadata: It is either (1) information about a data set which is provided by the data supplier or the generating algorithm and which provides a description of the content, format, and utility of the data set; metadata provide criteria which may be used to select data for a particular scientific investigation; or, (2) information describing a data set, including data user guide, descriptions of the data set in directories, and inventories, and any additional information required to define the relationships among these. Source: ESADS, EPO, IWGDMGC; http://podaac.jpl.nasa.gov/glossary/.
5. def: data: The collection of material or facts on which a discussion or an inference is based. Data are the product of measurement. The word "data" is the plural of datum. Compare information (as referred to as a "Lexikon definition"); http://www.merrea.org/glossary%20d.htm.
6. Refer to footnote #715 (shown on the previous page).
7. Thanks (in part) to my wife who presented me with this idea when discussing this chapter.
8. 5 U.S.C. §552(b)(1).
9. 3 C.F.R. 333 (1996), reprinted in 50 U.S.C. §435 note.
10. Congressional Research Service — The Library of Congress, Report for Congress, RL31547, Critical Infrastructure Information: Disclosure and Homeland Security, January 29, 2003. http://www.fas.org/sgp/crs/RL31547.pdf

11. http://www.fas.org/sgp/crs/RL31547.pdf
12. Exec. Order No. 12.958, § 1.2(a)(4).
13. See White House Memorandum for Heads of Executive Departments and Agencies Concerning Safeguarding Information Regarding Weapons of Mass Destruction and Other Sensitive Documents Related to Homeland Security (March 19, 2002); reprinted in FOIA Post (posted 3/21/02).
14. See Memorandum from Acting Director of Information Security Oversight Office and Co-Directors of Office of Information and Privacy to Departments and Agencies (March 31, 2002); reprinted in FOIA Post (posted 3/21/02).
15. Congressional Research Service — The Library of Congress, Report for Congress, RL31547, Critical Infrastructure Information: Disclosure and Homeland Security, January 29, 2003. http://www.fas.org/sgp/crs/RL31547.pdf
16. http://www.fas.org/sgp/crs/RL31547.pdf
17. http://www.fas.org/sgp/crs/RL31547.pdf
18. http://www.fas.org/sgp/crs/RL31547.pdf
19. http://www.fas.org/sgp/crs/RL31547.pdf
20. See CRS Congressional Distribution Memorandum, American Law Division, Freedom of Information Act: Statutes Invoked under Exemption 3 by Gina Stevens (July 11, 2002).
21. Congressional Research Service — The Library of Congress, Report for Congress, RL31547, Critical Infrastructure Information: Disclosure and Homeland Security, January 29, 2003. http://www.fas.org/sgp/crs/RL31547.pdf
22. Congressional Research Service — The Library of Congress, Report for Congress, RL31547, Critical Infrastructure Information: Disclosure and Homeland Security, January 29, 2003. http://www.fas.org/sgp/crs/RL31547.pdf
23. http://www.fas.org/sgp/crs/RL31547.pdf
24. 5 U.S.C. § 552(b)(4).
25. Congressional Research Service — The Library of Congress, Report for Congress, RL31547, Critical Infrastructure Information: Disclosure and Homeland Security, January 29, 2003. http://www.fas.org/sgp/crs/RL31547.pdf
26. http://www.fas.org/sgp/crs/RL31547.pdf
27. Public Citizen Health Research Group v. FDA, 704 F.2d 1280, 1290 (D.C. Cir. 1983).
28. See, Nadler v. FDIC, 92 F.3d 93, 95 (2d Cir. 1996) (term "person" includes "individual, partnership, corporation, association, or public or private organization other than an agency" (quoting definition found in Administrative Procedure Act, 5 U.S.C. §551(2)).
29. See, Allnet Communications Servs. v. FCC, 800 F. Supp. 984, 988 (D.D.C. 1992).
30. Congressional Research Service — The Library of Congress, Report for Congress, RL31547, Critical Infrastructure Information: Disclosure and Homeland Security, January 29, 2003. http://www.fas.org/sgp/crs/RL31547.pdf
31. FOIA Post, "Critical Infrastructure Information Regulations Issued by DHS", February 27, 2004.
32. FOIA Post, "Critical Infrastructure Information Regulations Issued by DHS", February 27, 2004.
33. Exemption 3 of the Freedom of Information Act, 5 U.S.C. §552(b)(3) (2000).
34. "Systems or assets, whether physical or virtual, so vital to the United States that the incapacity or destruction of such systems and assets would have a debilitating impact on security, national economic security, national public health or safety, or any combination of those matters." P.L. 107–56, section 1016.

35. Congressional Research Service — The Library of Congress, Report for Congress, RL31547, Critical Infrastructure Information: Disclosure and Homeland Security, January 29, 2003. http://www.fas.org/sgp/crs/RL31547.pdf

36. FOIA Post, "Agencies Rely on Wide Range of Exemption 3 Statutes," February 16, 2003.

37. P.L. 107–296, §212(3).

38. P.L. 107–296, §212(3).

39. Congressional Research Service — The Library of Congress, Report for Congress, RL31547, Critical Infrastructure Information: Disclosure and Homeland Security, January 29, 2003. http://www.fas.org/sgp/crs/RL31547.pdf

40. http://www.fas.org/sgp/crs/RL31547.pdf

41. Congressional Research Service — The Library of Congress, Report for Congress, RL31547, Critical Infrastructure Information: Disclosure and Homeland Security, January 29, 2003. http://www.fas.org/sgp/crs/RL31547.pdf

42. http://www.fas.org/sgp/crs/RL31547.pdf

43. http://www.fas.org/sgp/crs/RL31547.pdf

44. http://www.fas.org/sgp/crs/RL31547.pdf

45. http://www.fas.org/sgp/crs/RL31547.pdf

46. http://www.fas.org/sgp/crs/RL31547.pdf

47. The Federal Advisory Committee Act (FACA) requires that the meetings of all federal advisory committees serving executive branch entities be open to the public. The FACA specifies nine categories of information, similar to those in FOIA, which may be permissively relied upon to close advisory committee deliberations. 5 U.S.C. App. 2.

48. Congressional Research Service — The Library of Congress, Report for Congress, RL31547, Critical Infrastructure Information: Disclosure and Homeland Security, January 29, 2003. http://www.fas.org/sgp/crs/RL31547.pdf

49. http://www.fas.org/sgp/crs/RL31547.pdf

50. http://www.fas.org/sgp/crs/RL31547.pdf

51. http://www.wasc.noaa.gov/wrso/security_guide/intro-5.htm#Sensitive

52. The U.S. Department of State uses "Sensitive But Unclassified" (SBU) as a document designation comparable to "For Official Use Only."

53. The Freedom of Information Act (FOIA) establishes a presumption that records in the possession of agencies and departments of the executive branch of the federal government are accessible to the people. This was not always the approach to federal information disclosure policy. Before enactment of the FOIA in 1966, the burden was on the individual to establish a right to examine these government records. There were no statutory guidelines or procedures to help a person seeking information. There were no judicial remedies for those denied access. With the passage of the FOIA, the burden of proof shifted from the individual to the government. Those seeking information are no longer required to show a need for information. Instead, the "need to know" standard has been replaced by a "right to know" doctrine. The government now has to justify the need for secrecy. The FOIA sets standards for determining which records must be disclosed and which records may be withheld. The law also provides administrative and judicial remedies for those denied access to records. Above all, the statute requires government organizations to provide the fullest possible disclosure of information to the public.

54. http://frwebgate.access.gpo.gov/cgi-bin/getdoc.cgi?dbname=106_cong_reports&docid=f:hr050.106.pdf

55. Information taken from the NOAA Web site, in which information posted on the various categories of sensitive unclassified information, is based on a research report prepared for PERSEREC by John Tippit & Associates.

56. DoD Guide to Marking Classified Documents, DoD 5200.1-PH, April 1997, Assistant Secretary of Defense for Command, Control, Communications and Intelligence. http://www.wasc.noaa.gov/wrso/briefings/DOD%20Marking%20Guide.ppt
57. http://www.wasc.noaa.gov/wrso/security_guide/intro-5.htm#Sensitive
58. DoD Regulation 5200.1-R, Information Security Program
59. http://www.wasc.noaa.gov/wrso/security_guide/intro-5.htm#Sensitive
60. http://www.wasc.noaa.gov/wrso/security_guide/intro-5.htm#Sensitive
61. http://www.wasc.noaa.gov/wrso/security_guide/intro-5.htm#Sensitive
62. http://www.wasc.noaa.gov/wrso/security_guide/intro-5.htm#Sensitive
63. http://www.wasc.noaa.gov/wrso/security_guide/intro-5.htm#Sensitive
64. http://www.wasc.noaa.gov/wrso/security_guide/intro-5.htm#Sensitive
65. http://www.wasc.noaa.gov/wrso/security_guide/intro-5.htm#Sensitive
66. http://www.wasc.noaa.gov/wrso/security_guide/intro-5.htm#Sensitive
67. http://www.wasc.noaa.gov/wrso/security_guide/intro-5.htm#Sensitive
68. http://www.wasc.noaa.gov/wrso/security_guide/intro-5.htm#Sensitive
69. http://www.wasc.noaa.gov/wrso/security_guide/foia.htm
70. http://www.wasc.noaa.gov/wrso/security_guide/foia.htm
71. http://www.wasc.noaa.gov/wrso/security_guide/foia.htm
72. http://www.wasc.noaa.gov/wrso/security_guide/foia.htm
73. http://www.wasc.noaa.gov/wrso/security_guide/foia.htm
74. DoD Regulation 5200.1-R, Information Security Program
75. http://www.wasc.noaa.gov/wrso/security_guide/foia.htm
76. http://www.wasc.noaa.gov/wrso/security_guide/foia.htm
77. http://www.wasc.noaa.gov/wrso/security_guide/foia.htm
78. http://www.wasc.noaa.gov/wrso/security_guide/foia.htm
79. http://www.wasc.noaa.gov/wrso/security_guide/foia.htm
80. http://www.wasc.noaa.gov/wrso/security_guide/foia.htm
81. http://www.wasc.noaa.gov/wrso/security_guide/foia.htm
82. http://www.wasc.noaa.gov/wrso/security_guide/foia.htm
83. http://www.wasc.noaa.gov/wrso/security_guide/need-2.htm#Need-to-Know
84. http://www.wasc.noaa.gov/wrso/security_guide/need-2.htm#Need-to-Know
85. http://www.wasc.noaa.gov/wrso/security_guide/need-2.htm#Need-to-Know
86. http://www.wasc.noaa.gov/wrso/security_guide/need-2.htm#Need-to-Know
87. http://www.wasc.noaa.gov/wrso/security_guide/need-2.htm#Need-to-Know
88. http://www.wasc.noaa.gov/wrso/security_guide/need-2.htm#Need-to-Know
89. http://www.wasc.noaa.gov/wrso/security_guide/fouo.htm#For Official
90. http://www.wasc.noaa.gov/wrso/security_guide/fouo.htm#For Official
91. http://www.wasc.noaa.gov/wrso/security_guide/fouo.htm#For Official
92. http://www.wasc.noaa.gov/wrso/security_guide/fouo.htm#For Official
93. DoD Regulation 5200.1-R, Information Security Program
94. http://www.wasc.noaa.gov/wrso/security_guide/fouo.htm#For Official
95. http://www.wasc.noaa.gov/wrso/security_guide/fouo.htm#For Official
96. http://www.wasc.noaa.gov/wrso/security_guide/fouo.htm#For Official
97. http://www.wasc.noaa.gov/wrso/security_guide/fouo.htm#For Official
98. http://www.wasc.noaa.gov/wrso/security_guide/fouo.htm#For Official
99. http://www.wasc.noaa.gov/wrso/security_guide/fouo.htm#For Official
100. http://www.wasc.noaa.gov/wrso/security_guide/fouo.htm#For Official
101. http://www.wasc.noaa.gov/wrso/security_guide/fouo.htm#For Official
102. http://www.wasc.noaa.gov/wrso/security_guide/fouo.htm#For Official
103. http://www.wasc.noaa.gov/wrso/security_guide/fouo.htm#For Official

104. 5 USC 301 - Departmental Regulations: DoD Regulation 5200.1-R — The Information Security Program; DoD Directive 5400.7 — The Freedom of Information Act (FOIA) Program; DoD Regulation 5400.7-R — The DoD Freedom of Information Act Program; DoD Regulation 5400.11-R — Department of Defense Privacy Program.
105. http://www.wasc.noaa.gov/wrso/security_guide/website.htm#Pre-Publication
106. http://www.wasc.noaa.gov/wrso/security_guide/website.htm#Pre-Publication
107. http://www.wasc.noaa.gov/wrso/security_guide/website.htm#Pre-Publication
108. http://www.wasc.noaa.gov/wrso/security_guide/website.htm#Pre-Publication
109. http://www.wasc.noaa.gov/wrso/security_guide/website.htm#Pre-Publication
110. http://www.wasc.noaa.gov/wrso/security_guide/website.htm#Pre-Publication
111. http://www.wasc.noaa.gov/wrso/security_guide/website.htm#Pre-Publication
112. http://www.wasc.noaa.gov/wrso/security_guide/website.htm#Pre-Publication
113. http://www.wasc.noaa.gov/wrso/security_guide/website.htm#Pre-Publication
114. http://www.wasc.noaa.gov/wrso/security_guide/website.htm#Pre-Publication
115. http://www.wasc.noaa.gov/wrso/security_guide/website.htm#Pre-Publication
116. http://www.wasc.noaa.gov/wrso/security_guide/website.htm#Pre-Publication
117. http://www.wasc.noaa.gov/wrso/security_guide/website.htm#Pre-Publication
118. Web Site Administration Policies and Procedures, November 25, 1998, Office of the Assistant Secretary of Defense (C31). Approved by the Deputy Secretary of Defense, December 7, 1998. The full document is available on the Internet. www.defenselink.mil/webmasters/dod_web_policy_12071998_includes_amendments_from_04262001.html
119. Executive Order 12923 Continuation of Export Control Regulations, 30 June 1994: Title 22 USC 2778 et seq. — Arms Export Control Act; Title 50 USC 2401 et seq. — Export Administration Act of 1979 (as amended); Title 50 USC Appendix, Section 10 — Trading With the Enemy Act of 1917; Title 15 CFR Export Administration Regulations, part 770; Title 15 CFR part 779 Technical Data; Title 22 CFR (Dept. of State) Subchapter M, The International Traffic and Arms Regulation (ITAR) Part 121-130.
120. http://www.wasc.noaa.gov/wrso/security_guide/export.htm#Export-Control
121. http://www.wasc.noaa.gov/wrso/security_guide/export.htm#Export-Control
122. http://www.wasc.noaa.gov/wrso/security_guide/export.htm#Export-Control
123. http://www.wasc.noaa.gov/wrso/security_guide/export.htm#Export-Control
124. http://www.wasc.noaa.gov/wrso/security_guide/export.htm#Export-Control
125. http://www.wasc.noaa.gov/wrso/security_guide/export.htm#Export-Control
126. http://www.wasc.noaa.gov/wrso/security_guide/export.htm#Export-Control
127. http://www.wasc.noaa.gov/wrso/security_guide/export.htm#Export-Control
128. http://www.wasc.noaa.gov/wrso/security_guide/export.htm#Export-Control
129. Title 41 USC 421 — Federal Acquisition Regulatory Council; Title 41 USC 423 — Procurement Integrity; FAR Part 3.104-1 — Procurement Integrity, General (48 CFR); FAR Part 3.104.3 — Statutory Prohibitions and Restrictions (48 CFR); FAR Part 3.104-5 — Disclosure, Protection, and Marking of Proprietary and Source Selection Information; FAR Part 14.401 — Receipt and Safeguarding of Bids (48 CFR); FAR Part 15.407 — Solicitation Provisions (48 CFR); FAR Part 27.4 — Rights in Data and Copyrights; FAR Part 52.215-12 — Restriction on Disclosure and Use of Data (48 CFR).
130. http://www.wasc.noaa.gov/wrso/security_guide/source.htm#Source_Selection
131. http://www.wasc.noaa.gov/wrso/security_guide/source.htm#Source_Selection
132. http://www.arnet.gov/far
133. http://www.arnet.gov/far/facsframe.html

134. http://www.wasc.noaa.gov/wrso/security_guide/source.htm#Source_Selection
135. http://www.acqnet.gov/far/current/html/Subpart%2014_4.html#wp1090681
136. http://www.wasc.noaa.gov/wrso/security_guide/source.htm#Source_Selection
137. http://www.acqnet.gov/far/current/html/Subpart%203_1.html#wp1139379
138. http://www.acqnet.gov/far/current/html/Subpart%203_1.html#wp1139379
139. http://www.acqnet.gov/far/current/html/Subpart%203_1.html#wp1139379
140. http://www.acqnet.gov/far/current/html/Subpart%203_1.html#wp1139379
141. http://www.acqnet.gov/far/current/html/Subpart%203_1.html#wp1139379
142. http://www.acqnet.gov/far/current/html/Subpart%203_1.html#wp1139379
143. http://www.acqnet.gov/far/current/html/Subpart%203_1.html#wp1139379
144. http://www.acqnet.gov/far/current/html/Subpart%203_1.html#wp1139379
145. http://www.wasc.noaa.gov/wrso/security_guide/privacy.htm#Privacy Information
146. http://www.wasc.noaa.gov/wrso/security_guide/privacy.htm#Privacy Information
147. http://www.wasc.noaa.gov/wrso/security_guide/privacy.htm#Privacy Information
148. Title 5 USC 552a — Records Maintained on Individuals (Privacy Act); Title 12 USC 3417 — Civil Penalties; Title 18 USC 1905 — Disclosure of Confidential Information Generally; Title 41 CFR 201-6.1 — Federal Information Resources Management Regulation; E.O. 12564 — Drug Free Federal Workplace; OMB Circular No. A-130 — Management of Federal Information Resources, Appendix 1, Federal Agency Responsibilities for Maintaining Records About Individuals; P.L. 100-71 — The Supplemental Appropriations Act of 1987, Section 503; P.L. 104-13 — Paperwork Reduction Act of 1955.
149. http://www.wasc.noaa.gov/wrso/security_guide/privacy.htm#Privacy Information
150. http://www.wasc.noaa.gov/wrso/security_guide/privacy.htm#Privacy Information
151. http://www.wasc.noaa.gov/wrso/security_guide/privacy.htm#Privacy Information
152. http://www.wasc.noaa.gov/wrso/security_guide/privacy.htm#Privacy Information
153. http://www.wasc.noaa.gov/wrso/security_guide/privacy.htm#Privacy Information
154. http://www.wasc.noaa.gov/wrso/security_guide/privacy.htm#Privacy Information
155. http://www.wasc.noaa.gov/wrso/security_guide/privacy.htm#Privacy Information
156. http://www.ftc.gov/privacy/glbact
157. http://www.hhs.gov/ocr/hipaa
158. 42 USC 2168 — Atomic Energy Act of 1954; 10 CFR Part 1017 — Identification and Protection of Unclassified Controlled Nuclear Information; DoD Regulation 5200.1-R, Information Security Program.
159. http://www.wasc.noaa.gov/wrso/security_guide/ucni.htm#Unclassified Controlled
160. http://www.wasc.noaa.gov/wrso/security_guide/ucni.htm#Unclassified Controlled
161. http://www.wasc.noaa.gov/wrso/security_guide/ucni.htm#Unclassified Controlled
162. 42 USC 2168 — Atomic Energy Act of 1954; 10 CFR Part 1017 — Identification and Protection of Unclassified Controlled Nuclear Information; DoD Regulation 5200.1-R, Information Security Program.
163. http://www.ferc.gov/legal/ceii-foia/ceii.asp
164. http://www.ferc.gov/legal/maj-ord-reg/land-docs/ceii-rule.asp
165. http://www.ferc.gov/legal/ceii-foia/ceii/nip.asp
166. http://www.ferc.gov/legal/ceii-foia/ceii/classes.asp
167. http://www.ferc.gov/legal/ceii-foia/ceii/classes.asp
168. U.S. Department of Energy, Environmental Safety and Health (http://www.eh.doe.gov/ll). U.S. Department of Transportation, Federal Transit Administration (http:// www.fta.dot.gov/transit_data_info/reports_publications/publications/project_construction_management_guidelines/11143_ENG_HTML.htm). National Aeronautics and Space Administration (http://llis.nasa.gov). U.S. Department of Homeland

Security (http://www.llis.dhs.gov). U.S. Department of Health and Human Services (http://www.usability.gov/lessons). U.S. Department of Energy, Project Hanford (http://www.hanford.gov/lessons/sitell/sitehome.htm) Lawrence Livermore National Laboratory (http://www.llnl.gov/es_and_h/lessons/lessons.shtml). The Library of Congress (http://memory.loc.gov/ammem/award/lessons/lessons.html). Federal Aviation Administration (http://www.asu.faa.gov/lesslrnd/).

169. U.S. Department of Justice Federal Bureau of Investigation INFRAGARD Frequently Asked Questions (FAQ). http://www.infragard.net/about_us/faqs.htm
170. http://www.infragard.net/about_us/faqs.htm
171. http://www.infragard.net/about_us/faqs.htm
172. http://www.infragard.net/about_us/faqs.htm
173. http://www.infragard.net/about_us/faqs.htm
174. http://www.infragard.net/about_us/faqs.htm
175. http://www.infragard.net/about_us/faqs.htm
176. http://www.infragard.net/about_us/faqs.htm
177. http://www.infragard.net/about_us/faqs.htm
178. http://www.infragard.net/about_us/faqs.htm
179. http://www.infragard.net/about_us/faqs.htm
180. http://www.wasc.noaa.gov/wrso/security_guide/intro-5.htm#Sensitive.
181. The U.S. Department of State uses "Sensitive But Unclassified" (SBU) as a document designation comparable to "For Official Use Only."
182. DoD Regulation 5200.1-R, Information Security Program
183. DoD Regulation 5200.1-R, Information Security Program
184. http://www.wasc.noaa.gov/wrso/security_guide/fouo.htm#For Official
185. http://www.wasc.noaa.gov/wrso/security_guide/fouo.htm#For Official
186. http://www.wasc.noaa.gov/wrso/security_guide/fouo.htm#For Official
187. http://www.wasc.noaa.gov/wrso/security_guide/fouo.htm#For Official

Index

C